A Hard Journey

A Hard Journey

The Life of Don West

James J. Lorence

UNIVERSITY OF ILLINOIS PRESS

URBANA AND CHICAGO

© 2007 by the Board of Trustees
of the University of Illinois
All rights reserved
Manufactured in the United States of America
C 5 4 3 2 1
♾ This book is printed on acid-free paper.

Library of Congress Cataloging-in-Publication Data
Lorence, James J.
A hard journey : the life of Don West / James J. Lorence.
p.   cm.
Includes bibliographical references (p.   ) and index.
ISBN 978-0-252-03231-8 (alk. paper)
ISBN 0-252-03231-4 (alk. paper)
1. West, Don.
2. Authors, American—20th century—Biography.
3. Appalachian Region—Social life and customs—20th century.
I. Title.
PS3545.E8279Z75   2007
811'.54—dc22 [B]   2007011385

In memory of my father, a working man

Contents

Illustrations follow page 142

Acknowledgments

This book would not have been possible without the generous support of several institutions. Essential to the completion of the work was the funding provided by Gainesville State College, which made research in North Georgia history a central feature in my teaching position. Travel to distant manuscript repositories was underwritten by the Gainesville State College Eminent Scholar Research Fund. The technical support provided by the college, especially the work of instructional technology specialist Alfred Barker and librarian Becky Webb, is also gratefully acknowledged. In addition, a Lubin-Winant Research Fellowship from the Franklin and Eleanor Roosevelt Institute facilitated research at the Franklin D. Roosevelt Library in Hyde Park, New York. The Georgia Historical Society generously granted permission to publish material on West that originally appeared in the *Georgia Historical Quarterly*.

A project of this magnitude could not be carried out without the assistance of skilled archivists and library personnel at a variety of archival repositories. Especially helpful were Kathy Shoemaker of the Emory University Special Collections, Pamela Hackbart-Dean and Lauren Kata of the Georgia State University Pullen Library's Southern Labor Archives, Harry Miller of the Wisconsin Historical Society Archives and Manuscripts Division, Charles Barber of the Hargrett Rare Books and Manuscripts Library at the University of Georgia, Susan Williams of the Highlander Research and Education Center Library, Peter Filardo at the Tamiment Institute and Robert Wagner Labor Archives at New York University, Karen Anson of the Franklin D. Roosevelt Library, John White of the University of North Carolina–Chapel Hill's Wilson Library Southern Historical Collection, Nat DeBruin of the J. Glenn Beall Archives at Frostburg State University Special Collections, Ned

Irwin of Eastern Tennessee State University Archives of Appalachia, Michael Smith and William LeFevre of the Archives of Labor and Urban Affairs at the Walter P. Reuther Library, Clara Potter at Morehead State University, Jacque Roethler of the University of Iowa Library Special Collections, Amy Fitch at Rockefeller Archive Center, David Palmore and James Gifford of the Jesse Stuart Foundation, Leanne Garland of Lincoln Memorial University Library Archives and Special Collections, Mark Rosenzweig of the Reference Center for Marxist Studies, Debra March of Young Harris College, Ann Salter of the Oglethorpe University Archives, Rebecca Roberts of Berry College Archives, Timothy Engels of Brown University Special Collections, Mary Hogue of the West Virginia Library Commission, Sandra Peck of Tuskeegee University Archives, Cathy Lynn Mundale of Atlanta University Center Special Collections, Ronald Bulatoff of the Hoover Institution on War, Revolution, and Peace, Christine Weidemann of Special Collections at Yale University Sterling Memorial Library, Delinda Buie of Louisville University, Claire McCann of the University of Kentucky Special Collections and Archives, and Amey Hutchins of the University of Pennsylvania Special Collections.

In Washington, D.C., the resources of the Library of Congress were useful in tracking West's political activities in the 1930s. Communist Party USA (CPUSA) Records from the Russian State Archive of Social and Political History were made more accessible through the assistance of John Haynes at the Library of Congress Manuscript Division and Harvey Klehr of Emory University. Special thanks are also due Ronald Bachman of the Library of Congress European Division, who aided me in accessing materials from the Communist International records available in Moscow. On-site research in Russia was performed by Dasha Lotareva, and assistance with translation was provided by Timothy Sergay and Olga Hebert. Finally, at the National Archives, Eugene Morris eased access to the records of the Works Progress Administration (WPA) and National Recovery Administration (NRA).

A key component of my research was a wide range of interviews with family, friends, and acquaintances of Don West. Among the persons who allowed me into their lives were Yvonne Farley, P. J. Laska, David Stanley, Warren Doyle, Helen Lewis, Frank T. Adams, George Brosi, Mildred Shackleford, Donald Rasmussen, Merry Tucker, Margie Hutchens, John Crawford, Jane Ross Davis, Michael Ross Jr., Kenneth West, William Best, Mark Pace, Gwen Chapman, Genevieve Duncan, Bobbie Moore, Clyde Moore, Ruth Tribble Forestor, John David, Herb Leslie, and Philip and Mildred Greear. Without access to their personal recollections, it would have been impossible to develop a balanced understanding of West's life after the 1950s.

Another source of both encouragement and wider knowledge of evidence was a group of colleagues who shared their own work with me, gave valuable advice, and provided criticism of this study at earlier stages in its development. Among the most helpful were Christopher Green of Marshall University, Alan Wald of the University of Michigan, Rachel Rubin of the University of Massachusetts–Boston, Carl Weinberg of Butler Univesity, James Smethurst of Amherst College, Paul S. Boyer of the University of Wisconsin–Madison, Mark Solomon of Simmons College, Robin D. G. Kelley of Columbia University, Martin Halpern of Henderson State University, Paul Buhle of Brown University, Carol Boggess of Mars Hill College, Ernst Benjamin of Silver Spring, Maryland, Helen Lewis of Morganton, Georgia, and Jeff Biggers of Macomb, Illinois.

While all have encouraged me to pursue this study, I must acknowledge the critical role of Jeff Biggers in the completion of the project. His invaluable work, with George Brosi, in bringing Don West's literary contribution to the attention of scholars has been both an inspiration and a challenge. Although his writing has been instructive, even more significant was the persistence with which he insisted that I look further into the career of Don West. Equally important was his generosity in sharing research files, which were important in persuading me that an adequate base of sources for a biography was available. Once the task was undertaken I also benefited from the professional guidance provided by the editors at the University of Illinois Press, especially the advice offered by Mary Giles and Laurie Matheson, both of whom saw the project through to a successful conclusion.

Invaluable as sources were the members of Don West's family, especially Hedy West of Narberth, Pennsylvania, and Ann West Williams of Charleston, West Virginia. By discussing their experiences with me they made a key contribution to my understanding of the contradictions that were central to Don West's character. Both shared correspondence, memorabilia, and memories, thereby enlarging both the paper trail and the oral history record of life with a complicated man. My extensive correspondence with Hedy played an important role in the effort to bring order to an incomplete record of the past. Equally valuable was her large collection of transcribed interviews with Lillie and Don West, which were critical in my reconstruction of early-twentieth-century mountain life as well as West-Mulkey family history. Since Hedy's death her daughter, Talitha, has kindly eased access to the West papers at her mother's residence. I thank Ann and Hedy for their contributions to the completion of this project. It is my hope that the book will call attention to their father's role in building a modern, nonracist South as well as to his place in Appalachian history and culture.

Finally, as has been true throughout my long academic life, I owe my greatest debt to my wife, Donna, who encouraged my commitment to scholarship from the very beginning. Without her, there would be no book; and I thank her for her unfailing support.

Prologue A Lifetime of Radicalism

Some say that in the fullness of his mature years Don West was an "opinionated cranky old man." Others found him openly hostile late in his career. Indeed, one of his most sympathetic critics acknowledged that he had gone through a productive life with a noticeable chip on his shoulder. If West was blunt and provocative, his edgy demeanor resulted from impatience over the unfulfilled promise of American life. From a very early age, the rugged mountaineer with craggy features had tested the limits of democracy and insisted on social justice for the laboring masses, black and white, who struggled to enjoy the full benefits of citizenship. West had, in the words of Ken Sullivan of West Virginia's *Goldenseal* magazine, "made it his business to afflict the comfortable" throughout a lifetime as "a radical of considerable standing." Hounded by government and private authorities alike, he lived long enough to become, in his declining years, a "local institution."[1] Loved and respected by the people of his adopted West Virginia home, Don West outlived and outshone many of the critics who pursued him relentlessly during a controversial career as poet, preacher, teacher, and labor organizer. By the time of West's death in 1992, both his literary work and myriad contributions to an Appalachian renaissance were gaining the recognition denied him for most of his life.

For years, Don West's life and work were underappreciated by a literary establishment that denigrated his commitment to art that elevated the common people and the Appalachian culture he valued and sought to preserve. Although some scholars have discounted West's poetry as didactic and even agitprop, there has been a revival of interest in his writing, best represented in the work of Jeff Biggers, George Brosi, Christopher Green, Alan Wald, David Duke, Rachel Rubin, Cary Nelson, and James Smethurst.[2] This outpouring of scholarship promises to bring West's literary contribution out of

xiv • PROLOGUE

the shadows and enhance his standing as a writer whose work marked him as the Walt Whitman of his time, a spokesperson for common people.

West's commitment to socially and politically engaged art set him apart from many literary figures of his time. One of a creative triumvirate of Kentucky writers who passed through the classes of Harry Harrison Kroll at Lincoln Memorial University, a circle that also included Jesse Stuart and James Still, West alone chose the path of radical agitation. His medium was poetry that expressed the anguish and hopes of the impoverished southern masses, whose suffering contributed to the South's dubious distinction as the nation's number one economic problem in the troubled 1930s. His distinctiveness was clear in his relationship with the better-known North Georgia poet Byron Herbert Reece, with whom West debated the ends of literary art. Consistently criticizing what West thought Reece's mistaken belief in "art for art's sake," he insisted that prose and poetry were useless if they were not "art for humanity's sake."[3] He never wavered from that conviction.

West's emphasis on the cause of humanity reflected the diverse roots from which his work grew, including his own peculiar brand of applied Christianity. An ordained minister of the gospel, West had imbibed deeply in the mountain religious traditions of his youth. He was the product of a large extended family with a rich religious heritage that counted more than one preacher in its number. Influenced by his mother's practical sense of fairness in human relations and familiarity with scriptural injunctions, the young man developed his own brand of religious commitment. Impressed by the social gospel teachings of reformer Alva W. Taylor, his Vanderbilt mentor, West soon modeled his personal life of social activism after a clear vision of the radical Jesus. With Jesus as comrade in revolutionary struggle, West worked to apply his own version of Christian humanism in a world populated by too few Christians who understood the need for radical social and economic change.

This growing conviction that the true social gospel required bold action in everyday life propelled West into the world of political radicalism in the early 1930s. After a series of encounters with raw economic power in the struggles of Kentucky and Tennessee miners, he moved rapidly into the Communist Party orbit, starting in 1933 with a prominent role in the defense of the young unemployed organizer Angelo Herndon, who stood accused of insurrection by Georgia authorities. This decision resulted in early immersion in both the secret and public worlds of American communism as well as a personal commitment to work as a party organizer in Georgia, North Carolina, and Kentucky during the dark days of the Great Depression. Having read deeply in Marx and Lenin, West made an intellectual and political commitment that was to energize his work over the years and expose him to unending surveillance and persecution for his beliefs and actions. Although later in life he would deny Communist Party membership, his commitment to Marxist ideology remained steadfast until the collapse of the Soviet Union caused him to entertain doubts in his last years.

Never doubting that his political religion would help alleviate the poverty he saw around him in countless mill villages and within the oppressed African American community of the rural South, West built a life as itinerant radical, dedicated artist, and reform-minded educator. At no time did his loyalties and sentiments depart very far from his roots in the North Georgia mountains. Throughout a long career as both organizer and teacher, the most consistent theme in his work was a dedication to the education of Appalachian youth and the fight against the denigration of mountain culture. From the founding of the Highlander Folk School in Tennessee through his work with outreach education in the Peoples Institute for Applied Religion to the establishment of the Appalachian South Folklife Center at Pipestem, West Virginia, West's fight for the integrity of mountain culture and improved lives for mountain people was the central feature of his intellectual life.

The clearest expression of his beliefs may be found in the gritty yet simple truthfulness of his poetry. West's poetic eloquence was rooted in a sense of both the pain and simple nobility of the common people's lived experience in the Appalachian South. Their struggle had intensified as industrialization transformed the mountains and the lives of mountain folk in the late nineteenth and early twentieth centuries. West's writings are filled with a mixture of anxiety and anger over changes in a way of life that was disappearing before his very eyes. As his people were drawn into the trap of industrialism, there developed a vicious stereotype depicting them as depraved, uneducated, and even defective human beings, an image that outraged West. His poetry consistently counters that image by portraying Appalachian people as active agents in their own lives and fortunes as well as inheritors of a rich culture in danger of obliteration. To West, this culture of southern Appalachia had rejected the brutal institution of slavery and the genteel society so often understood as the "old South" of myth and legend. His literary work contained a personal repudiation of that South, as well as an open embrace of working-class whites and blacks who stood against it. In his work and in his life, Don West was living evidence that a New South could be built on the basis of the interracial harmony first envisioned by the ancestors of the much-maligned Appalachian poor.

For West, the cornerstone of this new social edifice was to be found in the inherent wisdom of common people, whom he fervently believed capable of understanding their oppression and acting to overcome it. Hence, his poetry spoke to the working poor of the South in their own idiom. Although his earliest work employed vernacular imagery rooted in youthful experiences, the later poems never abandoned topical material and images that remained accessible to a wide, working-class readership. Through a variety of means to be explored in this volume, West's work reached an extraordinarily large audience, including significant numbers of readers found beyond the halls of academe and the eastern literary establishment. Although it is difficult to confirm his often-repeated claim that his most notable work, *Clods of Southern Earth*, sold upward of a hundred thousand copies, records do reveal its unusual financial success for a poetry collection. Aided by the involvement of the CIO, Southern Conference for Human Welfare, and Peoples Institute for Applied Religion in the promotion and use of *Clods*, West's words reached an unprecedented working-class audience. Wide distribution was consistent with the author's goals and beliefs, which were reflected in his encouragement of paperback editions and disinterest in copyright protection. West was certain that his works were read and understood by many people not normally exposed to poetry. This outcome reinforced his firm conviction that an accessible peoples' art opened new horizons to the common folk who would become agents in the transformation of their own lives. The message emphasized hope, pride in culture, and confidence in self; the medium was Don West the activist.

I was drawn to West's story as a result of research on the history of American radicalism in the South. Engaged in work on a study of community organizing in Georgia during the 1930s, I frequently encountered West as an actor on the political stage whose utterances and actions belied the prevailing image of southern whites in that age of economic disruption. So fascinating and important did he seem that I determined to explore further the life of this unconventional southerner. I soon concluded that close attention to his career could reveal the sometimes ignored role of radicalism in advancing the cause of the exploited workers of the South. In recent years the work of Robin D. G. Kelley, Mark Solomon, Robert Craig, John Egerton, and Anthony Dunbar have taught us much about the important role played by the Left in the popular struggles of the depression era.[4] This volume complements their research by providing in a study of Don West a life history of commitment to the fight against racism and for impoverished southern workers. It also places West squarely in the tradition of American radicalism and demonstrates the power of literature to inspire, when matched with the courageous actions of a socially committed artist as agitator.

Indeed, it is not an exaggeration to say that Don West's career was emblematic of an alternative version of southern history and literature, one that challenged the South of the "plantation illusion" and substituted a narrative of resistance to racism and discrimination. West's ongoing struggle for the rights of laborers, impoverished farmers, and oppressed African Americans made his life and work a living contradiction to the accepted wisdom about southern folkways and class relations. Too long neglected, his writing explodes the myth of a monolithic southern agrarian tradition that expressed reactionary literary and cultural preferences as the dominant social and economic story line of the nation's most troubled region. Influential as the Nashville cultural nationalists were, and powerful as the area's old and new elites remained, there was another south, populated by the working poor and characterized by resistance to planter-manager coercion. It was these southerners and their cause that West embraced; and through his work, simmering class tensions came to the surface in an alternative reading of southern history and the future of the South's working poor. Close examination of his career therefore allows us to reexamine the politics, social relations, and literary life of a modernizing south, including the poorly understood role of radicalism as a force for progressive thought and action.

From his college years on, West searched for the most effective tool with which to promote the goals of cultural renewal and social advancement. At an early date, he concluded that education was the key that unlocked the door to human improvement, social justice, and pride in culture. Exposed to the folk school model while studying in Denmark, West became convinced that the best hope for Appalachian community life rested with cooperative education that reinforced cultural heritage. For the rest of his life he worked to create institutions through which that ideal might be realized, first at Highlander, then in Georgia, and finally at Pipestem, where he was able to create the learning environment he had dreamed of throughout his career as an organizer, teacher, and artist. Here he devoted the last twenty-five years of his life to the preservation of Appalachian culture and the education of mountain youth to understand their forebears and lead their communities toward a better future.

It is clear, therefore, that a sense of place is essential to understanding the life and work of a gifted man who made a major contribution to regional literature, Appalachian cultural awareness, and the improvement of everyday life for the hardworking people who struggled to win a living from the land and resources of colonial Appalachia. In order to provide an accurate account of this extraordinary life we must return to the North Georgia mountains and the nurturing community that shaped Don West's development as spokesperson for a world that was fast disappearing at the time of his birth. And so to Appalachia.

part one

A Man in a Hurry:
The Roots of Commitment

one

Shaping a Value System: Family, the Mountains, and the Wider World, 1906–26

The rugged mountains of North Georgia form the southern extension of the Appalachians, which separate the Piedmont from the plateau and lowlands sloping down to the Mississippi Valley. By the mid-nineteenth century, the Southern Appalachians were home to a distinct culture independent of the Old South and often strongly unionist during the Civil War. Between the Civil War and the 1920s, debate raged over the very existence of a distinct cultural entity called Appalachia. Finally, with the advance of industrialism and the migration of mountain people to piedmont textile mills, many observers concluded that there was in the mountains a rich culture worthy of preservation. Since the 1970s, most modern scholars have assumed that the notion of "Appalachia" was a product of the northern intellectuals' imagination, but it is equally true that contemporary observers, both outsiders and native-born, were essentially correct in concluding that a distinctive people and overwhelmingly rural mountain culture had existed in relative isolation before 1930.[1]

While the pressures of industrialism threatened to alter that unique culture, the pull of traditional values remained strong even as the old way of life disappeared. The determined fight to preserve mountain culture, as reflected in the life of one of its strongest defenders, constitutes the central theme in this study. Don West's story begins with his family's struggle to maintain mountain values in the face of a shattering economic and social transformation well under way at the time of his birth. By the dawn of the twentieth century, Appalachia was already immersed in an irreversible transition that strained the bonds of family and community that had sustained mountain people for more than a century.

Into that changing world was born Donald Lee West on June 6, 1906. The eldest son in a family of eight, young Don seemed at first destined for the agricultural life in his Gilmer County home. Like other farmers in the small rural community near Cartecay, Georgia, his parents, James Oliver and Lillie Mulkey West, worked the land and hoped for better times that might lift them beyond their marginal existence. Descended from Carolina Scotch Irish emigrants, the West and Mulkey families were comfortable with the rural life and the agricultural economy that had sustained generations of mountaineers. Very early in Don's life, Oliver moved the family to the Gilmer County up-country, occupying a plot of land not far from Turkey Creek at the foot of Burnt Mountain. Here Oliver and Lillie labored in close proximity to the farms of Don's grandfather and uncle. Just fifteen miles from the county seat at Ellijay, the original West home place was a world unto itself, still somewhat removed from the forces of industrial development that were transforming rural life in the Appalachians. Don later recalled a life of poverty that matched that of the surrounding rural community, where all people were "just poor hill farmers" struggling to master the rugged terrain.[2]

One product of rural isolation in the mountains was the absence of ethnic and racial biases found elsewhere in the South, especially in tidewater areas. From an early age Don learned tolerance based on an assumption of human equality everywhere evident in the equality of hardship encountered by poor people striving to survive and care for their families within a supportive community setting. Free from the lowland dependence on cotton culture, the Scotch Irish of the North Georgia mountains felt little need to introduce the institution of slavery, which meant that in the early twentieth century the African American population was negligible. West often recalled that he had never seen a black person until his fifteenth year (twelve is more likely), when he encountered an African American at the Ellijay railroad yards.

After the family removed to the Cobb County cotton country in 1918, the population was much more diverse. In the Kennesaw and Douglas County areas, the Wests' neighbors were people of color. Carrying on beliefs and traditions rooted in family history, Lillie and Oliver interacted easily with the local population, which meant that blacks were frequent guests in their home. When confronted with local suspicions about her social relations with African Americans, Lillie's response was, "They're our neighbors," a reaction rooted in generations of mountain community life. Neighborliness, hospitality, and community had been part of her family experience. The West family's willingness to embrace an advanced concept of racial equality was rooted in a mountain tradition that assumed the dignity that came with hard work, independence, and self-sufficiency. Don West's decision to embrace a progressive view of race relations and a lifetime commitment to the fight for social justice mirrored his upbringing as well as the values of the mountain culture of which his family was a product.

Like their neighbors in the mountains, Oliver and Lillie practiced subsistence agriculture during the early years of their marriage, hardscrabble farming supplemented by the occasional sale of crossties to the railroad and marketing surplus crops in Ellijay, Rome, Marietta, and Atlanta. When his father traveled to the villages and towns to sell produce, Don was an eager companion, always interested in the outside world. This intellectual curiosity marked him as the member of the growing family most likely to achieve prominence in the wider community beyond Gilmer County. His love of learning was nourished by Lillie, who despite limited formal education was an avid reader blessed with acute native intelligence. Often over the objections of the more short-sighted Oliver, she encouraged Don's keen interest in reading at every turn. It is clear that in plotting his future and seeking education, Don was truly Lillie's son.

Although he loved his father, Don's perspective on Oliver is best described as one of sympathy and understanding. Limited in outlook, Oliver West was consumed with the problem of survival, constantly working to provide a day-to-day existence for a growing family. Try as he might, he was never a financial success; Lillie frequently attested to his inability to handle money and plan for the future. Her recollections are filled with critical comments on her hapless husband's financial failures and peculiar ideas on child-rearing. It is likely that Oliver's lack of financial acumen and failed effort to provide for the family influenced Don, who found it hard to observe and accept his father's impractical approach to economic life. To see his father crushed by circumstance and humiliated before a disapproving mother was to feel humiliation himself. Under the circumstances, Don had difficulty fully respecting Oliver as head of the family; rather, he looked to Lillie for strength and leadership as he plotted his own future. She recalled that she and Oliver "worked like slaves all of [their] lives" and "never did have much to show for it" until her years as a widow. Always a striver and planner, Lillie provided a model of agency and determined acceptance of responsibility that remained with Don throughout a life in which he welcomed responsibility for uplifting the poor and elevating the downtrodden. To Don, Oliver's life provided a textbook case in victimhood, whereas Lillie stood out as the family's problem-solver.[3]

Lillie exerted a strong influence on the development of Don's character, but there was another important figure in his young life. As revealed in his later literary work, West was deeply impressed at an early age by the towering presence of his maternal grandfather, Asberry Kimsey Mulkey. He was, Don recalled, a "marvelous man," who "exercised a great influence on my early attitudes." A giant of a man, old Kim Mulkey taught the impressionable youth the importance of tolerance, honesty, and independence. Always an informal instructor, Kim impressed on Don the importance of human equality before God. In his later poem "Unity Is an Ax," West addressed Kim Mulkey's vision of a better world: "forget your skin is black or white / Pull back the scales / That hide you / From the future!" And in nearly every interview granted in later years West acknowledged the profound influence of his grandfather, whose "blood burn[ed] in [his] veins and crie[d] for justice." His mother remembered that Don idolized Kim, that he "believed in him, just as strongly as anybody could."[4]

Not only did Kim offer clear moral direction but he also impressed Don with the validity of traditional Appalachian values, a lesson he never forgot. Part and parcel of this intergenerational dialog was immersion in the history of the region and its people. Kim stressed opposition to slavery in the mountains and the diversity of opinion on the Civil War, which led family members to serve in both Union and Confederate armies.[5] Fueled by stories of mountain unionism, West tended to oversimplify the complexities of a mountain economy that in some parts of the Southern Appalachians did incorporate the peculiar institution. The history that stuck in Don's mind, however, emphasized both human dignity and the depravity of slavery. Another lesson transmitted by Kim Mulkey was the importance of community life, in which he had played an important role as local blacksmith, justice of the peace, and deacon in the Baptist church. This nourishment of community solidarity and sense of place, characterized by religious commitment, sharing, hospitality, neighborliness, and mutual dependence, was central to the mountain culture that Don West absorbed as a youth.

The church, in fact, had been a key feature of both the Mulkey and the West family history. Lillie's grandfather, Philip Mulkey, deeded the land for the Ebenezer Baptist Church and the adjoining cemetery. Moreover, West family history is peppered with Baptist preachers, some of whom served Ebenezer Baptist in the mid-nineteenth century. Lillie raised her family in the Baptist religious tradition but with a healthy suspicion of unbounded authority. The family attended a small Primitive Baptist Church, where Don absorbed Lillie's common-sense, pragmatic religious attitudes. Alternately impressed by and skeptical of preachers as a class, she developed her own knowledge of scripture but never coerced her children in matters of faith. As a child, Don was deeply impressed by the genuinely human preacher Larkin Chastain of Gilmer County, so much so that later in life he attributed his decision to enter the ministry to Chastain's influence. What appealed to Don the most was his emphasis on a "God of compassion and love . . . a very understanding God" capable of overlooking human foibles and grasping secular problems.[6] Thus, Don grew up outwardly religious but more interested in the application of religious principles in the here and now than in the search for an entry pass into an afterlife. Over the years, West's humanistic religion evolved into a commitment to the Social Gospel that emphasized a revolutionary Jesus without embracing trinitarian doctrine or even the divinity of Christ, whom he preferred to regard as the "Great Teacher." This Christian humanism was rooted in the evangelical traditions central to mountain religion but characterized by a clear understanding of Jesus as a leader of people seeking a better life on earth.[7]

Intimately connected to the West family's church activities was the role of music, ballad, and lyrical poetry in religious experience. Music, including the singing of hymns, was an integral element in Baptist worship, which often became demonstrative as the excitement created by the music escalated. Not surprisingly, fiddles and banjos were also present in both the Mulkey and later, the West, homes. Lillie was, in fact, an accomplished musician from a family of "working class music makers" who "continually added whatever music they heard and liked or made to what they already knew."[8] Nourished within this environment, Don West became a performer of mountain music, which he often used later in life as an organizing tool. In Appalachia, words, music, and oral tradition had long been a means for intergenerational transmission of knowledge, culture, and history. It was therefore a logical extension of that cultural memory when West used them to inform young and old of their long history of independence and agency.

This educational process was a reaction to the vicious stereotyping of mountain people that Don West abhorred. Contrary to the image projected by the media and outside critics, the inhabitants of the community in which Don grew up valued education very highly. For Don, moreover, home was yet another educational institution, largely due to the tireless efforts of his mother to expand her son's horizons. Indeed, the West place became an informal educational center where neighbor children often gathered to listen to Lillie's singing, storytelling, and reading.

Although Don was a quick learner who took advantage of the educational opportunities available in Gilmer County, his family concluded that the schools left much to be desired. Oliver had attended school for only two grades and Lillie five, but there had been educated people in the family's history. The intellectual richness in that history, the supportive environment created by Lillie, and even Oliver's grudging aspirations for the children's futures were factors in the Wests' migration to the lowlands in 1918.[9] Although they preferred the mountains and pined for their home territory throughout their lives, Oliver and Lillie saw both economic improvement and potential benefit to their children in the move and as a result relocated in Cobb County, a decision that was to have a profound impact on their son's future.

The shift meant economic hardship as the Wests became sharecroppers, but it also advanced Don's intellectual growth by affording greater educational opportunity. Proximity to Marietta made inexpensive books more accessible, and the learning environment improved in the town school at Douglasville. Here, Don and his sisters were "green" and stood out with their overalls and calico dresses. West recalled vividly the ridicule he initially endured because of the bib overalls he wore. Yet because of his early academic and athletic successes Don soon became a role model for his classmates, who abandoned dress pants for the overall style he set. Although the criticism of his "hillbilly" roots had been disturbing, he renewed his determination to wear his cultural heritage proudly.[10]

While Don excelled academically, the family struggled economically. Eventually, most extended family members joined the army of displaced mountaineers who supplied the labor that fed the industrial development revolutionizing the New South. Like many mountain families, the Gilmer County Wests participated in what Don remembered later as the "exodus." While most members of the West clan moved to the cotton mill country near Cartersville, Oliver insisted on making his way as a farmer. Lillie vowed that she "never intend[ed] for one of [her] children to go into the cotton mill." Sharecropping meant that day-to-day existence was a family matter, which required Lillie, Don, and the children to work together in the cotton fields at hard, sometimes dangerous labor. It was, for example, in the Cobb County fields that Don lost three fingers in a dynamiting accident. Never comfortable as flatlanders, Lillie and Oliver dreamed of a return to the mountains, but it was not to be; Oliver remained a cropper until his death.[11] Later in life, Don often asserted that his father's death had been hastened by the hard life imposed on him by an agricultural economy that placed a higher value on limitless labor than the quality of human life. Oliver's sad experience was an important factor in his son's developing social consciousness and commitment to relieve the suffering of the capitalist system's castoff victims, both rural and urban.

So difficult was family life in the sharecropping system that eventually Don looked for a way out. As he moved into high school, he contemplated a dramatic change. Only sixteen, he knew that a departure from home would have violated the old custom that young men were bound to work for their father until they reached the age of twenty-one. Although Don had independently explored both a local agricultural and mechanical school and Berry School in Rome, it was Oliver who approached him with an acknowledgment that the long walk from school and the exhaustion of working was simply too much for a young man of academic promise. If Don could find the tuition money, Oliver was prepared to release him from his traditional obligation. After securing a $75 tuition loan from his uncle, Horace Mulkey, and making arrangements to work while studying, Don was off for Berry in 1922, where in Lillie's words, her son "made 'is own chance."[12]

For Don West, Berry presented both an opportunity and a challenge. Founded by Martha Berry in 1902 on inherited land, the Berry School for Boys was one of several educational outreach missions launched, often with the support of the Protestant churches and northern money, to bring education to mountain children. Driven by "compassion for the poor white hill people," Martha Berry hoped to break the cycle of poverty and remove the academic deficit that limited her students' opportunities. As noted by the modern scholar David Whisnant, however, such cultural intervention effectively deprived mountain people of their cultural heritage in the name of academic and professional advancement.[13] It was this dimension of the Berry enterprise, together with the influence of Henry Ford's money, that led West to resist the school's efforts to shape his education. The result was an ongoing struggle that ended in Don's decision to break with the discipline and paternalism that he perceived as an intolerable cultural burden.

Like many Berry students, Don participated in the work-study program at the school farm to pay his tuition and board. After one year, however, he took time off to work in order to pay expenses for his sister Elsie, who joined him at Mount Berry as a student in 1923. Once he returned to the academic life, he excelled in the classroom and on the athletic field, where he became a mainstay on the track team. Although he chafed under the institution's strict disciplinary regimen, Don seemed headed for success, at least until his sense of cultural pride and a growing independent streak embroiled him in controversies that ended in a premature departure from Berry.[14]

Although he had been aware of his distinctiveness as a mountain youth after his family's migration to Cobb County, the cultural differences between flatlanders and hill people were accentuated at Berry. Here Kim Mulkey's teachings concerning human equality and the history of mountain opposition to slavery clashed with the more conventional views of students raised in cotton country. What resulted was a controversial incident in which West led the opposition to a screening of the racist film *Birth of a Nation*. To Don's dismay, one misguided instructor prepared his students for the film by indoctrinating them in the then-current Dunning school of southern history and arguing that slaveholding was their heritage. His words contradicted everything Don had learned about slavery, Reconstruction, and the hated Ku Klux Klan at the feet of old Kim Mulkey. Angered by both the film and the teacher's distortion of history, West organized a protest, during which he said "some pretty sharp things" about the racial stereotyping in the movie.[15]

Long before *Birth of a Nation* embroiled Don West in controversy, he had begun to buck the system. As he later admitted, he was a "rebel" who "resented certain things." Chief among his grievances was the paternalism of Henry Ford and the "civilizing" mission assumed by the Berry authorities, who, he believed, worked to strip Appalachian children of their culture. He was convinced that one of their main purposes was to "separate the mountain youth from their real heritage." Conscious of his grandfather's example, Don felt obligated to "take a stand on principles" when important issues arose.[16]

As the high school years passed, the intensity of West's grudge against both the Fords and the Berry administration increased. In the process, his anger turned to resentment against the inequities found in the capitalist system. He had little doubt that Ford's millions were given "with the idea that he was helping to keep the pure attitude of the mountain people separated from any kind of ideas of organization, union." West also saw the school as a recruiting station for Ford, who frequently gave summer jobs in Detroit to Berry students, who were properly warned to resist organization. In hope of snaring generous contributions to the school, moreover, Berry students were routinely forced to welcome the "New England pilgrims" as well as the "Ford entourage" with "carefully coached smiles" and a rustic charade complete with prearranged oxen teams to underscore the pastoral image so appealing to the nostalgic Ford.[17]

Don's disdain for the Fords and their money was matched by suspicions about Martha Berry's objectives. Although Berry was southern, her willingness to accept northern dollars and faculty to carry out what seemed a project of cultural annihilation disgusted Don. He regarded Berry's founder as "very conscious of her superior aristocratic position." His angst was exacerbated by the ultimate humiliation of living with Berry as her "personal clean up boy" for a semester. This frustration, together with resentment against the Berry School's strict discipline, rigid demerit system, religious piety, and careful separation of the sexes, filled the young rebel with hostility toward it and the cultural intervention it represented.[18]

As West's frustration increased, his academic performance suffered. In April 1926, during his last year at Berry, Don announced to one of his instructors that "he thought he was degenerating" because he simply "[could] not seem to learn anything." Objecting that his assigned roommate, Burton Parks, was a cynical "bad spirit," Don felt that a change was warranted, a suggestion ultimately followed by the institution. Despite this accommodation, Don was among those students the faculty believed "lacking in earnestness."[19] Not long thereafter, the film incident further complicated West's troubled existence at Berry, which was destined to end in confrontation.

While West became increasingly uncomfortable at Berry as his high school years careened toward a premature conclusion, it was yet another clash with authority that led to his final break with the campus. His departure has been variously described as expulsion and personal protest. In later years Don often recalled that he was expelled after he had protested against the dismissal of a popular counselor. What Don regarded as expulsion was not quite that simple. Close scrutiny of the record reveals a more complicated set of circumstances and outcomes. Although the film incident jeopardized his position, it appears that West left Berry as a protest against the firing of the Rev. Melville Gurley, a chaplain and faculty member accused of "fraternizing" with the student body.[20]

Years later, Don remembered Gurley, who had originally recruited him for Berry, as a "very excellent" chaplain who connected with students on their level. The son of a prominent Philadelphia family, the Presbyterian minister enjoyed southern music and often invited students to his quarters, where they listened and discussed what they heard. Unfortunately for Gurley, many faculty members believed it inappropriate to "associate with the students," which they regarded as unacceptable behavior. In an action that many students deemed unfair, he was unceremoniously fired at the end of the 1925–26 academic year.[21]

There was a strong negative student reaction to Gurley's dismissal. In July 1926 at least three young men, including Don West, left the school in protest against Berry's callous treatment of their mentor. Don recalled that the three "took up for him," which meant that they "were let out, too." West later insisted that it was a matter of principle in which it was his responsibility to defend a man unjustly accused. The school's principal, G. Leland Green, saw his reaction as a matter of emotional attachment, asserting that "Donald was bound by strong ties of friendship to Mr. Gurley" and therefore "felt obliged to leave Berry."[22]

Although Don typically described the incident as his expulsion from Berry, Green's letter to Oliver suggests that the faculty and administration regarded his decision to leave as a "mistake" and encouraged him to "return for the opening of school ready to finish his course." What is certain is that within two weeks of his departure Don wrote to Principal Green, asking for a letter of recommendation and the transfer of his work credits to his sister Elsie, who would eventually graduate from Berry. Because he requested a transcript, it seems clear that he was already planning another academic endeavor. Green responded with a cordial assurance that he would supply a reference and an encouragement to complete his education. He also urged Oliver West to "advise Donald to return" to Berry, which suggests that the young rebel was indeed welcome should he have wished to re-enroll. Yet despite the niceties expressed at this time, Martha Berry later asserted that Don had indeed been expelled, after which he turned socialist and began "working with the Reds."[23] It is reasonable to conclude that West was expelled in 1926 with the option of re-enrolling at a later date to complete his high school education.

Although the departed students were encouraged to return, Gurley was gone for good, having been judged "indiscreet in his relations with students." The nature of that indiscretion became clear in Green's letter to another Gurley supporter (and donor), in which the principal defended the school's actions by detailing a litany of alleged sexual transgressions on the part of the beleaguered chaplain, including a series of occurrences that suggested either homosexuality or pedophilia. Charged with sleeping with, fondling, and photographing students, Gurley reportedly admitted that the charges were true but dismissed them as "grave indiscretions and not moral lapses." Don later alluded to unproven charges of homosexuality but neither confirmed nor denied their validity.[24] For him, the case seemed to boil down to a matter of fairness, and he remained unwilling to jettison a man for whom he had great respect.

West's loyalty was eventually acknowledged when Gurley tried to assist him in finding employment after he left Berry. In Atlanta, Gurley introduced him to an executive at Southern Bell Telephone Company, who subsequently offered Don a job stringing telephone wires from Gainesville to the North Georgia mountains near Tallulah Falls. He spent several months as a lineman, working on a railroad gang and earning $10 per week, which he dutifully sent home to assist the chronically ill Oliver in making ends meet as a hard-pressed sharecropper. A summer as lineman only whetted his appetite for education, and before long he was busy contacting colleges and universities, seeking admission to a postsecondary institution.[25]

Don had not graduated, but he had performed well and completed seventeen units of work at Berry, which qualified him for attendance at several institutions. Because of its location in the mountains of East Tennessee and its commitment to Appalachian youth, Lincoln Memorial University (LMU) drew his immediate attention. Informed that his work at Berry would satisfy entrance requirements, the itinerant scholar hitchhiked to Harrogate, Tennessee, with high hopes and a severely diminished bankroll. Eager to enroll, he approached Dean Charles D. Lewis with a story of ambition, intellectual curiosity, and financial embarrassment. Assured by the dean that a solution could be worked out, West jumped at the opportunity to work his way through college. Don subsequently paid his expenses and maintained his assistance to Oliver by working at the LMU campus farm, carrying laundry, digging ditches, and serving as a general laborer. Later, by taking a semester off to work on the campus farm, he also accumulated enough financial credit to bring Elsie to LMU.[26] That sacrifice demonstrated Don's internalization of traditional mountain values in that as the family's eldest son he felt a special obligation for the education of his siblings. This concern for familial well-being was a trait that would resurface periodically throughout his life, as he often found ways to assist his family, including not only his brothers and sisters but also his father and mother. It was the mountain way, and it was Don West's choice.

two

Expanded Horizons: Lincoln Memorial University as Seedbed of Creativity, 1926–29

Lincoln Memorial University (LMU) in Harrogate, Tennessee, was an institution tailor-made to suit Don West's emotional, spiritual, and educational needs in 1926. Founded in 1897 in recognition of mountaineers' contributions to the Union effort during the Civil War, its commitment to the education of Appalachian youths for service to their region matched West's developing concern for the preservation of mountain culture. In a missionary vein, Dean Lewis asserted that "prosperous America" desperately needed the blood of young mountain people, which at LMU would be "made ready to be transfused into [the nation's] polluted social blood stream." And very important to West, the campus commitment to the education of mountain students meant flexible entrance requirements that reflected the deficiencies in academic preparation often found among its clientele. Because of his academic potential, Don West essentially talked his way into the university's program.[1]

For West, LMU was liberating after his struggle with the Berry School, a needed breath of fresh air. Despite fairly rigid regulations, he "really felt great freedom when [he] first got there because they didn't tie you down." The relative openness at LMU was exhilarating, so much that by his senior year West was again deeply involved in "activities demanding more rights and privileges" for students.[2] Always testing the limits of the system, he married in violation of campus regulations and eventually organized students to promote the liberalization of policies on student social relationships.

When he arrived at LMU, West had no clear academic program in mind, yet a combination of factors predisposed him toward a career in the ministry. Deeply conscious of a family history filled with clergy and people of faith, he already thought of himself as a self-taught preacher. Driven by a personal calling to share his concept of Jesus the great teacher, Don plunged into religious activities from the outset of his college years. Before long he had become a fixture as he preached around the Cumberland Gap, spreading the gospel according to West. Moreover, although there was no clerical training program at LMU, he took courses in the Bible and excelled at them. He was also active in the Student Volunteer Band, an association that held regular prayer meetings and carried out social service projects in neighboring communities.[3]

West's work in the Student Volunteer Band reveals an early interest in socially committed religion. During his years at LMU he became well known in the schools and churches in nearby communities such as Poor Valley, where he established a Sunday school program. His preaching and teaching were short on piety and long on social service. In his words, he was never "piously religious" or "superstitious." Rather, he moved toward the ministry "as a way of serving my people" in the way he had seen mountain preachers in North Georgia meet the needs of their communities. That sort of social service was, in his view, "part of our mountain culture."[4]

There was substantial opportunity for apprenticeship in this field at LMU, where three Christian organizations were "doing a great work among the student body." Don West embraced them all. The Volunteer Band, the YMCA, and the YWCA all worked to serve students and take the campus to the community. By 1928 West had served as president of the Volunteer Band, the YMCA cabinet, and the Bible Study Club, in which he gained a reputation as the student who did "more outside work" than any other in "neighboring churches and Sunday Schools." Not only was Don a "leader in all religious activities of school life" but he was also "known and loved" by the younger boys and girls in "the most remote districts miles away from school."[5] LMU provided a useful training ground that nurtured West's instinct for common-sense religion and service to the poor.

While Don expended enormous effort on part-time religious work, the practical side of college mandated the selection of an academic major. Because his other passion was literature, his decision to focus on English was a natural choice. At LMU he began to "feel the effects of a little education" and "broader and deeper reading," not to mention a number of personal contacts that expanded his intellectual horizons. Among the first was a gangling Kentucky mountain boy, Jesse Stuart, whose intelligence and rebellious spirit made him a close friend. Their relationship was cemented by shared academic and literary interests that included mutual aspirations to become poets. Wandering the beautiful East Tennessee mountains, sharing their work, and dreaming dreams, they embodied the innocence and idealism of youth. Although his admiration would fade with the years, Stuart remembered West as "the finest man [he'd] met in Lincoln Memorial."[6] Together with classmate James Still, Stuart and West formed a remarkable literary triumvirate that reflected well on the small campus that nourished them during their formative years.

As aspiring artists, all three benefited enormously from contact with a gifted English professor, Harry Harrison Kroll. Once a sharecropper himself, Kroll served as an inspiring role model for young men in a hurry. An accomplished teacher and sensitive mentor, he was a successful writer in his own right, eventually producing more than twenty novels and works of nonfiction, including the very successful *Cabin in the Cotton* (1931), which was later made into a motion picture. He wrote from hard personal experience and sketched vivid portraits of class conflict and interracial unity in a modernizing south, providing images that fired the imagination of cultural chauvinists like West. Kroll encouraged students to write what they knew in the local vernacular, to emphasize "things in [their] own back yard that need[ed] to be written." For West, Kroll's background in a sharecropper family and literary emphasis on the lives of poor whites were most impressive. An "unusual teacher," he demonstrated for students the legitimacy of Appalachian culture as source material for successful literary work, a lesson Don West was primed to embrace.[7]

To both Stuart and West, Kroll was a model and more. Recognizing their potential as writers, he invested his own time and energy in their development. Stuart recalled that Kroll understood their financial need and tried to alleviate it with part-time employment. West's memory of Kroll, who knew of sharecropping firsthand, focused on his empathy for West as a sharecropper's son, an understanding that was the product of apprenticeship in the school of hard experience. He recalled that "no other major writer about the South has given us as understanding a portrayal of the poor white and black."[8] For West, it was Kroll's understanding of the poor that counted most, his treatment of sharecroppers as characters who possessed "dignity and self-respect." In Kroll's work, the poor white had a claim to equality, which he regarded as "every man's right."[9] That assumption was the central feature of Don's developing worldview.

Kroll's dismissal in 1929 came as an especially hard blow for West. After a mysterious figure haunted the campus for three days, one key LMU administrator and several faculty members were summarily fired for reasons unknown to the student body. Faculty understood that Kroll's vulnerability was related to controversy over the sexual content in his well-received novel *The Mountainy Singer* (1928). Although Stuart and West, who was devoted to Kroll, seemed unaware of the rationale behind the firing, the faculty purge coincided with a year of campus disturbances. Kroll was one of several faculty who had supported student demands for greater autonomy in a protest led by Don West. Following the professor's dismissal, Stuart visited Kroll, who concluded that he "must leave without reason and there's nothing that can be done about it."[10] West and Stuart were crushed by this blow to their mentor, a guiding light throughout their undergraduate years.

Under Kroll's guidance the two young writers had grown in self-confidence, creative powers, and participation in campus activism. West, more than Stuart or Still, had become a central figure on campus. Beyond his religious voluntarism, he soon emerged as a campus leader in a variety of activities; within two years he had become class president, YMCA president, literary society president, president of the Georgia Club, staff writer for *The Blue and the Grey*, and captain of the track squad. An "outstanding leader," he was "highly respected by the students." While compiling this record he also managed to turn in a respectable but not outstanding academic performance, all this while working his way through college, supporting his sister Elsie at LMU, and sending money home to assist the struggling Oliver.[11]

Of his many college activities, the literary societies were the closest to West's pretensions as a poet and writer. As treasurer of the Grant-Lee Literary Society in 1928, he was an active participant in campus literary and social events. A year later, as president of the new Howard Literary Society, the social activist West warned the aspiring writers to "not get so much form that the substance must suffer," advice he was soon to follow in his own literary work. At this early date *The Blue and the Grey* concluded that both Stuart and West were men who "speak through their pens."[12]

That observation was no exaggeration, for while at LMU the two apprentices had learned much from Kroll. Stuart penned five hundred poems before graduation, and West wrote extensively, publishing in campus magazines and local outlets. While a student, he was engaged in the work that was to appear in 1931 with the publication of his first major work, *Crab-Grass*. Harry Kroll's impact on West's work was substantial, most clearly in his employment of the vernacular to underscore the authenticity and homely beauty of mountain culture. Much more than Stuart, West would emulate Kroll's outrage at the injuries of class daily inflicted on the poor whites and blacks of the South.[13] West, Stuart, and Still were destined to make their marks on the American literary scene, albeit in dramatically different ways. Yet from the beginning, its sense of outrage at social injustice and contempt for accepted conventions would set West's work apart from that of his colleagues.

Don West's disregard for regulation and indifference to authority had surfaced during his turbulent years at Berry, and a thread of continuity in the LMU years demonstrated that he had grown no more willing to accept external discipline. One of the clearest examples may be found in his view of the campus regulations governing social relations among students. In contrast to the strict discipline at Berry, which discouraged interaction among boys and girls, the new freedom at LMU was a tonic and an opportunity soon taken. The first woman he dated was Mabel Constance (Connie) Adams, who had come to the university in 1926 on a scholarship from a nearby orphanage. Theirs was a tumultuous courtship punctuated by petty squabbling and extended periods apart. After Connie severed the relationship to date a student Don regarded as "about the worst guy on campus," the two were reunited and remained a couple for the rest of Don's college years.[14]

Connie Adams, a promising young art student, was the product of a difficult childhood. Beautiful and talented, she was both outgoing and popular. A native of Corbin, Kentucky, she was the daughter of a railroad engineer who spent much of his time on the road. After her mother's death, her father concluded that her best interests would be served by education in a Catholic orphanage, the Grace Nelson Home for Orphans, a decision that brought her to Harrogate. Her father, who "hated preachers" because his preacher stepfather had mistreated his mother, presented a major challenge for Don. Because he regarded the aspiring young preacher with suspicion, Don "had a rough time with the old man." Although Don recalled him as being unfriendly, that was not always so. In April 1928, after a visit in Corbin, Don wrote to Lillie of his relief at a cordial reception in the Adams home.[15]

The reason for Don's concern became clear the following year when the young lovers slipped away from the Lincoln Memorial campus to be secretly married in Middleboro, Kentucky. With Jesse Stuart and Mabel's sister, Addie, as the only witnesses, they broke one of the unwritten rules at the university, which "didn't like their students to get married." Concerned about the official reaction, the Wests succeeded in keeping their secret for six months, at least until early 1929, the year Don was scheduled to graduate. At first, they resided at their respective dormitories, but later the two began living together. The first penalty came when LMU withdrew Connie's scholarship, which made her senior year a significant financial challenge. By March 1929 the marriage was no longer a secret.[16] By then graduation was just around the corner, and it seemed safe enough to disclose the marriage without jeopardizing the couple's academic futures.

Although this minor transgression might well have been tolerated, other issues made it impossible for the LMU administration to ignore Don West's tendency to challenge authority. For West, a constant irritant was the presence of northern faculty who—from his point of view—failed to respect the mountain people who made up the student body. Again the old resentment welled up, sensitive as Don was about outsiders who viewed mountaineers as culturally inferior. Beyond that, he chafed at LMU's treatment of students in loco parentis and the denial of a meaningful student voice in campus affairs.[17]

Asked by LMU's board of trustees to make recommendations, West presented a set of suggested reforms to the faculty, most of which dealt with allegations that the administration treated students as uncultured "hillbillies" rather than the proud mountain people they were. To this argument was added a protest against its paternalistic approach to student life. Stuart remembered that Don stated the case "candidly," but Business Manager C. P. Williams recalled his suggestions as the result of a West-instigated whispering campaign against the administration. Finally, West sealed his own fate with a fiery speech to student supporters in which he "told them too much about [the] place." In defiance of campus authorities, he blistered the administration for its callous treatment of mountain people and calculated devaluation of the Appalachian cultural heritage that was the birthright of the student body.[18] His words reflected not only the rhetorical style learned from the country preachers of his youth but also the heightened resentment against cultural intervention that was the product of a maturing intellect.

The student strike essentially closed the campus for three weeks, causing the administration to flounder. At that point Harry Kroll and a few other faculty rallied to the students' side, only to be dismissed. According to Williams, a disenchanted West now proclaimed that he would not return to campus in the fall, but the rebel was never formally expelled although he was persona non grata the following semestser. In Stuart's account, Williams hesitated, then reversed himself with an announcement that Donald West, as protest leader, had been expelled from the university. By that time West had gone home to Georgia, where his mother had been reported seriously ill.[19]

While visiting Lillie, Don received a telegram from Lincoln Memorial announcing his expulsion and warning that he would not be allowed back on campus. In a defiant response, however, he returned to Harrogate, where he had many community supporters. Meanwhile, faculty and local citizens peppered the LMU administration with demands for the young dissident's reinstatement. In Stuart's words, "The students rose in revolt," determined to "wreck the damn school" if they failed to "have Don West back." In a contrasting version of the struggle, Williams recalled that a magnanimous Chancellor

John Wesley Hill had reinstated West with full academic standing.[20] What resulted was Don's triumphal return to Lincoln Memorial, from which he was graduated in 1929.

The student strike at Lincoln Memorial reinforced Don West's confrontational style, which was becoming a theme in his ideological journey. An important feature of West's thinking during his college years was a maturing consciousness of capitalist oppression, which he observed during the bitter labor disturbances of 1929. Part of the broader education gained at LMU was a sharpened awareness of social and economic change in other parts of the southern Appalachians. That social concern led West and other students to observe and engage in some of the workers' struggles sweeping the mountains. On weekends, for example, they sometimes went into Harlan County, Kentucky, to walk picket line with strikers. Similarly, the textile strikes at Elizabethton, Tennessee, and Marion and Gastonia, North Carolina, drew their interest and became hot topics at student discussion sessions back on campus. Gastonia in particular left an impression on West, who was struck by the "tenseness of the situation." Sensitized by the violence that erupted, he concluded that religion must be a tool "for helping the poor people that [he] came from."[21]

Determined to pursue activist religion, West left after graduation to explore graduate study opportunities. Planning to prepare for the ministry, he first considered the Presbyterian Theological Seminary in Louisville, but a cold reception from a dormitory house mother disillusioned him. As a result, he left for Vanderbilt University in hopes of enrolling there. Again identifying a sympathetic dean, O. O. Brown, and stressing his willingness to work, West talked himself into divinity school. Brown helped him land a job coaching basketball and other athletics at the Martha O'Brien Settlement House near Fisk University in Nashville's black district. Here his salary made life at Vanderbilt pleasant, yet again his thoughts turned to home, family, and obligation. He wrote home in November 1929 to tell his parents that he was conscious of "putting off year after year the time when [he] would go to work to help some." He then reasserted his main purpose in seeking higher education: to "help [his] people, do something that [would] make life a little more worth living."[22] To achieve his goal, he concluded that a divinity degree was essential. As a result, West set out on a new path that would end in ordination in the Congregational Church. Although he was to achieve his professional goal, Don West's Vanderbilt experience would be transformative in ways that he could not possibly have foreseen as he embarked on his next academic journey.

three

Social Gospel and Educational Mission: The Turning Point, 1930–33

The Vanderbilt School of Religion that Don West entered in 1929 was much more than a mere training ground for prospective clergy. Although induction into the clerical profession was its primary function, exposure to the Social Gospel was an important current in the research and teaching of an activist faculty. More than he knew, Vanderbilt in the early 1930s would become an intellectual and spiritual home for West, who was searching for a career that would unite his religious instincts with a determination to improve the lives of his people. Here he met engaged professors whose teachings fired him with hope for applied Christianity, and here he joined a coterie of idealistic young clergy-in-training, including Claude Williams, Ward Rogers, and Howard Kester, who were to remain friends and partners in the pursuit of social justice. Under the spell of the faculty social activists, West also took a sharp turn toward the political Left on the road to an ideological utopia that offered a solution to the problem of poverty in a land of plenty.

While seeking credentials as a preacher West also perfected the literary skills that had been nourished at LMU by his mentor Harry Kroll and encouraged by close friendships with Jesse Stuart and James Still. By fortuitous circumstance both Stuart and Still also found their way to Vanderbilt, where they continued their respective literary apprenticeships under the guidance of the Nashville Agrarians, including Donald Davidson, John Crowe Ransom, and Allen Tate. It was this influential intellectual circle that produced the classic exposition of the southern agricultural tradition *I'll Take My Stand* (1930), and it was this literary movement that West rejected in his own work. To Don, the Nashville school longed for a south that had never existed for the free men and women of his mountain home. Nor did they address the needs of the rural poor, whose plight drove his maturing political conscience. As West veered toward social activism, he parted company with his old friend Jesse Stuart, who had set off on his own ideological journey into political conservatism.[1]

During Stuart's one unhappy year at Vanderbilt he and West reestablished contact. The two, Stuart recalled, by this time had "clashed and were held apart," but at Vanderbilt they "tried to patch things up." Because Jesse was without resources, Don offered what help he could, starting with the purchase of a meal ticket that kept his friend alive for a year. But Stuart was appalled by West's growing radicalism and "ideas about the U.S. Government." By the time of their first campus meeting in 1931 West had already changed. He told Stuart that since Lincoln Memorial he had been kicked out of three churches and seen so much human suffering that he had "grown bitter." From then on, West announced, he intended to "save human beings on earth instead of preaching to them of a reward in heaven." Although he differed ideologically from Don, Stuart later maintained that West was "recognized as an unusual fellow" at Vanderbilt and soon "one of the leaders in the graduate class."[2]

Before Stuart showed up at Vanderbilt, West had already begun to absorb the teachings of a band of liberal theologians, including Alva W. Taylor and Willard Uphaus, scholars who exhorted the divinity students to immerse themselves in the communities they hoped to serve. Of these, none had greater impact on West's thinking than Taylor, a social reformer whom West regarded as "a great spirit" and a "tremendously dedicated, able person." Ordained minister and secretary of the Disciples of Christ's active Board of Temperance and Social Welfare, Taylor "brought Jesus to life" and "fitted him into the picture of today." A firm advocate of the Social Gospel, his active support of striking unionists in Tennessee, Kentucky, Illinois, and Virginia as well as his other activities eventually cost him his teaching job at Vanderbilt, thus providing stark evidence that, in Taylor's words, "It was dangerous to preach too much of the gospel message." Completely devoted to the advancement of human welfare, he "inspired his students to get out into things that were happening." Influenced by Taylor's courses in Christian ethics, West immersed himself in the survival problems of Tennessee and Kentucky mining communities, where he worked as a teacher and helped deliver relief supplies to suffering families. Under Taylor's guidance, Don also researched and wrote a senior thesis on

Knott County, Kentucky, while teaching at the Hindman Settlement School in 1930 and 1931. The example and teachings of Alva Taylor were key factors in moving West toward Christian socialism as the solution to the problems of the dispossessed of southern Appalachia.[3]

By the end of West's first year at Vanderbilt the economic distress of the mountain poor and mining communities of Tennessee and Kentucky had worsened as the nation fell into the early stages of the Great Depression. Subsistence farming sustained some, but the collapse of the market economy destroyed the livelihoods of miners, textile workers, and other laborers who had been drawn into the industrial system then transforming the South. As a result, the most dramatic crisis of the 1930s centered on the loss of jobs in the mines, mills, and forests, employment on which displaced rural families had come to depend. Further complicating a volatile social situation, employers were convinced that the only way they could stay competitive was to exploit a non-union labor force. As the pulse of the union movement quickened in the 1930s, competition for jobs and management resistance contributed to violence and instability in labor relations. With farm income down from an already abysmal level and mining counties depressed, eastern Kentucky and Tennessee were headed for long-term dependency status.[4]

It was this grim world that Don and Connie West entered in mid-1930 when both took jobs at the Hindman Settlement School in Knott County, Kentucky. Although Don loved the mountains and his students, there was something unsettling about his experience at Hindman. In October 1930, West wrote to James Still of his exhilaration over mountain life, teaching, and preaching. Despite the compensatory benefits, however, West expressed alarm over a local population "going down physically and otherwise," which meant that without a change they would become "a bunch of degenerates in a few generations." Social problems abounded, including intermarriage, illegitimacy, alcoholism, tobacco addiction, and malnutrition, all of which cried out for community uplift. Although shaken, he still had "faith in [his] purpose and ability to some day put across some of [his] ideals."[5]

Plagued by self-doubt, West told Still that he was not likely to return to Hindman the following year. Not only was he engaged in researching a thesis for his Vanderbilt degree but he also longed for a return to the more traditional academic life he had left behind. Equally important was a growing uneasiness with the Hindman approach to the education of mountain children and the cultural intervention he had opposed ever since his years at Berry. Finding a sympathetic listener, Don embraced Still's "proposition that mountain schools are conducted on false principles and are failing to a surprising degree." Only the John C. Campbell Folk School at Brasstown, North Carolina, seemed on the right track, an assessment that reflected West's growing interest in the Danish folk school as a model for the education of mountain people with an eye to cultural conservation.[6]

Closely linked to this interest in folk culture was West's thesis research, which was well underway by December 1930 in anticipation of a return to Vanderbilt and Alva Taylor. Scouring Knott County on horseback during a twelve-day tour, he compiled a detailed demographic, economic, and social study of the county's population that contained hints of his future political orientation and cultural project. The thesis described a community held together by common heritage but in need of education, social opportunity, and economic liberation. Yet he saw hope for a self-conscious rebellion that would lead to community resistance against an "inhuman system" that was "grinding out the blood of the people." This cultural revival was possible if only the mountain folk would "see the advantages of cooperation—Socialism." Although they had been "missionarized, pauperized, and sentimentalized," the common people could be "awakened to their responsibilities." Viewed against the remainder of his career, the Knott County study offered a blueprint for Don's contributions to cultural revival in Appalachia.[7]

Research in hand, West prepared for a return to the academic life as summer approached. Still driven by the conviction that "the only thing in life worthwhile is service, giving yourself for others," he was determined to follow the "hard road."[8] Although he was asked to become principal of the Pine Mountain Settlement School, Don rejected the offer in favor of other plans for the advancement of mountain education. By March 1931 he had accepted a scholarship to study the Danish folk schools in Copenhagen and Elsinore, where he intended to observe cooperative community enterprises, collaborative education, and methods of cultural preservation. Already familiar with the writings of John C. and Olive Dame Campbell, West believed the folk school model "offered some hope for Appalachia." With support from Yale University, probably engineered by Willard Uphaus and Alva Taylor, he planned to learn the Danish system with an eye to "raising to a higher level the standard of living among our mountains." West turned down several lucrative job offers, preferring to explore ideas applicable to Appalachian cultural uplift. He told his friend Jim Still that he would "never worry over money," which he spent "just about as fast as it [came] in."[9] This was a luxury he could afford because Connie was employed at Hindman, where she would teach during his European tour.

Because of its reputation for progressive education, workers' schools, the cooperative movement, and community outreach, Denmark was the center of attention for American educators interested in worker problems, extended education, and folk culture. Because the Appalachians had come to be viewed as the home of a genuine "folk culture," progressive educators were drawn to the Danish folk school movement as a model for the improvement of regional rural education. As early as the administration of Theodore Roosevelt, proponents of the country life movement had embraced folk schools as instruments for preserving a vibrant rural culture. Just as the traditional way of rural life began to disappear from the South in the 1920s, proponents of southern mountain schools, such as Hindman, advanced the idea of rural education based on traditional crafts and community service. The Council of Southern Mountain Workers, the voice of folk, mission, and settlement-school workers, now endorsed craft-based education that bore a strong resemblance to the Danish folk school model.[10]

To better understand the Danish approach, West spent several months in 1931 studying at the International People's College at Elsinore, where he was deeply impressed by what the Danes "had done for an illiterate people, an oppressed people, the serfs, the peasants, how they brought them up to high dignity and cultural development." This program, he recalled, had been started by Bishop Nikolai Gruntvig of the Danish state church, who insisted that illiterate peasants were just as capable of learning as others. Gruntvig saw folk schools as a means of "enlivening" farmers and workers long subjugated by an oppressive feudal system. Given free rein, Don visited farms and schools, where he witnessed the integration of folk music, oral tradition, the performing arts, and cooperative experience rooted in the soil.[11]

When he returned to the United States in the fall of 1931 West resolved to apply the Danish folk school model to the needs of Appalachian mountain people. After a brief stint teaching at Hindman, Don found himself penniless but full of ideas for improving the lives of the Appalachian poor. While completing his work at Vanderbilt he also published his first volume of poetry, *Crab-Grass*, which drew the attention of his mentors. In February 1932 the *Vanderbilt Alumnus* magazine ran a short feature on West's literary work, including poetry "of real value," which demonstrated that the author had "a fair ability to picture the mountaineer's life." Even the *Berry Alumni Quarterly* took pride in a former student's achievement, noting that *Crab-Grass* was "attracting wide-spread attention." Berry found in West's work a model for other Berry students who would pursue their goals with "unlimited pluck and determination." Dismissing the unpleasant circumstances surrounding his departure from the campus, the voice of Berry now saw the school's "noblest ideals . . . realized in Don West's life."[12]

The unanticipated notoriety was a matter of some pride as well as a source of limited income. In April 1932 West completed a successful tour of the

Southeast, presenting poetry readings in Louisiana, Mississippi, Alabama, and Georgia. Even more satisfying was his triumphant return to Berry, where his poetry "profoundly impressed students and faculty alike." Closest to his heart was his lecture to the agriculture school, which extolled the Danish folk schools for having "lifted the peasantry" to a "very high level of intelligence and culture." By this time both *Crab-Grass* and *Deep, Deep Down in Living* were in print, and, the Berry alumni magazine maintained, critics had begun to identify West as a rising literary star.[13]

West's poetry was an artistic extension of a young man's rising conscious-ness of human inequality and the disproportionate burden shouldered by the common people, whose exploitation at the hands of corporate capital weighed heavily on a troubled mind. Still searching for answers, he told Still that he was "trying to find out what all this life's about." At Vanderbilt, he sought the solution in the company of militants like Williams, Rogers, and Kester, all of them imbued with Alva Taylor's Social Gospel teachings. Ordained a Congregationalist minister in 1931, West excelled academically, compiling the highest grades in the School of Religion in 1932.[14] By the time of his gradu-ation in June 1932 he was prepared to bring his concept of the revolutionary Jesus to bear in solving human problems.

A Christ-centered evangelicalism was a central feature of the Social Gospel advocated by Taylor and the Vanderbilt activists. Impressed by the work and writings of Walter Rauschenbusch and other advocates of applied Christian-ity, who in the early twentieth century had sought to revitalize the church by inserting it into the communities it served, Alva Taylor called students to a social mission higher than personal salvation. Insisting that the church deal with human problems, advocates of the new religion called for the realization of the kingdom of God on earth, which required a revolution in human behav-ior modeled on the example of the historical Jesus. Theirs was an optimistic religion based on the belief that through education and adherence to moral principle, human beings could create a new social order that valued all people and elevated them spiritually. Firmly grounded in the evangelical Protestant-ism of the nineteenth-century home missions, the Appalachian Social Gospel "broke new ground" in the twentieth-century effort to engage the church in the solution of social problems.[15]

Inspired by Taylor's teaching, a young Texan, Ward Rogers, applied Social Gospel theory to international relations, urging that the church and clergy dedicate themselves to the preservation of world peace and social justice. Even more radical in applying his theology to the problems of the South was a Virginia-born advocate of racial accommodation, Howard "Buck" Kester. An activist in YMCA work, Kester spoke on college campuses of his determination to integrate the churches of his native region. A promoter of interracial social and religious events, he managed to alienate his mentors at a variety of institutions. Stricken from the list of candidates for Presbyterian ordination in Virginia, he attended Princeton Theological Seminary long enough to reject its conservative intellectual atmosphere. Kester's search for a socially relevant educational experience brought him to the side of Alva W. Taylor. After a contentious experience at Vanderbilt, he dropped out to engage in organizational work for the Fellowship of Reconciliation as youth secretary. By the time he returned to Vanderbilt in 1929 Kester had been sufficiently radicalized to discuss with West possible membership in the Communist Party. Kester's close friend, Claude Williams, was another Vanderbilt student who, under Taylor's influence, began to develop a liberal theology featuring emphasis on meeting the needs of the poor. The son of a Tennessee sharecropper, Williams had preached traditional fundamentalist religion for several years before his conversion to the gospel of interracial unity and compassion for the dispossessed.[16] His political journey toward Marx matched the leftward drift of Don West in the early 1930s.

Under the spell of Alva W. Taylor, this band of activist students was drawn into the grim world of labor-management confrontation. As early as 1929, Taylor exhorted his followers to become engaged in the labor struggles sweeping the South, first as observers during the bitter Gastonia strike and later as participants in the demonstrations. He urged his social ethics classes to become engaged witnesses to worker resistance to oppression and the damaging impact of industrialism on mountain people not far removed from rural life. West recalled that Taylor "had the knack for challenging and stimulating students to get into the things that really mattered."[17]

To Taylor and his students, nothing mattered more than the plight of the worker community and families of Wilder, Tennessee, where a bitter strike divided labor and management over a series of wage cuts going back to 1930. Here the United Mineworkers of America (UMWA) had successfully organized a union at the Fentress Coal and Coke Company, which had won at least one contract before the collapse of the wage structure under the combined pressures of a depressed economy and management determination to break the union. When the contract expired in June 1932 the company began a systematic firing of union members, who then went out on strike. After some miners reluctantly returned to work in October, violence broke out between scabs and striking miners, which led Gov. Henry H. Horton to send in the National Guard, ostensibly to maintain order but essentially to protect company property. Faced with hopeless odds and powerful enemies, the union ended the work stoppage in the spring of 1933, leaving worker families jobless and starving. In late 1932 several outside groups took an active interest in the miners' plight. Among them were Alva Taylor's student volunteers, including Don West, who brought supplies to Wilder on weekend excursions into the world of industrial warfare. By fall 1932, Kester's Emergency Relief Committee and Taylor's Church Relief Committee had skillfully organized support for the destitute worker community.[18]

The Wilder crisis coincided with West's deepening commitment to Marxism as an ideology that explained the degradation of his people and provided hope for a solution to their problems. Like Kester, West had read Marx, Engels, and Lenin and begun an ideological journey into the world of socialism. By this time, Rogers, Williams, and West "were considered the radicals . . . the ones that they [the Vanderbilt authorities] thought would come to bad end in the future." For West, the imperative to aid the needy, rooted in a sense of community ingrained in his very being by youthful exposure to mountain values, was the germ of a collective consciousness that fed his social activism. Under Taylor's spell, West melded the teachings of his own culture with a socialist perspective encountered in his mentor's classes at Vanderbilt. Impressed by Taylor's endorsement of Christian socialism as well as the charismatic leadership of Norman Thomas, who also came to Wilder, West joined the Socialist Party (SP) and became its Tennessee state organizer in late 1932. Confident of a collectivist future, he enthusiastically embraced a radical solution to the problem of poverty and exploitation.[19]

After a brief period in early 1932 as pastor of a Congregational church in Crossville, Tennessee, West threw himself into relief work at Wilder and socialist organizing activity wherever he could find an audience. Following a pattern set early in their marriage, Don was temporarily separated from Connie, who spent time with Lillie in Georgia while her husband traveled the state before landing in Tennessee in September 1932. To his dismay, prospects for socialism in Wilder were slim. In November, Howard Kester observed that Wilder workers were basically "conservative in their social and economic views," which initially made them cautious because they "didn't want any 'Reds' in their midst."[20]

Eventually, however, they came to trust Kester, who took up residence in Wilder, as well as the regular visitor, Don West, who spoke to local audiences on behalf of the SP on several occasions in late 1932. It is clear from Kester's correspondence that the primary impetus behind the Wilder relief program came from the Tennessee socialists, a tightly knit group that grew very close to the mining community. In December 1932, Taylor launched a new organizational effort, which began with a significant contribution from Norman Thomas. Meanwhile, Kester carried out a political education program stressing

Wilder as an example of "what [was] happening . . . to all wage earners living under our anarchistic, capitalistic, individualistic, competitive society." While focusing on relief, he had "not neglected to do the very important thing of distributing ideas."[21]

In the wake of a collapsed economy, the appeal of radicalism was on the rise throughout the United States. Given the strong dose of Christian socialism administered by Alva W. Taylor, the response of his students was predictable. The fact that the chief national spokesperson for socialism, Norman Thomas, was himself a member of the Protestant clergy merely reaffirmed their predisposition to adopt an ideology that promised relief to the suffering of capitalism's dispossessed. Although relief efforts and political work were well underway by September 1932, West envisioned a complementary scheme to promote the economic salvation and cultural preservation of the Appalachian South through cooperative education based on the Danish folk school model he had observed firsthand. The result was an educational experiment that created one of the most significant institutions for the advancement of southern social justice and racial equality to appear in the years before the development of the modern civil rights movement: the Highlander Folk School.

By the summer of 1932 another southern radical, Myles Horton, had also concluded that a people's school could serve the cause of workers and hasten the arrival of a socialist revolution while preserving Appalachian culture. Already engaged in fund-raising to that end, the Tennessee-born Horton relied largely on northern capital and the powerful endorsement of his mentor at Union Theological Seminary, Reinhold Niebuhr, who helped generate financial support for the scheme. Embraced by Niebuhr, Horton enlisted the support of Thomas and the Socialist Party, Kirby Page of the Fellowship of Reconciliation, educator John Dewey, Roger Baldwin of the American Civil Liberties Union (ACLU), and President Frank Porter Graham of the University of North Carolina. He also began to recruit a teaching staff that soon would include two classmates, southern-born James A. Dombrowski and John B. Thompson, both Union graduate students who were to join the Highlander faculty shortly after its opening.[22]

Although Horton had launched the fund-raising task, it was Don West who first identified the location and property near Monteagle, Tennessee, where the school would eventually be established. West had long nurtured the dream of a folk school to foster pride in culture among the people of the Appalachian South. To this end, in the spring of 1932 he took the first halting steps that were to end in the opening of the Highlander Folk School. Shortly before West's graduation from Vanderbilt, the southern superintendent of the Congregational Church, Fred P. Ensminger, who had ordained Don and was familiar with his folk school obsession, informed him that there was an elderly woman who might be willing to donate her farm near Monteagle for educational programming in that area. West, at this time pastor at Barton Chapel in Crossville, expressed immediate interest in exploring with her his plans for a new cooperative education program. Enslinger introduced West to Lillian Johnson and her fellow teacher, the children's writer May Justus, thus establishing a relationship that ended in Johnson's offering the property to the school. A Wellesley graduate and progressive educator who had studied under John Dewey at the University of Michigan, Johnson had compiled an impressive professional record as a college teacher and president of Western College for Women in Ohio. She also had a long history of interest in cooperatives and collaborative education, which had led her to convert her house and grounds into a community social center for mountain people near Summerfield, Tennessee. She and Justus recalled meeting West in the spring of 1932, before Horton was on the scene. As a result of their initial meeting Johnson agreed to turn over the property and buildings to West for the purpose of starting the folk school he envisioned. Thus, before encountering Myles Horton, West had begun the negotiating process that resulted in the provisional land grant that made Highlander possible.[23]

During the summer of 1932, while the Wests were participating in a YMCA summer conference at Blue Ridge, North Carolina, Don received a call from Horton, who expressed interest in discussing their separate plans for southern folk schools. Horton had been referred to West by Will Alexander of the Committee on Interracial Cooperation in Atlanta, who was aware of West's plan for a folk school. After exploring mutual interests, they spent several days scouring the South Appalachian area for a site suitable for Horton's project. Joined by Horton's classmate John Thompson and John's sister Dorothy, they shared visions of cooperative education in the Appalachian South. After several sites in Tennessee, Kentucky, and North Carolina proved unsatisfactory, Don invited the group to the Summerfield property for a talk with Lillian Johnson, which made perfect sense to him in view of his own endorsement of collaborative principles. According to West's account, Horton then suggested becoming a partner in the Summerfield (Monteagle) project already in its planning stages, a proposal to which Don, a proponent of cooperation, readily agreed. At the time, Horton recalled, they both "felt that within two or three years there would be a school like Highlander in every state" and that "the idea would spread very rapidly."[24]

By the time West and Horton formally launched the project in September 1932 they had already rethought its name. Although the initial fund-raising letter carried the letterhead "Southern Mountain Folk School," the institution had become the Highlander Folk School before West and Horton completed negotiations with Lillian Johnson. After considerable debate, Connie West suggested that the label "Highlander" accurately represented the mountain culture and people that were to be their central concern. In his autobiography, Horton acknowledged that although he thought the original name satisfactory, the Wests "decided that we needed a better one" and that he acceded to their wishes.[25] With a one-year lease in hand, the new partners launched an educational institution that was to change the history of the South and influence both the twentieth-century labor movement and the modern civil rights movement.

Both founders aspired to "enrich the lives of mountain people," but West, always the more politicized of the two, proclaimed that Highlander "educate[d] for a socialized nation" that would advance "human justice, cooperation, a livelihood for every man and a fair distribution of wealth." Horton, who shared West's goal as a *long-term* objective, was more cautious in articulating the school's purposes and emphasized a narrower goal of educating farmers and workers for a new society based on human brotherhood and social justice.[26] West and Horton glimpsed the outlines of a better future for their people, but in temperament they were fire and ice. Before long, their differences threatened the stability of a struggling institution.

Delighted with the initiative, Highlander board member Alva W. Taylor counted the school among the most significant "social experiments" to appear in the South in the early 1930s. Citing Commonwealth College in Arkansas and the John C. Campbell Folk School in North Carolina as examples, he told *Christian Century* readers that the Appalachians were "rich in material for such undertakings." With emphasis on the importance of the Danish folk school model, Taylor took pride in the work of the "two young Galahads" who had embarked on "an adventure of faith." At Highlander, he insisted, mountain youths and their mentors would soon "live and work together in an earnest and utterly unconventional manner to find what life is all about and how to live it in a manner most serviceable to their fellow man."[27]

Fueled by a belief in Christian socialism, cooperative education, and the richness of Appalachian culture, the partners now worked to convert a dream into reality. The adjustment brought many problems, beginning with difficulties in recruitment that hampered the full-time program. Although both worked to win the confidence of the surrounding community, local suspicions died hard. Consequently, while community outreach efforts brought respectable crowds, faculty outnumbered students in the first class. Surviving on a steady diet of potatoes and beans, West and Horton struggled on, Don as organizational director and Myles as educational director. West endured constant travel and external criticism while, according to one student observer, Horton bore relatively little work responsibility beyond fund-raising. Don traveled through Tennessee, Kentucky, Georgia, and Alabama, "beating the bushes," but he attracted few students. Although the results were disappointing, West's recruitment work contributed to his political education by further immersing him in rural poverty and the lives of forgotten people in the mining towns of Appalachia. Despite heroic efforts, only one resident student, the son of an Alabama miner, showed up for classes on November 1, 1932, when the program began.[28] Highlander seemed headed for hard times.

By most accounts, West's perspective was more regional than that of Horton, who retained his ties with Niebuhr and Union, including the financial supporters who kept the program afloat with seed money in the early months. West thought of himself as "more locally oriented," in contrast to Horton, who retained a cosmopolitan outlook. Their first student recalled that Don's southern contacts and the reputation "he had attained as a radical" placed him on a level of equity with Myles. According to this observer, it was West who shouldered responsibility for clubs and classes in outlying communities, and he also bore most of the community's criticism when the program raised concerns over the goals of social action and politicization.[29]

In view of Highlander's avowed intent to "train *radical* labor leaders who [would] understand the need of both political and union strategy," community resistance was to be expected. The attack was not long in coming. Latent suspicion was already present due to the Wilder relief efforts. Equally provocative was the community outreach work that brought the program "severe criticism and misunderstanding," much of it directed at West. Typical was Grundy County school board chair W. J. Jossi's assertion that the "political matters being taught were 'Red' or communist in appearance." As a result of this notoriety the local board denied Highlander faculty the use of school facilities. Although "ordinary poor people" were friendly, "the ones who had power were pretty anti-Highlander in the beginning and it got worse." Their hostility was evident in the words of A. L. Henderson, cashier of the First National Bank of Tracy City, who charged that "athiests, infidels, and agitators" were "stirring up trouble" with "lectures on how to successfully conduct a strike, lectures on how the capitalists cheat the workers out of the rightful fruits of their labor, and the Russian form of government." These charges drew an angry response from West, who disputed charges of communist instruction but issued a ringing defense of socialism together with an invititation to the interested public to attend sessions and make an independent judgment.[30]

Although these criticisms were a reaction to Highlander's outreach program they also reflected concern about West's active socialist organizing. By now state organizer, he had thrown himself into the difficult task of building socialism in Tennessee. Horton reported to Clarence Senior of the national SP that in neighboring Palmer, Tennessee, Don and one of his students had been holding socialist meetings just outside the mine village, a provocation that led directly to the county school board's action against Highlander for "advocating Communism." Despite the setbacks, miners and workers in several communities were "asking that Socialist locals be organized," and Highlander faculty tried to respond.[31]

The notoriety drew the attention of not only the local press but also Highlander's key benefactor, Lillian Johnson. The daughter of a Memphis banker, Johnson brought a distinctly elite perspective to the issues raised by the school's radical activity. West's proselytizing and Horton's arrest at Wilder for relief activities raised public awareness of Highlander's work, which was taking on a form not envisioned in Johnson's original understanding of the project. Alarmed by the negative publicity, she warned Horton not to teach "theories and slogans that are divisive." She clearly separated her ideas from socialism, which was, in her mind, "connected with loose living . . . political failures . . . and the worst kind of trade unionism." Despite the reservations, she defended the Highlander experiment in a strong letter to the *Chattanooga Times.* Insisting that cooperation was "a form of brotherhood that would bring all classes together," she embraced the school and characterized West and Horton as selfless men who gave themselves to the people of the Appalachian South in "a truly Christ-like spirit."[32]

Four days later, a distressed Lillian Johnson told Horton that the *Times* editor claimed that Highlander's directors embraced communism and distributed radical literature. Worse yet, in a public lecture West had allegedly "decried anyone having any right to accumulate property." In her letter to the editor she had staunchly defended what she thought was Highlander's brand of cooperation, including its relief work at Wilder, as an effort at "breaking down the antagonism between modern methods of business and the principles of Christianity." She gamely reiterated her endorsement but recommended that the school "let socialism, which does not seem to be getting anywhere, alone."[33]

Not long thereafter the strife at Wilder refocused public attention on Highlander and its leaders when violence erupted anew. Corporate control of local churches, medical facilities, and law enforcement had long been part of the local scene, as had the ominous presence of the National Guard. After Horton's arrest in November 1932, threats against the life of union president Barney Graham intensified the atmosphere of fear that gripped the community. As of early 1933, West maintained, the main Highlander contribution to the union cause had been to "stir up a lot of hell." In January, Graham told

West that the Guard was still in Wilder, but the men "were sticking just like they [had been] when [Don] was up [there]." Because of the tense situation, however, he did not "think it would be wise to teach until we see what they [the guard and the company] do."[34]

If teaching was difficult, the pace of socialist organizing quickened. Kester wrote to Senior that a successful organizational meeting had been held, at which Don was again appointed state organizer. Hoping to capitalize on SP interest in the Wilder crisis, West now helped Kester persuade Thomas to visit the beleaguered mining community. Concerned over Highlander's growing radical reputation, Don proposed that Kester arrange the event but agreed to play a role in the program. Convinced that "the time [was] ripe for Socialism" in Wilder, the comrades coordinated the program with relief distribution to emphasize the Party's commitment to the strikers. Relying on the mountain ballad tradition and a long-standing union practice of building solidarity through song, West joined country musician Ed Davis to perform "The Davidson-Wilder Blues," a lyrical attack on the scabs whose labor eventually enabled the company to break the strike. Thomas responded with a stirring speech placing the Wilder struggle in the context of organized labor's history and destiny.[35]

Not long after the rhetoric faded, however, the workers sustained a fatal blow when on April 30, 1933, Graham was murdered by two company guards as he walked down Wilder's main street to the company store. Although official accounts maintained that the gunmen fired in self-defense, the union and the Highlander activists were unconvinced in view of the four bullets that hit Graham in the back and the fact that the handgun found near his body still had its safety on. Moreover, Horton had learned the previous week that Jack Green, a company man, was a "hired assassin" from Illinois whose mission it was to kill Graham. West recalled the murder as "unprovoked," except that Graham was "provoking them by being union president."[36]

In response to the violence, the Kesters stayed with the Graham family that night to comfort them. Soon thereafter it became necessary to make funeral arrangements, but so dominant was corporate influence in Wilder that no local church would consent to hold a funeral, nor would a local preacher officiate. Again, the Highlander group responded. West and Kester helped conduct simple funeral services in the Graham home and at the cemetery, following a somber procession of seven hundred miners and their families through Wilder. It was at the Graham residence that West conducted his first funeral as an ordained minister, in what he later described as "a grim situation."[37]

Company-sponsored violence in Wilder had an immediate effect. One day after Graham's murder, three hundred disconsolate miners returned to work without a union contract. Those who refused work on company terms were blacklisted, and by fall the worker community existed in a near destitute state. Once the troops left, the company refused mediation, the strike was lost, and union miners remained jobless. Despite residual sniping, the strike was broken and the union was destroyed. Not surprisingly, the killer was acquitted of all charges. After years of deprivation, some miners were hired by the Tennessee Valley Authority (TVA); blacklisted families relocated to homesteads in Crossville, Tennessee, under the authority of the Resettlement Administration's Cumberland Homestead program, which was administered by Vanderbilt refugee Alva W. Taylor.[38]

The murder of Barney Graham and the Wilder strike made an indelible impression on Don West, whose mind was filled with resentment against the exploitation of the poor. When asked years later why he had gone to Wilder, the deep feelings poured out: "I was interested in them because they were being oppressed. I had grown up oppressed. I came from the poorest of the poor." As David Duke has shown, what West saw at Wilder "clarified what he had known for most of his life—that there was a tremendous gulf between the haves and have-nots, the oppressed and the oppressors." Don never forgot Graham, his widow, or the children he left, including young Della Mae, who as a twelve-year-old followed mountain tradition to pen the lyrics of the plaintive "Ballad of Barney Graham." For West and his comrades, Wilder stimulated a new southern radicalism rooted in the Populist tradition but updated by industrial warfare in the New South.[39]

Demanding as it was, relief and community organizing in Wilder was only one facet of the work undertaken by Taylor's young activists in 1933. Highlander was growing, and by spring, twenty-five community resident students had enrolled in a variety of classes, including Don's social literature course and Connie's arts and crafts program. Moreover, Don's sister, Elsie (Johnnye), had arrived at Monteagle and was working with Dorothy Thompson and Horton's sister, Elsie Pearl, to present dramatic productions. With the arrival of Zilla Hawes and James Dombrowski in the spring of 1933, a start was made toward financial stability. Horton recalled that until Dombrowski signed on, Highlander was little more than "a group of dedicated would-be liberal adult educators." With little to eat save beans and greens, the resident staff brooded and sometimes clashed over programs, policies, and personalities.[40]

In February 1933, West, who never doubted his role as organizer, found himself in the midst of a labor disturbance at the Peerless Textile Mill in Rossville, Georgia, near the state line. Working to assist in the organization of a union at the mill, Don told the Rossville workers that the country's economic conditions made unionization more important than ever. Clubbed from behind, he was knocked cold. Denounced as an "outsider and an agitator" and battered by a "blue streak of oaths" labeling him a "son of a ——- and a 'God-damned Red,'" he persisted. By summer the United Textile Workers (UTW) had organized a strong local at Peerless, which secured union recognition once the National Recovery Administration code went into effect.[41] For West, the main outcome was reaffirmation of his reputation as a radical agitator.

West's and Horton's activism threatened to undermine the support they had received for the Highlander experiment. Even their mentor Alva Taylor expressed concern over the young radicals' "apostolic zeal that makes socialism and every other good thing synonymous" to them. Ignoring Lillian Johnson's warning, Horton and West had made socialist organizing the central feature of the program, so much that the renewal of the one-year lease seemed in doubt. In preparation for the worst, they began to explore new locations for the program in anticipation of a conflict with their benefactor. Horton favored property in Allardt, Tennessee, 150 miles to the north, while West explored a site in Benton County, although he thought more and more of returning to Georgia to start a folk school in his home state. He was back home near Kennesaw as early as April 1933, scouting locations and making plans for a new outreach program. On April 1, Don left for Georgia, intending to build a chain of workers' cooperative libraries and establish another school "to educate farmers and industrial workers for the cooperative commonwealth."[42]

Beneath the debate over Highlander's future home lay a simmering dispute between West and Horton, an ill-concealed conflict rooted in deep differences over the best means to achieve the educational and social objectives both endorsed. Short on money, dispirited over the relentless attacks on the program, and increasingly divided over tactics, the two concluded that it was in the best interest of the project that they part. Almost from its outset their partnership had been plagued by conflicting egos, a rift exacerbated by West's impatience with Horton's pragmatism as well as the pace of social change. As John Egerton has noted, West was "more politically and ideologically moti-vated than Horton," which led to a struggle for leadership. The conflict was clear to at least one student, who as early as November 1932 perceived that their "personalities and fundamental makeup" simply "would not admit . . . unity." In a clash over the program's future, Horton attacked West's "individu-alism" and West criticized Horton for unilateralism in decision-making and the tendency to hog credit for the school's existence because of his financial ties. Because of his fund-raising capacity, the student observer recalled, Myles "could wield the economic club." Although both made "great contributions," he asserted, the two "[didn't] work together."[43]

While West and Horton sparred over strategy and tactics, interpersonal relationships at Highlander deteriorated. Shared living arrangements were complicated by Connie's pregnancy, which led her and Johnnye to move to separate quarters. To Connie, it seemed that Horton made things "very unpleasant." In effect, the two women were evicted in April 1933, an action that infuriated Don, who believed that the original agreement with Johnson meant that he was to be associated with the program until September. Yet the frequency of West's absences as he followed the social struggle wherever it led lends some credence to Dombrowski's claim that Don failed to see that "he neglected his women." In contrast, the observations of the anonymous Highlander student support West's claim that Horton made Connie uncomfortable with "abuse and insinuations."[44] The social fabric at Highlander had worn thin.

Efforts were made to conceal the rift, but the finality of the divorce was clear in West's sharp letter of May 12, 1933, written from Nashville, in which he upbraided Horton for his "insinuating remarks" about their working relationship. "Deeply hurt and disappointed" by his partner's alleged criticisms, Don reaffirmed his commitment to cooperate in the larger fight to advance socialism in the South. The letter reveals resentment over Horton's emphasis on his own fund-raising prowess, especially in view of West's work in recruitment and extension education and the "adverse criticisms" he had borne due to his high profile. Driven by anger over Connie's eviction, Don asserted that Horton had "let something get away with [his] sense of manhood." Asking for a "square deal," West promised "every bit of cooperation possible," but it was clear that the bond had been broken.

The entire episode raises questions about West's character, motives, and sense of mission. In a May 20 letter filled with concern for Highlander's future, Dombrowski told Horton that Kester had "spilled the beans" by informing Don of Horton's criticisms. A conversation with resident student Walker Martin made it clear to Dombrowski that Don nursed a grudge over Horton interpreting the original agreement in a way that ousted Connie. Although it seemed wise to smooth over the differences, Dombrowski thought it impossible due to Don's "mountaineer individualism," which drove him to "bury the hatchets in everybody's backyard." There is some truth in his frank assertion that West was plagued by "eccentricities," including a "chronic martyr complex" that often caused him to feel victimized by others whose vision of the future differed from his own. What Dombrowski missed was West's growing conviction that the primary perpetrators of his victimhood were to be found less in his timid socialist comrades than in capitalism and the possessors of great wealth who exploited and oppressed the poor. The truth is that West, much more radical in his social analysis, had concluded that Horton's measured vision of social change was inadequate to meet the challenge of the hour. A man in a hurry, Don West was already moving toward a more active expression of Marxism than his partner could accept.

It was Myles Horton, the survivor in their ideological struggle, who was privileged by history to tell the story of Highlander's origins. He maintained that West's departure resulted from a long-standing desire to establish a folk school in his native Georgia, but the explanation was far more complex and related to West's advancing politicization. In his letter to Horton, he countered the charges and admonished his collaborator for undermining his reputation. Demanding open discussion, he promised future cooperation in the common cause but informed Horton that he was securing affidavits from Highlander students and others "who know the situation," to be shared with others interested in building the southern labor movement. He also underscored the importance of maintaining a "harmonious front presented to the public." The letter ended with a plea for "cooperation in our labor movement" as the two worked to build a new social order "whether through Socialism or Communism."[45] With that cryptic but telling remark West sent an unmistakable message: Socialism had failed the test, and it was time to make way for the wave of the future.

four

Radicalization: Baptism of Fire, 1933–34

In early 1933, while still at Highlander, West read in a Chattanooga newspaper that Angelo Herndon, an African American unemployed organizer, had been arrested in Atlanta and then tried and convicted under a Georgia insurrection law dating from the Reconstruction era. In June 1932, after a series of Communist Party (CP) failures in Atlanta, Birmingham-based District 17 sent the charismatic young organizer to revitalize the Party organization in Georgia. After one extraordinary demonstration had brought a thousand unemployed Atlantans, black and white, into the streets and forced the extraction of $6,000 from the public purse for relief, Herndon was incarcerated and bound over on charges of violating an archaic insurrection statute, primarily on the basis of large quantities of radical literature found in his possession. The same Reconstruction-era statute had been used in 1930 to arraign and charge another group of radicals (the "Atlanta Six"), accused of similar activities. After a brief trial in January 1933, Herndon was convicted and sentenced to eighteen to twenty years of imprisonment, an outcome that enraged Atlanta liberals, radicals, the unemployed, and the wider African American population.

By West's account it was Herndon's plight that brought him back to Georgia on a mission to investigate and help with the defense. After hitchhiking down to Atlanta, he hunted for a contact who might inform him about the Herndon case. His search took him to Auburn Avenue in the black district, where he finally located the provisional defense committee in a "little hole-in-the-wall office" and offered assistance. West told African American attorney Ben Davis Jr. that CP district organizer Nat Ross had sent him and that he needed to know more about the Herndon case. Ross, a New Yorker and the son of Russian immigrant Jews, had undertaken graduate study at Columbia University before joining the CP in 1929 and working as an organizer, first in southern Illinois and then in Birmingham. A rigid disciplinarian and committed Leninist, he nonetheless saw the fiery and independent West as a prime prospect. Immediately grasping West's potential value as a white Georgian, the Herndon committee in Atlanta urged him to attend an upcoming defense meeting and asked that he chair the gathering, which he agreed to do. At the meeting, African Americans complained that because the only whites on the committee were New Yorkers, liberal southern whites would suspect its deliberations. Their concerns, as well as the persuasive powers of Ben Davis, were enough to convince West that he should assume a leadership role.[1]

Support for Herndon was firm in the black community, but the whites on the defense committee quarreled over tactics and leadership. The divided socialist contingent, which had been active in the defense, was soon uneasy about the prominent role that communists played in committee deliberations. The lethargic socialist local, primarily petit bourgeois in composition, spelled trouble for any effort to coordinate liberal and radical efforts on Herndon's behalf. Mary Raoul Millis, the leading figure in the Georgia SP's conservative old guard, quickly recognized that the International Labor Defense (ILD) and CP were the active forces in the battle to defend Herndon, which prompted her dramatic resignation as defense committee chair at a large public meeting on Sunday, May 7, 1933. At this point, a young scholar, C. Vann Woodward, found himself in charge of a disrupted meeting, which announced plans for yet another gathering a few days later at the Royal Theater. It was this follow-up meeting that introduced West, as chair and chief speaker, to the Atlanta liberal-radical coalition supporting Herndon. After further discussion with key committee members West agreed to head the defense committee once he was permanently established in Georgia.[2]

Before assuming responsibility for the Herndon defense, West decided to visit Communist Party headquarters in New York to explore the Party's commitment to the defense and to the interests of southern workers. It soon became clear that the ILD had succeeded in creating a broad-based defense committee that united church leaders, labor figures, social service organizations, socialists, communists, and liberals, but Don had a broad agenda and "wanted to see what the Communists had to offer." At this point he had not yet made the formal switch from the SP to the CP, but that subject was foremost in his mind as he contemplated his new role as Atlanta coordinator of the Herndon campaign. Rather than squander his meager resources on a train ticket, West chose to purchase and ride an Indian 85 motorcycle, which would be useful upon his return. After more than one accident en route, he arrived in mid-May at CP headquarters in New York, where he met and talked with both Clarence Hathaway, editor of *The Daily Worker*, and party chair Earl Browder. Hathaway impressed West as a sympathetic listener who not only gave him temporary lodging but also clarified the role of the ILD in the Herndon defense, thus firming his commitment to lead the Atlanta committee. He returned to the South ready to become a communist activist.[3]

Pleased to have escaped the impersonal character of New York (his negative impression of the city was to remain with him throughout his life), West returned to Monteagle on May 26, 1933, one day after Connie gave birth to their first child, Ann. The two now planned a move to Georgia, where they would take up temporary residence with Oliver and Lillie, who had purchased a small farm in Kennesaw, not far from Atlanta. Although West's energies were devoted primarily to the defense committee, he and Connie also launched their own folk school at this time. Work for Herndon was difficult due to the "police terror" that intensified because of the communist presence in the movement. Once Don had spoken publicly, he was "labeled right off as a Red," thus acquiring an image that would follow him for the rest of his life.[4]

West soon learned that the provisional defense committee was a broad-based coalition. Spearheaded by the ILD, which worked assiduously to raise a legal defense fund, the committee brought together blacks and whites of all political ideologies. By September 1933 it included African American clergy, university faculty, American Federation of Labor (AFL) representatives, merchants, and representatives from the National Association for the Advancement of Colored People (NAACP), all determined "to spread the Angelo Herndon case before the white and Negro masses" and provide an "effective defense." To that end, the committee engaged the young and aggressive Davis, whose father was a prominent Republican community leader. Independent of partisan activity, a spontaneous movement among black Atlantans stood ready to challenge the Herndon prosecution, which was widely perceived as an effort to quell activism among the city's unemployed. The black press and the NAACP were important elements in this coalition, which incorporated the "leading negroes" of Atlanta, many of whom lent financial support to the defense. Although there was a conscious effort to deemphasize party identification, CP organizer Caroline Drew reported sympathy for her cause in the black community, where at least some NAACP members were "with [the CP] ideologically."[5]

The Communist Party's central role in the Herndon defense highlighted its growing activism in the Atlanta area. Although several well-attended mass meetings occurred in the black community, party work among whites remained relatively weak, especially among workers. Because of the importance of an interracial coalition among the unemployed, Drew insisted that white party members, who could not be attacked as outsiders, must be placed in control of organizational work. Asserting that it was "very difficult for a Northern white woman to work in the South," she proposed in July 1933 that her replacement be "comrade Don West who could . . . take [her] place and do the work with the close guidance, help, and cooperation of the district bureau."[6]

By this time West had returned from his conference with Hathaway, ready to change party affiliations and assume further responsibility as both coordinator of the Herndon defense and a CP operative. As section organizer in Atlanta, West's primary activity involved leadership of the Herndon committee, which he accepted after Ben Davis impressed upon him his importance as a native-born southern white willing to challenge the system. The work appealed to West's keen interest in both the unemployed movement and the advancement of interracial organization in Georgia. On June 6, 1933, the Party's Birmingham (District 17) organizer reported to the Central Committee Secretariat in New York that West was considered useful as one of several "native Southern whites with mass connections" through whom the CP could get "a clear feel of the attitude of many of the white workers and farmers towards the movement." Three weeks later, Nat Ross, soon to become Don's brother-in-law, informed New York that West had joined the Communist Party under an assumed name and been assigned to Atlanta. To Ross, West "really look[ed] like one of the best white workers [he] had come in touch with in the South."[7]

After cutting ties with Highlander and removing to Georgia, Don and Connie threw themselves into organizational activity with renewed enthusiasm. While living with Oliver and Lillie, their chief local activity focused on the new folk school in Kennesaw. The Southern Folk School and Libraries was an outreach program that established lending libraries and offered extension courses "to educate farmers and industrial workers for the cooperative commonwealth." As early as March 1933, Howard Kester expressed active interest in West's plans as a counter to the Alabama CP; on March 27 he told Myles Horton that "if we don't get these folks the Communists will, for they are doing things and I don't mean maybe." Still working as an SP organizer, West approached Norman Thomas for help before he left Highlander, and both Thomas and Upton Sinclair responded by contributing periodicals and other materials to the project.[8]

Although resources were limited the Wests stubbornly persisted in their effort to extend worker education. Among family and friends lending moral support were "professional advisors" Howard Kester and Ben Davis, "farmer advisor" and "worker advisor" Manuel Sutton and Harve West, and "directors" Clyde Johnson and Willis Sutton. By November 1933, eleven libraries had been established, and "community classes" were underway, courses intended "to arouse, educate, and organize Southern toilers" for a society in which "cooperative, collective endeavor" would replace "selfish, dog-eat-dog competition." A full partner in the folk school project, Connie published an article in the *Cumberland Empire*, appealing for support of their program and the mountaineers, croppers, tenants, and farmers it served. She argued that the "forgotten people of the South" who produced "all the wealth" were the "people the Southern Folk School and Libraries are established for."[9]

For some residents of northwest Georgia, too much advice and assistance had already come from the Southern Folk School. During the summer of 1933, Don's cousin Willis Sutton, a student at Berry, became interested in the National Student League, a militant student organization sponsored by the Communist Party. Disturbed by their work assignments and a student pay cut at Berry, Sutton and several dissidents came to Don to ask for help in organizing a student union. West declined to become involved, but he did propose an alternative. Clyde Johnson, a student of Columbia University economics professor Donald Henderson, who had been fired for National Student League (NSL) activity, had already come south as a communist organizer. Born in Minnesota, he had been a student activist in the NSL at the City College of New York, where he became radicalized, joined the CP, and moved south on party assignment in 1933. To both West and the students it made sense to send Johnson to Berry as organizer, so Don picked him up on his Indian 85 and took him to the home of a relative in Snow, Georgia, not far from the Berry campus. Berry officials soon apprehended Sutton and Johnson and hauled them off to jail in Rome. Released the next day, Johnson was arrested again and threatened with lynching unless he left the area.[10]

Evidence suggests that there was indeed dissatisfaction with the Berry system among some students. Sutton and the other dissenters chafed under the school's rigid social restrictions as well as recent reductions in work credit, which seemed insensitive in view of depression conditions. More than seventy students sympathized with the rebels, who launched a labor action to demonstrate solidarity by boycotting work on August 28, 1933. The protesters, angry over what they labeled "forced labor" at substandard wages, appealed to the community with charges that Berry undersold local farmers with produce raised by a "captive" labor force. Upon close examination, their argument revealed the fine hand of Don West. The students criticized Berry for telling "sob stories" in the North and East about the "poor little country boys and girls" who were told to be "thankful . . . to RICH men for giving money." Turning to Floyd and Bartow County farmers for support, the resisters charged that Berry took a few promising students to be educated and lost to the city rather than "return to their communities."[11]

Although the actual strike lasted no more than two days, that was not the end of the story. After Johnson's unceremonious expulsion from Rome, West contacted the National Student Association and requested intervention. Not to be deterred, the NSL distributed a critical leaflet to students, Berry trustees, and school supporters throughout the United States. And in a coordinated attack, letters of protest against the school's practices poured into Berry from NSL chapters, several unions, the Commonwealth College Student Body, and the Socialist Party of Atlanta. They included an attack on Berry's "undemocratic treatment" of students from an unnamed college fraternity in Atlanta, signed by David Lee (one of West's aliases). West followed up with a letter to *The New Republic* in which he upbraided Berry for its paternalism, authoritarianism, and exploitation of student labor. Attacking the Berry administration for imposing a gag order on students, West denounced the "missionary institutions with which the South [was] cursed." In a similar vein, Walker Martin, West's Highlander protege from Alabama, now fully radicalized, asserted that "the wealth at Berry [had] been wrung from the working people by the capitalist class and exhibited as proof of their superiority."[12]

Confronted by West's open challenge and the NSL assault, Berry responded with its own offensive. Not only did the school deny the charges but it also made inflammatory accusations of communist treachery, at least a partial truth because West's influence on the strike and subsequent controversy was clear. Moreover, the student body adopted resolutions repudiating "Don West and his fellow agitators" and, under heavy pressure from the Berry faculty, launched an effort to flood West's mailbox with their own letters of protest. Meanwhile, in a national public relations campaign the school addressed only that portion of the struggle that had occurred after West's involvement began. Part of the counterattack was a demand that *The New Republic* print a retraction of West's story. It was, in the words of Jesse Stuart, "a fine mess that old Don got into with the Berry Schools." Despite their differences, however, Stuart's "heart went with him wrong or right," and he grudgingly acknowledged that West was "absolutely fearless." In response to an inquiry from the magazine's editors, West suggested that an independent observer be sent to Berry to research the incident. To clear the air, the liberal journal now promised an investigation.[13]

Concern over the negative publicity induced Martha Berry to contact supporters, trustees, and the interested public with her own version of the events that had transpired. Among the many recipients of her letters was Alva W.

Taylor, who replied that he "deplored Don's radical attitude and especially his denunciatory temper." Although his mentor defended West as a man of "unwavering moral courage," Taylor confirmed that Don had "gone Communist with all the trimmings" and that his outburst in *The New Republic* suggested that he had "gone blooie." The school's matriarch denied that any strike had occurred, but an inquiry by a South Carolina author, Hamilton Basso, sustained the essence of West's charges. Basso confirmed the issues at stake, the reality of the strike, and the likelihood that it was a "student's movement."[14]

Basso's conclusions were widely shared at Highlander. Horton asserted that the Highlander Folk School was "very sympathetic to any effort Don or any one else may make to point out situations where workers are not given justice." In its pursuit of West, the Berry administration launched an indirect assault on Highlander, due largely to *The New Republic*'s error in listing Don's address as Monteagle. Under increasing pressure due to Berry's threat of a seditious libel prosecution, an exasperated West told Horton that a letter of support to *New Republic* editor Bruce Bliven would strike a blow against Berry paternalism. Although Horton pointedly noted that West had left Highlander, he did tell Bliven that Berry's denials were "an obvious evasion." He maintained that both Georgia and Tennessee press reported that a strike had occurred and that Martha Berry maintained "a dictatorial policy toward her students." Taylor added his own support with a letter to Bliven endorsing West's character and integrity. In a related letter to Horton, Howard Kester asserted that he was anxious to "save Don from cynicism." He noted that "some people want to run rough shod over him," a solution that "simply [wouldn't] do." Kester then reminded Horton that there was a relationship between the "creed of Communism" and the ideas of socialists, so it was wise to "be careful about what we say about our comrades in the movement who are wearing their guts out for it."[15]

The plight of the Berry students briefly engaged West's attention, and the work of the Southern Folk School expressed his deepest cultural and educational objectives, but it was the Angelo Herndon case that captured most of his attention during the summer and fall of 1933. The intensity of Don's commitment to Herndon's defense reflected the devotion of a recent convert to communism as the political ideology most likely to hasten the liberation of the poor and to Marxism as the social analysis most consistent with his personal view of the human condition and the remedy for economic injustice. Disillusioned with what could be accomplished within the prevailing limits at Highlander, Don was deeply impressed by the "militancy of the CP, the Scottsboro policy, and the party stand on the Negro question." By that he undoubtedly meant communist insistence on the creation of an interracial united front, which was so evident in its approach to unemployed organizing, the Atlanta case, and the Herndon defense. Once he joined the Party, he chose to conceal his membership, which made perfect tactical sense. In late spring, district CP officials acknowledged that because the Party "function[ed] illegally in Atlanta," it was impolitic to ask recruits like West to openly declare their new affiliations.[16] Despite his underground status it is clear that by June 1933 West had chosen communism, a shift wholly consistent with his parting remarks to Horton, which strongly implied that activists must choose the brand of radicalism that held the greatest hope for social transformation. Asked many years later why he had moved sharply to the Left in 1933, West asserted that the communists "were doing things" and "were committed." In his view, CP activists "stuck their necks out" and took chances, always maintaining "terrific discipline."[17]

For Don and Connie the new commitment meant hard, uncompensated labor, beginning with organizational work for the Herndon committee. Moving to Atlanta, they took a basement apartment on Georgia Avenue in the black district, short on furniture but long on energy. Forced underground, both Connie and Don labored tirelessly to publicize the case through mimeographed newsletters, handbills, and newspapers, most of them produced in their spare quarters. Understating the scope of this work, FBI informants reported that Don West's activities in Atlanta "consisted of holding meetings in the houses of negros and poor white laborers" and "distribution of Communist literature in the vicinity." Because of the "police terror," the work was deeply underground, their literature delivered in the dark of night, cautiously slipped behind doors and on porches in Atlanta's black community where their most loyal following was to be found.[18]

Once engaged in organizing the defense forces, the Wests experienced major problems due to the heavy hand of police surveillance, which limited the opportunity to operate publicly. Nonetheless, the Herndon committee succeeded in building a strong organization linking African Americans, white liberals, the ILD, and the American Civil Liberties Union, not to mention a cautious NAACP. The ambivalent response of the NAACP reflected its belief that the CP "stirred up more racial discord than anything else." The association was convinced that "sensible Negroes in Georgia [could not] afford to line up with the Communists as Communism [would] never succeed in Georgia." Yet NAACP cooperation was a reluctant admission that the legal defense had brought "great admiration" for Herndon's advocates, including the CP. Anxious to capitalize on broad-based support, Don and Connie launched an educational effort to frame the issue and publicize the real reasons why Herndon was "singled out" for his "fight on behalf of both white and black poor people." As partners in activism, the Wests concentrated on building local grass-roots support, which although predominantly black included at least a dozen white workers from Atlanta's Fulton Bag Mill, men and women forced to work secretly to avoid loss of employment. Among the white participants, women were especially active, including CP firebrands Nannie Leah (Young) Washburn and Annie May (Young) Leathers. Washburn, a veteran of the Atlanta unemployed movement, greatly admired Herndon for his role in the 1932 demonstration that had forged an interracial link, a bond that, in her words, had revealed that "the blacks was just like us poor whites." In addition to these committed working-class radicals, several white university students and professors, including Vann Woodward and Mercer Evans, showed "real courage" by taking a public stand for Herndon.[19]

Support within the African American community was rock solid. Here, West found his most effective backers among the clergy, who had originally directed him to Ben Davis's office in May 1933, when he was still exploring the case. Among the black ministers, the outstanding leader was the Rev. J. A. Martin of the Wheat Street Baptist Church, who was fearless on Herndon's behalf. Although a broad coalition of African American leaders embraced the cause, West later asserted that it was the "black ministers, particularly" who were most deeply "concerned with the Herndon case."[20]

The watchful eye of public officials made it "very difficult to work in Atlanta at that time." The Atlanta police blanketed the African American community and devoted special attention to "anybody who undertook to do anything for the benefit of black people." On more than one occasion Don and Connie were almost snared in police raids. Once, when they were working on protest materials, the Red Squad of the Atlanta police invaded the home of Max Singer, a Jewish merchant who permitted the committee to keep its mimeograph machine in his store. Connie, who had been reproducing handbills when the police arrived, calmly deposited the evidence in a wastebasket and donned an apron. Similar discipline was evident in the word-of-mouth notification of meetings in private homes, which often frustrated official efforts to break up defense committee deliberations. Don recalled that self-discipline was essential because "people's freedom depended on it—sometimes people's lives."[21]

West's high profile in the Herndon defense made him a prime target for the police, whose Red Squad pursued him with a vengeance. Much more than Clyde Johnson, the tall, handsome Don West was a charismatic figure who drew supporters to his side, which meant that authorities deemed him especially dangerous. West contributed to his notoriety with publication in the March 13, 1934, *Daily Worker* of a revealing and militant poem, "Listen, I Am a Communist." It was a flaming declaration of radicalism that was to follow him for the rest of his days as part of an extensive FBI file and a weapon for the southern press as well as congressional investigators. In words dripping with resentment against capital and entrenched wealth, he defiantly announced:

I am a Communist
A Red
A Bolshevik!
Do you, toilers of the South,
Know Me,
Do you understand?

Invoking the spirit of old Kim Mulkey, West declared himself the "son of my grandfather," whose "blood pounds through my veins, and cries out for justice!" Embracing comrades in the Soviet Union, he implored the South's oppressed toilers to "organize to be free" and heed his words:

I, the poet
Don West
Communist
Bolshevik
Red . . .
Working man
Southern toiler . . .
You will hear me
And you'll believe
Because I am you,
You are me.
　　And
　　We
Are power!

It was such words that moved *Daily Worker* editor Mike Gold on January 13, 1934, to embrace West as a revolutionary poet who followed the "road from poetry to action." Like Robert Burns, Gold argued, Don West possessed that "sensitivity" that made people's poets "feel acutely the bitter lot of their brothers." Armed with Marx and Lenin, he was organizing Georgia workers into "that solemn union" certain to "end all exploitation, slavery, and race hatred, and make a world of beauty, such as poets [could] truthfully hymn."

The poem's publication coincided with Don's presence in New York to attend the CP National Training School, where he studied the history of the trade union movement, the development of capitalism, the evolution of the Communist Party, the rise of imperialism, and the applicability of Marx to the crisis of capitalism. It was at the Workers School that West first met Hosea Hudson, an African American originally from Georgia, who became a lifelong friend. Hudson, who had worked for the Party in both Alabama and Georgia, was a genuine working-class radical and judged by party officials to have great potential as an "effective worker," which was realized when he was assigned to organizing in Atlanta in 1934. While studying in New York, Don became a mentor for Hudson, who recalled that it was West who taught him to read. On the last day of school West prepared for his return to Atlanta by publishing "Angelo Herndon Dreams" in the March 17 *Daily Worker*, a bold prediction of a new Georgia of "black kids and white / Singing songs together." Once the training session closed in mid-March, West, Hudson, and two other African Americans from Birmingham drove back south together although they were arrested in Philadelphia in possession of large quantities of communist literature. Confronted by a police investigator, West informed him that he was a minister from Georgia, to which the officer replied, "And these are your God damn disciples you got here!" Freed with the assistance of an ILD lawyer, the group was ordered to get out of Philadelphia lest they be charged with insurrection. Hudson remained in Birmingham until he was reassigned in July 1934 to Atlanta as a replacement for West and Clyde Johnson following the Red Squad raids in June.[22]

His open declaration of radicalism only made West's work in Atlanta more difficult. Although Don and Connie jointly coordinated support activities for Herndon, Don also involved himself in unemployed organizing on the federal government's Public Works Administration (PWA) projects and those of the Civil Works Administration (CWA) with the help of Clyde Johnson, whom he assigned to work with the Atlanta Unemployed Councils. Because of the Party's aggressive tactics as well as the militancy of desperate workers, especially displaced African Americans, suspicions of revolutionary activity and racial paranoia strained police-community relations to the breaking point. Within this atmosphere of anticommunist hysteria and interracial tension, the position of radical organizers such as Don West deteriorated under increased state pressure.

As the Red Scare escalated, organizing for Herndon became more difficult. Most of Atlanta's ten CP clubs were exclusively black, so door-to-door activities were subject to close official scrutiny. More important for Don, who needed to maintain close liaison with party troops, it became increasingly difficult to meet with subordinates without attracting attention. In April 1934, police harassment escalated, often in the guise of efforts to enforce segregation statutes. Consequently, both West and Johnson experienced narrow escapes from the law, which was intent on enforcing Jim Crow. By May 1934, West had become the primary target of raids calculated to undermine both unemployed organizing and the Herndon defense committee.[23]

Shortly after the Georgia Supreme Court upheld the lower court's harsh sentence to Angelo Herndon, the pressure on West increased dramatically. Confident that the state court had given its imprimatur to his antiradical campaign, Atlanta's assistant solicitor, John Hudson, launched a new "reign of terror" that featured regular raids on private residences and ILD offices in working-class districts to harass communists while pursuing West. Facing charges of "inciting to insurrection," West eluded adversaries for the moment, but the heat was on. On one occasion he evaded the police by escaping into the woods from the back door of defense committee activist Walter Washburn's home; at another point he lay concealed in a cellar beneath a rug in the home of Murray Branch, an African American minister.[24] Time was running out.

The scope and intensity of the raids reflected Hudson's successful infiltration of the defense committee, which had been facilitated by the inside work of Ansel Morrison, a somewhat unbalanced former radical who betrayed West and his comrades. Morrison, once a student acquaintance of Don's at Berry, was an Atlanta lawyer who had worked for the Pinkerton agency and then professed a conversion to communism to gain the confidence of party activists. For a brief moment Morrison may have believed a communist revolution inevitable. The fact that he had worked as a legal assistant to Ben Davis, together with his school ties with West, helped him gain acceptance in Atlanta's radical circles. "Not any too well supplied with brains," according to Mary Raoul Millis, Morrison was also dangerously erratic, as evidenced by his betrayal of West and the committee in May 1934.[25] In an act of considerable gullibility the committee had concealed its records at Morrison's residence, which was thought to be safe from the long arm of the Red Squad. What West and his comrades failed to understand was that the middle-class attorney was actually a police agent, which meant that he promptly turned the materials over to Hudson's office. Consequently, the committee lost everything, including precious membership lists that soon guided the police to the homes of party members and the CP activists who had helped organize Herndon's defense.[26]

For West, the intensified police presence in the African American community made it impossible to carry on his work for the defense. He consistently eluded adversaries, but it was "hard to go through a working class neighborhood because on almost every corner a cop or a detective was stationed." Workers, he claimed, were threatened in the official effort to "get [him] dead or alive and burn Communism out of Georgia." After a year of organizing for the Communist Party, West was a hunted man. Anxious to avoid arrest, he discussed the situation with defense committee members, who concluded that it would be wise for him to get to New York, where he might confer with party leaders and the coordinators of the Herndon defense. In the words of *The Daily Worker*, Don West chose to execute a "fadeaway."[27]

Spirited out of Atlanta under cover of night (and concealed by blankets and canvass sacks), West escaped in the back seat of Ben Davis's Ford. Before his departure he arranged for Connie to vacate the Georgia Avenue apartment and take Ann to Kennesaw, where they could live safely with Oliver and Lillie. After Davis deposited his passenger near Decatur, it was a simple matter for West to catch a bus for North Carolina—and, finally, New York—for a conference with party leaders. Once beyond the reach of Georgia authorities, Don compared the state's suppression of radicalism with Adolph Hitler's fascist dictatorship in Germany in that both regimes were brutally effective in "destroying workers' freedom."[28]

Safe in New York, West carried on as advocate for Angelo Herndon with an assault on Georgia's "ruling class justice" that had demanded his arrest as one of those "furriners" who were "Roosian Reds!" Branded a "dangerous criminal" for committing the "unforgivable crime of organizing Negro and white workers together," he pledged to carry on the fight. As frequent speaker at Herndon rallies, West worked with the ILD and the National Committee for the Defense of Political Prisoners to publicize the shortcomings of Georgia justice.[29] Never fond of New York and reluctant to be exploited for political purposes, he now hoped for a new party assignment that would allow him to return to the South he loved and the woman with whom he shared his life.

Since June 1934, Connie had made her home with Oliver and Lillie in Kennesaw, a refuge in difficult times. She had been Don's willing partner in the struggle for justice, although the strain and uncertainty of underground life placed an unwelcome burden on both mother and daughter Ann, whose infancy was complicated by a ever-shifting home environment. Connie had known from the beginning that married life with a rolling stone like Don West would be stressful, and she was ready to meet the challenge. Most important, her family background prepared her to share Don's economic and social outlook. Her father, a railroad engineer, had instilled in her a concern for social justice and empathy for the less fortunate as well as respect for the union tradition. Moreover, her Kentucky roots made her fully sensitive to the injuries of class visited daily on the hard-pressed Harlan and Perry County miners then struggling to build a union. That consciousness of social and economic disparities was the underpinning of her lifetime partnership with Don West. It also enlivened her creative life as an accomplished artist whose work told the stories of the mountain people among whom she lived.

Because of her father's position Connie always had some of life's finer things, although her educational experience in a Catholic convent school had been unpleasant. She would have been willing to lead a bourgeois life but accepted the hard choices that came with marriage to a committed social activist. At LMU she had shared many of Don's interests, including activities in the Student Volunteer Band, which reflected the deep roots of their mutual Social Gospel inclinations. The couple often discussed the political commitment they were making, including the very real sacrifices it entailed. Indeed, throughout their married life it was the financial stability provided by Connie's relatively steady employment that enabled the family to survive economically.[30] Theirs was a sexual division of labor accepted by both as essential to the economic health of the family and important to the fulfillment of their long-standing dream of founding an educational institution dedicated to the preservation of the mountain culture they revered.

Not only was Connie's earning capacity vital to the couple's survival at several junctures in their married lives but her labor was also critical in carrying out the political goals they worked to achieve. While Don organized workers and supporters, Connie often turned out the propaganda material disseminated by the Herndon defense committee and helped distribute it, sometimes at personal risk. Although they went through life at a frenetic pace that left Connie sometimes frazzled and apparently disorganized, her "fractured personality" was matched by Don's impatient yet often sympathetic acceptance of her discomfiture.[31] Theirs was a partnership that somehow worked on both interpersonal and political levels, yet underlying tension was ever-present.

By the standards of the time, the Wests' marriage was relatively modern in that both partners understood the other's contributions, accepted separateness, and valued independence. Don's expression of those goals was more public and vigorous, and Connie would have preferred greater stability, but the two were united in their pursuit. Although their views of sexual independence were in part informed by the Communist Party concept of the "woman question," it is important to note that the Old Left's renunciation of male chauvinism was somewhat limited in scope. It argued that bourgeois culture and morality helped perpetuate the class system, but the Party's treatment of women's roles was relatively conservative. Traditional Marxist theorists maintained that the relationship between gender and class was rooted in the concept of women as property subject to domination, an assumption Don and Connie rejected—at least in theory and often in practice. Their adaptation of the sexual division of labor, including the assignment of political work, reflected assumptions within the Party in the 1930s, which meant that Connie performed many menial functions essential to successful organizing and Don assumed leadership. In accepting their respective roles they acted according to the social conventions of their time and place.[32]

The Wests' commitment to work for political change was also influenced by Connie's close relationship with Don's siblings, especially Elsie (Johnnye) and Belle, who had independently chosen the path of radicalism as the road to a better world. In part because of their political decisions, the two married Nat Ross and Bart Logan, both of them key party activists. Connie's personal history with an absentee father and needs as a caring mother also drew her toward Lillie, who consistently provided shelter, comfort, child care, and the close family ties previously missing in Connie's life. Lillie was occasionally critical of Don's "Communist work" but invariably was a willing caregiver when called upon for help.[33] Yet in the final analysis the theme that penetrated this untraditional situation was the concept of family and mutual obligations drawn from the history of mountain culture and society. It was this tradition that held Don and Connie together when the tensions and risks experienced during the perilous Atlanta years tested their marriage. Lillie and the Kennesaw refuge bridged the gap created by Don's conflicting obligations to party and family at a moment of great personal danger.

— —

In a brief fifteen months Don West had traveled a significant distance from the convictions he embraced after his departure from Vanderbilt. His journey from socialism to communism was marked by an ever-stronger sense of outrage at the exploitation of the small farmers, sharecroppers, and workers then caught in the industrial transformation of the New South. West's hostility toward great wealth and rejection of capitalism had become a worldview that hardened as he moved through successive stages of a personal struggle to advance the revolution. His friend, New Deal administrator Aubrey Williams, believed that he acted because he "hunger[ed] for beauty that [would] replace the ugliness of poverty." Other observers were convinced that hunger had turned to anger in 1933. Martha Berry, for example, saw Don's behavior as the result of hostility to the school. Given his antipathy toward Berry's attempt at cultural intervention, it may be that she understood too well West's actions as a way to expose an illegitimate effort to erase Appalachian culture.[34]

But an attack on cultural interventionism cannot explain Don West's departure from Highlander and accelerated rush toward communism. The rapid dissolution of the partnership with Horton and abrupt return to Georgia in May 1933 reflected deeper concerns and motivations. Both Dombrowski and Horton emphasized Don's headstrong insistence on militant political engagement and accurately explained it in terms of intense impatience with the pace of social change. West's state of mind was captured by his mentor Alva W. Taylor, who told Martha Berry in October 1933 that Don had converted to communism and gotten "more temperamental as he [went] on." Taylor then diagnosed the psychological illness: "he seems to have a smouldering [*sic*] temperament that broods over the wrongs of the working people, coupled with a highly individualistic ego" that made "any constructive team work impossible." In a companion letter to the Commission on Interracial Cooperation's Will Alexander he asserted that West had "gone clear wild" in the belief that "all that is must be destroyed before a better social order can be builded [*sic*]." Despite West's inability to work with others, Taylor declared admiration for Don's "sincerity, his moral courage, and his sacrificial life."[35]

It was these characteristics that made West an enormously popular figure among Atlanta's dispossessed as well as observers on the Left. He was widely admired because of his sense of moral rectitude and charismatic presence. At the same time, he could be an intimidating figure whose deadly serious personal commitment made supporters and subordinates uncomfortable when approaching him with regard to Party work or defense committee activities.[36] Some recall him as impatient with those less competent than he, a person whose ideological commitments drained him of the capacity for empathy. Paradoxically, he is also remembered as generous to a fault and selfless in commitment to his causes, a truly inspirational leader.

Alva Taylor came as close as any observer to understanding the roots of Don West's radicalism, including his conversion to communism. He was clearly a young man on a revolutionary mission by 1934. Angered by the inequities he saw around him and inspired by the Social Gospel teachings he had internalized at Vanderbilt, West was psychologically incapable of accepting gradualism, including the democratic socialism embraced by Horton, Dombrowski, and the more cautious Highlander group. A convert to revolutionary socialism, Don West had become a "true believer" in the Gospel according to Marx. Claiming Jesus as comrade, he now waited in New York for his next opportunity to spread the word in his homeland, which soon came when he reentered the house of southern labor.

five

On the Road: Party Activism and Organizational Work, 1934–37

By July 1934 Don West was prepared to recommit himself to the protection of workers' rights in a new venue. After a brief stay in New York, he received a new party assignment as trade union organizer in North Carolina, based in the textile community of Burlington. Meanwhile, Connie and Ann remained with Lillie in Kennesaw for the summer, rejoining Don in North Carolina in the fall. Because he was wanted in Georgia as Don West, he assumed an alias, Jim Weaver, which he would use until August 1935, when his true identity would be revealed. As early as July 1934 he was cooperating with CP district organizer Paul Crouch in an effort to conduct "opposition work" within the conservative United Textile Workers (UTW) as an entering wedge for the eventual organization of the CP-dominated National Textile Workers Union (NTWU). The Party still followed the "dual unions" line, so the overriding goal was to build the NTWU at the expense of the UTW. Working with "small forces," Crouch and Weaver awaited instructions from New York on the right moment for this activity to accelerate. Within a month, West was busy expanding CP presence among textile workers in Burlington, where both unions were notoriously weak although the opportunity seemed great.[1]

His work in Burlington was not West's first exposure to textile unionism in North Carolina, which had a conflicted history going back to the organizational drives in Marion and Gastonia in 1929. While still a student in Alva Taylor's classes, West had visited Gastonia during the violent struggle of 1929, an assignment that left him profoundly impressed by the sharp class struggle he observed. Here, where he met the soon-to-be martyred Ella May Wiggins, he identified with the cultural war that had enveloped transplanted mountain people. By the time West reappeared in North Carolina the union movement in textiles had fallen on hard times. As the representative of the Trade Union Unity League (TUUL) it was his task to rekindle the fires of resistance while enhancing the Party's role in advancing class struggle.

Not long after returning from exile in New York, Don drove to Kennesaw to pick up Connie and Ann, who were at his side, at least temporarily, in Burlington. Once again, Connie fulfilled the supporting role in a political partnership as the master of the mimeograph machine. Yet by the end of 1934 financial reality impinged upon Don's existence as an activist and forced Connie to find work teaching at Conawaia Folk School in Arkansas in order to supply their basic needs. As a consequence, the family was again separated, and it was Connie who supplied the stability that allowed Don to pursue his political mission. Meanwhile, other family ties grew stronger. Don's sister Belle, who in 1932 had joined the Communist Party in Alabama, was assigned to work with the Young Communist League (YCL) in North Carolina, and Elsie (Johnnye), a party member since late 1933, engaged in organizational work in Birmingham, where her husband, Nat Ross, was District 17 organizer.[2]

By August 1934 West and District 16's organizer, Paul Crouch, had relocated the CP district offices to Greensboro, which provided a more central location for organizing textile workers. Active in Greensboro, Burlington, Danville, Winston-Salem, Concord, Charlotte, and Gastonia, the organizers concentrated on the crisis soon to break out during the great national textile strike of 1934. Placed "in general charge" of strike preparations in Burlington, West built an organization that was "stronger there than anywhere else—so far as work inside the mills [was] concerned."[3] Here, Jim Weaver (West) immersed himself in mobilizing workers in a united front with the UTW at the massive properties operated by J. Spencer Love. Like other southern textile firms, the Burlington mills became a target when the general strike broke out in September 1934. The dramatic work stoppage lent special urgency to the new effort to bring NTWU activists into the UTW, a key priority for party organizers.

The UTW's leaders predicted 90 percent participation, but Crouch feared that because of previous strike failures many workers would "be inclined to remain at work." A huge combination of fourteen factories, the Love properties encompassed a complex of corporate paternalism that impoverished the operatives who inhabited the neighboring mill village. At the E. M. Holt Plaid Company, sweatshop conditions prevailed and the hated "stretch-out" made life miserable for those who worked long hours in oppressive heat for declining wages. Conditions were ripe for rebellion.

Violence flared when the nationwide uprising of 1934 broke out, especially in southern mill towns where workers had long paid the price for industrial development in discounted wages that gave the South a competitive advantage. From the Carolinas to Alabama, Tennessee, and Georgia, wildcat strikes and aggressive "flying squadrons" of aroused workers challenged the authority long wielded by paternalistic mill owners and autocratic managers. Bitter clashes between the National Guard and strikers took place in the important strike center of Burlington, and strikers succeeded in closing most factories. On September 4, 1934, the union's flying squad reached the E. M. Holt plant, where "the power of men and women in the streets" induced night-shift workers to pull the switch and walk out. West recalled that rank-and-file workers were even more important than committed union activists in the work of flying squadrons. Vann Woodward, who believed that the only way to learn anything about American labor was "through first hand observation," wrote to his Atlanta colleague Glenn Rainey that he had helped West "organize some protest of the terrorism." Although Love insisted that socialists and communists had "taken charge of the situation in Burlington," Woodward concluded that "communism was pretty much eclipsed in the strike." Perhaps so, but the radical undercurrent was always present. The settlement reached after three weeks of industrial warfare provided for the rehiring of all strikers. Although workers were persuaded to return to the mills with promises of National Recovery Administration (NRA) intervention and adjudication of disputes, what resulted was disappointment as management ignored the agreements made to end the strike. Yet to West, the extreme militancy of the work stoppage had been a "remarkable thing" that revealed deep class feeling. He recognized that pro-labor sentiment "got very deep," yet the struggle resulted in "very little organization."[4]

In the wake of the failed strike, the Communist Party convened a National Party Textile Conference, which met in New York on October 6, 1934. Addressing the delegates, West acknowledged that there were "very difficult problems" in the South. In his view, the weakness of the CP was the "Negro problem," which made solidarity hard to achieve. Moreover, he argued, party publications were too often written at a level that "flies over the head of the southern textile workers." A further complication lay in UTW conservatism, including its unwillingness to organize African American workers and condemnation of the flying squadrons that had led the attack.[5]

What his postmortem failed to emphasize enough was the imposition of state authority that quelled disturbances and ultimately crushed the strike. For West, the most significant intervention was the prosecution of eight mill operatives who had been framed as participants in an alleged bomb plot at the E. M. Holt Plaid Mill. On September 15, 1934, a dynamite bomb, which management assumed to be the work of striking workers, exploded in the Holt mill yard. Dissatisfied with the pace of local justice, the company imported four private detectives from Pennsylvania to build a conspiracy case against the union leadership. The Burlington case was, in fact, part of the sweeping repression that followed the ill-fated strike of 1934 as management attempted to smash unionism throughout the South. Local sheriff H. J. Stockard assumed that the explosion was the "work of communists," but no firm evidence exists to support his conclusion.[6]

Although the strike was already collapsing, the Holt bombing destroyed residual worker and community support for the struggle in Alamance County. Most significant for the union was the arrest and detention of the eight workers, who were brought to trial on November 28, 1934. After a disastrous weeklong court proceeding in which three defendants turned state's evidence under dubious circumstances, seven workers (four of them UTW members) were found guilty, including alleged ringleader John "Slim" Anderson, who was sentenced to eight to ten years' imprisonment. The verdict resulted in widespread anger in the North Carolina liberal community, especially among University of North Carolina (UNC) faculty and staff. A series of campus meetings led by members of UNC's English department protested the verdict and ignited a campus controversy. At the urging of West, the trial also produced an immediate response from the International Labor Defense (ILD), which pledged to handle the Burlington appeals. In early December the ILD moved to organize a Burlington defense committee and mobilize the state's liberal community.[7]

In view of his experience with the Herndon defense committee, Don West was the logical choice to coordinate the ILD's effort. Already active in North Carolina and Virginia "textile work," West quickly assumed leadership of the Burlington Workers Defense Committee and launched an effort to broaden the group's support base. Joined by thirty workers at the first meeting, West and the committee planned to raise funds for an appeal, disseminate publicity to a wider public, generate support in UTW locals, and provide financial assistance to the jailed defendants. Attacking UTW officials for abandoning the defense, the committee threatened to bring down "the wrath of the rank and file" on the union's timid leaders.[8] In order to maximize pressure on the UTW, Walt Pickard, president of Burlington Local 1777, and his supporters drafted a sample resolution seeking to force International president Thomas McMahon's hand. The Burlington workers asked the national leadership to "go on record officially for support of the Burlington Six" and against the attempt to "discredit and smash our union."[9]

One of the strongest weapons in the union's arsenal was the pen wielded by Don West and his collaborator Walt Pickard in their pamphlet *The Burlington Dynamite Plot*, a spirited defense of the union and the defendants. Clearly West's work, the ILD publication told Pickard's "tale of grim struggles . . . of Southern workers fighting for better conditions." Truth be told, the pamphlet expressed a radical political perspective more extreme than that of most local citizens or the UTW national leadership. Blistering the company for employing labor spies, intimidating defense witnesses, blacklisting, and using stool pigeons, it exposed company tactics in securing convictions on the basis of purchased testimony. Pickard and West also denounced management for retaliating against union workers who dared to testify on behalf of the accused, many of whom lost their jobs for doing so. This labor manifesto, written in a persuasive, vernacular style, documented West's determination to "show up [the] whole rotten frame-up for what it [was]."[10]

Not long after the convictions, West urged Crouch to relieve him of other duties so could devote full time to the Burlington defense. West had been scheduled to "get inside the union for active work" but considered the Burlington defense more urgent. Moreover, financial support had again become a pressing issue. As a result of heavy travel expenses and assistance to the Pickard family, the Wests were "flat."[11] The ILD provided legal assistance and the union local strongly backed the defense committee, but West's most effective allies were drawn from the liberal communities at Durham and Chapel Hill, especially the UNC faculty. At Don's behest, a committee of academics came over to Burlington in January 1935 to investigate the handling of the case. Among those most active in this effort were the playwright Paul Green, J. O. Bailey of the UNC English department, historian C. Vann Woodward, writer Olive Stone, underground communist E. E. Ericson, and W. T. Couch of the university press. After meeting in John Anderson's home with union members and defense committee members, the liberals concluded that the accused had been the victims of a frame-up and were being railroaded into extended prison terms. Reporting on the outcome, West told "Slim" Anderson that things were "going splendidly" as a result of the meeting, which resulted in resolutions endorsing the ILD's involvement in the defense, new publicity measures, and concrete plans to raise bail money for the incarcerated defendants.[12]

The central figure in the liberal group, Paul Green, told West that if he "could just be convinced" that the workers were "framed up" he would "really throw in and do everything [he] could." True to his word, he followed through by putting up $20,000 for cash bail in an act that "really shocked" West, who retained a "very warm feeling" for Green years later because of his willingness to "put his money where his sentiment was." Green in turn remembered West as a complex man, who although imaginative was "slightly unreliable." He admired West as a committed activist but expressed mixed feelings about his "volubility," including the "need to express himself." Their "hearts were all tied up in knots over these poor devils and there was sort of an enjoyment in West in participating in this."[13]

Green and West remained on good terms during the appeal, but their differences over political exploitation of the defense persisted. At a subsequent meeting of the defense committee, which several Chapel Hill liberals attended, the public relations problem created by circulating communist literature broke into the open. Insisting that such publicity would hurt the cause statewide, Green wanted to know "just how many people of the Defense Committee are communists." West responded from the chair that if Green was a communist, he "would be proud of it."[14] Confirming liberal vulnerability, James Spencer Love angrily told his sister in Chapel Hill that the CP was behind the defense and that "if Green [was] not a Communist he [was] certainly beyond the slightest question associating and affiliating with them in this matter."[15]

Although West shared CP organizational responsibility with Crouch, "the defense work was the chief thing" that occupied him in 1935. He viewed this activity as a great opportunity for political consciousness-raising that would enable exploited workers to better understand the importance of solidarity. In January 1935, for example, he reminded Anderson that the contribution of ILD lawyers to the defense demonstrated that "we must do things *collectively*" and that only through "united, collective efforts" could workers "hope to effectively fight [their] oppressors, the mill owners." West went on to suggest that "this [was] why we try to do away with what we call 'individualism,' or conceit of self importance."[16]

On the front lines in the struggle to promote collective consciousness, radicals focused on the wider worker community. One of the most active groups in the battle against the local power structure was the Young Communist League (YCL), which urged members of the National Guard on duty at plant sites to refuse to act as strikebreakers and instead prevent scabs from entering the mills. In mid-February, Don wrote to Crouch that things were "sort of sliding along" but money was short. At that time, he was housing Belle, the key figure in the YCL's effort to make Burlington a party "concentration section." Although ready to support Belle, Don told Crouch that it was unfair to have the trade union organizer "always foot the bill for the YCL."[17]

Despite the Party's critical financial situation, the ILD maintained pressure for a successful appeal. Announcing its formal entry into the battle on February 1, 1935, the organization recounted the dismal history of the case and asserted that conviction had been obtained through "faked evidence" and prejudice from the bench. Behind the frame-up, the ILD maintained, was the "burning question of the right of workers in the South to organize into unions" and a "vicious hatred on the part of the mill owners for unions and those who join them." The ILD's national secretary, Anna Damon, denounced the Burlington conviction by a "hand picked jury from which all union members and union sympathizers were barred."[18] When the appeal reached the North Carolina Supreme Court, the ILD's performance justified the liberals' worst fears when New York attorney David Levinson launched a broadside attack on North Carolina justice in general, emphasizing the denial of "equal justice" to the working classes. After Levinson's diatribe against the state, the case was essentially lost and the sentences confirmed.[19]

The impact of the strike, the dynamite incident, and the subsequent legal proceedings on Burlington workers was profound. When Homer Brown, the U.S. Labor Department's conciliator, visited Burlington to investigate the union's complaints of employment discrimination, he found Holt Plaid Mill's vice president Lynn B. Williamson uncooperative and unrepentant. Brown was told that the defendants were "allied with the more radical elements among the workers." The analysis was consistent with West's experience as a speaker at a Chapel Hill religious meeting, where nearly every presenter supported the communist position, as did most listeners. He later speculated to Crouch that a socialist presenter who sat in stunned silence "must have thought we had the whole audience in the C.P. from the way they spoke up."[20]

West's passing reference to the troubled socialist signaled growing differences among communists, socialists, and the UTW's leadership, always reluctant collaborators in the united front built by the Burlington Defense Committee. Cooperation with the SP was complicated by factional strife among competing leaders, including what West regarded as a "reactionary group" led by the local socialist activist Jack Fies. He had, West reported to CP leader James Ford in New York, no rank-and-file following, and, meanwhile, the North Carolina communists had "won over the best the [state SP] had." In March 1935, West also opened lines of communication with the editor of the *Carolina Times*, an influential black newspaper that reached a large African American audience. Commending Jim Weaver and his "associates" for their "great work toward liberating the fettered masses of the South," editor L. M. Austin promised to carry a weekly column from the writer Don West, which he thought would "create quite a bit of interest through the South."[21]

While he worked to gain influence among socialists and liberals, West struggled with the UTW leadership. Overcoming stubborn opposition in Burlington, the defense committee finally persuaded national president McMahon to declare belief in the defendants' innocence. By March 1935, however, the prominence of the ILD reignited resistance among UTW leaders, including the officers of Burlington Local 1777. Incensed by the accused workers' willingness to "become involved in the activities of the International Labor Defense and apparently the Communist Party," the local executive board cut off all support for the defendants. On March 2 the board declared that it would do nothing on their behalf and urged the AFL to deny them any assistance as long as they "maintain[ed] their present connection with the ILD and the Communists."[22]

Despite Local 1777's foot-dragging, West continued to work with the UTW in an effort to breathe life into the weakened North Carolina united front. Consequently, five UTW representatives were among the ten delegates he led on May 26 to the All-Southern Conference for Civil and Trade Union Rights in Chattanooga. Responding to a call from James A. Dombrowski, Howard Kester, and Lee Burns of the Bessemer Trades Council, West assembled a delegation that included Walt Pickard and George Eliot of Burlington, three other UTW members, socialists, members of the North Carolina Unemployed League, and Workers Education groups. Jim Weaver (West) chaired a resolutions committee that advanced a wide range of defiant proposals endorsing labor unionism. But the key proposal for the North Carolina delegation was a demand for the immediate and unconditional release of the Burlington defendants. The meeting, although disrupted by an unwelcome American Legion delegation, embodied the Popular Front policy embraced by the CP and formally adopted at the Seventh Congress of the Communist International in summer 1935. The Chattanooga conference unified southern radicals and liberals in defense of civil liberties and the "rights of unmolested organization" to "win a higher material and cultural standard of life for Southern people."[23]

Despite momentary unity, however, North Carolina's Left was dividing into warring factions that spelled trouble for West. In June 1935, Paul Crouch observed that the UTW was near collapse as workers deserted the organization due to the "refusal of the leadership to carry on any struggles." Worse yet, he argued, the union had mounted a "vicious 'anti-Red' campaign" that was undermining the Burlington defense. The key figure in this drive was Leonard Green, a nominal socialist whom the UTW had sent into North Carolina to reorganize Local 1777 and bar from membership any union member who refused to repudiate the defense committee and the ILD. Meanwhile, the CP struggled in Greensboro, where only seven members, including the Wests, held forth.[24]

West was fully aware of tensions within the united front and also faced internal conflict within the state CP. Because of illness, Crouch had been unable to carry on full-time work, which meant that party organizers in the state essentially operated as individuals. In April, West complained that the CP's Southern Committee had formed a negative impression of his performance because he had not sent in "regular reports smearing on the bull about wonderful work with rank and file workers." Worried about finding resources to care for Connie and Ann, he was depressed by overwork on the Burlington defense. "Hell, I'm all alone," he asserted. West told fellow organizer Jim Crews that the Party's back-biting "gets a man's goat sometimes." What made him "sore" was the role of the Southern Committee in "spreading such goddamned bull about [him] not doing anything."[25] It was clear that all was not well on the front lines of the people's struggle.

West's concerns finally led to a direct appeal to the organizing committee in New York. Charging Crouch with "ineffectiveness" due to health problems and noting Sylvia Crouch's weakened physical condition, Don maintained that security had been compromised and the Party's influence reduced. He claimed that other North Carolina communists shared his views and expressed pessimism over the Party's outlook with Crouch in the position of district organizer. The beleaguered Crouch, who had seen West's letter, asked the Central Organizing Committee for an organizing secretary to ease his workload. In a not-too-subtle reference to Don, he also asserted that the new organizer be a "comrade without family responsibilities."[26]

This exchange, which grew out of West's frustration over workload, criticism of his work, and lingering personal animosities, was revealing in at least two ways. First, his criticism of Crouch began a conflict that would return to haunt him in later years when an unstable Crouch was to turn against the Communist Party and become a government witness. Even more telling in an effort to understand Don West's personal character was the reemergence of his difficulties in working with strong-willed colleagues. Internal party correspondence reveals West's growing conviction in 1935 that party comrades failed to appreciate the magnitude of the sacrifices he and his family were making. Moreover, it demonstrates that although he labored tirelessly for his political cause he could be inattentive to details, a flaw that caught the attention of others in the organization. The situations differed, but the rising tensions were reminiscent of the conditions surrounding his break from Highlander in 1933. An open breech might well have occurred had not other complications arisen to hasten his departure from North Carolina.

The roots of West's decision to move on during the summer of 1935 may be traced to a serious rupture that undermined the solidarity of the united front in North Carolina. Tensions between communists and socialists escalated in August 1935 due to intense factionalism within the state's Socialist Party. The catalyst for this disruption was the meddler Leonard Green, the New England socialist determined to discipline SP members inside Local 1777. Green, with his old guard ally Jack Fies, led the conservative wing of the state SP in an effort to discredit the Burlington defense committee. On August 3, 1935, West retaliated with a letter to the *Burlington Times-News*, attacking the interloper for joining hands with mill owners to make "malicious attacks on the Burlington defense." To refute Green's charges of ILD–CP domination as well as personal attacks on himself, West challenged his adversary to a public debate. At a statewide socialist conference in High Point a day later Green led an anticommunist revolt that exposed the factional rift within the SP and drove another wedge between Local 1777 socialists and the Burlington defense committee. In an attempt to further discredit the committee, Green escalated the conflict on August 12 by disclosing Jim Weaver's identity as Don West, a fugitive from Georgia justice.[27]

Mounting a counter-offensive, North Carolina CP activists responded with an effort to undermine the "social fascists" by exposing Green and Fies as class collaborators. Allen Johnson of *The Southern Worker* suggested that the CP focus on the socialist right-wing leaders' ties to management but admitted that Weaver was West and backed him.[28] Green, meanwhile, responded to West's challenge by denying that it came from a legitimate organization and refusing to consider it. He added that if he ever did "decide to debate a jack-ass," he would surely not pick a "straw one."[29]

Behind Green's bravado lay the reality that he had overstepped his authority so far as his Socialist Party credentials were concerned. Although West's relations with Howard Kester were strained by Don's communist ties, he made a successful appeal to his old friend in the name of socialism. "Shocked and disturbed" about the disclosure of Jim Weaver's true identity, Kester realized that Green's blunder jeopardized West's position in North Carolina. As a follow-up, he wrote to both Norman Thomas and the Socialist Party's chief labor organizer Clarence Senior to complain about Green's and Fies's treachery. Senior's initial response was equivocal, but he acknowledged that socialists were in a "serious dilemma in North Carolina."[30] What resulted was the SP's removal of Green from the state as a disciplinary measure.

It was too late, however, to help the beleaguered Don West. Fearing extradition to Georgia, where he was still wanted on insurrection charges, West again went underground. Meanwhile, after a failed appeal to the North Carolina Supreme Court, the Burlington defendants began serving their sentences in November 1935. No longer in a position to work effectively in North

Carolina, the original architect of the defense fled the state to become a labor organizer in the conflict-ridden coal fields of Kentucky, where he renewed his personal struggle for economic and social justice.[31]

Well before moving to Kentucky, West attended to an important item of family business. Don had become worried about his sister, Belle, who was active in YCL organizing in North Carolina. Characteristically, he took his responsibility as eldest son seriously, which led him to question her sexual liaison with Durham CP organizer Jim Crews. By April 1935, Belle had fallen under Crews's influence and become his *"de facto* wife," a matter of concern to Don because of her partner's criminal record. West's reservations had more to do with unhealthy ideological influence than moral issues. Convinced that she had "let him [Crews] have too much sway over her," he worked to have Belle transferred to District 17 in Birmingham, where Johnnye resided and her husband, Nat Ross, presided over party activities. At first "demoralized" over her separation from Crews, Belle later saw the wisdom in the Party's decision, which was confirmed when he was disciplined for stealing from party coffers. In 1937 she would return to North Carolina as YCL leader when her husband, Bart Logan, became Carolina district organizer.[32] In September 1935, this last problem resolved, Don slipped away to undertake a new assignment in Kentucky.

The relocation was in one sense a homecoming because West had studied and married in Kentucky. More significant for his organizational activity, he had visited Harlan County as a student during the bitter National Miners Union (NMU) struggle of 1929, in which communist-backed unionists battled mine operators and gun thugs bent on preventing labor organization of any kind. Don and Connie settled temporarily on Greasy Creek in Bell County, where there were a few scattered remnants of the earlier NMU drive. And scattered they were. As early as March 1935, District 23 organizer Jim Garland of Pineville had sent an urgent SOS to the Politburo in New York, asserting that the local party was "dying and dying fast." Unable to "hold [the] district together," Garland begged the Party to send a new organizer lest the organization "disintegrate." A "convinced Communist," he desperately wanted the Party to achieve "its historical task of leading the working class to victory against their oppressors."[33]

Four months later the solution to the CP problem in Kentucky emerged when West's identity was dramatically revealed in North Carolina. Even before then, however, he had clashed with other radicals, both socialist and communist. Substantial internal divisions had weakened the state CP, and Don was at the center of those disputes. Therefore, when Crouch informed him of the Party's difficulty in finding the right person for the Kentucky assignment, West readily volunteered his services. In August 1935 he told the Central Organizing Commission that given his experience in the state, he was "willing to take a try at Kentucky." By mid-September, West had relocated to Pineville, where he set about the task of reviving CP fortunes in an area where he found that "there was nothing organized."[34]

When he arrived in the eastern Kentucky coal fields West entered a world beyond the bounds of established order and amicable labor-management relations. Ever since the coal wars of the late 1920s and early 1930s, "Bloody Harlan" had symbolized the most brutal management efforts to stifle unionism in the non-union era. Here, labor relations had historically been carried out at the point of a gun as workers and the coal operators' gun thugs contested for control of the work place. It was this violence that offered an opening to the Communist Party, which had built the NMU into an effective competitor in the organizational battle. With the defeat of the NMU in 1931, the operators reestablished their dominant position in the class struggle, but the union spirit remained in the hearts of workers who sought parity at the bargaining table. Once the New Deal established the NRA in 1933 the fires of resistance flared anew, rekindled by what seemed a more receptive government. Under the aegis of the NRA's bargaining structure, the United Mine Workers of America (UMWA) built a powerful union juggernaut that would change the terrain of labor-management relations for years to come. Yet despite both the NRA and the Wagner Labor Relations Act, coal operators fought a vigorous rear-guard action that throughout the depression era frustrated the efforts of John L. Lewis and UMWA to win labor's right to organize and to quell the spirit of democratic unionism expressed by the Progressive Miners of America in labor's internal war.

Into this struggle came the labor revolutionary Don West. Going to the workers in September 1935, he and two other organizers took jobs in the Kayjay mine in order to "talk union" with the miners. Because the NMU was a dead letter by 1935, West worked to organize a United Mine Workers of America local, which, he claimed, included a membership of two hundred by late October. Deeply impressed by the descent into the depths of the earth, he carried the memory of that work experience throughout his life. His job at the mine afforded opportunity to organize undetected—or so he thought. The subterfuge was necessary due to the heavy repression imposed on the work force by company thugs whose presence made public events and home meetings dangerous. West consequently visited miners under cover of night to coordinate efforts to plan a general strike in late 1935. As he organized, it was hard to conceal his political agenda because "every comrade who lives here is widely known as a Red," which made it "difficult to work with them without being spotted." Close surveillance was an obstacle, but West reported to New York that the prevailing attitude among local comrades was "hell yes, we are Reds, and proud of it, and don't give a damn who knows it!"[35] Although West and his partners had gone into the mines as scabs in order to reach the rank and file, they were subject to constant monitoring. The "degree of actual fascist brutality and terror in Harlan" went "even beyond [his] expectation." In Bell County, once he entered a miner's home there would soon be a knock on the door from a company gunman who asked, "What are you doing here buddy? You don't live here." One FBI watchdog reported that at this time West was a party-line communist spurred by a "martyr complex" and a conviction that "laborers [were] the very backbone of the United States."[36] Such indictments of his radicalism failed to deter Don West, who undoubtedly agreed with the second premise.

West's organizing strategy was to work as an ordinary miner, assume union leadership, and identify militants for recruitment into the Party. Confident of worker support, he benefited from a widespread assumption among eastern Kentucky miners that red-baiting was to be expected from management. He later summarized the workers' perspective as an attitude that "anybody that's for us is gonna be called a Communist." To miners, it followed that "if somebody's called a Communist, that must mean he [was] for [them], or for poor people." In short, depression conditions, economic exploitation, and human suffering neutralized the local impact of red-baiting attacks.[37]

Probably more dangerous to West was that he openly preached the Social Gospel, which typically featured a forceful argument that "American citizens had a right to join any organization they wanted to." Once Kayjay miners walked out on strike in October 1935, West's message caught up with him when gun thugs and deputies arrested him in Bell County. Armed with six-shooters, they invaded the Wests' two-room shack on Greasy Creek. Unfortunately for West, one of his Kayjay partners, Fred Gooden, turned out to be a company agent who had betrayed him to the authorities. Both Don and Connie were hauled off to jail in Pineville, and Ann was taken in by neighbors. Connie was freed a week later, but Don was placed under a peace bond of $5,000, which, if no one made bail, was tantamount to a one-year sentence. Held on charges of criminal syndicalism, Don came in for special treatment and was accused of "conspiring to overthrow the government by use of the churches." After he spent six weeks in a filthy cell, local citizens put up the money that allowed him to go free on the condition that the Wests leave the state of Kentucky.[38]

Before his release, West devised a plan for Connie to accept temporary exile as a condition of her freedom. From his jail cell, he wrote to Charlotte

Moscowitz at Commonwealth College in Mena, Arkansas, that both Connie and her brother, Jack Adams, would make excellent students, both "pulled right out of struggle in the front lines" to learn how to "build a revolutionary organization that will stand against all the fascist brutality we know here in Kentucky." He told Moscowitz that although both were "fearless" they needed "more theory and understanding." Before long, Connie was on her way to Arkansas, where she resumed the familiar role of breadwinner once her talents as both student and art instructor were recognized.[39] After she became established at Commonwealth she brought Ann to Mena, where she spent three months on staff before returning to Kentucky to rejoin her husband and share his struggle against capital.

Although the Bell County community stood by him, West was less successful with some of his long-standing acquaintances. During Don's incarceration he was allowed but one visitor, an old Vanderbilt classmate who came to verify his predicament. His guest was a fundamentalist preacher who "just wanted to make sure it was [him]." Expressing similar skepticism, Jesse Stuart wrote to James Still to announce that Don was in jail for "working as a spy in a mine near Pineville." Stuart, who complained that West would not "get out of Communism," was ready to "fight over the racket he [was] in." At this time West asked him for a loan to ensure that Ann was well nourished, only to be rebuffed by Stuart, who refused to advance a cause he abhorred.[40] The incident starkly revealed the distance that had come to separate the two friends because of Don's political obsession and Stuart's distaste for communism.

Once Don was free, the Wests left Pineville to comply with the letter of the law. After their departure, they narrowly averted disaster when on a mountain road all four wheels fell off their car, the lugnuts mysteriously loosened. Like many other incidents in the coal fields, the event merely strengthened Don's stubborn commitment to the organization of the poor and dispossessed. Observing the court order in the very narrowest sense, the Wests landed just across the border in Tennessee. Soon thereafter Connie departed for her learning and teaching stint at Commonwealth College while Don tackled new responsibilities as party activist. A few weeks later, Hazard gun thugs administered a severe beating on Black Mountain, where they left Don for dead. An elderly mountain couple rescued and comforted him, however, and he lived to organize another day.

In his underground life West remained district organizer for the CP in Kentucky, but in June 1936 he assumed a more public role as a leading figure in the Kentucky Workers Alliance, a growing organization dedicated to meeting the needs of the unemployed through collective action. At the national level the Workers Alliance had initially been a socialist body in a few midwestern and eastern states, but by 1935 it had grown into a major national organization with a membership of four hundred thousand in eighteen states. By this time, the alliance had largely eclipsed the CP's Unemployed Councils and various other jobless groups, including the Trotskyist National Unemployed Leagues (NUL), as the leading voice of the jobless. In keeping with the Popular Front strategy, the councils merged with the alliance in 1936 to create a powerful national unemployed union capable of influencing New Deal social policy, jobs programs, and welfare provision. Although the board was ideologically diverse, the expanded Workers Alliance was strongly influenced by its communist national executive secretary, Herbert Benjamin, who worked with socialist president David Lasser to advance the interests of their jobless constituency in Washington. Acting on both personal social commitment and party ideology, West devoted most of his attention for the next two years to building the Kentucky affiliate of this organization.[41]

West's active involvement in organizing the unemployed was clearly in tune with the CP's Popular Front strategy and wholly consistent with his abiding faith in collective action and collaboration among oppressed groups. In February 1936, aware of the Party's emphasis on the creation of a "united mass unemployed organization," West approached the state secretary of the Kentucky Socialist Party with a proposal for a united front on several issues, one of which was unemployed work.[42] Although he wooed the socialists, he also did what he could to ensure CP influence in the national unemployed union then in formation. Communists worked assiduously to ensure a strong voice in the new united front group, but Benjamin's accounting system revealed that the Unemployed Councils and Workers Alliance were, as of 1936, relatively small in Kentucky, where the National Unemployed League was more influential. On March 2, 1936, recent communist convert Arnold Johnson of the NUL suggested to Benjamin that the time was right for West to approach the Kentucky League with a merger proposal to win delegates to the side of the CP caucus at the upcoming national unity meeting. By April, the Party had gained working control of the Kentucky delegation, so no further concessions to Trotskyist holdouts were necessary.[43] The result of these maneuvers was strong support for the merger that created the new Workers Alliance of America, including the power-sharing arrangement that made Lasser its president and Benjamin its secretary. The enlarged Alliance quickly became the leading voice of the jobless in dealing with government agencies, whether the Works Progress Administration (WPA) or local relief agencies.

In early 1936 the largest group of the unemployed in Kentucky was the independent Wage Earners, Inc., based in Lexington and dedicated to advocacy for WPA workers or those employed by the federal government's Public Works

Administation (PWA). Not long after the national unity meeting, a young union leader, Roy Swanson of the Hod Carriers, brought to a Wage Earners meeting a tall, handsome man named George Brown, a "stunning friend of the working class with some organizing skill" who was asked to address the meeting. Brown (West) gave a speech endorsing a united front for the jobless, a stirring presentation that deeply impressed the leadership.[44] Seizing the opportunity, West joined Wage Earners, Inc. and quickly emerged as a leader.

In order to consolidate ties with the new national unemployed union, the state's disparate jobless groups met in June 1936 to forge a united front organization, the Kentucky Workers Alliance (KWA). In an analogue to the national unity movement, the state conference blended the Workers Alliance, Unemployed Council, National Unemployment League, and Wage Earners into a pressure group more than twenty thousand strong. By this time a trusted activist, West was named organizational secretary of the newly established KWA. Working with state chair Giles Cooper and secretary-treasurer Allen McElfresh, the newcomer used his eastern Kentucky contacts to help mold the alliance into an influential pressure group by uniting warring factions into a body that spoke with one voice, usually in support—and sometimes in advance—of the Roosevelt jobs and welfare programs. KWA leaders recalled that in this important formative period West's southern roots, Kentucky contacts, organizing experience, and charismatic presence made him a "tower of strength to the effort."[45]

The Kentucky Workers Alliance crafted a sweeping program of "simple and reasonable demands," including WPA jobs for all unemployed at union scale, adequate pensions and relief for the disabled and aged, the right to organize freely, a $5 million direct-relief program, minimum old-age pensions, and an end to racial discrimination in job and relief programs. To publicize the KWA program West took to the air waves in 1936 to expose the shame of the inadequate state wage rate for WPA workers and ask the jobless to "join the army of the organized." Citing the six million organized workers in the United States, he asserted that "in union we are strong" and "by unity we shall win!" Determined to fulfill his prophecy, West scoured the countryside and rallied the destitute for political and social action. Preaching a "social class conscious Jesus . . . a mountaineer's Jesus, a worker's Jesus," he was "fiery in his advocacy of human rights." Wherever George Brown stopped in eastern Kentucky, friends and supporters appeared to embrace the cause of the dispossessed. In deeply depressed Paintsville, for example, the elderly union man John Mollette, also a state legislator, pledged enthusiastic support for KWA demands. In the same locality a fundamentalist preacher and veteran miner, Elihu Trusty, opened his simple home to West and lent powerful backing from the pulpit. A strong union supporter, the illiterate Trusty "could make a moving speech and he understood the issues, the purposes, and the principles" for which the alliance fought. And it was here that West was temporarily jailed, at least until three hundred angry relief workers and miners forced a local judge and sheriff to free him before the crowd took over. In this instance, Don wrote, "[my] attorney was mass defense."[46] All these encounters were filled with the spirit of community that for so many years had influenced Don's view of the world and those who did the nation's work.

Many years later West looked back with satisfaction on the foresight displayed by the urban poor, rural dispossessed, and unemployed of Kentucky in advancing a program for unemployment insurance, welfare, and social security, all ideas that became "an integral part of our society." His reminiscences confirm his basic endorsement of New Deal social provision, which he consistently supported while calling for more generous expenditures than the administration could possibly deliver. Even late in life the lesson of the alliance was, for West, that those victories were "won by poor people in united struggle" and it was still possible "to win greater victories in the future by similarly uniting in struggle."[47]

Solidarity was an absolute necessity in depression-era Kentucky in order to bring pressure to bear on chronically dilatory relief authorities and WPA representatives. Alliance veterans later remained critical of public officials who addressed workers' needs "only when the workers protested loud and long." With West serving as organizational secretary, the KWA "quickly acquired a good bit of political clout," which meant that grievances were successfully handled and the organization gained "respect from those it dealt with."[48] This grudging acknowledgment reflected the power of unity and numbers, often displayed in demonstrations, sit-ins, and "hunger marches" that dramatized the needs of the unemployed and dependent. Whether the target was Kentucky's evasive Gov. A. B. "Happy" Chandler or the sympathetic WPA administrator Aubrey Williams in Washington, West was typically at the center of the actions.

By mid-summer 1936, the KWA had become a force in Kentucky's relief politics. In August, organizer George Brown reported "degrading poverty and misery among the mountain counties of Kentucky, where whole families . . . [were] living in rock cliffs and caves." Among people "ripe for organization," he organized fifteen new eastern Kentucky locals and revived several old NUL groups. Those advances were matched by accelerated organizational activity and militancy in Louisville, Lexington, and Paducah. By fall, Alliance president David Lasser was trumpeting an endorsement from AFL president William Green and reporting that the Kentucky organization was an Alliance stronghold, one of the "nerve centers of the nation."[49]

Before long, West and his allies also exerted new and intense pressure on WPA officials in the nation's capitol. Incensed by both federal job cutbacks and the demeaning wage differential that discriminated against laborers south of the Ohio River, the KWA sent a delegation to Washington to press their case with Aubrey Williams, himself an Alabama-born mountaineer and a strong advocate of social justice. The petitioners argued that Kentucky WPA workers faced the same living costs as those in Ohio but received only $22.40 per month instead of the $60 paid on the north bank of the river. Williams understood their outrage but told West and his followers that he was powerless to act without legislative authorization. Their only course of action was to rally support in Kentucky for the New Deal. West "knew that Aubrey was not responsible for the discrimination," so the delegation "went back home" to "raise some hell."[50] Eventually, Kentucky workers received the desired change.

Acting on Williams's advice, the KWA turned up the political heat. At a Lexington relief demonstration West blistered the mayor for the city's tardiness in providing local matching funds to secure federal job funding and accused the officials of "callous indifference to human want." In October 1936 the alliance urged passage of a new relief bill and threatened "to compel Governor Chandler to meet its demands." Delegates at the organization's first convention visited the capitol, but the governor was nowhere to be found. Acting on a tip, West and the group treed their quarry at the governor's mansion. There, a hot session ensued that was climaxed by a verbal duel in which the governor's wife attacked McElfresh as a "crippled s.o.b." and roundly "cursed him out."[51]

After this confrontation, which spread more heat than light, the KWA increased the pressure on state and local authorities. At a rousing demonstration in Lexington, for example, West called for "militant action to enforce the demands the alliance [was] making on local relief officials." He insisted that it was now necessary to "show the WPA city and county officials that the workers [were] hungry" and that the alliance's demands "must be granted." West also built alliances with other worker organizations. In December 1936, he addressed the Lexington Hod Carriers Union, which followed up by endorsing the KWA's plans for further demonstrations. The following year, West's organizing activity went on unabated in various locales, including Lousville, Lexington, Bowling Green, and Paintsville. Eventually, success came in 1938, when, under intense pressure from the national alliance, the WPA raised wages for its employees in the South, thus reducing the sectional disparity in work relief compensation that had so angered Kentucky workers.[52] The victory confirmed the Workers Alliance's status as the recognized union of the unemployed, a result fully consonant with WPA labor relations policy.

West's active engagement in Workers Alliance organizing was a logical extension of his concern for the poor and voiceless, his awareness of eastern Kentucky's poverty, his experiences in the coal fields, and a rock-solid conviction that collective action was essential to any meaningful attack on systemic poverty. Moreover, the fact that the KWA was racially integrated mirrored his faith in cooperation across racial lines. Those factors notwithstanding, it is equally true that the Communist Party was a strong force in both the national and local Workers Alliance, which was a prime example of the Popular Front's philosophy in operation. By 1936 the state CP was what KWA veterans recalled as an "out-in-the-open establishment," headquartered in Louisville and active in both Lexington and eastern Kentucky. Typically circumspect about his party work, West told the *Louisville Courier-Journal*'s Herbert Agar in 1937 that the Communist Party had a "very practical approach to programs in the American labor movement," but he did not "propose that the Russian government be put over on the U.S." Given his party responsibilities as district organizer, West's energetic work on behalf of the alliance must be understood in part as an expression of his political views, which were firmly held and helped guide his actions. Communist influence on West, Arnold Johnson, and other CP members in the KWA also help explain the Kentucky Alliance's support for a farmer-labor party in 1936. This position was clearly stated in West's radio address calling for independent political action through a farmer-labor party that would serve the "general welfare" and "build a system of planned plenty."[53]

Although West eventually endorsed the communist ticket in 1936 and was a member of the National Unemployed Committee for Earl Browder and James Ford, most Kentucky workers were enthusiastic about the New Deal and hoped that it would expand. In short, the pull of the Roosevelt program doomed minor party agitation to failure. "Nothing came of this political activity" in 1936, but McElfresh and Cooper saw the farmer-labor movement as part of a long-term formative process that climaxed in the Progressive Party movement of 1948.[54]

Closely related to West's party activity in 1936 and 1937 was the recruitment of volunteers to serve in the Abraham Lincoln Brigade during the Spanish civil war. The very embodiment of the Popular Front, this group of idealists embraced the cause of democracy and antifascism at a time when Gen. Francisco Franco's forces fought to dislodge the legitimate Loyalist government in Spain. The Lincoln Brigade was a key priority for the CP, which enthusiastically supported the Loyalist regime. Consequently, Don was instrumental in organizing a statewide fund-raising event at the Brown Hotel in Louisville, at which Herbert Agar was featured speaker. West recalled "a good bit of sentiment over the state of Kentucky for Loyalist Spain."[55] The result was twenty-three volunteers, including Connie's brother and alliance member

Jack Adams, who was killed at the Battle of Ebro Crossing. Convinced that it acted in solidarity with the world's working class, the KWA believed that it compiled a "noble record at assisting the Spanish people in their struggle" despite the steep price paid by these unemployed workers.[56]

As he pursued his goals, West's literary skills proved a valuable asset to the unemployed movement. He continued to publish poetry and prose that dramatized the plight of the dispossessed in Kentucky. A regular contributor to *Southern Worker*, West called for a "new South of peace, jobs, security and plenty for all." Throughout his Kentucky years he advanced this argument with frequent speeches and performances of his own work, which were delivered with animation and eloquence that thrilled audiences. Even more accessible were his *Songs for Kentucky Workers*, published by the KWA in 1937, which "expressed thoughts of people towards unionism, bosses, [and] exploitation." Drawing freely on familiar music as well as many songs that originated in "bloody Harlan," West substituted locally relevant words that articulated the sentiments of the downtrodden toward the elite who dominated their lives and inspired them to collective action.

Among the songwriters whose work Don borrowed were Aunt Molly Jackson and Jim Garland, his original CP contact in Pineville. Their work has subsequently been recognized as part of the long history of American labor music that inspired workers to action over the years. Despite his role in familiarizing a new working-class public with Jackson's music, West eventually came to regret her prominence when she became a favorite of New York radicals who "spoiled" her by embracing her mountain creativity. West denounced the exploitation of Appalachian artists and their music but was prepared to employ them in support of the revolutionary cause. His introductory poem in the songbook celebrates the sacrifice of workers and promises to voice their concerns:

> Up, up, you toilers
> And hear what I tell.
> In a world of plenty
> We're hungry as hell!
>
> We dig and we shovel.
> We weave and we sweat.
> But when comes the harvest
> It's little we get!
>
> Oh this is the story
> of you and the rest—
> And if I am lying
> My name's not Don West.[57]

After two years of organizing for the KWA, West left the alliance in late 1937 and returned to his native Georgia. Connie was pregnant again, and he wanted to devote more time to the family. Several factors influenced his departure from Kentucky, including the pregnancy and Ann's need for a more settled existence as she prepared to start school. Don's account of this period typically stressed gradual improvement in the economy, which, he argued, made organizing the unemployed a less urgent matter (a dubious claim in view of the recession of 1937–38).

In addition, the red-baiting and blacklisting he had encountered in eastern Kentucky made it increasingly difficult for West to function effectively as an organizer. What he never acknowledged was a sharp conflict with the CP organization in New York over his performance as district organizer. The Party's Central Control Commission (CCC) later reported that in late 1937 West had been "dismissed, since he was ill suited for district organizing work and tried to devote all his time to the writing of a book." Party bureaucrats claimed that he had filed inaccurate membership reports, forgotten to submit financial reports, and failed to create "an effective district committee." Following his dismissal, he became inaccessible, but when contact was reestablished, West told party officials that he had underestimated his "obligations," undervalued the importance of "collective leadership," and experienced difficulty in contacting "comrades living in remote areas." He also expressed interest in working with farmers' organizations, with the Party's approval. Reviewing West's party status in May 1939, the CCC concluded that he did not demonstrate "responsibility and organizational capabilities in the discharging of his duties as Kentucky district organizer and left his highly important work there in a chaotic state." As a result, it recommended that the Party not "appoint him to work requiring organizational responsibility without the consent of the CCC." The "decision dating from autumn, 1937, to dismiss him" would remain in effect.[58]

The statement reflected the extent to which New York party leaders failed to grasp the substantial difficulties encountered in a hostile environment, not to mention the limitations placed on rank-and-file workers by insufficient financial support and backup personnel. At the same time, the description of West as committed to his literary work and dismissive of bureaucratic reporting responsibilities accurately portrays him as a thinker and doer with little time for matters of insignificant detail. It is equally true that Don West never responded positively to directives from faceless authority figures geographically removed from his world of day-to-day activism and confrontation. Finally, as was evident in his previous organizational experiences, it was not unusual for West to clash with other committed activists despite mutual commitments to shared goals. In short, he was an independent individualist operating within the framework of a structured collective institution. In this instance, his insistence on freedom and independence coincided with family considerations and the desire to attain a measure of respectability. The result was a return to his Georgia home and a search for stability.

SIX

A Poet in Formation: The Creative Impulse

An important dimension of the conflict between Don West and the CP bureaucracy was his commitment to writing, which outweighed dedication to organizational detail. This tension reflected West's stubborn insistence on making room in his crowded world for a literary life that expressed the creative impulse so vital to his existence since his college days at Lincoln Memorial University (LMU). It also concealed the extent to which in his inner life he consistently gave priority to the preservation of Appalachian history and culture as well as a lifelong project to celebrate the common folk of Georgia. During the 1930s, West's poetry evolved from work that expressed love for the rural mountain culture of his youth to sharp social criticism aimed at exposing the shortcomings of capitalism and the damage it inflicted on society's discards, the poor and dispossessed at the fringes of an industrial system then transforming his beloved south. As he proceeded along the path of radical activism, Don West assembled a body of work that challenged the agrarian tradition of the Vanderbilt fugitives and sketched a new vision of a modern south that valued the humanity of the underclass.

Until recently, scholars of modern poetry have ignored the cultural production of once obscure poets and writers who sought to use their art to promote social change. As Cary Nelson and Michael Denning have demonstrated, literary gatekeepers have consistently undervalued a huge body of work by categorizing radical and working-class writers as "minor poets" or denying the admission of their writing into the canon that represents the gatekeepers' literature of value. Too often these judgments have been influenced consciously or unconsciously by racism and class bias that prevented protest poetry like West's from being accepted into the realm of legitimate art. The decision to ignore working-class poetry coincided with a complementary determination to dismiss southern Appalachian culture as unworthy of academic attention. As a result of these assumptions, West's work, although it enjoyed an unusually wide readership and included large non-elite audiences, never gained a place in the canon. Nor was West typically regarded as even a "minor poet" of significance.[1] Such are the politics of cultural memory.

The process of rescue must begin with an examination of West's concept of poetry's purposes. In March 1941 he told another north Georgia poet, Byron Herbert Reece, that the task of a writer is to incorporate "more and more of concrete realism" in literary work and give that realism "social breadth." West insisted that poets are obligated to "evoke life" in its "totalities," focusing on the tremendous social currents "changing the face of the world." For West, the "individualism of a rising young nation of capitalism" was "utterly out of place in the new period." On the contrary, it is the poet's duty to "raise up in literature the collective drama" and bring the masses to the stage as a new protagonist. The artist, therefore, must take "the side of the oppressed, against the oppressors . . . the exploited against the exploiter—openly, clearly, honestly!" "Art for art's sake," he chided Reece, was "as far outmoded as the 'rugged individualism' of Herby Hoover!"[2]

This pronouncement underscored West's conviction that literature of value must be socially committed and anchored in day-to-day human experience. Acknowledging that he had an "aim" in his work, he contended that for poetry "to be worth a damn" it "must eat right down into the bone and marrow of living."[3] This commitment to the depiction of human life, the daily struggle and the fears and hopes of everyday people was the essence of West's early work. The result was a Whitman-like earthiness and humanity in the poetry West published at the dawn of his career. From the earliest publications on his work exhibited flashes of insight and human understanding that marked him as a people's poet gifted with empathy drawn from personal experience.

While a student at LMU, West began writing poetry that addressed the lives of the mountain people from whom he had come. Under the wing of Harry Harrison Kroll, he began to develop a storyteller's skills, which he employed with simplicity and power as he wrote of common people caught up in the task of earning a living from the products of the soil and the use of their hands. Because his work focused on what he knew, it reflected intimate familiarity with the simple ballad form to which he had been exposed in a family and community that honored oral tradition and lyrical expression through music.

West's choice of ballad format was rooted in family history. From early childhood, he listened to the song-stories passed on in tunes played by Lillie West, a musician as well as a virtual storehouse of cultural history. Exposed to literature and the arts at home, Don followed his interest by creating his own art and sharing it with LMU's other aspiring writers, Jesse Stuart and James Still. Nurtured in the southern Appalachian ballad tradition, West soon turned to the lyricism of short poems rooted in the human struggle.[4] The experience on which he relied in his first works was that of family and community, particularly admiration and idealization of his grandfather, Kim Mulkey, who inspired much of West's literary production over the years. Likewise, he acknowledged his parents' influence in the dedication of his first book, *Crab-Grass*, published in 1931 for "my mother and father/mountain woman and man."[5]

By the time West reached Vanderbilt University in 1929, his work was already being published in literary journals, and he was preparing larger works. *Crab-Grass* extolled the rural Appalachian culture he valued above all else and celebrated the family that had guided his intellectual development. Written in mountain vernacular, the volume was the first of many in which West would celebrate his cultural roots, which he perceived to be under attack from a variety of sources. As Stuart noted in the introduction, it was the work of a man who had "lived the things he writes."

The book was filled with the sights, sounds, and people of the mountain society that West had known as a child. Because of his appreciation of Appalachian cultural values, he was deeply offended by the hillbilly/cracker stereotype that denigrated mountain people and devalued rural southern whites. Not only were his people unfairly maligned, he believed, but the community and culture of his youth were also disappearing before his very eyes. Already, the forces of greed and class exploitation were undermining the values he held to be true. Mourning the passing of "Bill Dalton's Wife," West describes death in childbirth because

Th' babe was crossed, Bill sed
Th' doctor wudn't cum
Bill wuz powfly in debt
An' cudn't pay th' sum.[6]

By framing the poem in simple dialect he makes "a statement about the dignity of the Appalachian poor."[7] Similarly, in "Laid Off" he laments the fate of Tom Wilson, who "stole money and bought / Corn bread for his children

/ When the wolf stalked the door." For his crime, Wilson rotted in prison, a convicted thief who took bread when laid off while his employer, Cornelius Vandermeulin, worked his men "on death colored wages" and "made a thousand dollars a day." Ominously, West warns of "working men with a tiger light in their eyes."[8] The stark realism in these lines reflected the early influence of Alva W. Taylor on West's social thought. Already on the road to radicalism, he nursed a grudge against the faceless capitalists whose intervention in the economy of the Mountain South was producing what he considered a generation of wage slaves who were disconnected from the self-sufficient culture and economy of his childhood.

Despite clear indications of a rising social conscience, the predominant theme of West's first books is the celebration of family, friends, and mountain culture. His several tributes to Kim Mulkey revealed the awesome presence of a man who did much to shape young Don's character, providing a role model and respect for education that he found lacking in the hapless Oliver West. Even broader in scope, West's overriding argument was encapsulated in his tribute to the entire mountain community that sustained him:

My people are a sturdy race
With simple honest ways
They labor hard among the hills
And sing their mountain lays.[9]

The quiet dignity afforded the folk was not missed by reviewer May Smith, who observed that in *Crab-Grass* "one can recognize real people and real situations" as well as genuine "acquaintance" and "affection." These people were not the stereotypical "crackers" or "hillbillies" that so offended West. In 1933 he undercut that image with arresting irony when he called the much-maligned but poorly understood common people to action: "Clodhoppers of the World Unite! You have nothing to lose but your clods!"[10] This preoccupation with worker unity was a recurrent theme in much of West's early work and continued to appear as his writing became more politicized after 1934.

From 1932 on, West began redirecting his work toward deeper commitment to social activism. His escalating outrage at the exploitation of the poor took concrete form in poetry that revealed both anger and doubt about the commitment of mainstream religion to the way of Jesus as he knew it. West wondered how any deity, vengeful or benevolent, could tolerate the abuses that daily insulted the laboring masses. A hint of new militancy may be detected, veiled though it was, in "I've Seen God." In a sensitive expression of a personal search for understanding, he declares:

I've Seen God—
In the gaunt eyes
Of a factory worker,
Bound by chains
Of circumstances.
I've felt God's pulse beat,
I've seen his soul
And heard him groan
From the hungry throats
Of miners children
In a Kentucky coal camp.
And God was in prison![11]

This dark observation, brimming with doubt, presaged West's next stop on the journey into radicalism and disbelief.

West's formal entry into movement culture came on January 13, 1934, with the publication of "The New Song" in *The Daily Worker*. In these militant verses he left behind

Songs of flowers
And mountains
Songs of crab-grass
And maple tree
Leaves.

Moving beyond a concentration on sorrow and grief, he announces:

Today I sing
A new song
A song of revolution.
Hear, O my people
Who wrestle with
Death!

I sing to rouse you
Dreamy sleepers.
Snoring like cattle
And struggling
For breath.

Tomorrow—
Ah, Tomorrow . . .

I shall shout:
"A new people.
Who sing out their
Gladness
And laugh in
Their joys."

This poem drew the enthusiastic attention of CP intellectual Mike Gold, who welcomed its author into the radical fold with a ringing column embracing his work as evidence of "the great currents moving in the South." Gold also observed that West's heightened political consciousness reflected a "painful transition." In his estimation, Don West was destined to emerge as a "new revolutionary poet" who would "sing the song of the Southern mountains and factory towns." Two months later, West decisively broke the bonds of tradition with a militant declaration of political independence in "Listen, I Am a Communist."[12] Although he later insisted that he intended the poem to express an element of irony, the clarity of its assertion exposed him to extensive public criticism.

Despite his party affiliation in 1934, West did not hesitate to criticize the Party on several points, most notably its ignorance about his south and the misplaced missionary zeal of some CP outsiders who came to enlighten it. This critique reflected the underlying significance of his Appalachian cultural chauvinism, which was to remain a key theme in his lifetime body of work. Personal politics aside, West generally remained autonomous from party dictation and party-sponsored literary organizations. Like many intellectuals in the 1930s, he initially regarded communists as "Socialists in a hurry," an analysis that matched his own political trajectory.[13]

West's personal manifesto coincided with the emergence of "proletarian literature" in 1934, the year a cadre of young radical artists and intellectuals declared themselves "proletarians" and "revolutionaries" dedicated to victory in what some called the "literary class war." This movement, which was to enliven literary discourse for a relatively brief period, inaugurated what Michael Denning has called "a proletarian renaissance that stamped an indelible working class imprint" on American cultural life in the 1930s.[14] For a brief moment of possibility, poetry became a vessel for revolutionary activism. Although nascent southern radicalism was but one current in a broad national stream flowing through the literature of the Left, it was unquestionably consistent with the larger movement. Don West's work was part of that cultural project.

West's induction into the radical literary pantheon of his era was confirmed in 1935 by his inclusion in *Proletarian Literature in the United States: An An-*

thology, which was published with CP support. A massive anthology of stories, poems, plays, and essays from the Left, the volume soon became a benchmark in the advancing literary class struggle of the 1930s. His work appeared in other party-sponsored publications, including *The Daily Worker, New Masses*, and *Liberator*. One of the poems selected for the anthology pointedly employed the vernacular as an act of revolutionary defiance that tested the limits of literary acceptability. In "Dark Winds," nonstandard speech strengthens the protest against incorporating mountain people into the expanding industrial economy of the New South:

Sad Winds
They've blowed sorrow an' sufferin'
Frum northern mills
An' drug my people
Down from th' hills.

These words express West's bitterness over mountaineers trapped into lives hated by most but accepted out of economic necessity. Equally significant was the use of spoken language and nonstandard speech patterns, which "declared in their very existence a resistance to class, regional and/or national oppression."[15]

The other West verses in the anthology built upon his declaration of ideological independence. "Southern Lullaby" called a recently born generation to take up arms in the class war. In a sharp attack on economic oppression, the poet counsels anger over the injuries of class as well as personal engagement in struggle:

Eat, little baby, eat well,
A Bolshevik you'll be,
And hate this bosses' hell—
Sucking it in from me . . .

Hate, little baby, hate deep,
You musn't know my fears.
Mother is watching your sleep,
But you don't see her tears.[16]

Words like these have led some literary critics and scholars to dismiss West's work as excessively didactic and fundamentally ideological. If didacticism was defined as a commitment to teaching, Don West would have pled guilty, for he was at heart a teacher who employed every tool at his disposal to stimulate independent thought. If a poem could encompass a lesson, especially concerning pride in culture or sharpened political consciousness among the rural poor, he thought it foolhardy to miss such an opportunity to communicate an alternative vision of a new and radicalized south to readers.

To West's dismay, other visions of the South had dominated literary discourse for years, most clearly in the writings of the renowned Vanderbilt agrarians, the "fugitive poets" who turned away from an industrial future for their section. These writers, based at Vanderbilt University, coalesced in a conservative reaction to the ascendancy of modernism by the 1920s. The "fugitives," including Robert Crowe Ransom, Donald Davidson, and Alan Tate, met regularly to discuss their mutual disenchantment with the coarse aspects of industrial society and eventually published a sweeping agrarian manifesto, *I'll Take My Stand* (1930). In that volume they rejected the modern South in favor of a return to their peculiar version of traditional southern values, most of which West rejected.[17]

In contrast to the fugitives' backward vision, West looked to the future of a revolutionized south that would throw off the yoke of agrarian conservatism and embrace his vision of economic and social equality. He had little time for the "professional agrarians" willing to establish their position by "turning the wheels of history back" to a time of "murder, lynch, and iron hand." In his biting attack "They Take Their Stand (for Some Professional Agrarians)," West ridicules nostalgia for a society long gone and disdain for political engagement in the modern world:

They never delve in politics,
    That's all too commonplace, they say.
Their thoughts must go to subtle tricks
    Befitting noble gents like they.

In Dixie land there's many an ass
    Braying loud in every school,
But never sees the growing grass
    That might be had by any mule.

Come, sift the star dust off their stars—
    See coal dumps where our children play.
They sing of ancient Greece and Mars,
    We'll show them starving kids today![18]

Behind the sharp critique of the agrarians lay West's love affair with the South of his personal experience. Moreover, there was in his work a didactic tendency that even he acknowledged. Later in life, he frankly acknowledged that he regarded poetry as a "medium of communication" into which a lesson could be incorporated. He also believed poetry that didn't communicate was of little use to anyone. In his early work, he tried to reconcile his emotional attachment to the South with an acknowledgement of its shortcomings. "My South," published in *The New Masses* on April 10, 1935, cites the many aspects of southern life to which he was drawn while asserting "deep sorrow" over unsung songs capable of "slashing" at the "cruel chains of hunger." West recognizes a south whose "eyes were blind" and "hate was old," which drives him to the point of despair:

Oh, my south,
My cold-blooded south
With a Negroes' blood
Smeared over your mouth

And a Negroes' bones
Which you blindly make
A few charred coals
By a burnt off stake—

Despite its social pathology, however, West's south held out hope of a redemption he believes his words would advance:

Tomorrow you must wake
And white hands
Will clasp
Ebony
Bowed over a few charred bones
By a burnt-off stake . . .!

You are my south—
And I love you . . .[19]

The ambivalence in West's affection for his homeland was evident in his review of Albert Bein's play *Let Freedom Ring*, published in *The Daily Worker* on November 18, 1935. Based on Grace Lumpkin's powerful novel set during the bitter Gastonia strike of 1929, Bein's work (later published with an introduction by West) captured West's imagination as a realistic account of the southern class struggle that provided a clear picture of "ruling class brutality." West knew the play was not likely to be seen in the South, but, he speculated, had there been a free marketplace of ideas, southern worker-viewers would have been "stirred to greater struggles" by Bein's work.[20]

By the time the review appeared West had moved to Kentucky. During his organizing years among the miners and unemployed there, the character of West's literary output shifted. Work as union advocate, district organizer, and unemployed activist swallowed his time, yet West did manage to adjust his creative life to new circumstances. Confronted by new challenges, he devoted more time to prose and music lyrics in 1936 and 1937, literary pursuits directly related to Kentucky organizational activity. Likewise, his poetry mirrors the grim life experiences of the workers with whom he lived and worked. Typical of this work was "Miner's Widow," which is filled with anger at the fate of Barney Graham's family following his murder during the bitter Wilder strike in 1933. "Super's gunmen" are held responsible for the family's privation, while mainstream preachers also come in for their share of blame:

> Preachers come a-peddlin'
> Thur tales about a prayer
> Leave me here a-grievin',
> You have done your share;
> You preachers of the bosses,
> Take away yore prayer.[21]

Like Joe Hill, West placed little faith in organized religion, which had, in his view, been co-opted by corporate overlords.

More directly connected to his organizational work was West's expression of solidarity with the "Harlan County Coal Digger, 1934," whose humanity penetrates early stanzas devoted to a portrait of a miner's simple abode and home life. Its stark images and flat declaration of private despair convey the simplicity of the worker's daily experience. Cognizant of the terror and intimidation that were also part of a miner's existence, he warns of "company gun thugs" and prescribes a solution:

> If you are not a union man . . .
> you ought to be. . . .
> It takes unity . . .
> to build the union strong.[22]

In the context of the mining wars of the 1930s and West's role as activist and agitator, the call for union solidarity made perfect sense. Yet the optimism of the union organizer was tempered by "Portraits of Harlan, Kentucky," which asserts that "beauty / Is a stranger / To the coal camps." These poems revealed ambivalence toward coal mining and its deleterious effects on workers caught up in the industry, a sense of paradox that matched Don West's lifelong love-hate relationship with an America that was half dream and half nightmare.[23]

An even more graphic portrait of the miner's life, "Thoughts of a Kentucky Miner," appeared in *Mountain Life and Work* (published by the Council for the Southern Mountains [CSM]) in January 1936 over the byline of one Mack Adams. This short essay, which West composed while he languished in the Pineville jail, used the pen name because the CSM would never publish the piece knowing that its author was a prisoner who had also organized for the CP-dominated National Miners Union. The story describes the drab, dangerous life of the miners, whose "lives [were] dark" and minds "cramped." It ends with a ringing statement of worker defiance:

> But this is America! We are part of her. Our fathers hewed the wilderness and fought the revolution. Our fathers were dangerous men. They believed in right. They took their guns and went barefooted to Washington. They made a revolution. And there may come a time when we are dangerous men, even the one-armed brother. For every day we look up and say: 'God, must our children follow our stumbling feet! Is there not sunshine of new life, of intelligent learning, ideas that will penetrate even the dismal depths of Dark Hollow?' Our kids, they're all that matter now.[24]

The article drew widespread praise, including an endorsement from John L. Lewis, who pronounced it the most accurate description of a miner's life he had read. West had great fun with the scheme, which included his own follow-up suggestion that he write a similar piece under his own name. The editors said "nothing doing," not with his name attached to it. Reprinted in the UMW journal and *Literary Digest*, the Mack Adams piece was enormously successful, a result that West attributed to his mining experience. Despite the favorable response, the story's author remained a mystery until 1961, when it was reprinted over the pen name in *Mountain Life and Work*, whose editors were still uncertain about the author's identity. At that point folk musician Hedy West wrote to inform them of her father's authorship, which revealed "how close his thinking ran to the feeling of the coal miner."[25]

West's ties with eastern Kentucky mining communities served him well once he moved on to organizing the unemployed in 1936. Equally valuable was his vast knowledge of mountain music and its history, which became a key weapon in the battle of the KWA on behalf of the jobless. Like the union movement, the unemployed movement was a singing movement, and the alliance understood the galvanizing potential of songs that told the truth. The executive board authorized *Songs for Southern Workers*, confident in the belief that Don's verses, set to familiar tunes, would "inspire people to keep struggling" for their goals.[26]

Because of his personal background, Don West was uniquely qualified to advance those objectives through the medium of music. From his earliest days he had been exposed to the Appalachian oral tradition in which cultural history was passed from generation to generation, sometimes through story and sometimes through song. Lillie West sang at home and in the fields, so much that music was closely integrated into daily life. This "legacy of song" helped shape Don into "both artist and political activist," and it was this tradition that enabled him to give new meaning to familiar tunes by crafting contemporary political lyrics that spoke to the experience of Kentucky's unemployed workers and blacklisted unionists. Patterned after the Industrial Workers of the World's *Little Red Song Book, Songs for Southern Workers* was widely used in union organizing throughout the South in the 1930s and 1940s.[27]

West's first effort to advance organization through song predated the formal publication of his work in 1937. In 1936, he drafted a mimeographed version of politicized union songs, which the KWA distributed. Entitled "Songs for Kentucky Workers," the song sheet was geared to the interests of Kentucky workers, featuring such unfamiliar verses as "Going to Kick Old Goodman Out," which was a direct attack on the state's Works Progress Administration administrator George H. Goodman, long a KWA target. The handout also included several songs by Jim Garland and Molly Jackson, including "Build the Union," "Give Me Back My Job Again," and "Poor Miner's Farewell," all of which were familiar to Kentucky's jobless, especially eastern Kentucky miners. The remainder of the packet blended traditional union songs with the state-oriented material, closing in a defiant gesture with "The Internationale." Most of these tunes survived in the print version, with the notable exception of the attack on Goodman, apparently deemed too parochial.[28]

The inclusion of "The Internationale" in the song book reflected an ideologically driven determination that influenced most of West's work in the mid-1930s. It was this missionary spirit that alienated his old friend Jesse Stuart, who was convinced that Don's politics had tainted his art. Their deep differences over literary work were evident in West's critique of Stuart's "old romantic sentimentalism which outsiders hook[ed] up with the mountains." He was convinced that because of his romanticism, Stuart's writing would "surely not endure." In a related comment, Don also criticized Still's work as "romantic' although he felt that because Still was honest, "there [was] still hope for [his] writing." For his part, Stuart considered some of West's poetry "sentimental mush," akin to "puppy love." In a letter to Still in September 1937, Stuart asserted that Don's political ideology had become a "religion" that endowed him with a "spirit unbreakable." Yet he insisted that as a poet, "Don will pass as a blowing wind unless he does a book of his own."[29] Stuart thought that unlikely unless West turned away from political activism and toward a writer's life. Although they met occasionally and tried unsuccessfully to set aside their differences in the interest of civility, the disagreement over the nature and purposes of literary art only deepened with the passing years.

What Stuart could not have been aware of in 1937 was Don's growing rift with CP officials in New York and the imminence of his decision to abandon the burdensome details of organizing the unemployed for rural life in his native Georgia. At this time, West also reached for literary respectability by submitting a substantial packet of his poems to Lillian Smith's *North Georgia Review*, a magazine published by a woman who represented the soul of mainstream southern liberalism in 1937. Included were many verses penned during the perilous mid-1930s, including several Harlan County pieces, several poetic love notes addressed to the South, and the haunting "What Shall a Poet Sing." Written in 1933, the poem documents the raw brutality of southern folkways and challenges literary artists to accept social responsibility:

What is a poet saying
Down by a Georgia pine
Where a broken body's swaying
Hung to a cotton line . . .

What of a pile of ashes
Scattered around a stake
And bones that can't show lashes
Which leather horse-whips make . . .

Where working children's crying
By a cupboard cold and bare,
Their mother slowly dying
Working for a millionaire . . .

With his folks all lean and stark,
Pinched by hunger's pain.
Whether he's white or dark,
What shall a poet sing . . .
   Georgia, 1933.[30]

Deflecting the glancing blow contained in this pointed query, the *Review* rejected the poem while accepting the less graphic "Southern Nights" for publication. Dedicated to African American communist Benjamin Davis Jr., this piece speaks eloquently of the South that West both loved and hated. Lyrical and filled with rich imagery, "Southern Nights" is daring as it moves effortlessly from visions of a beautiful evening to the

Cruel south
A cold hearted south
With flesh in her teeth
And blood on her mouth.

Here the poet offers the image of "slow southern rivers" murmuring gently over the "bones / of dead negroes," victims of the lies spoken in the "drawling voice" of the ruling south."[31] The publication of the poem, with its implicit references to lynching, did place the magazine on record in criticism of the South's social system as it existed in 1937. It remained for Hagglund Press of San Benito, Texas, to publish most of the poems originally sent to Smith, this time in West's fourth book, *Toil and Hunger* (1940).

Although the *North Georgia Review*'s editors had "enjoyed reading" West's work, there was an element of suspicion in their acceptance letter, in which Smith's editorial associate, Paula Snelling, apologized for a long delay in considering the poems. She told him that they had "been interested in the bits of information [they] had about [him]," including a "little folder" about West sent to the *Review* by an unnamed correspondent. Snelling closed with an invitation to visit the editorial offices so that they might talk at greater length and a request for "a little more recent information about yourself."[32] Although West would stay in communication with Smith, they were eventually to part ways as she veered toward anticommunist liberalism after World War II.

The cautious attitude of Georgia liberals suggested that West was in for more trouble in his native state. For the immediate future, he contented himself with a return to the agrarian life. When the opportunity presented itself in 1938, he purchased the old family property near Cartersville at Cass Station, where Grandpa Benjamin (Bud) West had lived while working at the Atco Mill. For the next year, West relied on his considerable skills as a farmer, marketing produce in both Cartersville and Atlanta, with special attention to consumers in the African American community, where he retained substantial popularity due to his organizing work in the mid-1930s. He later shipped out of Memphis as a deckhand on a Mississippi riverboat while he looked for steady work. Yet for Don and Connie, Cass Station was a welcome retreat, and it was there that their second daughter, Grace Hedwig (Hedy), was born on April 6, 1938.[33]

In 1938 West also met Mike Ross, another dedicated labor activist and soon to become a member of the extended family when he married Don's sister, Ann (Buddie). Don, who seemed bigger than life to young Mike at this time, again assumed leadership as the unofficial family patriarch in view of the dying Oliver's debilitating illness. A "giant" in Mike's eyes, his brother-in-law was truly "impressive" to a novice union organizer aware of his record in Georgia, Kentucky, and especially North Carolina, where Mike had worked briefly with Bart and Belle.[34]

Life on the farm was a welcome change, but West soon became restless with the sedentary life and the minimal opportunity it offered to advance the cause of social justice, always the driving force behind his relentless political activism. Equally important to the Wests was the need for income, which compelled Don to seek a temporary solution to their financial problems. From the moment he returned in late 1937, he began to seek teaching positions and other employment. Simultaneously, he enrolled as a graduate student in education at Oglethorpe University. Although he continued writing, his literary production slowed during this rural interlude.

Nonetheless, faculty who supported his job applications generally agreed on both his teaching potential and his substantial literary skills. While Alva W. Taylor predicted that West would "make a name" as a literary figure, Dean Robert L. Ormsby of Oglethorpe confidently predicted a "future for him in the field of creative writing." Almost as an aside, some of Don's reference letters mentioned his religious convictions as a "spiritually minded man," who, in the words of H. H. Taylor of the Knott County Public Schools, was "destined to be a great leader in religious work."[35]

Before long, West's record as a preacher and graduate training in religious studies produced a short-term answer to his financial difficulties. Aware of the opportunities in religious work, he maintained ties with regional church institutions that might lead to employment. In October 1938, West attended the Tennessee Congregationalist Conference in Crossville, where he contacted his one-time sponsor, Dr. Fred Ensminger, and met Methodist elder A. M. Pierce of Dalton, Georgia. Always promoting progressive religious activity, he worked to publicize the new Fellowship of Southern Churchmen, a reform caucus of religious activists led by his old friend Buck Kester. Upon return, he informed Kester of his Cass Station address and tried to reopen their relationship, which had cooled considerably due to West's political activities in North Carolina and Kentucky.[36]

As the result of an extended job search, West finally found employment when in 1939 an interdenominational consortium of church groups in Bethel, Ohio, called him to serve as pastor and youth counselor. At the Christian Fellowship Parish in rural Bethel, he was responsible for both preaching and supervision of the Department of Education and Young People's Activities. In view of his YMCA experience as a youth, religious training, and educational experience, Don seemed an ideal choice for the position. Although the new job took the Wests a great distance from their Georgia home, Don embraced the opportunity it gave him to teach "Christian social ethics" to a fresh audience. So it was that economic necessity and professional interests ended in yet another geographic dislocation for a family accustomed to life on the move.

part two

Transitional Years:
Finding the Way

seven

Refuge and Respectability: From the Pulpit to the Classroom, 1939–42

When Don West arrived in Bethel, Ohio, he hoped to leave behind him the political infighting that had been an important factor in his early exit from Kentucky. It was not to be. Although the battle took on new forms, West's personal history and political commitments guaranteed that there would be little respite from the ideological wars. While he immersed himself in youth organizing and ministerial duties in Bethel, he found time to participate in CP-backed groups such as the American Peace Mobilization following the signing of the Nazi-Soviet Pact in 1939. No longer a party operative, West nonetheless continued to support principled positions on issues that were consistent with his own moral and religious beliefs. Never one to inquire into the political backgrounds of others, West was perfectly willing to cooperate with individuals and groups that sought to promote social justice, economic equity for workers, and world peace. It was inevitable that this work would also put him in touch with Ohio Communist Party members, including Columbus party secretary Steve Grattan and former communist journalist Martha Edmiston, who would later identify West as a party member in the southwestern Ohio area. Before one year had elapsed, he was the subject of an FBI investigation by the Cincinnati Field Division, which reported him "active in Communist circles in the Cincinnati Section of the Party and in the Peace movements."[1]

The Bethel years were also the occasion of a sharp rift with his old friend Howard Kester over West's allegations that Kester had shut him out of the Fellowship of Southern Churchmen (FSC), a liberal social action organization dedicated to bringing the living church closer to a meaningful relationship with southern poor. West asserted that Kester was "so prejudiced against the CP" that his suspicions "could not be allayed." For this reason, Don thought his own inquiry about the FSC had been ignored, which in his view was "no way such an organization builds itself." Denying any exclusionary policy, Kester responded to the charges in late 1939 with a packet of FSC literature and an acid assertion that West was "intolerant of those who don't see things the same way as [he did]." Angered by West's "bitterness and self-righteousness," Kester admitted fatigue with his old friend's "strutting," as if he was "the only person in all the world with any insights" or commitment to the labor movement. Kester's pointed accusation that Don had not "graduated from the Communist kindergarten" suggested that despite the denials, he had probably kept West out of the organization for ideological reasons.[2]

The crux of their disagreement was West's adoption of a neutralist position after the announcement of the Nazi-Soviet Pact of August 1939, including a spirited defense of nonintervention in the European war. Although Don expressed willingness "to take the verdict of history for the correctness or incorrectness of the Soviet policy," Kester interpreted his apparent acceptance of the Party line as "someone always calling the balls" for him. Where Kester saw subservience, West emphasized an independent vision of Christian principles on the pursuit of peace. He countered the charges against him by embracing the peace movement and chiding Kester for red-baiting when other issues were much more important than allegations of radicalism.[3]

In a follow-up letter, West assured Kester that he had severed his "former political connections" with the CP some two years earlier and saw "no use to argue over politics." In a moment of unusual frankness, he acknowledged that he "had been given more hell by those former associates" than Kester had administered in his rebuke. Yet his account of a definitive break with the Party was disingenuous in view of his discussions with the Central Control Commission in May 1939. In reality, he would soon establish contacts with Cincinnati communists, and he continued to cooperate with proponents of social and economic justice, which sometimes meant adopting positions embraced by the CP and forming working alliances with radicals of all persuasions. Two years later, after the Nazi invasion of the Soviet Union had changed the calculus of international politics, he was still denying formal party involvement, this time in a letter to Alva Taylor in which West insisted that he was "no Red" but reserved the right to support the CP when "the Reds happen to be right on things."[4]

Although he refused to jettison party-endorsed ideas when they fit his own social and political analysis, it is clear that by late 1939 West had moved beyond committed organizational work to a broader Popular Front liberalism more attuned to his personal situation and changed relationship with the CP. He was still the religious radical who regarded the man Jesus as "the first guerilla Christian," and, like his old Vanderbilt compatriot Claude Williams, his revolutionary theology set him apart from most Social Gospel adherents. In 1939, however, there was a subtle change in West's strategy for living God's word in that he increasingly relied on moral suasion from the pulpit or the pen to change people's hearts. Simultaneously, he attempted to distance himself from participation in the day-to-day work of the Communist Party as he reached for respectability and acted out his belief in the revolutionary Jesus.[5]

One avenue that West pursued led to deep involvement in the peace movement, including active work for the Cincinnati branch of the American Peace Mobilization, a "party-inspired and party-controlled organization." Although the organization was the antiwar arm of the American Communist Party, Don's commitment to its activities stemmed from the strong neutralist views he had expressed earlier to Howard Kester. His most important contribution to the peace movement was undoubtedly the role he played as publicist. In late 1940, for example, he published "Blessed Are the Peace Makers," an "urgent appeal to the peace lovers of the South," in which he invoked the "principles of Jesus Christ, the 'Prince of Peace.'" Excoriating General Motors, Ford, Dupont, Standard Oil, and General Electric as Adolph Hitler's accomplices, he warned against another "imperialist war" promoted by "false prophets" in the political arena. A frontal attack on the proposed lend-lease bill, West's essay constituted an emotional appeal to "Christians, working men . . . and common folks" to preserve their "dearly purchased personal liberties" by lobbying Congress to kill the legislation and organizing for peace.[6]

Throughout the year in Bethel, West planned other educational endeavors, most of them focused on a return to his Georgia home. As early as September 1939, he informed Myles Horton that he found himself in Ohio as "a purely temporary expedient" in preparation for the establishment of an "educational project in Georgia." He thought that the Cass Station farm would be the perfect place to undertake "special work in the agricultural field" with both tenants and industrial workers. Although Georgia was a "right tough nut to crack," he insisted that it "needed cracking." Horton immediately responded with a letter of encouragement. Warning against a large-scale operation, perhaps in self-defense, he restated support for their "original plan of starting a number of small schools, run on a small budget."[7]

At the same approximate moment, West also approached James L. Adams at Meadville Theological School in Chicago about the possibility of support for further study focused on making the church "an agency for putting the principles of Jesus into active reality in life." In early 1940, he told Adams that he wanted to make the proposed Georgia school an institution "with an appeal especially to the rural, more or less uneducated preachers and lay workers." The long-range goal would be to use his rural education facility to offer leadership training for farm and labor leaders in the South. West expressed concern over the threat of fascism and anti-Semitism in the rural South unless urban and rural workers could be exposed to the "right sort of applied religion." He closed with a suggestion that funds be supplied by "Jewish organizations" and an appeal to Adams for assistance in making the right contacts. The school never opened, but West stayed in touch with the Unitarian liberal for the next three years, well after his own professional activities had taken yet another turn.[8]

Side by side with his scheme for a southern folk school, West pursued a parallel interest in the problem of peonage in Georgia. In March 1940 he visited Oglethorpe County to investigate this subtle system of involuntary servitude, which locked African American tenants, sharecroppers, and day laborers in economic bondage to plantation owners. The inquiry convinced him that "the surface [had] not been scratched yet in that peonage situation." Determined to expand the study and expose the planters, he also wrote to W. E. B. Du Bois in Atlanta to arrange a meeting in April, when West was scheduled to address the Christian-Congregational Churches of Georgia in Buford. He informed Du Bois of plans to interview sharecroppers, preachers, planters, and court house officials to verify reports from Georgia refugees in Cincinnati who told stories of economic bondage that were "surely blood-curdling."[9]

West eventually published his findings in the June-July issue of *Protestant Digest* under the title "Slavery Returns to Georgia." The Oglethorpe County research confirmed the vestiges of economic bondage in labor-short areas of the state. Reprinted in *Negro World Digest*, the essay drew widespread interest and resulted in a request from *Christian Century* for a related article.[10]

While West completed the peonage investigation and laid plans for the proposed southern folk school, he maintained a high profile on the Left with an ongoing series of columns for the Birmingham *Southern News Almanac* a radical "united front" journal launched with communist support in January 1940. West used his regular column, "The Awakening Church," to proc southern clergy to become advocates for the cause of economic and social justice as well as world peace. Constantly returning to the theme of Jesus as a model for human behavior, he opposed a war that would be a "struggle for loot—colonies, markets, profits." West insisted that the church "cease to be a groveling apologist for nations with social systems that breed injustice, poverty, and war," and instead raise "a prophetic voice" that would "harmonize with that of the great masses of the oppressed of this earth."[11] These columns mirrored the Soviet antiwar position and also expressed the deeply held egalitarianism that had long marked West's opinions on class relations in America.

Typical of these views was his attack on sanctimonious "little town daddies" who wore a cloak of respectability but dominated small-town economies and political life, local overlords who could "pull the main string that makes the preacher jump." West's open criticism of cowardly church leaders won him few friends among established clergy. In one column, he recalled that at the 1939 Conference of Congregational Churches, Dr. William James Campbell of the Vanderbilt Divinity School counseled younger ministers to "quiet the troubled waters" and denounced West as a "rebel." Don accepted that label with pride and a comparison: "And so it goes, on and on. Jesus, the disciples, and the prophets were too old-fashioned. They opposed oppression and exploitation of their day and got arrested and put in jail. Such as that would be a disgrace for us modern preachers. We must smile with tolerance and tickle the ego of our Pharaohs with pretty words."[12]

Attacked for excessive idealism, West published a manifesto in which he affirmed his own belief system, which gave primacy to human welfare, endorsed the cooperative system, dismissed competition and warfare as misuses of energy, embraced an economy of abundance, and rejected a "defeatist philosophy of accepting things as they are."[13]

These remarks demonstrated that, if anything, his ministry at Bethel strengthened Don West's convictions concerning the church's social mission. Never really at home in Ohio, by September 1940 he was again seeking a new venue in which he might exhort believers to follow the path of the revolutionary Jesus. He told Paula Snelling and Lillian Smith of the *North Georgia Review* that Bethel had been a "temporary stop gap" and he was "tied to Georgia by sentiment and background." Asserting that he would "rather be in Georgia than up here," West again proposed a "school with the purpose of 'education for applied religion and democracy.'"[14]

By November 1940, West had returned to Georgia, where he again took up the cause of radical religion, this time as a proponent of the Rev. Claude Williams's new People's Institute for Applied Religion (PIAR). Close friends since their days with Alva W. Taylor at Vanderbilt, West and Williams shared a Marxist economic and political outlook that energized their commitments to the Social Gospel. Forced out as director of Commonwealth College in 1938 amid allegations of communist influence on his administration, Williams was an independent gadfly of the religious Left.[15] Like West, he was committed to the way of the revolutionary Jesus in service to the poor and dispossessed. In 1940, he was ready to act on that commitment.

Founded in late 1940, the PIAR was intended to be an "independent means of training the grass-roots religious leaders of the cotton belt in the principles of labor unionism." An amalgam of religious and political conviction, the institute proposed to "realize democracy and equality (of wealth and race) via the radicalizing power of religious literacy" for farmers and workers. Although organized throughout the South, its goals meshed well with West's plans for a new folk school in Georgia; consequently, Don readily agreed to serve as organizer and state director for "work among the 'grassroot' preachers" in his home state. In announcing his appointment, Williams cited West's "deep understanding of the Southern people" and asserted that "his entire ministry has been given to the things for which the Institute stands."[16]

Boldly interracial, pointedly nonsectarian, and thoroughly committed to working with the natural leaders of the southern poor, the PIAR began as an attempt to train lay preachers and rural clergy to teach and practice the "Gospel of the Kingdom of God on earth." Before long, however, its activities spilled over into collaboration with CIO efforts to organize southern industry. The organization brought together small groups of black and white farmers, workers, and preachers for brief workshops in shared learning. Meeting on common ground, many for the first times in their lives, these interracial cadres were to be at the forefront of the religious revolution that West and Williams envisioned.[17]

The institute was based on the assumption that political movements must "meet people with an openness to the positive convictions and yearnings they express within their own frame of reference." Institute leaders learned from the poor and integrated that knowledge into the larger radical movement of the late 1930s. From poor whites, they gained an understanding of "otherworldliness and fierce moralism" that expressed protest against intolerable conditions endured by people with no means of resistance. African Americans taught them about embracing misery while finding "joy in the present and hope in the future." In Georgia, West anticipated real progress among poor white farmers "frequently misled by such as [Gov. Eugene] Talmadge." Reporting on West's work, Williams expressed confidence in his ability to succeed because he was "of the people and spoke their language." Their liberation theology set Williams and West apart from most Social Gospel adherents of the time

Both were unreconstructed religious radicals who regarded Jesus as a "guerilla Christian" whose example inspired them to enlist in a revolutionary army.[18] They made the PIAR a key instrument in the struggle for social justice. For West, however, the return to Georgia opened another front in that battle. By January 1941, he had accepted a call to pastor a small Congregational-Christian church in the southwestern Georgia community of Meansville. Although his ministerial duties required full-time attention, he still managed to write for the *Southern News Almanac*, and before long he was also editing and writing a column for *The Country Parson*, an "independent journal of applied religion" published in Meansville. At the same time, he stayed active in the American peace mobilization, and in April 1941 signed the call to an American People's Meeting in New York to lobby against American involvement in the war. His views accurately represented one wing of liberal thought at the time, a principled antiwar perspective lauded by Horton and other southern reformers. West remained a penetrating critic of intervention—at least until the German attack on the Soviet Union in June 1941. Then, like the American communists, he reversed his stance and aimed his antifascist critique directly toward Nazi Germany.[19]

By this time, however, West's radical past had caught up with him and exposed him to increased criticism from both the human community he served and the literary community he challenged. In his largely favorable review of *Toil and Hunger* (1940), a rising young north Georgia poet, Byron Herbert Reece, noted that although some critics attacked West as a Red, all the book proved was that "there [was] hunger and toil all around us." He defiantly added that "if only a Red can recognize misery, and hate it and its causes when he sees them, then I'm Stalin's right hand man." Responding to Reece's "kind expressions" in March 1941, West denied being a communist and insisted that he did not advocate revolution. Rather, he asserted that he was merely a minister of the Gospel who "had confidence in the basic goodness of human beings." He also acknowledged an "aim" in everything he did, including his pursuit of peace.[20]

A week later, West followed up with a longer letter dismissing as irrelevant the comments on his politics by those North Georgia residents who "pretend to be intelligent." He wearily acknowledged that it was "natural these times for someone who takes a few matters like justice in our life and world seriously, to get labeled one way or another." West also agreed with Reece that if "to see misery and poverty" and "seek actively to eleviate [*sic*] them" was Red, he proudly accepted the label. As a follow-up, he launched a diatribe against "art for art's sake" and embraced realism in writing that would "portray our world in its time." Although Reece could not agree "poetically," he did say that

West "almost speaks my language when it comes to politics." The two seemed to reach an understanding at this point, but after a four-month lapse in their correspondence Don expressed hope that he had not offended his friend with his "sharp comments." In a rare moment of candor, West admitted that he sometimes got so "frazzled" in the "everlasting struggle" that he was "liable to make stronger words than [were] intended."[21]

As evidenced in his correspondence with Reece, West had no use for the views of establishment intellectuals, most of whom cared little for the wisdom of common folk. Included in his list of adversaries were mainstream clergy, who seemed bent on comforting the comfortable. In March 1941, for example, he wrote to Lillian Smith of his amusement at the "naive notion some folks seem to hold about religion and the church and its servants." His ten years as an ordained minister had worked to "dispel any illusions [his] early idealism might have built up." Even more reprehensible were intellectuals who tended to "look down their noses at the dumb 'uneducated people' who cannot understand their 'subtle philosophical distinctions.'" Instead of waiting for the uneducated to pay them homage, he argued, the "so-called intellectuals" needed to "go to the workers and learn there about the tremendous currents that [were] shaping and remaking a world."[22]

By July 1941, West had worn out his welcome at Meansville, in part due to his outspoken expression of political and social views and in part due to an explosive incident in which he again acted on his beliefs with disastrous results. One congregant later claimed that West engaged in "communistic activities" while "posing as a Congregational preacher" until his sudden departure after the German attack on the Soviet Union. More damaging, however, was Don's reaction to the beating of an elderly African American who had inadvertently brushed against some white women. What complicated matters was the report that one of the church's lay leaders led the mob, which spelled trouble for a preacher with a social conscience. Outraged at the deacon's behavior, West took as his next sermon's text "even as you have done it unto the least of these." Then he resigned, never again to pastor a church congregation for compensation.[23]

By August 1941, West again found himself with little economic future. As a result of his clash with the wayward deacon and his reputation as a Red, his comfortable relationship with the Meansville congregation was at an end. In late July, he wrote to Alva W. Taylor of his inability to be a modern pastor, which meant willingness to be "all things to all men." West attributed his "failure" to his perception of "the only Jesus I know," a "bothersome fellow" who "gets me in Dutch time after time." He thought that Connie must occasionally "wish that I'd met up with that other Jesus, the one most of the churches have up in the stained glass." On the contrary, Don had gotten "all tangled up with the one that stirred up the people" and turned out to be "bad medicine for a pastor in modern churches."[24]

Although firm in denying that he was a communist, West stubbornly refused to abandon his principles simply because the Reds happened to share some of them. In September 1941, however, he did complain that since the invasion of the Soviet Union had changed world politics, he had been the "victim of a slander campaign" that left him "labeled as a Hitler agent" and worse. Expressing frustration at the recent turn of events, he wrote to Byron Reece that his persecution was evidence that "if you couldn't defeat a man's logic you still had the resort of calling him bad names."[25] As a result, he told Reece, he was on the job market again.

Still dreaming of pursuing his research on Georgia peonage, police brutality, and prison practices, West now saw the necessity of providing for his young family, which meant that his next stop was the Cass Station farm. He then shipped out as a deckhand on a Mississippi River boat for the better part of a year. During a layover in Memphis, he learned how difficult his chosen path would be when he approached Donald Henderson, the communist president of the Food, Tobacco, Agriculture, and Allied Workers Union (FTA), for a job as labor organizer. An old friend, Henderson delivered the bad news: "I'm sorry. You're too Red for my union." The verdict was especially hard to swallow because it came from an ideological soul mate who may have been influenced by the Party's verdict on West's organizational work in Kentucky. If there was no room for him in a left-wing union, his place in the mainstream of American life was also in doubt. Two weeks before Pearl Harbor, the Department of Justice Special Defense Unit placed Don West in a category of "individuals believed to be the most dangerous and who in all probability should be interned in event of war."[26]

As the United States entered World War II, then, Don West's history of uncompromising struggle to aid the oppressed and build a progressive, democratic South had rendered him too hot for either the Left or the Right to handle, at least until the wartime revival of the Popular Front made his militant antifascism again acceptable politics. For a full decade he had provided leadership to the dispossessed as radical preacher, labor organizer, and communist activist. There can be no doubt that his peculiar brand of humanistic religious commitment and strong sense of personal moral responsibility were the wellsprings of his social and political activism. It is equally obvious that he had embraced Marxism and communism as the ideology most likely to hasten the advent of the people's commonwealth of which he dreamed. West never wavered in his belief that some form of collectivism would best enable the underclass to unite in the struggle to inherit the earth.

Although he broke formal ties with the Communist Party in 1939, his vision of a collectivist future remained clear, just as his lifelong passion for social, economic, and racial justice informed his poetry and prose during his formative years as a writer and when he matured as a creative artist. As the 1930s receded into memory, political and literary critics had witnessed only a hint of the work that was to come. In the early 1940s, West was on the brink of a fresh experience as an educational innovator, a career that soon assumed new and original outlines in response to changing conditions and unforeseen opportunities. The next step in his colorful career was far from clear when he returned from exile on the river, but the religious and social beliefs formed in the North Georgia mountains of his youth remained a constant influence on West's life, as did the painful memories of capitalism's systemic crisis during the Great Depression. For the farmers and workers of his home state, economic hardship was still a fact of daily existence. It was here that the next chapter in the life of Georgia's radical son unfolded in the unlikely venue of the public school classroom.

eight

Teacher and Learner: Don West and the Democratic Classroom, 1942–45

Following his brief but tempestuous stint as pastor of the Congregational-Christian Parish of Meansville, Don West and his family retreated in late 1941 to the Cass Station farm·refuge where they practiced sustainable agriculture while contemplating Don's contracting career options. During his brief employment on the Mississippi steamboat West had joined the National Maritime Union and, at least for a moment, considered a possible future in labor organizing before Donald Henderson of the Food, Tobacco, Agriculture, and Allied Workers Union effectively destroyed that illusion. By May 1942, West was back on the farm, living with the family and, according to one local FBI informant, studiously avoiding the public eye. During the summer of 1942 he worked on his poetry, participated in Baptist and Methodist church activities, and ignored politics.[1]

During this pastoral interlude Don's interest in literary matters intensified when he was contacted by the New York novelist Henrietta Buckmaster, who was then researching the book that was to become *Deep River* (1944). After talking with Don's North Georgia friend Byron Reece, Buckmaster found her way to Cartersville and finally the family property, where in the fields she came upon Don, whom she described as "a tall slender beautiful man" of intelligence, passion and experience . . . a Georgian rooted in the mountains from time immemorial." She later told Lillian Smith that West had given her "a priceless gift" by taking her up to Gilmer County, where he introduced her to "the exact people [she] wanted to write about." With Don's encouragement, they talked of the antislavery heritage and Civil War unionism in the mountains. The novelist was equally impressed with Lillie, "a flowing river of knowledge who was "proud of her grandfather's hatred of slavery," which she carried with her to the lowlands, where she was reviled as a "nigger-lover." After Buckmaster returned to New York, Don was helpful in "keeping folklore moving [her] way, good practical information on mountain farming and remembrance of family doings." She also cleared her use of mountain language with both Reece and West. Don West was the most important of several persons who became models for the composite character of Simon Bliss in her successful novel. West was unsure about her reliance on him in shaping Simon's character, but he definitely "sympathize[d] with Simon's attitude" and represented its analog in 1944.[2]

While West struggled to survive economically, educational enterprises were never far from his mind, including the hope that a southern folk school might somehow be established. Finally, in the summer of 1942 his employment prospects brightened dramatically when he was offered the post of school superintendent of the Lula-Belton Schools in North Georgia's Hall County. Recalling that Lula, a rather "run-down" district, "needed somebody" badly, Don later found amusement in his disqualification for work with a Red union followed by a position as a school administrator in anticommunist Gov. Eugene Talmadge's Georgia. West served as principal of the Lula-Belton High School and also had responsibility for the elementary school program in the small rural community. For the next three years West made an indelible mark on the history of that community and brought it into the national spotlight with a host of innovations that placed the tiny district at the forefront of rural education reform.

No sooner had West entered Hall County in September 1942 than rumors concerning his radical political activities began to circulate. Shortly after his arrival, "some snoopers" came by "checking up on [his] patriotism." Moving to quash the controversy, West disingenuously assured local supporters that he had never been a communist and that the "issue would be cleared up in the future." It was not long before the FBI was on the scene, probing his activities in Lula, but early reports indicated that there was "no evidence of subversive activity." When government agents checked on him, his landlady asserted that there was "no more patriotic men [*sic*] in the country than Professor West." Although one of West's strongest supporters, Postmaster John Ernest Jones, wondered why a man with such a "wealth of education" came into the community, he concluded that West was a "high type of person," active in both Baptist and Methodist churches and prominent in "social affairs." He "never suspected West in the slightest." Others were more critical. One less sanguine source claimed that he was "very radical" and "pro-labor," which led him to believe that West was a communist.[3]

Before long, West's performance as superintendent caused most Lula residents to "discredit the rumors," which, in Jones's words, were "almost forgotten by the greater part of our people." To Jones, whom West regarded as the "town radical," educational reforms, firm leadership, patriotic wartime commitment, and community spirit made the Lula school the "leader in the county." He later recalled that West was a "regular dynamo for action" and produced results that "any community would have to be proud of." Even the Hall County school superintendent, who possessed the "most advanced dope" available about his radical politics, approved of his work in Lula. Years later, after Jones, under government pressure, had reluctantly come to the conclusion that West was probably a communist, he remembered Don as a humanitarian leader, a ready donor to local causes, and a trusted friend who gave his time and tallent [*sic*]" to the community. As late as 1948, Jones assured the militant anticommunist crusader Ralph McGill that West's "influence was not bad."[4]

This assessment mirrored the views of many observers who marveled at the progressive reforms West introduced into a school system that had been a serious trouble spot for previous administrators. Like many of West's educational endeavors, the program was rooted in the democratic features of the Danish folk school system that had guided his teaching philosophy since his college years at Vanderbilt. At Lula, West at last had his opportunity to implement the strategy of cooperative learning in a community setting. From the outset, he embraced a democratic approach that started with a meaningful student role in planning and executing the educational program. Explaining to his students that he shared their rural North Georgia background, he assumed the role of "adviser, friend, and fellow worker" and encouraged them to organize the student body, draw up a code of conduct, and enforce laws that they themselves had crafted. Although some residents were shocked, West's patient explanations and the program's success won community support and brought national recognition to the small Georgia town.[5]

The new superintendent began by abandoning the hoary tradition of corporal punishment and strict discipline. Convinced that true discipline would stem from democratic peer judgments, he installed a student-based enforcement system that placed decision making in the hands of the student body. A new student council took responsibility for initiating programs, implementing student ideas, and meting out justice when called upon to do so. As a result, the council "relieve[d the superintendent] of all discipline worry" and had very little of its own. Under West's leadership a lively school newspaper, the *Monthly Scrapper*, became an important conduit for the expression of student opinion as well as a literary outlet for young writers. Although students accepted responsibility for the *Scrapper*'s financing as well as content, West was a regular contributor to its columns. To further cement ties with the community, he was instrumental in establishing a regular weekly radio broadcast over station WGGA in neighboring Gainesville, through which the school's programs and services reached the widest possible audience. Reaching the student body, the community, and a national audience of educators, the *Scrapper* epitomized the best product of student-generated work.[6]

Consistent with West's long-held enthusiasm for the folk school model, the program quickly became a community enterprise in which "a school [ran] a town." Lula, a small town seventy miles north of Atlanta, had a long history of economic disparities between the landowning elite and a large tenant-farmer population. Symptomatic of these class differences was underlying conflict over school funding, instructional policies, and disciplinary procedures. As a consequence, Lula had acquired a reputation as a burial ground for educational administrators. Determined to reverse the pattern, Don West enlisted local citizens by making the school the "focal point" for the community. Recognizing the importance of abundant field labor at harvest time in the South's rural economy, he released students to pick cotton at peak work periods, thus integrating school and society. Convinced that a school in a rural setting should be a "community center" immersed in outreach education, he also helped launch a cooperative, a welding shop to serve the town, a cannery where surplus vegetables could be processed, and, finally, six units of the National Farmers Union (FU). By 1945 Aubrey Williams concluded that the FU organizational situation in Georgia was "hopeful." In turn, the Farmers Union established a cooperative feed mill on school property capable of grinding local grain. The cooperative marketed locally produced sorghum in seventeen states, and three hundred local families eventually used the cannery. The school was thus the lynchpin around which the entire community was organized to meet the needs of its children and citizens.[7]

For West, no part of the experiment was more important than the effort to foster the cooperative ideal among the farmers and workers who were the backbone of the community. The cooperative enterprise expressed this objective, but its central feature soon became the development of the Farmers Union as a voice for the small farmers of North Georgia as well as a tool for all citizens of the Lula-Belton district. John Ernest Jones remembered hat at one time the organization constituted "a great movement in Georgia." Himself a former secretary of the Franklin County Farmers Union, Jones warmly endorsed the organizational drive and cooperated with West and several community residents in organizing the Lula local. Working closely with former New Deal administrator Aubrey Williams, now organizer for the FU and editor of its national press organ *Union Farmer,* West helped spread the gospel of collective action and self-help among farmers on the margin. Committed to the Farmers Union as a "dirt farmer organization" distinct from the more elitist Farm Bureau, West and Williams revived the FU in North Georgia. With Williams often at his side, West used his oratorical skills in launching new chapters throughout North Georgia, including Barrett (Lula), Tadmore (Gainesville), Hickory Flat (Lula), Brookton (Gainesville), Macedonia (Clarkesville), and Tallapoosa (Carrollton). Closer to home, the Lula organization fostered the cooperative spirit that lay at the heart of West's vision of community education.[8]

In the wartime environment, democratic education held special meaning for Don West, his community, and his students. Since the Nazi invasion of the Soviet Union in June 1941, West had engaged in a rhetorical and written assault against fascism and its threat to American institutions. His commitment to that struggle led him to volunteer for the army in 1942, but because of two missing fingers due to his childhood accident he was rejected for military service. Two years later, when reclassified 1A, he fully expected to be inducted and chose not to ask for the deferment he would have received, and he "regretted his inability to serve." Instead, he was destined to make his contribution to the war effort on the home front, and did so with enthusiasm. West led Red Cross campaigns, scrap drives, and other morale-building exercises in such an energetic and forceful way" that the Lula-Belton school "became the county leader on all such drives." Moreover, the school inaugurated a Victory Corps, an induction program for those seniors destined for military service. The curriculum included a heavy dose of antifascist literature from the War Department and wide discussion of the fascist threat to democratic institutions. In shaping the program, West consciously embraced the ideas contained in Vice-President Henry Wallace's well-known address on the "Century of the Common Man," which was used in the classroom to "increase understanding of and appreciation of the true meaning of democracy." West's students recall with clarity that he "hated fascism" passionately.[9]

A central feature of West's program for democratic education at home was the Southern Educational Service (SES), established in 1943 to promote better understanding of the democracy Americans fought to defend. Based on the conviction that there was no middle ground in a world divided into democratic and fascist blocs, the SES took aim at the "enemy within" that had destroyed other nations and launched a program to teach democratic institutions in Georgia communities. Warning against hate groups, anti-Semitism, and all forms of bigotry, it published pamphlets, planned a quarterly magazine, fostered "progressive educational groups," disseminated information through the media, and proposed to offer short conferences to teachers, students, churches and community organizations. With Don West as secretary and Ernest Jones as chair, the Georgia Educational Service began by publicizing the Lula experiment in education as a first step in "making education a more dynamic force for a better South." That initiative was consistent with other progressive innovations then being explored by southern educators, including deemphasis on localism in favor of a wider conception of the common good. A committed Social Gospel advocate, West envisioned an institute that mirrored a wartime trend toward the reconstruction of an "individualized goal of salvation" in the form of "education to save the state."[10]

Lula-Belton students shared their mentor's enthusiasm. Their homely radio chats emphasized communal involvement in the war effort and stressed the theme of "education for victory." Similarly, the columns of the *Monthly Scrapper* were filled with articulate discussions of democracy and fascism. In 1944, editor Genevieve Stephens admonished readers to debate "democratic principles" and also to "live and practice them in every day affairs." In the same year, one issue of the *Scrapper* highlighted a bevy of sophisticated letters to the editor describing the war as a worldwide crusade against fascism with a crucial home front dimension that included the school-community effort found in the Lula-Belton district.[11]

West, meanwhile, did all he could to support his students' effort to place the war in a principled moral context. In a farewell message to the 1944 student body he delivered a devastating attack on the noxious "fascist race theory" that denied equality. Denouncing Hitler's "master race" assumptions he commended the student community's "firm determination to wipe the last vestige of fascist poison off the earth." Like the *Scrapper*, the Lula High School radio program became a forum for disseminating the superintendent's view of the war. In March 1943, West spoke of children as the community's "most precious possession" whose future underscored "the righteousness in the cause for which America and her allies fight." The following year he asserted that individuals, institutions, governments, and churches would face the "supreme test": Did their deeds "contribute to the major task of winning the war against fascism?"[12]

Taking these words seriously, Lula students moved to implement the ideals they shared with West. In January 1945 the community youth club created the Youth League for Tolerance aimed at "breaking down [their] prejudices and intolerance toward different groups, races, nationalities, etc." As a follow-up, *Scrapper* editor Genevieve Stephens informed Byron Reece of student plans to act against fascism and the "intolerance, prejudice, and ignorance" on which it thrived. Reece, by this time one of West's close literary acquaintances, responded with warm words about both Don and his student acolytes. Applauding their efforts, he hoped that the Lula example would inspire similar programs in the state and nation as a "rebuke to those among us who profess to love democracy yet seek to subjugate certain minorities for their own gain."[13]

While students strengthened their commitment to the struggle against fascism, West moved in 1944 to implement his own ideas through active engagement in the Georgia political arena. His Marxist views notwithstanding, he was a Democrat in 1944, a choice reinforced by strong support for Franklin Delano Roosevelt and the war effort. In February, West announced his candidacy for state legislature on the Democratic ticket as a first step in a projected political career, which included long-term plans to run for Congress. He told his old Vanderbilt sidekick Claude Williams that although he had already made progress, a few more years "building ground work [would] make a difference." Working with the Georgia CIO's Political Action Committee, West established close ties with labor by cultivating a friendship with CIO-PAC regional director George S. Mitchell, who "was impressed with [West] personally" and contributed to his campaign. Because he had tried to promote unionism through his work as Georgia representative of the People's Institute for Applied Religion (PIAR), West was no stranger to the CIO. In response to West's suggestion, Mitchell also urged the Textile Workers Union to send campaign workers into the district. Concerned about his financial disadvantage, West then asked Mitchell for help in identifying contributors. He expressed justifiable concern that in such an isolated rural area, "trying to build progressively and wage a progressive political campaign seem[ed] like a voice crying in the wilderness."[14]

True to his word, West ran a liberal campaign that challenged the "reactionary Talmadgeites" and "big boys" who used "ring politics and money" to stifle "progressive political action." In an appeal to his Lula electoral base, he promised to "do [his] best for [the] schools" and address "the problems of farm folk." The cornerstone of his campaign was a commitment to the "principles of representative government—*democracy*." Consequently, his platform called for victory over fascism, cooperation with government agencies in the war effort, a liberal revision of the state constitution, wide access to educational opportunity, and broadening representative government.[15]

West's decision to seek public office drew immediate support from colleagues in the Lula-Belton schools. Proud of the widespread acclaim afforded their program by state and national educational leaders, teachers adopted a resolution attributing their successes to West's leadership and his cooperation with teachers and citizens, which demonstrated that "democracy can work as well in a school as in a state or nation." Although West was defeated in the July primary after critics raised the issue of his previous communist ties, he was able to command strong local support from those who knew him best. At the same time, he faced red-baiting, which was what West expected from "an open shop section with a lot of textile mills." Undaunted by defeat, he reminded Mitchell that despite the "Talmadgeite" attack, "progressives must carry on a relentless battle."[16]

During the course of the campaign, West was drawn to the side of Georgia's reform governor, Ellis Arnall. Arnall's opposition to the white primary and the poll tax coincided with West's own liberalism on the race issue, a key theme in his work with students at Lula. In 1943, Arnall embraced education as "the hope of the future . . . the cure for ignorance, poverty, prejudice, hatred, and demagoguery." The following year, West heartily endorsed the governor's "challenge to make the schools democracy's cradle, and to inspire, encourage and lead the people in blazing new trails for a better post war world." To West, Arnall's vision for the future placed him "along side of statesmen like Wallace and Roosevelt," men whose "feel for the lot of the common man" was clear.[17]

Admiration for Arnall and anger over the poison of race hatred were linked in West's political consciousness, which reflected deep concern over the stained reputation of the South. His concern over the state of race relations and outrage over the national perception of the region's rural white population, including mountain folk, compelled him to again challenge the widely held "hillbilly" or "cracker" stereotype that assumed hostility toward African Americans among the South's rural poor. West had brooded over this flawed image since his days at Berry and Lincoln Memorial University, and his fixation on the problem remained an important theme in his intellectual life. In 1943 he opened a friendly yet critical dialog with black poet Langston Hughes, whom he chided for a faulty understanding of mountain culture. Long an admirer of Hughes's work, he questioned the African American assumption that "working whites" were "the chief enemy of the Negro people." Criticizing Hughes for the pejorative use of "cracker" in both his poetry and a specific column in *The Chicago Defender*, West boldly reinterpreted the term by his own lights as a reference the original antislavery inhabitants of colonial Georgia. More to the point, he insisted that it was wrongheaded for an "educated Negro" to "single out the 'cracker,' 'poor white trash' and any other group of working white folks, as the chief enemy of the Negro people." Drawing on his own experiences, West maintained that poor whites were the "best potential ally of the Negro people in their struggle for equality in the South." Likewise, he argued that African Americans were the "best ally" of white workers in their fight for "better conditions" and "more democracy."[18]

Clearly interested in communicating with Hughes over the "cracker" character issue, West used his achievements at Lula as a wedge to launch the conversation. His first letter cited his experience managing a black school, including the atypical inauguration of the nine-month school year, as evidence of firm commitment to equal educational opportunity. He also informed Hughes that he had been attacked for his efforts to organize the Farmers Union and his criticism of shady collusion between Agricultural Extension agents and the Farm Bureau to the disadvantage of labor and small farmers. For his trouble, he said, he had been hounded by the FBI, but local supporters "told them they'd better go to Detroit or to the KKK headquarters and check on the real un-American, subversive activity." West reminded Hughes that the townspeople who supported him were "my own folks, they're hillbillies, they're crackers." Deploring fascism, West drove home his central point: "the damned leaders and big shots are the ones we must attack," not the common man. Rather, the progressive mission was to "drive a wedge of truth between the cracker and the bourbon, the common man who loves democracy, and the Tory."[19]

West's directness and honesty caught Hughes's attention because he, too, had argued for interracial struggle against the forces of racism and the injuries of class. Hughes wrote to Arna Bontemps at Fisk University about "a fan letter from the white principal of schools in Lula, Georgia (of all places)." Not long thereafter, he also suggested that West contact the Rosenwald Fund for possible support of his program to advance equal opportunity in Georgia. As a consequence, West followed up with a request to Hughes for guidance in applying for a fellowship.[20] Eventually, their friendship led to a year of graduate study that was to change the course of West's life as he returned to the academic world.

While Don corresponded with Hughes and maintained the many literary contacts he had developed over the years, his family began to sink roots in Georgia soil once again—not always a simple task for those who loved a restless man with visions of social, economic, and political revolution. At first the Wests resided in a remodeled school building adjacent to the cooperative cannery in Lula, and then they moved to a larger home that could accommodate the houseguests that were a regular feature of family life. One result of Don's commitment to intellectual and political life was a constant stream of visitors, some of them houseguests, as in the case of the German American communist Waldemar Hille, a former Commonwealth College faculty member who resided with the family for a time during the Lula years. Always a full partner in the marriage, Connie taught fifth grade and participated in other school and community activities. Although she maintained a sense of humor about her unpredictable and sometimes transient existence with Don, she preferred a more stable middle-class life. As a result of their diverse experiences, Connie developed a "fractured personality" that expressed itself in frequent bickering over family issues. It was during the Lula years, Hedy later noted, that she first became aware of her parents' "troubled relationship."[21]

In 1942–43, their first year in Hall County, the two children were enrolled in the Lula school, Hedy at the age of four. Ann remembers this period as her most difficult year in school due to the pressure to set an example as the superintendent's daughter. Yet there was something luxurious about a three-year stretch of stability and a permanent home. At the same time, for both Hedy and Ann it was in some respects enjoyable to constantly be the new member of a class, wherever it might be. Don taught the girls to be extroverts, ask questions, and actively participate in any classroom or social situation, which led to their ready integration into many a new group. His politics, however, occasionally impinged on childhood experiences in that his opinions sometimes affected their choice of friends. Hedy, for example, was discouraged from associating too closely with a local merchant's daughter, whose company she enjoyed, because her anticapitalist father saw the merchant and his family as "bourgeois" and therefore unacceptable social acquaintances. Despite its limitations, Connie created a culturally rich home environment. Deeply devoted to music and art (and an accomplished artist in her own right), she encouraged her daughters' interest in the arts and high culture, sometimes at great distance and expense. Exposure to music combined with her father's dedication to proletarian art later influenced the inquisitive and sometimes rebellious Hedy to launch a successful independent career as a performing artist, a scholar-musician whose work reflected deep appreciation of authentic Appalachian culture and tradition. Later in life she insisted that pressure from Don was the key factor in her career choice.[22]

Above all, Lula brought a measure of stability to what had been a disjointed and unsettled family life characterized by fragmentation and frequent separations. Here Connie supplemented Don's annual income of $2,200, which in 1940s' dollars provided a comfortable standard of living. Once they moved to the large house on the hill, a sense of permanence permeated family life. Don's students later asserted that "the whole family was part of the school community" as his programs integrated community, school, students, and parents. It seemed that by 1944 Don West had found a home. As John Ernest Jones remembered, however, he always had his mind on the next challenge, and by May 1945 West could write to Claude Williams that things were "progressing . . . beyond my hopes."[23] A new opportunity had presented itself when the Rosenwald Fund chose to support the educational work he had undertaken in rural Lula.

The Lula-Belton experiment in community education had drawn wide attention since 1943, when both the Georgia state school superintendent and the U.S. Office of Education commended West for Lula's publications program and an "outstanding war job." Together with national press coverage, the official recognition established West as a leading progressive educator with a vision for the future of rural education. Of equal significance to the Rosenwald fellowship board was Langston Hughes's encouragement. Hughes's imprimatur was especially important in view of the foundation's commitment to research and education in the South, with emphasis on the advancement of interracial harmony. By the end of 1944, West had earned the M.A. degree at Oglethorpe University and was enrolled as a graduate student in education at the University of Georgia. While at Athens, he so impressed the faculty that they independently urged him to seek Rosenwald support. In 1945, Kenneth R. Williams, dean of education at the University of Georgia, informed the Rosenwald Fund that he had encouraged an application. Endorsing West as "one of the most outstanding potential educational leaders in our rural southland," Williams told the foundation that the faculty had pressed West to apply in the belief that he would, after further study, "render a great service in leadership in rural Georgia."[24]

It was this commitment to rural life and education that kept West in Lula when other opportunities beckoned. John Ernest Jones told the Rosenwald committee that West's desire to uplift the underclass explained why he remained at Lula-Belton "instead of accepting other positions that would have paid him double the salary received [there]." Although reluctant to lose West, Jones argued that the foundation would not find a better candidate anywhere in the South. More attuned to the Rosenwald agenda, Georgia faculty member Jane Franseth stressed West's interest in "the improvement of intercultural understanding," which was evident in the Lula program, where West was doing much to help the people appreciate the contributions to society which have been made by various culture groups."[25]

Because of West's desire to deal honestly with the Lula board, he pressured the Rosenwald committee for an early decision. Anxious to rehire him, Lula had barely issued West a long-term contract when the news of the grant came.

At the time of his application to the Rosenwald Fund, West had emphasized his intention to return to "rural life and education in North Georgia" after completion of the fellowship work, a pledge that now prompted the Lula board to leave the position of superintendent open to West should he choose to resume his duties.[26]

The news of the superintendent's imminent departure came as a disappointment to the student body, which had grown to appreciate the enlightened leadership he provided. After West confirmed his decision, *Monthly Scrapper* editor Genevieve Stephens endorsed democratic education as experienced in Lula and editorially embraced its founder. Stephens spoke for her class, which would "never forget how much he [had] meant to [them]" as a patient advisor who had "never failed to offer a helping hand or offer friendly encouragement." Conscious of the poignancy of the moment, West responded with a column in May 1945. He had never, he told the seniors, "felt quite so close to a group of young people as [he] did these." Addressing the wider community, he also expressed appreciation for its help and cooperation in the task of promoting democratic education in Lula.

The community's intense involvement with its schools was not to survive intact, but West made a major contribution to innovation in rural education in Georgia. Lula residents had literally taken control of community life. When West's successor failed to follow through on the reforms, local citizens forced his removal and replacement by a more flexible leader, an exercise in democracy that West would undoubtedly have endorsed. Equally important was the Southern Educational Service's adoption of the Lula-Belton program as a model that might "help guide and inspire other Southern schools." For West, the Rosenwald fellowship meant an opportunity to "carry his message to all the rural communities, not only in Georgia, but throughout the South."[27]

Not all local observers shared his enthusiasm. The FBI continued its relentless pursuit of West in hope of documenting subversive activity. Following his defeat in the legislative race of 1944, government watchdogs observed that he was "still active in civic, social, and educational affairs," which might reasonably translate as carrying out his duties as superintendent. Although he had "publicly denounced Communism in Lula," one FBI informant observed that "from the subject's activities" it seemed that West was "probably active in Communist meetings," although he had "no concrete evidence to substantiate this belief." By 1945, West was considered "a key figure in Communist activities in the Atlanta Field Division" and erroneously charged with "organizing a branch of the Communist Party in Lula."[28]

West's students later confirmed the presence of local detractors, some of whom charged West with subversive activity. Similarly, Jones acknowledged a persistent undercurrent of suspicion concerning the superintendent's political background and activities but insisted that there was no hard evidence that West had engaged in subversion while at Lula. Although the students heard the rumors, they "never did believe those stories about him." One noted that when West insisted on "equality for all people" and "food and educational opportunity" for every child, "some people took that idea as Communism."[29]

What students did remember were the new horizons opened to them under Don West's guidance. He took students away from their isolated environment and exposed them to the wider world. Of particular importance was his emphasis on the value of postsecondary education. On the eve of his departure for the Rosenwald year of study he was still working to send one or more of the graduating seniors to a Youth Congress of Applied Religion in New York, sponsored by Claude Williams, head of the PIAR. He focused on Genevieve Stephens, an active Baptist youth leader as well as editor of the *Scrapper*, whom West regarded as "good stuff" and a student who had "developed wonderfully." As late as December 1945, when West was at Columbia University, he attempted to have Reece bring Stephens and another student to New York for the event.[30] Although the trip was cancelled at the last minute, West's perseverance revealed his commitment to progressive education for young people in the rural south.

Similarly, West's concern for individual students was evident in the way he handled an extraordinary student problem in 1944. When young Ruth Tribble was unable to complete a written assignment on time he looked for a solution that would enable her to grow intellectually. Harriet Buckmaster had completed her *Deep River* manuscript and was seeking a proofreader to complete copyediting. Because of his close relationship with the author, West was able to arrange for Tribble to meet an academic requirement by completing the task, which she did on schedule. Buckmaster was so pleased with the result that she agreed to finance a New York trip for Ruth and another student as delayed compensation. When no other student was able to make the trip, Don sent twelve-year-old Ann as traveling companion, which resulted in a "wonderful experience" for the two children from rural Georgia. The incident revealed the willingness to intervene in the lives of students that marked Don's approach to education; the student remembers him as "a great influence" who "shaped [her] future more than anyone else."[31]

West's innovations as administrator won him widespread national recognition as a leading progressive educator. The extensive press coverage of the Lula experiment in collaborative education, which placed a tiny community on the national map, documented the impact one man had on a community, the education profession, and the townspeople, whom West regarded as "his" in the sense that they represented the same rural underclass from which he had come. West's work at Lula was wholly consistent with the career interests, educational philosophy, respect for human dignity, and commitment to the enrichment of country life that had driven his religious, political, and professional actions since the early 1930s.

In a more personal sense, the Lula interlude also unlocked the door to Don's professional advancement because the favorable publicity drew attention to his initiative and creativity, thus bringing the recognition and status that propelled him toward the Rosenwald fellowship. In turn, the year of study not only enabled West to accomplish his stated educational goals but also afforded him the precious time needed to prepare a major collection of poetry, soon to appear as *Clods of Southern Earth* (1946). At this moment, his teaching skills, administrative acumen, and creative genius persuaded Oglethorpe University to offer West a teaching position, thus providing not only the hope of stability but also a fresh intellectual stimulus to a man who thrived on challenges.

It is no exaggeration to argue that the Lula experience was critical to West's maturation as a scholar, poet, and teacher. A revolutionary he had always been, but before 1940 his efforts had focused primarily on employing communist political tools and engaged art to improve the lives of the Appalachian poor whose struggle was his lifelong project. In Lula, however, West injected radical pedagogical theory into mainstream community life. A small Georgia town provided the platform from which to implement ideas he had cherished since his exposure to the Danish folk school movement at Vanderbilt. Although he never abandoned radical political beliefs, during the war years he subordinated revolutionary goals to the short-term objective of assisting the Soviet Union through supporting the Allied battle against fascism. The school and community became indispensable vehicles for vanquishing totalitarianism, class exploitation, and racial intolerance. Whether active in the classroom or the community, West worked tirelessly to move his students and backers slowly but surely toward a collective interest in a more humane, prosperous, and democratic postwar world.

Don West's achievements in Lula remain one of the most impressive yet overlooked dimensions of a variegated life experience. As the furor of cold war anticommunism came to grip the land after 1947, the luster of these wartime accomplishments faded and the Lula experiment all but disappeared from public consciousness. Once West's outspoken support of the presidential aspirations of Henry A. Wallace ignited the flame of intolerance among both conservatives and cold war liberals such as Ralph McGill, red-baiters would increasingly view his work in Lula as a cover for pursuing subversive goals. Yet in the hearts and minds of his students and community supporters, the only subversion involved in democratic education had been its challenge to a power structure disturbed by collective action and rejection of outworn class relations and racial assumptions. More significant in the long run was the role Don West played in inviting rural folk into a new society of educated people and the wider world of ideas that awaited them beyond their community. A man who "improved relationships among people," West exercised an influence on Lula residents that outlasted his presence among them. As red-baiting intensified in 1948, a stubborn John Ernest Jones reasserted his own liberal social views and reminded West's critics that at the time of his departure most had expressed regrets, especially the teachers, who concluded that "no one would improve on his record."[32] When the war came to an end in 1945, West bade farewell to "his people" and moved on to the next stage in his fight for their dignity as well as the opening of the next chapter in his literary life.

nine

Literary Achievement and the Academic Life: The Price of Social Engagement, 1945–48

By July 1945 West had undertaken his research project on the improvement of rural education through community outreach and had every intention of returning to North Georgia to implement his ideas. Although he was preparing for a year of study at Columbia University, he assured Claude Williams that he was "building [himself] into Georgia" in a "very effective and telling way" as he planned for the expansion of the educational institute. For a time, twelve-year-old Ann joined her father in New York, where she lived with his close friend Freda Brown and Brown's sister, Serena Stone. Her stay was brief. In contrast to the rural South, Manhattan was unfriendly, unfamiliar, and stifling; within one semester she was back in Georgia with her mother. By this time Connie had again found a teaching position, this time at Ringgold in Catoosa County, where she and the girls shared a rented room and later a shack in a rural area. Despite the limitations imposed by a modest income and rural isolation, Connie made sure that the small family enjoyed memorable cultural experiences in nearby Chattanooga. For the adventurous Hedy exposure to the opera, concert stage, and great art was a stimulus to career development that would eventually be expressed in a lifetime of accomplishment as musical interpreter of the Appalachian oral tradition to admiring audiences worldwide.[1]

West concentrated on his studies, but other projects occasionally occupied his time. Following a long-standing regard for Claude Williams's work with the Peoples Institute for Applied Religion (PIAR), for example, he interested himself in Williams's plans for the Youth Congress on Applied Religion, scheduled for December 1945 in New York, which he thought an excellent opportunity for some Lula students to grow intellectually and culturally. Although his plans to bring Genevieve Stephens and Robbie Jones, the postmaster's daughter, to New York fell through, a Georgia contingent was present for the deliberations. More significant was West's role at the PIAR National Council Meeting, which gave him a platform to promote the Georgia Institute, publicize the Lula program, attack southern reactionaries, and denounce Georgia liberal Lillian Smith for her insistence in *Strange Fruit* that white workers were responsible for lynching in the South. By now an active member of the PIAR's national board, West disparaged Smith's "movement," which clashed with his own view of southern workers. Although he acknowledged Smith's opposition to segregation, West contended that her brand of Bourbon liberalism was "one of the worst things that has ever come out of the South."[2]

As the PIAR became more active and Williams moved to Birmingham to refocus on fighting the class war and racial battle in the South, West intensified his participation in the organization's work, both on its board and as Georgia director. Thanks to the Rosenwald grant, he enjoyed flexibility in planning his study schedule, which facilitated a six-week interlude of labor work. In early 1946 a Tennessee factory owner invited him to offer workers a six-week course in trade unionism, an opportunity that appealed to West's long-standing interest in labor organization. The owner of the plant, which had been organized by the Amalgamated Clothing Workers (ACW) Union, wanted the employees to "know more about trade unions so they [could] do a more efficient job." Following his Tennessee interlude, West proceeded to Andalusia, Alabama, where he aided ACW strikers at a local textile mill. Outraged at the company's "using everything, including Jesus," to break the strike, West argued forcefully that the "union [was] on the Lord's side" but that it was "impossible for people to take care of their problems alone" and that they must "stand together." Stand they did, and eventually, West reported, the union workers "got their negotiations through without difficulty."[3]

During his year of independent study, the government's monitoring of West's activities went on unabated. Because of the FBI's assumption that he was a key figure in the Georgia Communist Party, government agents tracked his activities in New York, where officials at Columbia Teachers College obliged them by opening his personal files for inspection. Although Georgia FBI officers considered West one of the CP's four key figures in the Atlanta region, the New York office found little political activity in his record there, which indicated that, to their apparent surprise, he was a student.[4]

Like any enterprising graduate student, West soon became concerned about financing his studies. Therefore, in December 1945, he approached the Rosenwald Fund about an additional year of support, this time for research on southern folk culture with emphasis on the "historical relations between the poor nonslaveholding whites and Negroes prior to the Civil War." In addition, West planned to expand the scope of the Southern Educational Service, beginning with a program of antifascist education for Georgia teachers. By this time, he had secured a publisher's contract for the proposed book as well as a projected novel; he had also arranged for the publication of his fifth book of poems, soon to become the pathbreaking *Clods of Southern Earth* (1946). For good measure, one of his referees noted, West went beyond the course-work at Columbia, "speaking before many groups, bringing people closer in understanding of the South and its problems" while "inspiring others to work for racial cooperation."[5]

The fellowship was not renewed, but the original grant opened new opportunities for West, who returned to graduate study at the University of Georgia, where he completed manuscript preparation for *Clods*. With the publication of this volume, he became an important literary figure, at least to the organizations and people for whom his work was intended. As early as February 1946, West wrote to Myles Horton that "nothing succeeds like success," as evidenced by the publicity, propositions, and invitations that came to him as a result of his writing. By April, pre-publication sales had buoyed Don's spirits after "so damn many years of scraping bottom." A month later, he returned to New York to launch the book, which propelled West into the limelight as never before. The collection, a sharp departure from the often nonconfrontational American fiction of the immediate postwar era, became an instant success as an expression of the hopes and aspirations of the southern working poor and a challenge to the literary canon that it defied.[6]

The appearance of this work marked the fortuitous intersection of West's maturing body of work, well-developed labor connections, myriad organizational activities, and the insight of the aggressive left-wing publishers Boni and Gaer. Charles Boni had long been an innovator in mass marketing, and his publishing career had advanced public awareness of radical ideas, progressive politics, and the goals of militant unionism. His partner, Joseph Gaer, a veteran field director in the New Deal Federal Writers Project and CIO-PAC publicity director, was equally committed to labor's cause. In 1946 the two formed a business alliance that played a key role in publicizing progressive ideas in the immediate postwar era, starting with their first project, *Clods of*

Southern Earth.[7] Because of the intense regional interest and labor enthusiasm for West's work, the book provided a new chapter in the history of literary publishing.

From the outset it was clear that this was no ordinary venture. Before the book was released an estimated thirteen thousand copies were on advance order, a remarkable prepublication record for any work of poetry. Not only did labor groups fuel demand but also, by July 1946, Claude Williams had embraced the book and thrown the support of the PIAR and its state affiliates behind it with hefty orders for use in their programs. Equally significant in driving sales was the endorsement of the liberal Southern Conference for Human Welfare (SCHW), which informed West in March 1946 that it would offer the book as a premium with subscriptions to its journal, *The Southern Patriot.* A broad coalition of liberals, radicals, unionists, whites, and blacks, the SCHW brought together elite groups and working-class members in a mature Popular Front organization that bucked the tide of anticommunist hysteria in cold war America. Although the SCHW embraced a variety of progressive causes, in 1946 its primary emphasis lay in ameliorating racial differences and economic inequities in the South. As a consequence, the CIO became a key component of the membership base, and many of its member unions ordered *Clods* for use in their worker education programs. Determined to unite workers in a nonracist postwar union drive, the CIO readily recognized the usefulness of West's poetry as an organizing tool. As Operation Dixie, its southern organizing drive, unfolded immediately after the war, the CIO built bridges with the SCHW, a needed ally in the progressive struggle to promote racial harmony and economic justice.[8]

The bitterness of *Toil and Hunger* had been lost in the larger public fixation on the imminent war with Germany in 1940, but *Clods* found a ready audience in the optimism of the postwar era in which it was possible to hope for racial accommodation. Moreover, the book aimed to reach an audience typically ignored by the academic establishment and the literati who pronounced judgment on works canonical and otherwise. At this historical moment it was possible for West to argue for a new literature in which poetry was the property of the common people—the working poor, the dirt farmer, the struggling African American, and the mountain folk of his youth. In an earthy introduction to *Clods*, West reiterated his conviction that the South had an unknown history, a story of antislavery enthusiasm that rejected the "culture" of the "lost cause" and insisted on the dignity of every human being. There was no mistaking his goal, which was to "kindle little sparks that [would] grow into big flames" that would sweep across a new south born in freedom, interracial cooperation, and social justice.[9]

Although the hope of social amelioration was a key feature of *Clods*, another important theme is the rehabilitation of the mountaineer image, which had suffered severe setbacks because of the popularization of the negative stereotype projected by Al Capp's Lil'Abner, Daisy Mae, and their feuding clans. During the war, one of West's prominent targets had been his estranged friend Jesse Stuart, whose novel *Taps for Private Tussie* prompted West to pen a scathing review in *Mountain Life and Work*. It was, in the approving words of Myles Horton, "a scorching." West's analysis was, in fact, a rebuttal to a favorable review by Lawrence Bowling that had been widely criticized by many "mountain workers," according to the magazine's editor. In his response, West challenged the hillbilly stereotype and scored *Taps* as a "vicious picture of the Southern mountaineer" as "white trash." West wrote to Byron Reece that he considered Stuart's book "in the same class with 'Lil' Abner' in that it caricatured mountain people as slow and simple—uncomplicated in a hopelessly romantic sense. His sentiments also found expression in his poem "For Jesse Stuart," which reappeared in *Clods* as "Lost Leader." In it, West asks,

> Why does he mumble to himself
> The praises he loves to hear
> When all around are mountain men
> Who toil with hunger near?"

For his part, Stuart denounced the "bitter and vicious" review and reciprocated the ill-feeling with a blast at West, who had "worked to overthrow our present form of government."[10]

A collection of poetry, much of which had been published earlier in relatively obscure journals, *Clods of Southern Earth* takes aim at the denigration of mountain people that had taken root in mainstream American culture. The clearest repudiation of the "hillbilly" stereotype comes in the militant "Voice of the Cracker," which challenges critics who wrongly insist "I'm the lyncher / Of Negroes / The man with hood and night shirt." Turning the tables on the southern power structure, West chastises the occupants of the "big houses," men of wealth

> Who taught me to hate
> And say "Nigger,"
> And the Negro to hate
> And say, "white trash,"
> And both of us
> To despise the Jew.

But the days of racial division are numbered, he insists, because mountain people have come to understand the oppressor:

> Oh, I'm the cracker
> And I'm learning—
> Of *unity*, Not *hate*,
> To look
> And talk straight!

In the same volume, West also repeats his defiant invitation to the "Clodhoppers of the world" to "unite."[11]

West's call for worker unity remained clear, but the imagery in *Clods* had undergone a subtle change. When the book appeared, conspicuous by their absence were the endorsements of communism that peppered his militant revolutionary poems of the 1930s. The profession of ideological faith made in earlier work became the more acceptable "Listen, I'm an Agitator." Although the call to radical activism remained, the "communist" of 1934 had been replaced by the "agitator" of 1946.[12] In "I Am an Agitator," West alludes to charges of communism but confines himself to a reflection on a "submerged South" stirring with anger on her lips:

> I am speaking!—Listen!
> I, the poet
> In overalls, working man,
> Mountaineer
> Agitator!

West was convinced that a poet's social role is to promote revolutionary action, but his work now avoided a party identification that might alienate readers and alert the anticommunist critics whose voices were being heard soon after the war. Moreover, his circumspect relationship with the institutional Party after 1940 resulted in more muted allusions to Marxist ideology and political activism.

Although West's work became more cautious it never lost the radical edge evident in his poetry since his earliest literary efforts. At bottom, he labored tirelessly to promote a new cultural pluralism that incorporated working-class Americans into a society of equality and an economy of abundance. He was certain that social justice would not be won without racial cooperation in mutual struggle. Nowhere in West's writing is that conviction more clear than the piercing teaching poem "Look Here, America," which is filled with confidence about the inevitable victory over racism and bigotry. In *Toil and Hunger,* he asked the haunting question, "What shall a poet sing?" when "Down by a Georgia pine / Where a broken body's swaying / Hung to a cotton line?" That burning anger had not disappeared six years later, but West's message in *Clods* stresses hope for a better day. Grieved "By looking / At what I've seen," the poet challenges readers to look deep within, with an eye to the future in which "a Georgia Cracker / Can clasp the hand of the black man / And say: 'Brother.'"[13]

In *Clods* West developed a sweeping theme of cultural pluralism that spoke to the aspirations of an audience of workers, farmers, and African Americans, the "wretched of the earth" who stood ready to claim their inheritance as the producers who created the nation's wealth. The volume is the centerpiece in a lifetime body of work dedicated to "creating authentic working class poetry as proto-socialist culture through the creation of myths about himself and a new history of his region." This alternative regionalism was evident in West's emphasis on the historical distinctions between the Appalachian South and the more traditional Deep South. *Clods* establishes the "persona of the Southern mountaineer; proud, generous and free and committed . . . to working together 'for peace brotherhood and plenty for all.'" With this book, West emerged as a "peoples poet" who spoke for a "grass roots based cooperative culture that [had] a long history as part of the American counter-tradition that resists the excesses of capitalism."[14]

The critical response to *Clods* was mixed, due less to its ideological under-pinnings than to its sometimes strident didacticism. Moreover, a decidedly regional dimension in reviewers' reactions provided penetrating insight into the South's social dilemmas. Perhaps most enthusiastic was *Mountain Life and Work*, which despite its relative conservatism could applaud West's emphasis on cultural integrity and mountaineer independence. Likewise, the *Atlanta Constitution* caught occasional glimpses of "literary art" in the work of a poet reminiscent of "Walt Whitman in overalls." Equally enthusiastic was a predict-able endorsement from *The Daily Worker*'s Samuel Sillen, who welcomed the book as an "intense expression of a collective experience" from a poet who was "an important force in the creation of a people's literature."[15]

If regional observers found much to admire in *Clods*, mainstream critics were less enthusiastic. Dismissing him as a "homespun writer . . . with a strong didactic bent," Nash K. Burger of the *New York Times Review of Books* con-cluded that "the best thing that could be said of Mr. West is that he is earnest and coherent," attributes that were "not sufficient in themselves to make a poet." Burger ridiculed Don's view of his homeland as "a romantic, simplified South which will be readily recognized by every school boy from Moscow to Vladivostok." In a similar vein, Ruth Lechlitner's review in the *New York*

Herald Tribune excoriated West's poetry as "simplified and over sentimental-ized" regionalism. Even Harold Preece, *The New Masses* reviewer, criticized the use of dialect and disapproved of West's sentimentalism. He did, however, see the volume as a "fresh, clean wind" from an area where "we thought blood and rope to be eternal phenomena."[16]

For West, the only reviewers who counted were the thousands of readers who never looked at a New York newspaper or concerned themselves with the keepers of the canon. The real story of the book's initial impact was told in the fourteen thousand copies distributed to PIAR organizers and CIO unions in the year of publication. Over the years, its phenomenal sales documented the wide influence of *Clods* among people and with audiences seldom reached by poetic works. When a naysayer in Lula complained that his writings painted "an untrue picture of the South," West's supporter John Ernest Jones came to his defense with an assertion that his poems "help[ed] many of us to see our-selves" and "sharpen[ed] our zeal to make a better Georgia and a better South." After reviewing the correspondence generated by *Clods*, *Atlanta Constitution* columnist Harold Martin concluded that "Don West is one of us. He knows what's wrong with us."[17]

For the West family, the book's success promised great things, including employment opportunity. Rather than return to Lula or graduate study, Don accepted a teaching position in the human relations department at Oglethorpe University in Atlanta, where for three years he taught creative writing, sacred literature, and applied democracy. With Connie teaching at Brookhaven and Don at Oglethorpe, the family's financial problems came to an end, at least for the moment. Book sales remained strong, which meant Don's frequent in-volvement in promotional efforts, including one Atlanta signing at which 1,100 copies of *Clods* were signed and sold.[18] For a family that had endured separation and economic hardship, the arrival of postwar prosperity was welcome.

Before long, however, West's past began to haunt him again. In October 1946 he told Horton that he had been "under pretty terrific pressure" since the publication of his book due to anonymous letters received by Oglethorpe president Philip Weltner calling for an investigation of his personal history. To complicate matters, a controversy raged in the Atlanta press over a lawsuit filed against him by a "cat's paw for the most vicious Talmade gite Kluxer" in North Georgia, whose name happened to be the same as that of a miner whose name West used in "Harlan Coal Digger, 1934." Charles Lewallen of Gainesville, Georgia, a front for long-standing West foe H. O. Tate of Lula, sued West and his publisher for defamation of character in an action that was not only a nuisance but also an expensive diversion of his energies. To a discouraged West, it "look[ed] like the bastards [were] bent on doing their durndest [*sic*] to get at [him]." Upon reflection, he concluded that the libel suit was not just a personal attack but rather a "part of the total aggressive onslaught of fascist forces here in the South."[19]

Although West's lawyer regarded the lawsuit as "utterly ridiculous," legal action was a financial drain. Under increasing strain, Don complained to Claude Williams that southern liberals had not really offered much assistance, which tended to make him "cynical." The Don West Defense Committee was eventually created to raise funds and discredit the plaintiff, who acted for Tate, a prosperous poultry farmer, and the Constitutional Educational League, a proto-fascist organization left over from the wartime era. The Georgia Defense Committee embraced West as "a progressive and fearless leader of the Southern people . . . hated and feared by the hate-peddlers." Casting the defense as a fight against the Klan in Georgia, West's regional supporters argued that unless the bigots were defeated, "every democratic voice in America [was] threatened." Equally concerned were members of a national defense committee that included such luminaries as Langston Hughes, Erskine Caldwell, Arthur Miller, William Rose Benet, Aaron Kramer, and Millard Lampell, prominent literary figures who warned of Klan inspiration and the potential spread of fascism.[20] The lawsuit was finally dismissed, but it was the beginning, not the end, of West's postwar problems.

At first, Oglethorpe seemed an island of quiet sanity in a sea of never-ending controversy. Under the leadership of Weltner, an educational reformer with a vision of collaborative education and shared governance, Oglethorpe worked to nurture and prepare students for their roles as citizens in a democratic society. As professor of human understanding and citizenship, West emphasized respect for humanistic values, human dignity, and the oneness of all people, teachings consistent with the campus's experimental curriculum but at odds with the folkways of the segregated South. Combined with the explosive content of *Clods*, West's classroom constituted a challenge to the social system and an inspiration to those bold southerners who envisioned an alternative future for the region.[21]

From his first days on campus West committed himself to Weltner's experiment in academic democracy. Characteristically an engaged educator, West served as faculty advisor to the student newspaper, the *Stormy Petrel*, which soon became a voice for liberalism in its editorial policies. By January 1947 West had organized a new journalism course that brought to the Oglethorpe classroom such personalities as labor journalist Victor Reisel, *Atlanta Constitution* columnist Harold Martin, and editor William R. Smith of the *Macon News*. He also found time to organize a Folk Lore Club as well as a new course

"Southern Folklore," building on his deep interest in folk culture. As a teacher, West was a "daring soul." One of his first Oglethorpe students, Herb Leslie, remembers his class as a "phenomenal experience" with "a man who was in touch with eternity." Aware of the South's painful history, West remained an optimist who "appealed to the best in the human being."[22]

Given his close relationship with the students, it is not surprising that West was chosen as student body advisor in November 1947. The *Stormy Petrel* expressed confidence in his "many good ideas on student government," an assessment that reflected the national attention drawn by his work at Lula. Not long after Weltner challenged the student body "to function democratically and effectively," West was also named faculty sponsor of student activities, with responsibility for promoting a democratic student body. The appointment pleased the newspaper, which noted that West was "known especially for his sympathetic interest in students and their problems."[23]

No aspect of teaching gave West more satisfaction than the heavy responsibilities he shouldered in the areas of adult education, teacher preparation, and community outreach. Because of Oglethorpe's previous loss of accreditation it was essential that information on Weltner's reforms and the revitalization of the curriculum be shared with educators and parents throughout its service area. Consequently, West made frequent presentations in the effort to repair the damage, work that led field representative Martha Pope Brown to acknowledge the "fine response from [his] public appearances." Even more successful was West's summer adult education program for teachers, which grew from an enrollment of thirty-five to 350 during his three years as director. The program rendered a vital service to Georgia's teachers and created a "loyal and happy student body composed of hundreds of teachers placed strategically over the state," all of whom worked with future college students. It also gave West another opportunity to promote his concept of the community school that built its educational program "around the needs and resources of its area" and became a functional and constructive part of its social structure." In 1948 these successes led Weltner to commend West for the "wonderful job" he had done and assure him that he had a job at Oglethorpe "as long as [he wanted] it."[24]

In fact, West's position was always tenuous. From 1946 on, Oglethorpe's experiment in democracy was plagued by conflict over the tension between individual freedom and group welfare. West's insistence on freedom of expression tested Weltner's liberalism when his introspective poem "The Four Gifts for Man" addressed the question of sexuality in a way that resonated with the young men and women with whom he worked. His words, published in the *Stormy Petrel*, speak frankly of

the inner urge
compelling the male to seek
the female
and she him;
the love of a man for a woman
and she for him.

The sex in that force is "clean and holy" because "no function / under the sun / in the life process / [was] unclean."[25]

The publication of this poem prompted Weltner to issue a thoughtful memo exploring the limits of academic freedom while questioning West's public expression of liberal views on so sensitive a subject:

> Take for instance the subject of sex. You and I do not tear sex out of its social context of courtship, marriage, and family, the three institutions through which love have sublimated a function which otherwise sinks to the level of the malacious [sic]. How many young people understand this? How many of their parents? How many of Don's detractors reading his beautiful poem in the Stormy Petrel, if they understood it, would be honest enough to give him the benefit of their approval? We must stay in character; otherwise, we are useless. But we can stay in character and yet follow ways through which each will serve all and all will serve each.[26]

Weltner's careful words reflected a commitment to academic freedom and the concept of liberal education as Oglethorpe defined it but made it clear that West must ponder the delicate balance between personal liberties and the interests of the university community. Unspoken but real was concern over the sensitivity of potential contributors to an ongoing capital campaign. West told Claude Williams that Weltner was "awfully worried" about the poem and that it was "merely a matter of time with me [at Oglethorpe]."[27] For another two years Don West worked to reconcile commitment to social justice with responsibilities as a faculty member. In the end, it became impossible to bridge the gap.

Because of his passion for racial equality, West consistently engaged in activities that focused unwanted attention on Oglethorpe and its progressive administration. Not long after his arrival on campus, he became alarmed over the rise of the Columbians, a militant Christian fascist organization founded in Atlanta in August 1946. Composed of local white supremacists, the organization of vigilantes reacted violently to the postwar integration of working-class neighborhoods. Patrolling the Sells Avenue area on Atlanta's west side, the Columbians dynamited African American homes and attacked

black homeowners in an effort to reverse the trend toward residential deseg-
regation, all under the eye of a sympathetic police force. Before long, "White
Only" signs cropped up in front of homes for sale in the surrounding area.[28]
West regarded these developments with a mixture of alarm and outrage. He
considered the fledgling organization as an "almost exact replica of the KKK."
Seizing the opportunity for experiential learning, West escorted a group of
Oglethorpe students to a Columbian rally, where they were confronted by the
ugly racism present in the postwar South. Upon their return to the campus,
the *Stormy Petrel* reported the story extensively and the student body publicly
denounced the Columbians, a measure that challenged Weltner's commitment
to liberal education.[29] To West, the "dangerously serious" Columbian menace
made him "scared as hell" of "what may and can happen in the future." What
especially enraged him was the silence of Atlanta liberals who were "closing
up like clams" and refusing to "go to bat."[30]

A deeper concern stemmed from West's ongoing engagement with the
liberal SCHW, which since 1938 had struggled to promote racial and economic justice in the South. West had not been a central figure in the body's
early activities, but he took increasing interest in its deliberations after he
edged toward respectability in Lula and postwar Atlanta. By late 1946 he had
grown disenchanted with the timidity of the body, which failed to connect
with "grass roots people." Sharply critical of the SCHW's failure to expose the
fascism of the Columbians, he attacked its Georgia leader, Margaret Fisher,
whose "dictatorial" behavior caused some state supporters to pull out. Worse
yet from West's standpoint, she engaged in red-baiting that limited her ability
to perform effective work.[31]

The remark about dictorial behavior reflected a simmering dispute within
the Committee for Georgia, the state affiliate of the SCHW, over the place of
communists in the organization. Founded in January 1945, the committee's
250 members included prominent members of Georgia's education, religious,
labor, professional, and literary communities. Although West was not on the
advisory committee, he was an enthusiastic member and supporter, as were his
old associates John Ernest Jones, Willis Sutton, and George S. Mitchell. After
a promising beginning, however, the organization began to fragment when
socialist labor lawyer Joseph Jacobs of Atlanta raised the issue of communist
membership at the February board meeting and urged that the committee
withhold affiliation with the SCHW. Equally disruptive was the resignation
of a key supporter, liberal writer Lillian Smith, from the SCHW's national
executive board in May 1945. Smith's defection was a damaging blow from
one of the state's most prominent voices against racism. Charging the national organization with undemocratic leadership and unjustified openness to

communist influence, Smith told national executive secretary Clark Foreman that she feared CP opportunism, authoritarianism, and lack of intellectual integrity.[32]

Although he was on sabbatical at Columbia, West was sufficiently aware of Georgia developments to become alarmed at the anticommunist trend and the state committee's equivocation on both the race issue and foreign policy. Although Don had few regrets about the departure of his nemesis Lillian Smith, he told the SCHW's executive secretary James Dombrowski that Margaret Fisher's administration of the Committee for Georgia had driven veteran Macon liberals William R. "Pop" Smith and Harry Strozier away from the organization. His concerns were echoed by Harriet Buckmaster, who noted that the state group had balked at endorsing Georgia's new state constitution, which had abolished the poll tax. Acting on information from Lula's John Ernest Jones, a member of the committee's executive board, West and Buckmaster joined in an effort to persuade the SCHW that changes were needed in Georgia.[33]

Despite these concerns, red-baiting escalated in 1946—and with damaging consequences. Two weeks before the publication of *Clods* the delicate relationship between the SCHW and its primary financial supporter, the CIO, was rocked by Van Bittner of the CIO Southern Organizing Committee, who attacked the conference and repudiated support from "outside organizations." By so doing, Bittner undermined a carefully constructed cross-class alliance between the two groups, which Lucy Randolph Mason and the SCHW's leaders had built in the immediate postwar period. In 1945 and 1946 the CIO's Operation Dixie worked to establish interracial unionism in the inhospitable territory of the American South but often found it necessary to permit Jim Crow locals as a practical response to southern social conditions. That policy in turn, drew the attention of SCHW's first African American field representative, Osceola McKain, and resulted in a confrontation that ended with Bittner's apology. Although the CIO renewed support for the conference, its financial contribution was cut in half in 1946, just as the SCHW reached peak membership.[34] In short, at the very moment that West published *Clods*, with its definitive call for interracial collaboration and economic democracy in the South, a deep rift opened between the two organizations most committed to the new liberalism.

Hoping to move the SCHW in a radical direction and convinced that the organization must "get rooted among the masses of plain people," West nominated Horton for the executive board in October 1946. He also agreed to be considered for a board slot himself although he dismissed his chances as unlikely at best. West strongly supported the SCHW in principle but doubted "whether the thing will ever be the mass people's organization" unless its leadership learned to "talk the people's language and meet and cope with their problems."[35] West would never be nominated but Horton was successful, and as the SCHW shifted to the Left in 1947 and 1948 West found himself in a position to influence an organization that tilted more and more toward his view of a people's movement. As West's star rose, however, the national conference entered a period of instability that coincided with the collapse of Georgia's fragile liberal coalition under the dual pressures of red-baiting in the press and a new bid for political power by the Talmadge forces. Especially devastating was internal tension between the anticommunist and leftist factions within the Committee for Georgia. The conflict escalated at the very moment that Georgia politics became sharply fractious. Enraged by the end of the white primary, the elimination of the poll tax, and an upsurge of black voters, a terminally ill Eugene Talmadge captured the Democratic gubernatorial nomination and emerged victorious from the election of 1946, only to die before his inauguration and set off a brutal power struggle that resulted in Georgia's infamous "three-governors controversy" in early 1947. With young Herman Talmadge seeking the governorship after a rigged write-in campaign and a forced occupation of outgoing governor Ellis Arnall's office, Arnall relinquished his position to the constitutional successor, Melvin E. Thompson, and endorsed his succession. As these astonishing events unfolded, West went on air on February 5, 1947, with a radio address blistering the Talmadge power grab as incipient fascism that employed the "Hitler pattern" in a proto-Nazi takeover of Georgia government. Embracing equal political rights, educational opportunity, and economic justice, West urged citizens to eject Talmadge and demand that the legal successor, Thompson, be seated. His broader goal was to prevent the reinstatement of the white primary and guarantee political rights to all Georgians, including African Americans.[36]

Almost immediately, both the SCHW and PIAR began disseminating a reprint of West's remarks, which they hoped would be read by hundreds of thousands of Americans nationwide. With this address West made his debut as a key figure in the conference's effort to organize Georgia and, more important, set the stage for an activist role in the subsequent drive to ally the SCHW with Progressive Party candidate Henry A. Wallace in the election of 1948. West soon emerged as the leading figure in the Georgia progressive movement, in part as a result of his outspoken resistance to the anticommunist element inside the troubled Committee for Georgia.[37] The splintering of Georgia's Left was symptomatic of escalating anticommunism in the postwar era as a consequence of the developing international conflict between the United States and the Soviet Union.

Although West's concerns dated from the Lillian Smith controversy and his objections to Margaret Fisher's leadership, the postwar struggle grew out of a broader conflict between the preference of Georgia's mainstream committee members for independent state-level political initiatives over Clark Foreman's increasingly militant centralizing stance as the conference's chief executive. Starting with Foreman's success in restricting the activity of Conference Secretary James Dombrowski exclusively to the administration of the Southern Conference Educational Fund (SCEF), the SCHW's nonprofit educational arm, the conference engaged in a contentious debate over the extent of its political initiatives. Foreman's sweeping activism clashed with the more moderate Fisher regime in Georgia, which, although it had energized the state's liberal community, essentially resisted the logical extension of Lucy Randolph Mason's and Don West's plans for grass-roots organization in the state's SCHW affiliate. Foreman insisted that a "proper educational job" on the necessity for an "all-out, democratic organization in the South" had not been done at the state level. Attacking the Committee for Georgia, he told Aubrey Williams that renewed effort was required before the 1948 election. He also insisted that the "great job in Georgia remain[ed] to be done," and that it was "no time to be guided by the egotism of one person."[38]

Foreman's remarks underscored the Committee on Georgia's decision to maintain a low profile on the "Talmadge affair," which had prompted West's fiery "Georgia's Crisis" radio address. His critique of the Fisher regime also coincided with West's escalating feud with the state committee's inner circle over its increasing isolation from the world of grass-roots Georgians. In November 1946, after Dombrowski had offered, then withdrawn, a position on the SCHW board to West, Don also hurled a verbal invective at the SCHW, which he saw mired in a "crisis" due to the leadership's "mismanagement" as well as red-baiting by emerging cold war liberals. In Georgia, meanwhile, the timidity of the liberal movement was deeply disappointing. Angry over "fence straddling" by his old ally Ellis Arnall, West told Claude Williams that if Arnall ever intended to fulfill "national political ambitions" he must "definitely align himself with the *left*" and distance himself from the "Aubrey Williams type of thing." This remark revealed West's disenchantment with his old friend Williams, who had recently proposed that the SCHW "declare itself on the Reds or communism." Frustrated by liberal paralysis, West found himself "disturbed about the Southern Conference and its future."[39]

To West, the answer to the conference's problems had always lain in reorienting its work toward the needs of the "grass roots folk of the South" by a leadership capable of connecting with common people. His prescription for success dismissed the need for "big shot names on the board" who "aren't worth a damn," including figureheads like the recently departed Lillian Smith, whom West derided as a "damned old Red baiter" who had already begun to turn on the SCHW. In late 1946 his suspicion of Smith was heightened by an increase in the intensity of anticommunist sentiment in the writings of Ralph McGill and others at the *Atlanta Constitution*, criticism that in his view had cowed Georgia liberals, who now crept around "like mice on cat's feet."[40]

It was this equivocation and dissension that lay behind West's decision in early 1947 to force the white primary issue among reluctant liberals with his "Georgia's Crisis" radio speech. Yet the wavering Committee on Georgia refused to embrace Arnall's choice for governor and remained silent. Like West, Foreman was "furious that no stand was taken" by the SCHW's Georgia affiliate, which West believed to be the result of the "Fisher sabotage." It is equally true that Fisher was unwilling to break with the Democratic Party to support Wallace, which placed her on a separate track from the SCHW. Consequently, the SCHW was prepared to accept Fisher's resignation, together with a report that closed the offices of the Committee for Georgia. Simultaneously, a liaison committee was created to explore the resolution of issues separating the state organization from the national body. As a result, the Georgia committee continued to function under the interim leadership of a West ally, Frank Spencer.[41]

In the wake of the Talmadge affair and Margaret Fisher's departure, West moved quickly to promote a reconfigured role for the SCHW in Georgia and a tighter link with Foreman and the national organization. He saw Fisher's resignation as a clear opportunity to move the Committee on Georgia and the SCHW more sharply to the Left. Anxious to reshape the revitalized committee, he worked to persuade Foreman that the Rev. Joseph Rabun of McCrae was the best choice to replace Fisher at the helm. After some prodding from West, Foreman approached the wavering preacher, who expressed interest in working with the SCHW in some capacity. In September 1947 the SCHW employed Rabun to set up a meeting for Wallace in November and arranged for Spencer to head the Committee for Georgia. Although West bemoaned Foreman's failure to nail down Rabun as state director it is clear that the national office worked closely with West in reorganizing and staffing its revitalized Georgia affiliate. Finally, West was a central figure in establishing an Atlanta chapter of the SCHW, which was formed on October 30, 1947, at a meeting attended by Edmonia Grant, the conference's new national administrator. On a motion by West, temporary officers were chosen, and as an interim measure grass-roots organizational work was entrusted to West and three other members of an activities committee. With a provisional organization in place, the Atlanta chapter endorsed Wallace's impending appearance and laid plans to make the event a success.[42] It was impossible to miss the overtly political tone of the SCHW's Atlanta meeting, which was clearly intended to lay the groundwork for a Wallace presidential campaign in Georgia.

In preparation for Wallace's visit, Grant urged Rabun to consult with West and cooperate with him in making the event a success. The SCHW took the lead in arranging Wallace's southern tour, but key figures in Atlanta were West, Rabun, and A. T. Walden, an African American attorney and the NAACP's long-standing legal counsel, who agreed to lead the necessary fundraising drive. Walden's role in the effort reflected strong support for Wallace in the Atlanta black community, which provided a substantial audience base for Wallace's address at the Wheat Street Baptist Church. In response to pressure from Weltner, West agreed not to introduce Wallace at the rally and accepted the president's decision to deny Wallace a platform at Oglethorpe. But on November 20, 1947, thirty of West's Oglethorpe students ushered an integrated audience of three thousand, the largest nonsegregated gathering ever assembled in Atlanta. Wallace told the crowd that white prejudice was not inborn but fostered by employers bent on preserving their privileged status and dividing potential opposition. He also included a sharp critique of the Truman administration's foreign policy, which he attacked as certain to drive a wedge between the United States and the Soviet Union. These were welcome words to local communists, who embraced the Wallace candidacy as a campaign consistent with an independent tradition in Georgia traceable to nineteenth-century Populism.[43]

Communist enthusiasm for Wallace spelled trouble for both West and the SCHW, each facing the early stages of a red-baiting campaign that would dog West's every move for the next ten years and destroy the fading conference. Since its inception in 1938 the SCHW had welcomed participants who had varied political views, including a sprinkling of communists who aligned themselves with the organization in an effort to create a united front against racism in the South. The conference maintained that in view of entrenched reaction in the South, it made no sense to exclude any individual or group that espoused progressive views and supported the SCHW program.[44] Therefore its membership policy exposed the conference to criticism from not only the right but also the anticommunist liberals whose attacks became increasingly shrill as the cold war took shape after the Greek Crisis of 1947 and the articulation of the Truman Doctrine.

While the conference struggled to counter charges of communist influence by both the House Un-American Activities Committee (HUAC) and McGill West's role in the organization and other activities in Georgia soon drew the attention of the state's anticommunist activists, both liberal and conservative

From his prominent position at the *Atlanta Constitution*, McGill launched a two-year assault on West, whom he regarded as "an enemy of the country." A widely respected racial moderate, McGill made common cause with James C. Davis, a conservative member of Congress from Atlanta, who supplied him with inside documentation of Don's activities from the HUAC internal files. West's poetry left him vulnerable, but his other activities were equally provocative. His ongoing involvement as Georgia coordinator for the PIAR as well as his role in the SCHW and the Wallace campaign provided ample fodder for the assault launched by McGill and Davis, who by June 1948 were working in tandem to expose West's political history. For good measure, HUAC records revealed that in 1947 West was in contact with both Homer Bates Chase, state organizer for the Georgia Communist Party, and Nat Ross, southern organizer for the CP.[45] Over the next two years McGill used this information in a relentless assault on West that ended in his dismissal from Oglethorpe and banishment from the academic world as well as Connie's loss of a teaching job.

Defiant in the face of rising criticism, West followed a self-destructive path of principle in 1947 and 1948. Intent on making Georgia the point of concentration for the PIAR, he urged Claude Williams to concentrate institute activity in the state. Working with the new state director, a liberal Episcopal priest, Archer Torrey of Darien, West hoped to revitalize Georgia's PIAR program with a series of meetings devoted to "building God's kingdom on earth." In late 1946 Don objected to Torrey's "desire to tie his kite onto the tail of some social-democratic organization" but acknowledged that his partner had "much good to contribute." Taking aim at the Fellowship of Southern Churchmen, West told his party acquaintance Bert Gilden, a Darien writer, that these religious liberals and other social democrats took credit for involvement in his legal defense, conveniently forgetting that they had "blackballed" him as a Red before his work made him a minor celebrity. Moreover, they ostracized Claude Williams and the PIAR. West still hoped that Torrey would "recognize reality and forget a lot of the mumbo-jumbo . . . learned in the theological cemeteries" so that he could become an effective organizer for social justice. To complement the PIAR, West redoubled efforts to build the Farmers Union, focusing on economic improvement as a prerequisite to developing religious consciousness among the oppressed. "Preaching and agitating are alright," West told Claude Williams, but the FU made sense because "just to agitate without any organizational connections . . . will not be enough."[46]

On another front, West cemented ties with the Atlanta Unitarian Church, where in early 1948 *Clods* was a popular text with the Rev. I. J. Domas and racial integration became a local goal. Desegregation was too much for Unitarian congregant Thomas Barnett, who in April 1948 protested West's presence and influence as part of a plot to communize the church and spread the political message of Henry Wallace, all of which "would play into the hands of Soviet Russia." Both the PIAR and West's collaboration with local Unitarians were among the first activities to draw fire from McGill, who in June 1948 blasted Claude Williams as a "Red preacher" with a long record of communist activity. In the same column, McGill, a staunch Truman backer, attacked West as a "Georgia born member of the Communist Party" and the central figure in the state Progressive campaign. The series of columns that followed was designed to undermine the Wallace effort in Georgia by linking it to West and the CP.[47]

The race issue that simmered beneath the anticommunist rhetoric found expression in yet another aspect of West's commitment to social justice, his involvement in the widely publicized Rosa Lee Ingram case in 1948. Controversy swirled around the fate of Ingram, an African American, and her two sons, all convicted by a white jury of murdering a white man who in November 1947 had invaded their home with intent to rape the mother. The Ingram case became a nationwide rallying point for African Americans who loudly protested the convictions and subsequent death sentences as "legal lynching." As they planned for a public event in Macon to support the Ingrams, leaders of the Georgia black community hoped to find at least one white speaker but failed to locate such an ally, even in Atlanta. Asked to speak at the meeting, West hesitated, fully aware that his position at Oglethorpe would be jeopardized by open support of the accused. Turning to Connie, his lifelong partner in the battle for racial justice in the unyielding South, he looked for moral guidance. Her response was firm: "You really *have* to speak or we have to quit pretending we believe what we say we believe."[48] Under no illusions, he addressed an almost all-black audience in Macon in an act of courage that hastened the end of his Oglethorpe career.

What made West's position untenable was not only his socially explosive role in the defense but also the composition of the coalition supporting the Ingrams. The local effort was led by the Rev. W. H. Borders, a prominent figure in Atlanta's African American community, and the home-grown Georgia Citizen's Committee. External legal assistance, however, came from the Communist Party, the Civil Rights Congress, and the NAACP. Nationwide support for the Ingrams soon eclipsed the Georgia effort, as CP activists Ben Davis and Louise Patterson took up the case. Patterson headed the integrated Sojourners for Truth and Justice, which united black and white women in a gender-based appeal for legal relief that eventually succeeded in reducing the Ingrams' sentences to life imprisonment. Although the Communist Party led in this struggle, the defense coalition incorporated mainstream labor, a variety of youth groups, and the Progressive Party. The Wallace-for-President organization called for leniency, as did Wallace, who attacked Georgia justice as "the epitome of the traditional oppression of Negro womanhood" and demanded that the Ingrams be freed.[49] For the Wests, the Ingram case held dramatic ramifications. Don later asserted that it was his very public role in the defense, even more than his Progressive Party activism, that prompted his dismissal from the Oglethorpe faculty. Other evidence supports that analysis. Weltner's files contain a detailed account of West's political history, in which West was reported to have had "no connection or belief in communist organization in principle" during the previous ten years. Nonetheless, by April 1948 it was widely understood that his contract would not be renewed because of unnamed "activities in organizations and movements which [were] not approved by the university." Denying the rumors and defending the right of faculty to express their political beliefs, Weltner publicly confirmed the university's intention to honor West's contract *through August 1949*. But he was gone from the classroom by September 1948. West insisted that the Ingram case and Progressive Party politics did him in, but the veteran liberal Glenn Rainey was convinced that he "was getting the gate" due to his "alliance with the Communist Party." Those remarks demonstrate the blurring of progressivism, racial liberalism, and communism that made West's position at Oglethorpe untenable. Weltner acted reluctantly, under pressure from several trustees and, according to some accounts, because William Randolph Hearst threatened to withdraw support from Oglethorpe. Not long thereafter, Connie paid the price for her husband's notoriety when she, too, was fired by the Brookhaven school, where she had taught since 1947.[50]

By this time, Don had become deeply enmeshed in Wallace's presidential campaign in Georgia, which had local roots in an informal collaboration among West, Torrey, Gilden, Rabun, and Chase, who combined with the remnants of the Committee for Georgia in September 1947 to launch a "people's movement" in the state. The initiative reflected an effort by communists like Chase and Gilden to cooperate with sympathizers like West, who had gone underground, as well as such liberals as Torrey and Rabun, in an effort to revive the Popular Front of the 1930s and promote social change through political action. Summarizing the group's organizing principle, Torrey refused to exclude any communist from the liberal fold. "If we stand for the same things," he said, "we work together until he proves by his actions that he really stands for something different."[51]

As the rift deepened between Truman and Wallace over the president's hard-line policies toward the Soviet Union, West drew ever closer to the Wallace candidacy, which, he argued, offered the best hope for peace as well as racial reconciliation in America. In February 1948 at a statewide Wallace conference in Macon, West spoke eloquently for a third party and introduced the initial resolution in support of the Wallace candidacy. A month later his name appeared as a member of the national Wallace for President Committee. At this time, Georgia's Wallace for President Committee issued a call to convention, a bold statement that attacked the "big money boys" and blistered "one party rule" in Georgia, which had ensured "terror, lynchings, and discrimination" against African Americans. After leading the drive to create the People's Progressive Party of Georgia, West became executive vice chair of the new organization. Resisting pressure to run for governor himself, Don nominated James Barfoot of the University of Georgia for the position and opted for a personal role as grass-roots organizer. In late May, West capitalized on his labor credentials and north Georgia background by forging an alliance with the Rev. Charles T. Pratt of Dalton, moderator of the fiercely unionist Church of God of the Union Assembly. At a Wallace meeting marked by intense "religious fervor and fanatic zeal," Pratt, a committed pro-labor preacher and co-chair of Georgia's Wallace Committee, embraced West; he, in turn, likened Pratt to Jesus Christ and Henry Wallace. Insisting that workers were "coming together" in organization, West maintained that "we won't let the rich people split us up any longer."[52]

The theme of class interest and racial unity penetrated the Wallace campaign in Georgia, which featured such black leaders as W. E. B. Du Bois and the militant concert artist Paul Robeson. The African American response to Wallace in Georgia was impressive. The majority of the eighty thousand signatures on his nomination papers came from registered black voters, and the core of his support in the state was found in the African American communities in Atlanta, Macon, and Savannah. Engineered by West, the agreement of Pratt and the African American journalist Larkin Marshall to serve as co-chairs symbolized the idea of racial accommodation, which Wallace underscored by refusing to address segregated audiences. He emphasized the central point with the argument that Wall Street kept the poor separated and the races divided in a Jim Crow South in which capitalists could dismiss labor as long as workers fought among themselves.[53]

While Wallace and West emphasized the need for racial unity and class solidarity in the Progressive cause, the Communist Party saw an opening that would enable it to counter the Truman administration's militant anti-Soviet foreign policy. Convinced that the Wallace candidacy would facilitate the development of a permanent farmer-labor party, the CP threw itself into the effort to build the Progressive Party in the South. Although there is no evidence that West was engaged in party work, he welcomed all progressives and did all he could to expand the Progressive Party's reach. In April 1948, for example, he served as keynote speaker at the founding convention of the North Carolina Progressive Party in Winston-Salem, where local liberals joined with radicals to support Wallace. When the Progressives' stance on CP involvement in the campaign came up back in Georgia, Don was "inclined to think that it would be a mistake to deny Communist affiliation."[54]

A month later Ralph McGill began his series of columns blistering West and the Progressive campaign for their alleged allegiances to the Communist Party. Using documentary material leaked to him by Congressman Davis, McGill first attacked Paul Robeson and followed up with a battery of questions about West's past communist connections. By linking the Progressives with West, Robeson, and Claude Williams, McGill helped undermine liberal support for the Wallace campaign. His assault may have been driven by the *Constitution*'s battle with the *Atlanta Journal* for market share, but it is equally true that he was a mainstream Truman supporter who saw danger on the Left for the president's chances in November. Others have suggested that McGill hoped that isolating West and the progressives as extremists would allow him to pursue a more liberal line on gradual integration.[55] Whatever the explanation, McGill fashioned a systematic campaign to discredit the Progressives as their national convention drew near.

Even before West arrived in Philadelphia as a delegate the combination of negative publicity and persistent conflict over Communist Party meddling in the Progressive campaign had driven a wedge between West and Homer Chase, the Party's organizer in Georgia. By most accounts, Chase was an offensive and contentious tyrant who had made enemies among liberals, radicals, and conservatives alike. In July 1948 he and West clashed over the issue of Progressive distribution of CP campaign materials as well as Chase's insistence on the nomination of Floyd Hunter as the Progressive Party's congressional candidate. Later, Don was elected to the Progressive National Committee over the objections of the CP "vanguard element" in Georgia. Finally, when West reached Philadelphia he received a telegram from Chase, instructing him to resign as national committeeman. West replied, "you can tell Homer to go to hell!" He was furious with Chase for factional maneuvering, which he regarded as an exercise in self-aggrandizement by a "leader" who saw himself as a "junior Lenin," a "little fellow . . . taking himself too seriously." Another analysis of this friction would stress conflict between two strong egos, recognizing that it was not the first time Don West had clashed with an equally forceful personality. In August he wrote to his brother-in-law, Bart

Logan, that he was "disgusted" with the Party's leadership in Georgia. West was certain that both Progressives and communists knew that he would "not accept anyone's word as gospel."[56]

Dismissing Chase's backstabbing as a matter of "personal jealousy," West moved on to campaign vigorously for Wallace as election day drew near. Tireless in his work with union groups, he hammered at the "significance of the Progressive Party to Southern workers." In September he joined Barfoot for a rousing rally in Brunswick, where a large black audience confirmed widespread support for the Progressive Party among African Americans in coastal Georgia. The climax of West's campaign efforts came on October 16, 1948, when he cooperated with Pratt to promote a massive turnout in Dalton for Wallace's speech before a gathering sponsored by Pratt and the Conference of Ministers of the Church of God. In the presence of five thousand "poor, white mountain people," many of them Pratt's unionist followers, Wallace spoke in messianic tones of "bringing the kingdom of God here on earth." Preaching universal brotherhood, he challenged the church to "take up the mighty sword of moral conviction" and "cut down the evil forces of hate and exploitation." In an attack on Jim Crow and the poll tax, the Iowa prophet called his flock to follow the path of righteousness, which led to the "brotherhood of man."[57] At this climactic moment Wallace seemed the living embodiment of Don West's vision of a new South of common people united in the struggle for human dignity.

Ralph McGill viewed Georgia Progressives from another perspective. Two days after the Dalton gathering he unleashed a bitter assault on West featuring the words of the original "Listen, I Am a Communist" in an attack he envisioned as the definitive argument against the Progressive campaign. Allowing West to speak, McGill offered his subject's confession:

> I am a Communist
> A Red
> A Bolshevik!
> Do you, toilers of the South
> Know Me?

McGill closed his case by asking if Georgia's Wallace party was "Communist directed or not" and whether voters were ready to "allow [the] two-party system to be split up and destroyed by the Wallaceites and the Dixiecrats."[58]

McGill's concern was premature. Wallace failed disastrously in Georgia, garnering only 1,636 votes, just as his entire campaign withered before the effective Truman effort to paint him into a Red corner. Unable to carry an electoral votes, the liberals' great hope went down to a disappointing defeat. And for Georgia's Progressives the worst was ahead as the party moved toward collapse in a flurry of internal bickering. Although the integrationist message was unwelcome in Jim Crow Georgia, the Progressive fate was sealed by the destructive machinations of the communists, who were bent on making the Wallace effort the first step in the creation of a farmer-labor movement. Because they had embraced a legitimate presidential candidate, communists had reached a position of influence in mainstream American politics never before achieved. As a consequence, however, there was tension between communists and noncommunists throughout the campaign. In Georgia and the South, the result was the disruption of liberalism under the pressure of intense red-baiting. Not long after the election, the rift created by Foreman's decision to take the SCHW into the Wallace campaign became an unbridgeable chasm when Dombrowski and Aubrey Williams severed remaining connections between the SCEF and the conference. On November 20 the fund brought together an integrated assemblage of two hundred middle-class liberals who adopted a "Declaration of Civil Rights" and proposed to "bring American ideals and deeds into closer harmony."[59] The SCHW was unceremoniously laid to rest one day later.

In the months following Wallace's defeat, West and the Georgia Progressives struggled to breathe life into an organization already on life support. In early May, West declared that it was "no time for pessimism" in view of the Progressive Party's progress on issues of race and class. Despite that promise, a "dogmatic left-sectarian group" came to dominate the rump party by March 1949. Their tactics, as James Barfoot asserted, "made it impossible to build a broad-based, democratic people's party." Central to this outcome was the confrontational behavior of Homer Chase and his Atlanta ally Eunice Tontak of the Atlanta Federation for Jewish Social Service, who had become a "dominant force" in the Georgia Progressive Party. In June 1949, after a struggle against the vanguard element, Barfoot resigned and recommended that the national party no longer subsidize its Georgia organization. In so doing he joined both Pratt and West, who had also severed ties with the Progressive Party. Barfoot informed Progressive national chair C. B. "Beanie" Baldwin that West, the owner of a "long and outstanding progressive record," had told him that this was "the first group he [had] ever known that he was unable to work with."[60] Although West's claim was dubious, the resignation ended his personal effort to build an interracial workers' coalition through the Progressive Party.

Given the loss of his teaching position, West had little alternative but to return to the land. Weltner's decision to provide a year's salary as a buffer against short-term financial hardship eased the blow, but for Don, there was no academic employment on the horizon. As early as October 1948 his friend Archer Torrey reported him "tired" as a result of the attacks on him, which were "telling" in that he now contemplated a move north. After trading the Kennesaw property for a four-hundred-acre farm in Douglasville near Atlanta, the family retreated to rural Georgia, where they farmed while Don resumed writing.[61] For the beleaguered Wests, unemployed and harassed by liberals, radicals, and the Klan, it was time to move on, but their destination was unclear.

Old Kim Mulkey.
(Courtesy of Ann West
Williams)

The West family, Ellijay, Georgia, ca. 1911. Left to right: James Oliver West,
Donald Lee West, Lillie Mulkey West, and Bonnie Elsie West. (From copy in Hedy
West Collection, courtesy of Talitha West)

Jesse Stuart (left) and Don West, Lincoln Memorial University, ca. 1926. (Courtesy of the Jesse Stuart Foundation)

A youthful Don West, ca. 1930. (Courtesy of Ann West Williams)

Don West on his Indian 85, ca. 1933. From John Egerton, *Speak Now Against the Day* (Chapel Hill: University of North Carolina Press, 1994)

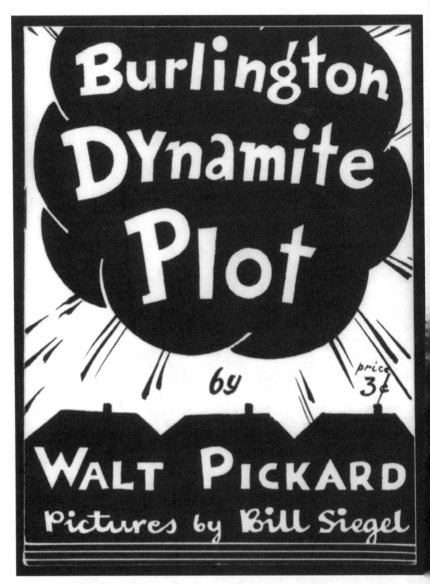

Cover illustration for the *Burlington Dynamite Plot*, 1935. (Courtesy of the Paul Green Papers, Southern Historical Collection, Manuscript Department, Wilson Library, University of North Carolina Library at Chapel Hill)

Communist Party labor organizer Don West, 1935. (Hedy West Collection, courtesy of Talitha West)

Janet West Ross (Johnnie Elsie West), sister and comrade, ca. 1940. (Hedy West Collection; courtesy of Talitha West)

Lillie West and Mike Ross at the West farm in Cassville, Georgia, ca. 1941. (Hedy West Collection, courtesy of Talitha West)

Superintendent Donald L. West, Lula-Belton High School, ca. 1943–44. (Courtesy of Gwen Chapman)

student body president Guinevere Cagle presents the Seniors Award Medal to Gov.
Ellis Arnall, 1945. Left to right: Arnall, Donald L. West, and Cagle. (From the *Lula
Scrapper*, 1944–45; courtesy of Gwen Chapman)

Connie West with her class at the Brookhaven, Georgia, school, 1948; Hedy West is at the far left in the front row. (Hedy West Collection, courtesy of Talitha West)

Lillie Mulkey West at the West Grocery Store, Blairsville, Georgia, ca. 1949. (Hedy West Collection, courtesy of Talitha West)

Tending to business, Pipestem, West Virginia, 1975.
(Hedy West Collection,
courtesy of Talitha West)

Addressing the audi-
ence at the Pipestem
Folk Festival, ca. 1975.
(Hedy West Collec-
tion, courtesy of Talitha
West)

Don and Hedy West prepare for Folk Festival at Pipestem, 1976. (Hedy West Collection, courtesy of Talitha West)

Teaching in the dining
hall at the Appalachian
South Folklife Center,
late 1970s. (Hedy West
Collection, courtesy of
Talitha West)

The quintessential Don
West, from the cover
of the first edition of *In
a Land of Plenty* (1982).
(Courtesy of John
Crawford)

Connie and Don West, ca. 1984. (Courtesy of Ann West Williams)

George Meyers, Don West, and Ann West Williams, West residence in Cabin Creek, West Virginia, late 1980s. (Courtesy of the George A. Meyers Collection, J. Glenn Beall Archives, Lewis J. Ort Library, Frostburg State University, Frostburg, Md.)

George Meyers and Don West at the memorial service for Connie West, Appalachian South Folklife Center, Pipestem, West Virginia, July 15, 1990. (Courtesy of the George A. Meyers Collection, J. Glenn Beall Archives, Lewis J. Ort Library, Frostburg State University, Frostburg, Md.)

Don West in retirement, ca. 1991. (Courtesy of Ann West Williams)

part three

Confronting the Great Fear:
Red-baiting and Response

ten

Before the Storm: Back at the Farm, 1949–54

The Wests' initial refuge was the family farm in Douglasville, where Don avoided the public eye and devoted himself to the practical business of supplementing the family income by working the land he loved. A successful farmer, he was able to market his produce in Atlanta, especially in the African American community, where he was a respected figure. Often accompanied by his daughter Hedy (and sometimes Ann), West peddled vegetables from a wagon to black customers who knew him as an advocate for their cause. Reflecting on this transitional period, even the FBI watchdogs later concluded that he had been "living a quiet life on his farm." Because Oglethorpe University honored his contract, the family economy was stable, if stretched. Although he was able to acquire a parcel of land at Lake Nottely near Blairsville, Don thought of these years as a period of "retreat."[1]

After almost a year on the farm, Connie again secured employment, this time in Fernandina, Florida, where she took the children in August 1949. At Fernandina, she remained silent about Don's background and reputation. For Hedy and Ann, the move meant yet another academic environment, to which they quickly adapted. Meanwhile, Don and Connie endured another long-distance relationship that, although not new to them, emphasized the fractured character of a marriage characterized by the unavoidable combination of separate career tracks. Always independent and more than ever sustained by her art, Connie managed the separation well, as did two children who were accustomed to periodic disruptions in family life. In 1967, Don told Hedy that "my kind of person . . . made it hard on [Connie]," which created "uncertainty" and "doubt" in their marital relationship, difficulties she accepted with "courage and strength." Always racked by internal tensions, in some respects the West family circle predated a modern concept of marriage, especially its acceptance of separate identities and individual autonomy. Throughout their marriage, Don had regarded his partner as the "solid source of dependability" that afforded him the opportunity to hold his "attitude and principles."[2] It is equally true that as the occupant of center stage, he often failed to acknowledge her contribution and sometimes belittled her intellectual efforts. But in the 1950s it was again Connie's earning power that ensured the family's economic survival.

When Don's prospects grew dim, he endured periods of self-doubt filled with emotions rarely expressed, even to family and friends. In November 1949, with Connie and the children gone, he did articulate these concerns to his friend and literary confidant, Byron Reece, with whom he shared the bond of North Georgia background. In a moment of candor he told Reece that he was "not doing so well" on his writing and that his financial situation bore down on him. Perhaps because he addressed another artist who had known adversity, West allowed his emotions to show in a way seldom seen at home. In a pensive mood, he poured out his feelings: "Last night was rather cold here. A big bright over-sized moon was out and before turning in I walked through the shadows down along the river and thought as I stumbled along about the mysteries of living and how a restless tide moves always through the lives of men, ever flowing, even as the little ripples of the river pull ceaselessly at the grass and dirt of the bank edge, also restless and never stopping." With his guard down, West went on to reconfirm the personal philosophy that had guided him since the Vanderbilt years, a belief system rooted in the primacy of love in the quest for meaning in life:

> The need of the human being is to love and be loved, and that is difficult of full realization, if not sometimes impossible in a world of so much treachery and distrust with its thwarted and twisted hopes. It can never be fully realized in this kind of world. So, the higher type human being has advanced to the higher form of selfishness—not new, exactly, been sticking around inside man's hopes for a long time. Jesus and the prophets talked about it—he realizes he can save himself only by saving others. He can live only when all men are guaranteed the right to live. The peoples of the East have learned this away ahead of us. They learned, and have tried to put into practice in their own lands.

But now—especially now—they, and many of us, realize that life cannot be guaranteed or secure in one country, two countries or a dozen nations unless all nations and peoples have it.[3]

In these words may be found West the humanitarian, the internationalist, and the unreconstructed advocate of human equality. Conscious of a divided world and fearful of "race suicide," he mourned unfulfilled human desire and advocated a changed reality. Yet he was ambivalent about the ultimate achievement of the new consciousness. As he "walked in wonder by the river in the night," not far from the city lights where men and women were "torn by doubts and full of fear," his heart "was full of all the negative and positive feelings of these people."[4] In this introspective letter, Don West revealed his inner hopes and fears with an eloquence seldom shared. His doubts also reflected the indignities showered on him as his Oglethorpe career came to a premature end.

Weary of the "slander" against him, West resolved to ignore Ralph McGill, Eugene Talmadge, and the Klan, all of whom seemed part of a "strange sort of anti–Don West united front" that was "united in giving [him] hell." He concluded that "somehow, something [was] wrong." Alone again and conscious of the liberal-radical coalition he faced, he prepared to leave his native state in search of financial stability. In 1950 Don traveled to Texas, where he combined work as a bill collector, part-time writer for *The Southern Farmer,* occasional trouble-shooter for the Farmers Union, and labor organizer among Mexican American migrant workers of the Southwest. By April 1950 he had landed a job with the Home Missions Council of the United States, working out of Lubbock and San Antonio to provide social services to the migrant community. Following the migrants, West spent summer months in South Dakota and Michigan, where he ministered to the needs of workers' families, monitored mistreatment of seasonal workers, and served as their advocate for better working and living conditions. Despite relentless surveillance, FBI observers were unable to detect any communist activity on the part of Don or the Home Missions Council. The evidence indicated that they were focused on alleviating distress and preaching labor organization—and no more. During his Texas stint West was reunited with his old friend Harry Koger of the Food, Tobacco, Agricultural, and Allied Workers of America (FTA), who had once worked in Georgia and Louisiana as a CIO organizer and now served as FTA regional director for Texas and Oklahoma. His experiences in Texas had a profound impact on West, who told Langston Hughes in April 1951 that he had seen "some terrific conditions among the migrant farm workers in the past year."[5] West's organizing duties kept him constantly on the road, and he disliked the vast openness of the Texas plains, concerns that ensured that this job would be nothing but temporary employment. While he organized in Texas, West rented his land to an African American tenant, Hardy Scott, who worked the farm in his absence. Scott, in the late 1930s a communist organizer of the unemployed in Atlanta, was an ideological soul mate in whom West could place his trust. Although Don occasionally visited the family in Fernandina, he returned to Douglasville infrequently. Then, during summer breaks, Connie and the family often joined him on the road from Texas to Michigan, meeting workers in the fields and ministering to their needs. Meanwhile, West returned to his writing and published several articles dealing with rural poverty. One, which appeared in *Southern Farmer*, graphically depicted the conditions under which Texas migratory workers and other small farmers lived, a problem regularly highlighted in Koger's *Agricultural Workers Bulletin*, which often featured excerpts from West's poetry on rural poverty. Even after Don's return to Georgia, Koger used his writing as an organizing tool.[6]

Nowhere in his travels did West find more deplorable conditions than in Texas, where the state refused to accept federal surplus commodities due to the cost of distribution. On one occasion a Methodist preacher asked him to deliver a Sunday sermon, which gave him an opportunity to highlight the hunger tolerated because of local government's unwillingness to accept federal aid. Confronted by disbelief, West persuaded the minister to organize a tour of the local migrant camp for his congregation. Once convinced of the severity of the problem, the group pressured the town to accept surplus food, thus winning a small victory in an ongoing struggle.[7]

Out of these experiences came West's next major publication, *The Road Is Rocky* (1951), a poetry collection simultaneously published as a trade book and in a chapbook edition used in Texas by the Home Missions Council as a fund-raising tool. Breaking out of the gloom he felt after his dismissal, West produced a volume of poems that spoke eloquently to the shame of rural poverty in America. Published in New York by a small house, New Christian Books, the book is filled with striking religious imagery that calls conscientious Christians to action and challenges the excesses of the early McCarthy era. In a sparse preface, Byron Herbert Reece conferred on West the mantle of "people's poet," a man possessed of that "particular kind of courage to speak up for those who have no voice of their own, no lobby." Reece also dismissed the political attacks on West, whose commitment to look ahead "validate[d] the integrity of the man" whose honesty found expression in the "honesty of his songs."

The volume opens with a powerful invocation of a lynching, based on a story West had heard during the summer of 1950. Returning from a visit to

Douglasville, he picked up a black transient and gave him a ride to Alabama. Gregarious by nature, Don drew the man into conversation, which yielded a chilling tale of a lynch victim cut down and thrown on his mother's porch. Don never forgot the story, which he recounted in "Anger in the Land," an expression of outrage later set to music and recorded by Hedy on the Folkways label:

> Oh, there's grieving in the plum-grove
> And there's weeping in the weeds,
> There is sorrow in the shanty
> Where a broken body bleeds . . .
>
> For there's been another lynching
> And another grain of sand
> Swells the mountain of resentment—
> Oh, there's anger in the land!
> And a woman broods in silence
> Close beside an open door
> Flung across the flimsey door-step
> Lies a corpse upon the floor!

With the scene set, West asks the reader to absorb the horror of a moment too often ignored:

> Did you ever see a lynching'
> Ever see a frenzied mob
> Mill around a swaying body
> When it's done its hellish job?

Recoiling from the horrific imagery, the reader shares the poet's revulsion:

> Oh, there's grieving in the plum-grove
> And there's sobbing on the sand
> There is sorrow in the shanties—
> And there's anger in the land."[8]

Anger turns to disillusionment in the poignant "Sad, Sad America" in which West reflects on the broken promise of a country betrayed: "Sad was the hour" in which "you rattle the atomic sword / And your bombs blast / Innocent brown babies / Eight thousand miles from these shores." Here West expresses momentary despair over the welling hostility toward America in Asia and Africa, while only "Decaying dictators / Look to America / With hope in their eyes."[9] Also in a dark vein, "Ballad of the Migrants" commemorates the deaths of a migrant family that had perished in flames as they huddled together for warmth on a cold Christmas eve in Texas:

Eleven skulls next morning
Were lying in a heap
The skulls of workers children
And workers flesh are cheap!"

Similarly, "I Saw a Hungry Child" and "I've Known Hunger" drew on West's recent experiences to expose unmet human needs.[10] These verses, with their stark images of poverty in the land of plenty, mark *The Road Is Rocky* as an eloquent statement on behalf of the forgotten underclass; they underscore West's artistic presence as a people's poet in the tradition of Walt Whitman and John Greenleaf Whittier.

So pointed was his advocacy that the FBI took notice of the book in late 1951, and the San Antonio office sent Director J. Edgar Hoover a complete copy together with a memo on West's previous communist activities and the Bureau's current interest in his movements. Local observers regarded *The Road Is Rocky* as a "bitter criticism of the alleged under-privileged conditions of and discrimination against the Negro and Mexican-American people." Calling particular attention to West's attack on the Korean War in "U.S. Inventory, 1951," regional officials believed the book to be of substantial interest to the agency's central research desk.[11]

The focus on the Korean War revealed another side of the book that domestic anticommunists found troublesome: West's open attack on the narrowing of civil liberties during the McCarthy era. His criticism of red-baiting posed the greatest potential challenge to the Cold Warriors of the 1950s and their enablers. In "Oh, Pity Those," written for "those who backed down under pressure," West feigns pity for the "liberal class / Once brave with words, now cowed by fears!" and chides them as pretenders to intellectual integrity:

Oh, pity those,
The liberal man
Whose words were brave when times were fair
But now their lips are tight and thin—
We cannot hear them anywhere!

Addressing the "little scared Christian" who signed a peace petition and then "sniveled and cried / To get a release," he sees a "soul for hire."[12]

His challenge to intellectual cowardice and confrontation with malignant anticommunism reflected West's personal experience in the late 1940s and early 1950s. After completing his assignment with the Home Missions Council in September 1951, he returned to Douglasville to seek a moment of respite. Not long thereafter, he learned that in 1949, Paul Crouch had named him before the House Un-American Activities Committee (HUAC) as a communist organizer in North Carolina and Kentucky in the 1930s, thus setting off a new wave of investigation and FBI scrutiny. West, who had been Crouch's factional rival in North Carolina party affairs, had "never had any confidence in him at all." Their strained relationship, however, did not prevent Crouch from asserting that the two were close collaborators during their organizing days. Then, in 1952, Harvey Matusow, a professional witness and inveterate prevaricator, testified that while in Bethel, West had been part of a communist plot to undermine the Boy Scouts of America, a claim that seemed to gain credence in view of Ohio informant Martha Edmiston's charge that West worked to subvert the Boy Scouts while carrying out communist work in Ohio. In an interview with *Atlanta Journal* reporter Celestine Sibley, West angrily dismissed the allegations as "lousy lies," the product of Matusow's fertile imagination. In a sympathetic account, Sibley quoted West's claim that he was "not doing anything now except trying to make a living." A frustrated West asserted, "I am not a Communist now. I am a Georgia farmer."[13] And there is no firm evidence to the contrary. Although he maintained ties to party acquaintances, West was not overtly engaged in CP activity in the early 1950s, a period during which numerous party people went underground in the wake of the Smith Act prosecutions and amid Communist Party fantasies concerning the imminence of fascist rule in the United States.

By 1953 West was struggling to make ends meet. In 1952 he was dropped from the regular staff of *Southern Farmer* just after his Home Missions Council employment came to an end, two actions that deprived him of needed income. In January 1953 he wrote to Aubrey Williams to propose a renewed connection with the newspaper and a fresh effort to popularize the Farmers Union publication in North Georgia. The response was not encouraging. Williams reported that his New York financiers had decided to "dispose of the whole shebang" because of insufficient revenues, so there was no newspaper for West to work for. Even more disturbing was Williams's conclusion that the Farmers Union had "sold out" on the peace issue. To Williams, the FU was "bankrupt of any real morality," having climbed "in bed with Harry Truman," who "pee[s] in his pants every time he sees a five star general."[14]

Without the Farmers Union outlet for his work West turned to another journalistic project that had long interested him. Since World War II he had been interested in purchasing a North Georgia newspaper, at first with Byron

Reece in mind as editor. Although Reece declined to participate in the scheme, West continued to explore the idea after the war, especially around 1950 after he had purchased land near Lake Nottely. There, he set up and stocked a general store for his mother, Lillie, to operate, thus providing her with a modest income. He also purchased a small newspaper, the *North Georgia News*, which provided work for his brother Rudy, who became editor and general manager. Later, in 1953, Rudy bought a part interest in the newspaper, a transaction that may have offered Don some temporary financial relief.[15] Fortunately for the Wests, between 1951 and 1953 Connie continued to teach at Fernandina, then Jacksonville, and finally in Murphy, North Carolina, again providing economic stability.

The Wests survived economically, but the relentless monitoring of Don's movements and activities bore heavily on him during the years at Douglasville. His frustration boiled over in early 1953, when medical bills and government agents seemed an intolerable burden. Both Lillie and Connie required hospitalization, and authorities at one "Christian Institution" refused to admit his mother until he paid cash in advance for her surgery. West suggested to Aubrey Williams that "the Lord, the McCarrans, McCarthys, and hospitals [were] all in cahoots." Equally troublesome were the periodic visits of FBI agents, who insisted that his future well-being was dependent on his willingness to provide information on his activities and those of his friends.[16]

During one particularly burdensome interview in March 1954 West complained that he was being persecuted for "honest beliefs," which he insisted were those of a "principled man." He told the inquisitors that since 1937 he had not belonged to the Communist Party but that he maintained "associations" with people whom he "believed to be Communists" as part of his objective of "accomplishing good" for others. West defended his support for Henry A. Wallace and attacked the communist operative Homer Chase for undermining the liberal movement in Georgia. He then asked the agents, "Do you think that if I were in the Communist Party at that time that I would be at liberty to differ with Chase?" As a result of West's diatribe his tormenters observed that he "did not appear to be very cooperative." In view of his response, they concluded that he would not be a "satisfactory witness," nor was he likely to serve as an informant.[17]

Constant attention from the FBI led West to be increasingly pessimistic about the nation's direction and his own future. Although government agents finally decided that he was merely "making an industrious effort to operate a successful farm," Don could not have known of that conclusion. At this time he reached out to his old mentor Alva Taylor for reassurance in an unfriendly world. He told Taylor that due to the pressures he experienced, he was in a "fix" that prevented him from following his interests. Moreover, his customary optimism seemed shaken by a belief that "in the US maybe we'll have fascism before we have democracy . . . a lot of dark before true daylight."[18]

While West was angry and depressed by the darkness of McCarthy era persecution, his accusers did not fare well. By 1954 Matusow had been exposed as a liar and Crouch was about to suffer a similar fate. As early as 1952, the Justice Department learned that the volatile Matusow had been diagnosed as neurotic but nonetheless continued to employ him as a witness. Likewise, Crouch, who had twice identified West as a communist, was also exposed as a prevaricator by Joseph and Stewart Alsop on April 16 and 19, 1954, in the *Washington Post.* Despite the exaggerations of Matusow, Crouch, and others like them, the paucity of admissible evidence caused the government to rely on such professional informers, often to its disadvantage.[19] For West, the short-term damage was limited. The increased intensity of the HUAC's interest in his background remained a long-term problem after 1955, however, when his activities drew attention from several government bodies. The revelations and petty harassment of the early 1950s marked the beginning of his running battle with the investigatory apparatus of the national security state.

When West's future seemed darkest, a ray of light came from an unexpected source. In 1954 the Rev. Charles T. Pratt, pastor of the Church of God of the Union Assembly, contacted him to propose a new Social Gospel alliance between the two old friends. Pratt urged West to join him in Dalton to edit a new newspaper intended to become the voice of the church and a force for social progress. A Wallace firebrand and labor activist, Pratt and his church were intense in their commitment to the gospel of unionism as the solution to their members' secular problems. With five hundred followers in Dalton and another ten thousand scattered around the South, Pratt taught his flock that union activism was a religious duty and that organization held the key to improving life on earth. As both Wallace supporter and proselytizer for labor, Pratt impressed West as a "terrific figure."[20]

Coming as it did at a time when Don's personal prospects were dismal, Pratt's offer renewed his faith in the future. He accepted the position, confident that he could not only use his literary skills but also fulfill his mission to improve the lives of the poor through militant unionism. Although the issues were not clear as West's tenure in Dalton began, his presence in that community was destined to produce rancorous political debate. Don West would soon emerge as a public figure as controversial as the man who sponsored him.

eleven

Trouble Brewing: The Great Dalton Red Hunt, 1954–56

Charlie Pratt's congregation seemed like home to Don West, who had long shared its pastor's conviction that Jesus was, in fact, a social revolutionary. A former Harlan County miner, Pratt preached the gospel of unionism as the doctrine of his church, which ministered to hardpressed miners and mill workers who came to accept labor activism as a religious duty. Illiterate but charismatic, he succeeded in building a church composed of loyal followers whose contributions launched a number of local institutions, including a co-operative supermarket, print shop, and several other businesses in the Dalton area. Pratt's enterprises raised questions about his activities, which prompted John G. Ramsay of the CIO's Committee on Religion and Labor to assert that "everything we have heard about him is anything but good."[1] Always an advocate for the poor, the preacher nonetheless earned the love and respect of his congregation, which identified with his background as a miner and embraced his doctrine of racial unity and worker solidarity. A spellbinding speaker, Pratt captured the essence of mountain religion as an antidote to the ravages of worker poverty.

Given Pratt's grass-roots appeal and broad-based support among workers West was instinctively drawn to his cause, and in October 1954 he proposed to join the Church of God of the Union Assembly and serve as a preacher. When asked to come to Dalton and start a church newspaper, therefore, West readily accepted the challenge. Don's brother-in-law, labor organizer Mike Ross, recalled that Pratt was so enamored of his new "intellectual leader" that he tried to bestow a variety of material goods on West. Uninterested in creature comforts, however, Don told his partner that if he wanted to reward him he might give him full responsibility for the newspaper. The new publication, christened *The Southerner*, was in West's estimation a "unique church paper" in that its primary theme was a clear union message. An instant success with Pratt's followers, the publication counted five thousand paid subscribers by the end of its first year of operation. The board of contributing editors reflected West's influence, counting among them Byron Herbert Reece, Aubrey Williams, and Alva W. Taylor. The first edition sounded its dominant theme in a joint editorial by Pratt and West, which declared *The Southerner's* purpose to be the pursuit of "freedom and right and justice for all regardless of race, creed, sex, or color." Moreover, its allegiance to labor was clear, a commitment that presaged controversy in the booming textile community. West told Taylor that although "it may seem risky . . . to begin such a journal in these times," he hoped for success. He was not far off the mark. From the outset, the newspaper drew the attention of FBI monitors, who promised to "follow closely the activities of this publication and the individuals connected therewith."[2]

By January 1955 West and Pratt were engaged in planning for *The Southerner's* debut—the first issue appeared in March of that year—as well as a new church college in Dalton that might provide workers' children with the educational opportunity often denied mountain youths. The projected institution, to be led by President Don West, was to be named Charlie Pratt College in honor of the people's preacher. Although the educational mission was important to West, he steadfastly maintained that other issues such as union organization must take precedence in pursuit of the church's social mission.[3]

For the moment, the newspaper remained Don's first priority, the realization of a dream. Flushed with anticipation, he confessed to Taylor that he "always [had] wanted something like this . . . by way of opportunity." Not long thereafter, *The Southerner's* outspoken advocacy of worker rights and the aspirations of local mill workers converged to spark a union drive in the chenille industry that would focus attention on West, Pratt, and the church and catalyze resistance among both local industrialists and community leaders.[4]

After a few issues, some Dalton workers, driven by working conditions and inspired by religious commitment and *The Southerner's* pro-labor message, approached West with a request to aid them in organizing a union in local chenille plants. At first hesitant, he insisted that he was an editor rather than a union organizer but could put them in touch with someone who would organize them. Subsequently, he contacted Boyd Payton of the Textile Workers Union of America (TWUA), who sent three union representatives to organize at the Lawtex Corporation and Belcraft Company. *The Southerner*'s firm support of organizing rights drew the immediate endorsement of other local unions, including the large and successful Local 185 at Crown Mills. Typical was a letter from Dalton Textile's Local 1376, which concluded that if workers would "all stick together" they would "have all the plants organized in Dalton." Many years later, union organizer Robert A. Freeman recalled the value of Don's assistance in the Dalton campaign and concluded that because of West's "ability to express [himself] through writings to the people" he became "an enemy to the plutocrats who controlled the lives of the chenille workers."[5]

Such sentiments were not welcome news in Dalton, especially among the business and community leadership. As Douglas Flamming has shown, Dalton's elite regarded the church's union activities and *The Southerner*'s outspoken support of organizing rights as "Protestantism gone afoul," whereas Pratt and West saw it as "Protestantism redeemed." Their message was clear and simple: "Christ sides with poor workers; unions offer poor workers a better life; Christ, therefore, favors unionization as a form of Godly retribution and justice."[6] The newspaper blended class leveling with union organizing: "We believe in the principles of organized labor because we believe in the life and teaching of Jesus Christ; because we believe in the principles of our founding fathers; because we believe in genuine Americanism."[7]

In Dalton, other definitions of Americanism held sway. By May 1955 local industrial leaders had organized their own resistance to the twin viruses of political radicalism and labor activism, which to management were inseparable. On April 28, Henry C. Ball of the Tufted Textile Manufacturer's Association (TTMA) alerted Cong. Henderson Lanham, a Democrat, to the subversive influence of Don West and requested assistance in accessing the contents of House Un-American Activities Committee (HUAC) files on him. In response, Lanham secured the West file from HUAC chair Francis Walter and forwarded its contents to interested constituents. Noting his recollection of West as "at least an extreme left-winger if not a Communist," Lanham thought it "too bad that this sort of thing is starting in our district."[8]

So alarmed was Lanham that he promptly informed David Burgess of the Georgia State Industrial Union Council that West, Pratt, and the newspaper were a threat to labor peace in Dalton. Lanham warned that the state labor movement would be "damaged" if textile unions continued their "close collaboration" with *The Southerner*. Equally alarmed after reviewing the West file, Burgess and C. H. Gilman, director of CIO Region 5, contacted TWUA national vice president William Pollock to urge immediate action to prevent

damage to CIO interests in North Georgia. Pollock followed up by instructing Jim O'Shea, manager of TWUA's Northwest Georgia Joint Board in Rome, to acquaint Dalton unionists with the problem. Acting on those instructions, O'Shea contacted both West and the Dalton locals to explore the situation. He also commended West for the newspaper's content and pledged to "clear up any misunderstandings that may exist."[9]

Confronted by a new challenge, West defiantly told O'Shea that he would "never waste breath in self-defense" and rejected any "Inquisition." More united than the union, he argued, the church and its followers backed the newspaper, and because they stood for "pure Americanism" they wanted to clear up any questions of loyalty. West might have been publicly open to discussion, but privately he fumed at Burgess's "stab in the back," which he thought motivated by Burgess's misguided desire to prove his own patriotism by "slandering and Red-baiting others."[10]

Faced by the public disclosures within the context of pervasive anticommunism, the TWUA saw a threat to its interests in the state as well as the future of the Dalton campaign. Moreover, the International Union had adopted an anticommunist stance during the CIO's internal struggle, which had, in 1949 and 1950, forced its left-led unions out of the national organization. Consequently, the International drew back from the tacit alliance with Pratt and West, starting with a series of meetings to warn local unionists against close ties with either *The Southerner* or its editor. At these sessions, O'Shea learned from Local 134 and 185 leaders that the TWUA would lose support if it made a public issue of the conflict, especially among the membership of the Church of God of the Union Assembly. Although Dalton unionists agreed to avoid a direct link between the union and the newspaper, O'Shea urged the TWUA's national office not to take any "drastic action" that might hurt the union locally. West summarized the outcome of his meeting with O'Shea as troublesome but not fatal. The controversy had "hurt [his] relations" with the union to some extent but "not severed them completely from rank and file members and local leaders."[11]

In the final analysis it was not the International that undercut the union cause and *The Southerner*'s pro-labor activism in Dalton. Much more powerful forces carried out a campaign of vilification that ended the pathbreaking collaboration between Pratt, West, the church, and the local labor movement. Recognizing a threat to their economic interests, Lawtex and Belcraft moved in July 1955 to undermine TWUA organizing efforts with their own antiunion campaign. In response to the presence of several International organizers in the community, management circulated questionnaires that included what seemed an innocuous query about church membership. Before long, a host of workers from Pratt's congregation found themselves unemployed. The selective firings resulted in a TWUA request for a Senate investigation, but national union officials distanced themselves from West and the newspaper. Some went further to attack Pratt for the church's business practices and alleged profiteering. Without strong backing from the International, West turned to B'nai B'rith's Anti-Defamation League with an appeal for intervention based on the similarity between Nazi persecution of the Jews and management's attack on Union Assembly workers. He also argued that because the mill owners were Jewish, the conflict was encouraging the growth of hostility toward Jews in Whitfield County. Although the League sent investigators, no action was taken, in part due to the Union Assembly's anti-Catholicism and anti-Semitism. Despite this handicap, the national Religious Freedom Committee, an ecumenical organization, did protest the firings at Lawtex.[12]

Pratt's union workers were the ultimate target, but the chenille industry leaders were shrewd enough to focus their attack on the Dalton labor movement's weak link: the radical reputation of Don West, who had become the public face of the Union Assembly Church and was recognized as widely as Pratt himself. Given West's history of communist activism, there was no need to criticize the church or the TWUA; management understood that the union could be undermined indirectly through encouragement of guilt by association, an all-too-common political stratagem in cold war America. Although the TTMA was clearly behind the campaign against West, the organization maintained a low profile and prefered to encourage public disclosure in the local press.

The key figure in exposing West's background was Mark Pace, a dynamic young journalist and editor of the *Dalton News* and *Dalton Citizen*. A racial moderate of the Ralph McGill variety, Pace became acquainted with West as a political figure during Henry A. Wallace's campaign in 1948, when Pratt and West brought the candidate to Dalton for the mass rally. At that time Pace regarded West as a misguided socialist, but by 1955 he had become convinced that he was a communist whose movements bore watching. Not long after West moved to Dalton, Don visited Pace to inform him that the Union Assembly was launching *The Southerner*. His initial impression of Pace was that he was "sort of pitiful . . . a weak little fellow who has a string around his neck." Following their first encounter, the Georgia Bureau of Investigation approached Pace to inform him of FBI-GBI surveillance of West and solicit his help in the effort. Ready to cooperate with law enforcement, Pace agreed to share his information on West's movements in Dalton. Aware of Pratt's union sympathies, Pace later insisted that he never opposed labor. Rather, he said, "for me, West's communist activities were always the issue, never his labor activities."[13]

The publicity barrage opened on August 21, 1955, with a full-page spread in the *Dalton News*, culled from HUAC files that Lanham supplied shortly after West's visit to Pace's offices. Asserting objectivity, the local press opened the public record so readers might judge West's actions. Subsequent issues were filled with a rehash of the old charges first leveled by McGill, all presented with a disclaimer denying any personal conviction concerning West's guilt or innocence. Like McGill, Pace quoted the 1934 version of "Listen, I Am a Communist," which spoke volumes despite West's numerous attempts to rebut the charges. To Mark Pace it was clear that "where there's so much smoke there must be some fire." Although Pace denied opposition to labor, his revelations coincided with the opening of the TWUA's chenille campaign and a wage increase announced by the TTMA.[14] As the summer came to an end the fat was in the fire.

In the wake of the publicity campaign, an *Atlanta Constitution* reporter journeyed north to Dalton to assess damage to the Union Assembly Church. West denied that he was a communist, and Pratt insisted that his intellectual leader would stay in Dalton, regardless of the accusations. Meanwhile, West maintained that "we had more unity than ever before." His private thoughts were darker. On August 25 he complained to Byron Reece of the "tremendous personal attack by the Dalton press," which he believed to be part of an effort to "work up a mob spirit of violence." In a reflective mood, Don admitted to his friend that he envied Reece's "quiet and peaceful life," which was so unlike his own experience of "hellfire and brimstone, toil and trouble." In early September, West complained that "a guy hardly has a chance when all the big dough is on the other side." Fully aware of his role as scapegoat, he understood the attack as an attempt to undermine the chenille campaign. In a moment of vulnerability, West confided that "a fellow feels terribly alone sometimes . . . not having . . . much spiritual or mental-intellectual fellowship."[15]

West considered himself a victim, but there was much truth in his perception of a bitter campaign against him. In a long letter to International representative Alton Lawrence, one TWUA organizer in Dalton recounted a tale of threatened violence against West that had Don "really scared, as well he should have been." Passing through Dalton on his way to an assignment in Copper Hill, Tennessee, he encountered the local fire chief, Luther Broome, who urged him to stay over to observe some "real excitement" when a "damn Communist" was lynched. Pace independently confirmed a local group's plan to "[pay] West a visit" but warned against mob violence. When the organizer caught up with West at the church, he found him "worried nearly to death" over the lynch-mob mentality abroad in the town. At a subsequent meeting with Pratt, the TWUA organizer persuaded the preacher and a large crowd of his flock that an attack on Don was an attack on the union. A day later he introduced West to Broome as "one of the finest men I have ever known." By the time they parted, the fire chief was agreeing with everything Don told him, and *"the lynching party was off."*[16]

Having foiled the incipient lynch mob, West's advocate began working on Georgia TWUA officials, whose maneuvers had inadvertently contributed to inflaming local opinion in Dalton. He contacted southern director Boyd Payton and Northwest Georgia Board representative James O'Shea and told them the chenille drive would collapse unless they halted their own attack on West because 50 percent of the affected workers were members of his church. The organizer insisted that Dalton workers "would choose their own friends and associates." After informing Payton and O'Shea that West was "100 percent ok in [his] book," he left for Atlanta to warn Burgess against any further effort to smear Don, whose efforts to "get these workers aroused" he fully appreciated.[17]

Although the immediate danger had subsided by early September, the episode left no doubt about the intensity of anticommunist sentiment in Dalton in the midst of the chenille campaign. Nor were West's concerns unwarranted. Galvanized by Pace's campaign, the local Veterans of Foreign Wars launched an assault with an open letter from Cmdr. Harry Campbell, whose position as manager of the Crown Mill Boylston plant could hardly have been coincidental. Campbell insisted that West address the HUAC record and answer charges of CP membership. Not to be outdone, Dalton American Legion Post 112 soon joined the fray with praise for Pace and condemnation for "those who in the name of religion and the church" were "acting as a front for foreign ideology seeking to destroy the very foundations of the Republic."[18]

West vainly attempted to answer the VFW's charges in a detailed letter to the *Dalton Citizen* on September 1. In it, he questioned the inquisitors' authority and presented a nuanced definition of the term *communist*, which, West argued, had been used to discredit a wide variety of reformers and seekers of social justice. Linking his cause with the history of political dissent, he attacked McCarthyism and denied that he was a communist. More to the point, he asserted the smear campaign was an ill-concealed effort to undermine the TWUA's chenille drive through an attack on his political beliefs and actions.[19]

The events that followed, including beatings, destruction of workers' property, and targeted job dismissals, sorely tested West's labor supporters. Even *The Southerner*'s offices were vandalized and its windows smashed and presses destroyed in an effort to intimidate Pratt and the church. Perhaps most devastating to Dalton's workers were layoffs at both Belcraft and Lawtex, where twenty-six workers found themselves jobless by September 8. In response to this escalation of the struggle Pratt forced Don to accept a .38 Smith and Wesson revolver as well as a shotgun, adding, "You might need these."[20] Subsequent events would bear him out.

The immediate problem for the union and the chenille campaign was the confusion and anxiety caused by the layoffs. In response, the TWUA claimed that workers had been fired for engaging in organizing activity and filed a protest with the National Labor Relations Board. The union also appealed to the Senate Judiciary Committee's Subcommittee on Constitutional Rights for an investigation of alleged religious discrimination against union workers. At the same time, John G. Ramsey and the CIO Committee on Religion and Labor expressed concern over the apparent linkage of religious persecution and antilabor actions.[21] To buttress its case the TWUA filed a set of worker affidavits charging that the dismissals were directly related to church membership. Workers insisted that "the company knew that if they got rid of the Church people they would get rid of our union members," thus removing those who were "advocating and encouraging organization among the chenille workers." Documenting West's role in the campaign, one member asserted that the church had been "encouraging and advocating the union in Dalton through its paper, *The Southerner.*"[22] Members of the Union Assembly Church paid a steep price for their convictions; the workplace implications of their religious preference were clear to the antiunion drive's victims.

No one felt the sting of religious discrimination more than the volatile Charlie Pratt. Incensed by the punitive layoffs, he called a mass meeting at the church on September 1. Pratt encouraged the organization of chenille workers but in the process delivered bitter anti-Catholic and anti-Semitic remarks that helped splinter support for the union. Such excesses persuaded the Anti-Defamation League that the Dalton struggle was a "good mess to stay away from." Completely missing the energizing role of West, Pratt, and the church, the League's representative Milton Ellerin reported that *they* were trying to "get in on the unionization efforts of the CIO Textile Workers Union," thus providing a flawed analysis of the union's actual dependence on the Union Assembly.[23]

In this overheated environment, the chenille campaign spun out of control. Although Belcraft workers remained on the job, the Lawtex group launched a strike that veered toward violence after a court injunction limited mass picketing. Once Gov. Marvin Griffin sent state troopers to police the struggle, the strike collapsed amid charges of union responsibility for the disruption of community life as well as growing recriminations concerning West's presence at the center of the storm. Although West and *The Southerner* played a central role in raising worker expectations and union consciousness in Dalton, the chenille campaign fell apart under the twin pressures exerted by the Red scare and the specter of worker militancy. In this struggle, Don West had been both a catalyst and an obstacle to realizing worker aspirations.[24]

As these events unfolded, Byron Reece offered West solace with a reminder of their comparable histories. On September 1 he wrote to express regret over "all this rehash of the old Communist charges," which paled before Don's "integrity of character." Reminding West that they were both "hill-born" with "liberty [as their] only heritage," he declared that although some in America thought it criminal to be free, they would never silence Don West. He also told his editor at E. P. Dutton that although West had been accused of being a communist, he was "not impressed," especially because holding people responsible for "an early flirtation with Communism" would force him to "hold most of the intellectuals responsible for the same thing."[25]

The good burghers of Dalton failed to share Reece's perspective. For the remainder of the year the battle ground on. In September, the local press launched an attack on Aubrey Williams and Alva W. Taylor, whom it linked with the nefarious Don West. It mattered not, West observed, that Williams was a loyal supporter of Franklin D. Roosevelt and a liberal *anticommunist*. In Dalton, West told Reece, "These boys don't care what *kind* of *communist* he is." The ongoing attacks led Don to suggest that "the fight be raised to a national level." In a letter to Claude Williams, he proposed a national press campaign to expose the red-baiters as enemies of religion and labor. West argued that the smear had become an attack on "American principles . . . *on a church paper because it is pro-labor.*" Denying that the question was communism, he now insisted that the issues were "as broad as the Bill of Rights."[26]

When West made this suggestion he was unaware of the extent to which the Dalton press was invading his personal right to privacy. A week after West's call for national exposure of the local anticommunist campaign, Pace wrote to J. Edgar Hoover to ask the Bureau for more recent information on West, Aubrey Williams, and Taylor, which might be used in proving that West had been a party member after 1953, when membership became illegal in the state of Georgia. Pace could not believe that "the organization would not cooperate in such a matter as vital as this."[27] The aggressive editor understood full well that the FBI could not pass information directly but suggested that the Georgia Bureau of Investigation might be a conduit for communication. FBI records confirm a "limited" but "cordial" correspondence with Pace but also indicate that the Bureau had no evidence that West was affiliated with the CP after 1950. In fact, he had been removed from its "Security Index" in June 1955 "due to inactivity on his part."[28]

The FBI was unable to clinch the case for Pace in time for an October grand jury in Whitfield County, but Washington did instruct the Atlanta field division to share all public source information at its disposal and put Pace in touch with the Legion's Americanism Commission and the Senate Internal Security Subcommittee for assistance. Subsequently, an Atlanta agent met with Pace to explain the Bureau's position and provide him with the available source material. During their conversation it became clear that although his campaign against West had been successful, the Dalton editor now feared that, having pressed the matter to the point at which a grand jury was to consider the case, there was "no hope of a successful prosecution."[29]

Pace was pleased with the FBI response, but he had hoped for more. He now informed Hoover that West had scheduled Aubrey Williams for a mass gathering of the Union Assembly, a tip he thought drew a "clearer picture of the Communist pattern operations" in Dalton. Challenged to a public debate of his charges against both Williams and Taylor, Pace refused to appear and instead turned to the FBI for documentation. Unfortunately, he was unaware of the FBI's conclusion that the controversy was "really a labor-management argument" in response to a "legitimate effort to unionize some workers in the chenille industry." Moreover, the Bureau had decided that given the prospect of a failed grand jury, the agency would be "extremely circumspect" in future contacts with Pace relating to the West case.[30]

The sweep of the Dalton struggle expanded in October when the Whitfield County grand jury took up the issue of communism, functioning as a local version of the HUAC to explore charges Pace had raised. The national scope of the story became obvious when Edgar C. Bundy of the Illinois American Legion's Americanism Committee came to Dalton to warn of the danger posed by Don West, whom, he alleged, had been identified as a communist by the FBI and exposed as a subversive. Widely quoted in the press, Bundy conducted a two-week informational campaign on Dalton radio, which further inflamed public opinion. He bitterly denounced West, observing that "a man does not have to be a card-carrying communist nor a member of the Communist Party in order to teach the Communist doctrine." The danger, Bundy insisted, was the silent cancer of infiltration "under the guise of religion, education, and labor unions."[31] Another apostle of Americanism who appeared in Dalton was Allston Calhoun Jr., a professional anticommunist from South Carolina who billed himself as the "working man's friend." Calhoun, representing the Foundation for Americanism Preferred, linked communism, unionism, and religion.[32] West's subpoena to appear before the grand jury came in October 1955, on the heels of the escalation in rhetoric.

He responded to the attack with an editorial disclosing Bundy's extremism as a critic of numerous respected national figures and an ally of Sen. Joseph R. McCarthy of Wisconsin. At the same time, he redoubled his effort to nationalize local issues by engaging the media in the Dalton story. Working through Claude Williams, Aubrey Williams, and several of his own contacts in Chicago and New York, West tried to interest the liberal press in the issues raised by the Dalton Red Scare and the chenille campaign. On October 17, the *National Guardian* reported West's expectation of a "frame-up" between the grand jury and the Dalton press. At this time, West told Claude Williams that it was "time some national magazines begin to take notice" of the situation and at long last become interested in the South.[33]

In a burst of frustration the beleaguered West complained to his old comrade that he was "damned tired fighting alone when the issues are, as I say, as broad as the Bill of Rights." Comparing himself to Jesus, he promised to "judge every tree by its fruit." Two weeks later he even questioned the usefulness of the People's Institute for Applied Religion, pointedly asking Williams, "Where is a concrete and definite thing it is doing—HERE IN THE SOUTH." By contrast, he asserted, *The Southerner* was "already doing a job . . . not just a theory . . . it is a fighting Southern newspaper that's right now in one hell of a fight."[34] The letter was classic West, a combination of anxiety and hubris that revealed a personal sense of mission as well as the impatience and self-righteousness of a martyred prophet.

Confronted by West's challenge, Williams responded in kind with a letter blistering his friend for the messianic tone of his diatribe. Although he acknowledged that West was "in a fight and an *important* one," he wondered if the Union Assembly preachers "say you are *messiah*." Reminding Don that he had been "born as near the cotton patch as [West]," he agreed *The Southerner* was important but asserted that it could not do the work Williams was doing at the grass roots. Criticizing West's "defensive complex" and tendency to "lash out like a caged bobcat at everything that comes close," Williams insisted that to change the South "every southerner needs *The Southerner* and *The Southerner* needs every southerner." Yet interdependence could not be realized if Don attacked "every one who is not as perfect as [he] conceive[d] [himself] to be." Rather, Williams suggested that West recognize that he was "not so all-fired perfect" as his "militant self-righteousness and feigned hardness would indicate."[35] These were the words of a friend, but coming on the eve of West's testimony they offered little comfort or reassurance.

Against the background of sensational charges, West's grand jury appearance was anticlimactic. Asked about both his past record and current activity in Dalton, he refused to answer questions on Fifth Amendment grounds. Although the grand jury commended Pace for his campaign, it was less pleased with West. Insisting that it recognized the right to invoke the Fifth Amendment, the panel expected "full cooperation" from law-abiding citizens, which it thought West had denied it. It then concluded that communist activities *could* be under way and that residents must be "ever watchful that communism does not infiltrate and spread into [the] community."[36]

As the chenille campaign came to a climax in December 1955, local unionists rallied to West's side at a mass public meeting to emphasize labor's commitment to Dalton as a good place to work and live. The event was intended to burnish organized labor's status in a tense community, but assembled workers not only pledged their support for the chenille workers but also denounced the press and business community for smearing the TWUA and Don West. Despite the brave words, the organizing drive fell short. Only 43 percent of the votes were cast for the union on December 15, a result that spelled trouble for Dalton's fragile labor movement. With the union threat quelled, Pace renewed his attack on West in late December with the revelation that West's writings had been featured in a communist book store in Chicago, complete with photographs supplied by the national commander of the American Legion. Relentlessly pursuing his quarry, Pace intensified the attack in January with a full resume edition recapping charges lodged against West since the previous summer.[37]

By escalating the battle, Pace effectively separated the Red hunt from the bitterly fought chenille campaign. With the major labor conflict resolved, the local press worked to rid the community of alleged subversion by forcing Pratt's hand. West later insisted that because "the old man had so much pressure on him . . . eventually I just told him that I'd better get out." Although pressure was intense, the explanation of Don's departure is more complicated than his account suggests. In fact, newspaper reports reveal that to clear the Union Assembly's name, Preacher Pratt required that all ministers publicly swear they were not communists. Should any refuse, he declared, "I don't want them in this church." In January, West appeared ready to testify on his local efforts since 1952, but he was unwilling to explore his activities before that time, a stance that failed to satisfy Pratt or Whitfield County solicitor Erwin Mitchell, who was to administer the loyalty oath. West maintained that he could not comply with the demand that he discuss his past associations, waiving Fifth Amendment rights in advance, and be faithful to his conscience or loyal to the Constitution. Citing the long history of forced confessions as violations of personal liberty, West refused to cooperate further. He then resigned from the Church of God of the Union Assembly, which expelled him the same evening. Pratt's diligence as guardian of public morality quickly earned him accolades from Congressman Lanham, who praised him for "disassociating [his] church from Don West." A key participant in the anticommunist campaign as a source of damaging information, Lanham also commended Pace and Mitchell for "eliminating Don West from [their] community."[38]

Following his resignation, West left Dalton for Blairsville in Union County, where his mother resided and operated the general store Don had set up for her. As he drove over Fort Mountain on a narrow, winding road, he noticed that a car was crowding him from behind. Aware of a similar incident that had forced several union organizers into a ditch a few weeks earlier, West reached for the .38 revolver on the seat beside him, emptied it into the front tires of his pursuers' automobile, and proceeded on his journey unmolested. With that sour episode, his bittersweet Dalton experience came to an ignominious end. A few months later West observed that few would ever know how much *The Southerner* had meant to him but the Constitution meant more. He simply could not accede to a McCarthyite interpretation of the Fifth Amendment, which was designed to protect the innocent with no intention that *"any guilt whatsoever should be attached to invoking it."*[39] With this principled stand on a matter of conscience, West closed a conflict-ridden chapter in an already controversial life. Returning to his refuge on the Douglasville farm, he expected to avoid the glare of publicity that had surrounded him throughout his sojourn in Dalton. It was a vain hope.

twelve

Economic Struggle: The Ravages of Anticommunism and Years of Exile, 1956–65

What was principle for West was pain for his family. By 1955 Connie was teaching in Murphy, North Carolina, where Hedy excelled academically and completed high school in June, just before the Dalton story broke. Once again, Don's political reputation spelled unemployment for Connie, who was dismissed by the Murphy schools. Buffeted by the economic blow and weary of involuntary career changes, her response was "oh no, not again!" After a temporary stay in Douglasville, she moved to St. Petersburg, where she landed a teaching position at a distance from her controversial spouse. Because of his continuing mobility, Ann remembered her father as essentially a "visiting guy" in the mid-1950s, when the family entered another period of economic hardship and separation.[1]

Safely ensconced on the Douglasville farm, West returned to the land and tried to restart his creative life. In the immediate aftermath of the Dalton struggle he devoted his intellectual energy to an accurate presentation of the circumstances surrounding his departure. One of his key allies in the media campaign was the Trotskyist journalist George Lavan Weissman, editor of Pathfinder Press and an important figure in the Socialist Workers Party (SWP). An active party functionary, Weissman had been a branch organizer in Boston and edited the SWP house organ *The Militant*. Eventually, Weissman and his wife, Connie, were counted among the Wests' extended political and social family, and over the years Don remained grateful for Weissman's loyalty when he was under attack in the 1950s. As early as November 1955, when West fought for national recognition of the Dalton crisis, Weissman had become interested in *The Southerner,* the Union Assembly Church, and the ill-fated chenille campaign. Alerted to the targeted dismissals, he began research on the Textile Workers Union of Ameria's effort to demonstrate that unfair labor practices had been employed in Dalton.[2]

The result of this work was a series of articles in *The Nation, The Churchman,* and *Commentary,* all appearing in 1956 and endorsing the Union Assembly, West, and *The Southerner* as Dalton labor's hope for the future. As evidence of their impact, Weissman cited local press reports that "the seeds sown by West still exist[ed]" and that the area was infected with "Westism" long after Don's departure.[3]

West's lingering influence in the Dalton working community was confirmed by the March issue of *The Southerner,* which carried a bevy of supportive letters side by side with a tirade from its new editor Charlie Pratt denouncing the writers. Meanwhile, Don's confidant Freda Brown told Weissman that West had received many "friendly and encouraging" personal letters commenting on his final column. *The Daily Worker* seized upon the published correspondence to highlight local protest against West's "betrayal" by church authorities. The party organ reminded readers that for a brief moment West had "stirred the hearts of the oppressed and impoverished slave-wage workers of this area" and that *The Southerner* lived on to support organized labor in a hostile community.[4]

In a signed statement defending his resignation from the Union Assembly, West pledged that the "spirit of *The Southerner* [was] a thing that [couldn't] die." True to his word, in March 1956 he revived the newspaper as *The New Southerner,* now published by Aubrey Williams's *Southern Farm and Home* with a little seed money from the People's Institute for Applied Religion and significant encouragement from Trotskyists Ferrell Dobbs and George Weissman, who developed a fund-raising brochure for use with potential supporters. Weissman's central theme was the idea that "one round doesn't end the fight . . . for civil rights, the right to form unions, and for all progress in the South." Moreover, he argued that it was "imperative to get *The New Southerner* off the press" to provide an "independent, liberal voice speaking for the rights and liberties of both Negroes and whites." West confirmed the urgency of ongoing support in a letter to Weissman asserting that the "situation [was] very tense in Georgia and Alabama," with white citizens' councils organizing against the Brown decision. He insisted that the new publication be "aimed first and primarily toward the southern poor white," with emphasis on the problems of the "common laboring people of the South." Accordingly, the first issue featured a dubious assertion that the Dalton chenille workers' union drive was alive and well. Equally strident was a sweeping editorial endorsement of a civil rights movement rooted in a deep love that "won't be quiet—as long as those rights are denied to anybody."[5]

No sooner had the April issue appeared than the Montgomery press launched an attack on the fledgling newspaper, focusing on the Dalton confrontation and West's past communist associations. The *Montgomery Advertiser* concluded that until West "cleared his record" he did not "merit the confidence of the community." The underlying concern in Montgomery was evident in the *Advertiser*'s observation that *The New Southerner*'s slogan—"truth, hope, love, brotherhood, non-violence and simplicity"—bore a close resemblance to the local bus boycotters' theme of "love your enemies, non violence, and passive resistance." Concerned about this response, West told Weissman that the Montgomery power structure was "bringing the squeeze" on Aubrey Williams in an effort to force him out of business. A frustrated West complained that "trouble just comes a looking for me even if I don't look for it," initiated by "rabid bad boys" who "would rather attack me than anybody in the South."[6]

Although *The New Southerner* was controversial in its own right, it was West's additional misfortune to launch it in the midst of the Montgomery bus boycott as well as the discontent attendant upon the Brown decision. Given the volatile social environment, West's newspaper was doomed from the outset. Clearly disappointed by the turn of events, he informed Weissman that Williams could no longer print *The Southerner*. Because the "tenseness of the moment [was] terrific," West saw no alternative but to change his strategy by starting a new southern newsletter and experimenting with pamphlet literature.[7] Defiant to the end, his lead editorial in the final, summer 1956, issue of *The New Southerner* forecast a revival of the Populist farmer-labor coalition that would demand social and racial equality in a unionized south. In his call for a south without poverty, prejudice, or demagoguery, West advanced an idea whose time had come. Yet caught between economic reality and social change in a dynamic south, *The New Southerner* passed quietly into the annals of southern history.

By summer 1956, West had returned to Douglasville, where he tried to extract a living from the soil while reorienting his writing toward the southern newsletter and his long-neglected history of the antebellum Appalachian South. When not so engaged, he found time for visits to his mother in Blairsville and a Christian cooperative farm community in Americus, then under attack because of its insistence on nonracist communitarianism. Sharing some of

West's assumptions, founder Clarence Jordan and the Koinonia community practiced a communal lifestyle based on the model of the early New Testament church. Because of its interracial composition and commitment to cooperative marketing, Koinonia became a target for proponents of the economic and social status quo. As a result, amid charges of communist infiltration its farm market was bombed in July 1956 and attacked by nocturnal visitors in the fall. In a show of solidarity, West visited Koinonia and welcomed its apprentices at his Douglasville farm in the years between 1956 and 1959.[8] During this period he was also regularly harassed by local vigilantes, government agents, and congressional committees.

The local situation was sometimes "not pleasant" as West tried to "pick up the pieces." In early 1957, for example, he faced the Klan, "out on a visit," followed by a confrontation with a local organization, "The Friendly Boys, Inc." Later in the year he endured two KKK cross-burnings on his property and a command performance before Mississippi senator James Eastland's Senate Internal Security Subcommittee (SISS). One day while West plowed his land near the Chattahoochie River, a U.S. marshal served him with a subpoena to appear on October 28, 1957, at a hearing in Memphis devoted to the subject of communism in the Mid-South. West, who had been subpoenaed but never testified in 1954, responded dryly, "Yeah, it looks like I'm doing some awfully subversive activities around here."[9]

Although West had not testified in 1954, Paul and Sylvia Crouch identified him as a communist labor organizer in North Carolina. Crouch, by this time a self-described "professional witness," named both Don and his sister, Janet Ross, as Communist Party members. Probably because West was no longer a central figure in the Southern Conference for Human Welfare, the subject of the hearing, he returned to Douglasville without taking the stand. In 1957, however, the situation had changed, and he was a featured attraction. He was also an openly hostile witness from his first statement, which clearly asserted his Fifth Amendment rights and presaged a refusal to name names or discuss previous political associations. The committee's files are filled with detailed memoranda on West, noting his family ties with Nat Ross, Janet Weaver (Ross), and Bart and Belle Logan and documenting his colorful political history. West was "considered to be one of the more prominent Communist organizers in the South over a period of many years."[10] Conspicuous by its absence was any evidence of party activity after 1950, which meant that the SISS was no more informed than the Whitfield grand jury had been.

As his interrogators peppered him with questions, West stood squarely on the Fifth Amendment, which led to a sometimes-testy interchange. Asked to identify himself as author of a CP organizing document, he answered firmly that he had "never seen nor heard that reading" and most certainly was not its author. A thoroughly unfriendly witness, West gave no ground and was finally dismissed after the committee contented itself with inserting extensive documentation on his political life into the record.[11] Among the most damaging entries was the product of faulty research by the Georgia Commission on Education (GCE), which had only recently launched a frontal attack on the Highlander Folk School in Monteagle. Established in 1953 to devise techniques to avoid the impending Supreme Court order on school desegregation, the GCE had by 1957 expanded its scope to include disseminating research material attacking integration, promoting massive resistance to the Brown decision, and exposing alleged subversive activity in the South. Probably the best-known product of this propaganda effort was a pamphlet attacking Highlander, which the commission linked with the civil rights movement and the communist conspiracy that threatened the "Georgia way of life." When Highlander planned a Labor Day program marking its twenty-fifth anniversary, the GCE sent a reporter-photographer to the event at Monteagle. Publishing a four-page broadside account of the program, the commission intended to "identify the leaders and participants of this Communist training school" and inform the general public in order to "combat this alien menace to Constitutional government."[12]

Among those figures prominently featured in the report were Don West, Aubrey Williams, Martin Luther King Jr., Myles Horton, folk singer Pete Seeger, and Abner Berry, an important black communist and *Daily Worker* correspondent. Although proud of his role in creating Highlander, West complained to Claude Williams about the GCE smear, which incorrectly placed him at the Labor Day celebration. The interaction of prominent civil rights leaders with a few communists was extensively displayed, together with images of interracial socializing that challenged the southern folkways the GCE hoped to preserve. Not only was the document widely disseminated among national newspapers, other state commissions, white citizen's councils, patriotic organizations, politicians, and businesspeople but the commission also shared its contents with the SISS and collaborated with the Eastland Committee's investigation before the Memphis hearings.[13] Signed by Georgia governor Marvin Griffin and billed as evidence that the civil rights movement was part of a communist conspiracy, the Highlander revelations and the clash in Memphis made West's position in Georgia even more precarious.

One of the first to exploit the story was his old comrade Charlie Pratt, whose retooled *Southerner* emphasized the Union Assembly's break with West and highlighted reports of his participation in the alleged "Communist training school" at Highlander. In the wake of recent events, the church organ now insisted that West was "well-known in the Northern part of Georgia for his Communistic and radical undertakings." Adopting the GCE tactic, it also viewed interracial fraternizing at Highlander as a prelude to further race hatred and violence in peace-loving Georgia.[14] Distancing himself from West, Pratt separated the Union Assembly from the preachers and educators then under GCE scrutiny as the "weakest links in the segregation chain." GCE executive T. V. Williams identified West as one of that group "engaged in ministerial studies and duties while advancing the Communist Party cause."[15]

Reeling under unending political pressure, West doggedly persisted in his attempt to support himself by selling farm produce in Atlanta. Simultaneously, he renewed his commitment to writing, publishing in *The New Southerner, The National Guardian*, and the new "Southern News Letter" issued in Louisville and edited by a former acquaintance, Eugene Feldman. He also returned to his long-standing interest in the flawed image of the southern mountaineer, which he tried to correct in "'Hill-Billy,' 'Plowboy,' 'Wool-Hats,' and 'Crackers,'" an attempt to deal with a subject he thought "misunderstood and misrepresented." While admitting that his people could sometimes be found among Klansmen and Citizens' Councils, he argued that they were not the primary source of race hatred, which could be traced to "those who own the wealth and means" to "twist the minds and spirits of the many." In a related shift, West also returned to his major project, a book dealing with the non-slaveholding whites of the antebellum South.[16]

Despite his desire to refocus his life, the tense political environment of cold war America made it impossible for West to achieve that goal. Not long after the Memphis hearings, the Klan burned crosses on his farm to serve notice that he was under observation. Troubled by these "nasty gestures," Don began to think the unthinkable. With no apparent alternative, he confided to Aubrey Williams, it might become necessary to sell the farm and relocate. In January 1958 he considered "selling out and leaving this confounded state." Uncharacteristically pessimistic, West sadly concluded that things had gotten "murky with hate and prejudice and ignorance."[17]

Just as the furor over Highlander and the SISS hearings subsided, the House Un-American Activities Committee (HUAC) launched an inquiry into "current techniques of the Communist Party operation," this time exploring the Party's inroads into the industrial areas of the South. In February 1958 West became the prime target of the American Legion's *Firing Line*, which publicized his political record, relying on material from Robert Morris, the SISS general counsel. Not long thereafter, West's name was placed on the docket as the HUAC prepared for its southern inquiry, scheduled for July 28 to 30, 1958, in Atlanta. As he contemplated the prospect of more testimony,

West was acutely aware that at that moment in Georgia history it was "worse to call a man an integrationist than to call him a Red," but "that issue was sure to be raised in one way or another."[18]

Before West could plot a course for the Atlanta hearings, however, an even greater personal crisis demanded immediate attention. On July 7, 1958, a telephone call from Bowling Green, Kentucky, informed him that Connie had been seriously injured in an automobile accident on her way back from the National Teachers Association convention in Cleveland. As she lay in hospital with a fractured skull and multiple broken bones in her face, Connie's survival was in grave doubt. Turning in desperation to Aubrey Williams, Don asked whether he thought it possible to be excused from the "damnable Un-American hearing" in view of the family crisis. Uncertain of his best legal strategy and in financial straits, he told Williams that he needed to talk with someone he could trust but that "in this spiritual Siberian desert over here there is no one."[19]

A faithful friend in this moment of crisis, Aubrey Williams advised Don to "stay by the bedside of [his] wife and tell the Committee to go and jump in the creek." He argued that since the HUAC had all the available information on him, the best course would be to "tell them very politely to go to hell." By this time a fatalist, Williams concluded that he and others like him would serve the liberal cause most effectively by serving jail time.[20] Despite the pessimism, Williams lodged a vigorous protest with Cong. James Roosevelt, intended to derail the Atlanta hearings by turning the tables with an investigation of the HUAC's intentions in the South. He told Roosevelt that there was plenty of un-American activity in the South, but that it was the result of Jim Crow, discrimination, and widespread violence against African Americans and liberal whites. Like West, he charged that "mere advocacy of equality for Negroes makes one a Communist" and that the primary victims of the smears were those who "openly stand with the Supreme Court." Aware of West's financial difficulties, Williams also helped establish a Don West fund administered by the Southern Conference Educational Fund (SCEF) in New Orleans.[21]

Under attack from the Legion, pursued by the HUAC, and concerned over his wife's grave injuries, West journeyed to Atlanta under arrest, supervised by a federal marshal who ignored his request to remain at Connie's bedside. Called to testify at a time when Connie's prognosis was uncertain at best, West suffered vilification from a hostile hearing-room crowd but was dismissed without taking the stand. Committee records suggest an element of harassment in the pursuit of West in view of the staff's long-held assumption that he would be an unfriendly Fifth Amendment witness, as evidenced by his Memphis appearance. When the HUAC excused him on July 29, 1958, the

FBI concluded that because he was "not considered a friendly witness, . . . it [was] not believed results of [a further] interview would be of value."[22]

The Bureau's analysis was on the mark. Don's first priority was now Connie, and his second concern the farm. At her side in Kentucky, he learned that her face had been horribly disfigured and months of convalescence would be required. In September, he took her to New York for consultation with a world-famous cosmetic surgeon, and later in the year she underwent several surgeries to repair damage to her face, a grueling regimen that kept her hospitalized in Louisville for weeks at a time. Although Connie suffered physically, the combination of her condition, financial stress, and a rapidly deteriorating situation in Douglasville also exacted an emotional toll on Don. As a result of the publicity surrounding the Atlanta hearings, the Klan and other troublemakers resumed their harassment in ever more petty ways: poisoned livestock, stolen equipment, and a dynamited dam. In December 1958 he admitted to George Weissman that the problem "makes a man sore, but sometimes little can be done to get at the bottom of the dirt because the dirt doers are themselves the 'investigators.'"[23]

West's momentary pessimism documented the reality of widespread fear in the South as the drive toward integration accelerated. It was a mean season for racial liberalism, and it took a toll on one of integration's staunchest proponents. In the words of Don's sister Belle, Don had more than "his share of trials and tribulations." Although Belle saw in her brother the "patience of Job," Don's patience was at an end. His correspondence was filled with announcements that he was ready to "close out" in Georgia and move to another state. In October he complained to Jim Dombrowski that Connie's accident and the Atlanta hearings had "set off a chain reaction of reversals and one bad piece of luck after another" that forced them to "look toward a new set up of some sort."[24]

By late 1958 West had come to see his plight as part of a larger pattern of violence and hatred sweeping the South, as evidenced by recent bombings of Atlanta synagogues. Both the temple incidents and the vigilante attacks on West's property expressed "the bombing and blasting spirit of our time and area." Years later Don remembered the McCarthy era as a period in which the "spirit of the thirties had just completely been beaten down." With few people willing to take a stand on any controversial issue, he waited for the heavy hand of government to fall, confident that his time of torment was imminent. With Sen. Joseph McCarthy and J. Edgar Hoover unleashed, "terror and fear" took hold, a "silent kind of thing" that moved Don toward noncooperation with congressional investigators. Although he recalled being "just one of many," he acknowledged damaging pressure on normal family relationships with the assertion that "it was a rough kind of life."[25]

Without a doubt, the Wests' road was rocky. With no other income in sight, Don resumed farming at Douglasville in 1959, where hunted political refugees sometimes found the West home a safe house in times of trouble. Although he stayed in touch with the New York Left and occasionally visited party offices in the city, he lived an isolated existence in an unobtrusive way. Connie was again teaching in Florida, but her world was shaken in May 1959 when her superintendent announced that due to Don's radical reputation she would not be rehired for the next year. Aware of the Atlanta hearings and the Highlander allegations, school officials in Florida considered Connie employable if divorced; her job performance was excellent. This news came on the heels of new medical reports of ruptured disks requiring spinal surgery. To Don, it seemed that the "poor girl [had] no end of tribulations."[26]

As a result of these setbacks West was finally ready to move out of Georgia. By November 1959 the family resided temporarily in New York at a Seventy-first Street apartment occupied by Hedy. Some FBI reports suggested that West sought employment in the New York public schools, and others maintained he had no visible means of support but traveled extensively between November 1959 and July 1960. Determined to restart his literary career in late 1959, West actively sought support for the projected Appalachian history book. By this time he had completed substantial preliminary research and was preparing to work on the full manuscript. Weary of a marginal existence, he longed to concentrate on writing.[27] To that end, he concluded that grant support might provide at least partial maintenance until he was able to find permanent employment again.

By June 1960 he had identified a possible source of financial support in the left-leaning Louis M. Rabinowitz Foundation in New York. With letters of endorsement from Aubrey Williams and C. Vann Woodward as well as concrete interest from Alfred A. Knopf in New York, West proposed to complete a book on the "anti-slavery, loyalist pro-Union thought in the South prior to and during the Civil War, particularly the people of the Appalachian South." Of the proposal and its author Williams wrote, "I have never known him to trim, or to sacrifice truth no matter how strong the pressures were for expediency. . . . He is one of those rare individuals in which is combined a fine intelligence with a clear social evaluator." In agreement with this assessment, the foundation awarded West $3,000 to pursue his research in July 1960, thus providing needed financial relief at a moment of transition.[28] Once again West returned to the world of scholarship and teaching.

Renewed work on the manuscript resulted in a dual benefit. Not only did it enable him to revive his acquaintance with eminent southern historian C. Vann Woodward, but extended stays in the Baltimore-Washington area also eased Connie's access to specialists at the Johns Hopkins University Hospital. The back surgery had been unsuccessful, which mandated treatment only available at a major medical facility. As a result, the Wests divided time between Douglasville, Blairsville, and Baltimore in 1960. Impressed by Woodward's work on racial amelioration, which he thought "could tie our land and our world together as civilized men," West benefited from the scholar's counsel as he pursued research at the Library of Congress and National Archives.[29]

More important from a financial standpoint was Connie's success in finding a teaching job in the Baltimore County school system. Starting in September 1960, she began teaching art in the Baltimore schools while Don worked on the book. The following year he secured a position teaching economics at the Talmudical Academy of Baltimore, a rabbinical training institution for orthodox Jews. For several years Don headed the social studies department and worked with young men, many of whom he found as prejudiced against African Americans as any poor white in rural Georgia. West thoroughly enjoyed the unique position because it enabled him to help young people understand that lynch mobs in Georgia targeted Jews as well as blacks, as in the infamous Leo Frank case. Eventually, his agitation for racial inclusion led the academy to hire its first African American, an English teacher.[30] Once again Don West had made a difference in the lives of the young.

Not long after establishing permanent residence in Baltimore, West sustained a blow that shook his faith in human nature to the core. In February 1961, while Don was at work in the Library of Congress, word arrived that his home in Georgia had been torched and destroyed by fire. Three structures were gone, but the most tragic outcome was the complete loss of West's library of ten thousand books, including a valuable collection willed to him by Olive Tilford Dargan. Dargan, a leftist novelist whose politics matched Don's had entrusted a large cache of books and manuscripts to him in an effort to avoid the fate that befell them on the West property. The fire was therefore doubly tragic in that it destroyed material that shed light on the careers of not one but two literary artists. West told his old friend Bert Gilden that he was "heartsick" and "dazed" over the fire, which left him "shaken with anger and disgust" over the "low-lifed, underhanded blow." Recalling Ralph McGill' ongoing smear campaign against him, Don noted that McGill "took care always to indicate just the specific location of my place." As much as anyone West "lay responsibility for this disaster to him" although he later speculated that the Klan was involved in the incident.[31] Even a retreat to the North, it seemed, could not insulate Don West from the incidental consequences of his personal history.

While living in Baltimore, West also reentered the academic world as a graduate student in education, first at the Johns Hopkins University's Mc-Coy College of Education and later at the University of Maryland in College Park, where he served as an instructor in education. Between 1963 and 1964 he worked as a student-teacher supervisor and graduate teaching assistant for the university's College of Education while also teaching at the McDonough School in Baltimore and Madison College in Harrisonburg, Virginia. Because the West children were independent and Connie earned a full salary, it now became possible to save for the future.[32] The Baltimore years were those of urban exile, a period of waiting for an opportunity to pursue Don's lifelong dream of building a folk school for the people of Appalachia.

During his years in the Maryland borderlands West was again drawn into the left-wing political movements that grew rapidly in the early 1960s as college students throughout the United States became political activists. One of the few "Old Left" figures to embrace the New Left, he endorsed the identity politics associated with the civil rights and antiwar movements, including black power and the American Indian movement. Although he remained suspicious of middle-class radical youth as transitory warriors, West served as a bridge between the activism of the past and that of the future. He also made periodic forays into the depressed areas of Appalachia to assess the Kennedy-Johnson programs to alleviate regional economic distress. At this time he encouraged the southern-born civil rights activist and SCEF leader Anne Braden to accelerate the organization's Appalachian initiatives after the African American leadership began moving toward black control of the movement. West told Braden that uplifting the poor whites of the South was a "prerequisite to any stable future for civil rights," a reality that made the SCEF's new focus critical to the movement for social justice in America. Although he acknowledged having been driven from his home country, he grimly insisted that he was "not giving up—never will."[33]

It was this determination that brought him to the Students for a Democratic Society (SDS) national council meeting at Pine Hill, New York, in 1962. There, West addressed a group of young skeptics, often disrespectful of the Old Left and suspicious of anyone over thirty. He applauded the youthful radicals for their idealism and dedication but warned that real progress required long-term commitment. His quiet demeanor and message of hope won him the grudging admiration of a new progressive generation. Don's commitment to the advancement of Appalachian people impressed those youthful activists who were determined to work for the preservation of mountain values within a framework of economic freedom. Always committed to an alternative social system, West was willing to transcend artificial boundaries and create new alliances to aid mountain people displaced by the ravenous industrial economy of modern America.[34]

As faculty adviser to the SDS chapter at the University of Maryland in 1964, West assumed the role of elder statesman, providing low-key guidance and counseling patience and determination in the quest for social change. By the time of the SDS national convention in June 1964, West had gained sufficient support to be an invited discussant at a session on the role of radicals in past, present, and future community organizing. Following this meeting, he told Claude Williams that he was greatly encouraged by "the way these students from colleges and universities all over America had gathered and were seriously searching for truth and determined to do something about it."[35]

A parallel development at this time was the organization of the Southern Student Organizing Committee (SSOC) to assess the needs of students on southern college campuses and launch a program to engage them in the struggle for civil rights. Acting in coordination with the SDS, the SSOC intended to "serve as the nerve center of the Southern movement" that would "reach into isolated Southern campuses and guide liberal students into the mainstream of the student movement." After a preliminary session in Nashville in April 1964, more than forty activists met in Atlanta the following month to create a permanent organization to bring southern students into the movement and establish a fraternal relationship with the SDS and Student Non-Violent Coordinating Committee. By November, the body had grown strong enough to field a conference in Atlanta attended by 144 students from forty-three southern campuses. An invited speaker at the SSOC conference, West discussed "The South of the Thirties and Forties" and provided historical background on the southern economy. He found the meeting stimulating, especially the implications of "native white Southern students seriously gathered to discuss and plan to labor for less prejudice and more understanding."[36]

Although the quickening of student activism encouraged West, his deepest interests in the early 1960s were in Appalachia and its forgotten people displaced by the onrush of industrial development. The clearest expression of that commitment was his growing interest in the Committee for Miners, an organization formed in 1963 to provide legal aid and economic assistance to unemployed miners in eastern Kentucky. Originally intended to raise funds for eight jobless miners accused of conspiracy to dynamite the L&N railroad bridge in Perry County, Kentucky, its purpose soon expanded to encompass protection of the rights of the unemployed in the depressed area around Hazard. To that end, West made numerous visits to Kentucky in 1963 and 1964 to confer with the local committee and assess economic needs. His major contribution was fund-raising for miners' relief, but by September 1964 he became disillusioned with the committee's unwillingness to make a substantial investment in the Hazard project. In 1964 Hedy joined the fund-raising effort with a series of benefit concerts in the Baltimore-Washington area. Equally committed to advancing social justice for Appalachian miners, she donated proceeds from record sales to the Appalachian Committee for Full Employment and in April 1964 performed at four area colleges and universities, committing all funds raised to the miners' organization. The result was music that "vitalize[d]" the miners' stories and "[brought] their meaning alive," an outcome in part related to Don's encouragement but more attributable to the trajectory of Hedy's social consciousness and personal commitment to the cause of Appalachian people.[37] Like her father (and partly due to his sometimes intrusive influence), Hedy had become interested in the use of folk music to reconfirm the self-respect of mountain people. Not the least of her concerns was the mercenary exploitation of folk themes by a "booming folk-pop industry" that generated "tremendous income" but returned "precious little of it" to those whose cultures "produced the folk material."[38] Benefit concerts were one way she attempted to redress the imbalance.

Although Don's primary interests never strayed far from Appalachia, other problems drew his attention, especially in 1964, a pivotal year for not only American politics but also the foreign policy of the United States. An outspoken critic of the Johnson administration's intervention in Vietnam, which he regarded as the logical extension of American imperialism, West feared descent into nuclear war. After the Gulf of Tonkin incident in August 1964 he denounced Johnson's "misdoings in Vietnam."[39] A student of domestic reform, West concluded that the most tragic aspect of the Vietnam War was its corrosive impact on the African American leadership of the civil rights movement, which failed to provide "leadership against the imperialist policy and actions against colonial peoples all of which are colored in one hue or another." Unless Martin Luther King Jr. and others bucked U.S. imperialism, he argued, "no basic and permanent changes [would be] effected on the domestic front." In his view, King had a wonderful opportunity to "teach a tremendously important truth" about American imperialism, which might actually justify a peace prize.[40]

Closer to home, West was plagued with doubts concerning Connie's deteriorating physical condition. In 1963, after breast cancer was detected, she underwent major surgery at the Johns Hopkins Medical Center, which was followed by months of exhausting therapy. Worse yet, she was given little chance of long-term survival, a diagnosis that colored Don's outlook on life. Despite a painful regimen, however, she proved remarkably resilient and remained in good spirits, producing some of her best art work. In September 1964 Don confessed to Claude Williams that the "poor girl . . . suffer[ed] more and more," a stark reality that left him "terribly bothered."[41]

Because of Connie's dependence on the medical facilities available at Johns Hopkins, as well as the financial advantages of employment opportunity in the Baltimore-Washington area, the Wests were place-bound and Don was forced to "stay and stew." Behind that terse comment lay a long-term plan to refocus his attention on the Appalachian South and eventually remove to the mountains. For ten years, one salary had been saved with an eye to the day when the years of exile would come to an end.[42]

By 1964 Don had become restless and weary of city life, which he had always detested, and in January he wrote to Bert Gilden of his determination to get back to the South, where he could "tell the story of the people." By this time he was deeply engaged in a plan to edit a regional journal, to be published by a cooperative of "hillbillies" located somewhere in the mountains. With all the contemporary concern about depressed areas, he thought such a publication would "take roots" once he reestablished himself in Appalachia.[43]

West thought the moment was right to launch the project that was eventually to become *Appalachian South*. Although he never regarded his position at Maryland as permanent, it enabled him to complete a large body of research on Appalachian history that was sure to be useful in the kind of journal he contemplated. His plan was not to make it a "radical thing" with "old worn-out phrases" but to stress the "rape of natural and human resources that was the genuine radical story." It was essential that the publication provide an accurate voice for the "folk" Don thought grossly misrepresented in the media, notably by "yankee progressives" and "city slicker folk singer groups." Still nursing his lifetime grudge against outsiders, the New York "muck hole," and Madison Avenue's "fast buck artists," he railed against the mischaracterization of poor whites as ignorant racists rather than victims of vicious stereotypes. Increasingly unhappy in Baltimore, West turned to Connie in 1965 and proposed an early retirement that would allow him to plan for the next stage in their lifelong journey together. After discussing the logistics of a change, they agreed that Don would retire and return to the South and Connie would work for a transitional period. As she had done so many times, she was to send Don money while he searched the West Virginia mountains for a suitable location not too far from Ann's residence in Charleston.[44] Fired with enthusiasm for an educational project that promised to elevate Appalachian history to a new level and instill in mountain people pride in cultural heritage, Don West set off for one more adventure that was to end in the final, climactic chapter in a variegated professional life.

part four

Coming Home:
Appalachia Again

thirteen

Pipestem: Old Left, New Left, and a New Educational Activism, 1966–82

Throughout a long career as preacher, teacher, organizer, and poet Don West never gave up his dream of an educational institution based on the Danish folk school model that so impressed him during his college years. The confrontation with Myles Horton over the direction of Highlander left him embittered, especially as the school matured and public awareness of his own pivotal role in its establishment became obscured, not entirely by accident. Moreover, the years of urban exile fueled West's determination to return to the mountains where he might fulfill his mission to counteract the stereotyping of mountaineers and build pride in culture among Appalachian youths. Although he continued teaching at Madison College in Harrisonburg, Virginia, after leaving the University of Maryland, his thoughts and energies soon turned toward the establishment of a new folk school. By spring 1966, Don was circulating a proposal for an educational program aimed at the academic reclamation of dropout students from southern Appalachia. Located at Pipestem, West Virginia, on a three-hundred-acre plot of land he acquired, the new school would be open to the children of mountain families and the rural poor, both black and white, who were to come on scholarship to a welcoming environment where they might be exposed to history, literature, and the arts, with complementary emphasis on folk art and traditional skills. West's highest priority was to provide educational enrichment to disadvantaged young people; in practice, that meant that a large portion of the students came from mining families whose need was great. The new Appalachian South Folklife Center (ASFC) focused on regional history, geography, economics, cultural awareness, and values-based education. His concept of "education by purposeful experience" emphasized frequent visits to cultural sites as well as regular participation in creative writing, editing, publishing, and artistic endeavors—all aimed at cultivating the whole person as a logical being with a commitment to human values.[1]

Don and Connie were intent upon offering a program distinct from most folk schools then in operation. Determined to build a unique institution, they relied heavily on the Danish model. The projected program, which would stress cultural awareness, was "dedicated to a mountain heritage of freedom, self respect and independence with human dignity to the end that people of all races, faiths, [and] nationalities may better understand one another's religion and culture and work and live together for peace, brotherhood, and plenty for all." The project was designed to attack problems missed by the Johnson administration's War on Poverty, which West believed to be aimed at the symptoms rather than the causes of Appalachia's problems. The Folklife Center focused on the restoration of self-respect and human dignity lost as a consequence of the region's colonial relationship with industrial America over a century's time. West proposed to use the "values of the traditional mountain culture" and a new awareness of Appalachia's place in history to rekindle the self-confidence of mountain people. By cultivating a sense of cultural pride among the young, he hoped to encourage mountain youths to remain in the mountains to "build a better Appalachian South."[2]

Although grimly determined to succeed, West was painfully aware of the potential obstacles, primarily financial. In a request for support from the Southern Conference Educational Fund (SCEF), he told civil rights activist and SCEF director Carl Braden that because he felt "stymied" in his "regular job" at Madison College he was willing to gamble and invest his personal resources at Pipestem. By April 1966 West had assembled a broad coalition of supporters who lent their names to the initial appeal for funding. Among his backers were Kentucky lawyer Harry M. Caudill, environmental activist Gordon K. Ebersole, journalist William C. Blizzard of the *Charleston Gazette* James L. Hupp of the West Virginia Archives, state senator Paul Kaufman dean Cratis Williams of Appalachian State College, editor Harry Golden of the *Carolina Israelite*, and several other figures from the world of regional journalism and music. Although Carl and Anne Braden found much to be admired in West's proposal, the SCEF's financial resources were sufficiently depleted to make a grant impossible at the time. They did agree to consider a fund-raising effort in the fall, and as an interim measure they forwarded West's appeal to James A. Dombrowski, who was in the process of setting up the Aubrey Williams Memorial Fund, another possible source of support. In response, Dombrowski told the Bradens that "you must admire the spirit of the guy" who, despite a long history of personal reverses, was "still able to come up with such a grand design for the good life."[3]

Despite the financial problems, West proceeded with his plans for the Folklife Center, which were not intended to bear fruit until the following year. Meanwhile, he worked to build *Appalachian South* into an open forum for discussing regional problems from a radical perspective. Even more significant was a more comprehensive project that took shape in 1966, the new Congress for Appalachian Development (CAD), an organization intended to break the colonial relationship that bound Appalachia's human and economic resources to eastern corporate interests. By embracing the concept of public utility districts (PUDs), CAD worked to restore regional economic independence through public ownership and control of natural resources. Deeply imbedded in this promising initiative was a shared commitment to renewing self-respect and affirming human dignity that were the hallmarks of the Pipestem experiment. Don West was a key figure in the organization and direction of CAD from the very beginning.[4]

West maintained that CAD grew out of *Appalachian South* magazine, but the origins of the organization may actually be traced to earlier collaboration between Caudill, Ebersole, and native Appalachian Ed Fraley, all of whom joined West in seeking a solution to the problem of regional colonial dependency. As early as January 1966, Caudill was preparing an article for *Appalachian South* calling for the creation of PUDs in Kentucky and West Virginia. With that goal in mind, Caudill wrote to West to propose organizing "sentiment for dynamic change on the college campuses" aimed at breaking the corporate grip on Appalachia. In August, when CAD's preliminary organizational meeting was in the planning stages, Caudill urged Ed Fraley to be sure that West was present.[5]

The CAD initiative surfaced at a critical moment in the history of both federal concern over Appalachian development and grass-roots organizing to combat the region's ingrained economic problems. Although the Kennedy-Johnson programs for area redevelopment and an attack on poverty had failed to deliver, indigenous movements had yet to fill the power vacuum. The Hazard project to assist unemployed miners had essentially collapsed by 1966, and the SCEF's new Southern Mountain Project had not had time to fulfill its promise. As the black power movement emerged, the Student Non-Violent

Coordinating Committee (SNCC) urged white radicals to refocus their efforts on the task of organizing persons of their own color, which prompted new emphasis on Appalachia and provided a new coterie of enthusiastic volunteers for service in the movement. Initially interracial in character, organizing teams were increasingly dominated by whites as blacks enlisted in SNCC under the banner of black nationalism. These refugees from organizing in the Deep South often clashed with their Appalachian host communities, and turnover escalated. Nonetheless, in 1966 West concurred in SNCC's judgment that its white members could best serve the cause of civil rights by working with poor whites in common cause. He later wrote to Anne Braden to express "sympathy with the black militants who finally told the whites to go do their own thing." West linked the new focus on organizing working-class whites with the need for mountain people to develop "self identity and awareness," which had always been his goal.[6] He resented the Left's attitude that organizing blacks must take priority in the South, a perspective that left poor whites to the likes of Lester Maddox, George Wallace, and the KKK. In his view, the problem of race would not be solved until "a sizable number of whites" were prepared to "go to bat on common problems" that confronted the American underclass across racial lines.[7]

Disillusioned over the flagging War on Poverty, West saw greater hope for CAD, which reflected a strong grass-roots determination to bring about social change through alternatives to capitalism. The new organization was an outgrowth of an informal meeting of Appalachian activists held at Bristol Virginia, in response to an invitation from Ed Fraley and Harry Caudill, who had discussed with Don the need for a new mechanism by which "Appalachian resources [could] be utilized for the benefit of the people within the area." Caudill's proposal for creating a PUD that would own coal mines and supply public power was, in fact, the same idea he explored with West and published in the summer issue of *Appalachian South*. More significant was creating a planning committee, of which West was a member, and deciding to hold a formal organizational meeting in Charleston, West Virginia, where CAD came into being.[8]

West was named to the planning committee, but his selection occurred in his absence due to a broken leg suffered in an auto accident en route to Bristol. For some of the organizers, West's high-profile participation seemed a mixed blessing. Reflecting on the outcome, his close friend Ed Fraley told Caudill that Don's presence on the committee could become controversial. When issuing invitations, Fraley intentionally omitted Ralph McGill from the list recognizing that "it might not be healthy for him to be in the same room with Don," whom he had been "hounding and harassing" for thirty years. Fraley went on to argue that in view of the activists' radical plans, coal companies and corporate interests were certain to be looking for "an Achilles heel" in the organization, some individual who might be labeled subversive and thereby undermine the entire effort. Despite admiration for West, Fraley concluded that his selection for the committee had been a strategic error that might be corrected by limiting the body to the original eight.[9] Such concerns aside, West took part in the October meeting in Charleston before diplomatically declining nomination to the steering committee.

Although the Bristol meeting and plans for a new organization were promising, some aspects of the session disappointed West. He wrote to Myles Horton that he preferred to see more miners and unemployed workers represented. Worse yet, he feared that as members of the more conservative Council for the Southern Mountains (CSM), some participants, such as Fraley, would be unwilling to mount a radical challenge to the economic order. Horton quickly responded with his own misgivings and for essentially the same reasons. At Bristol, Horton had argued that the new organization must be "fundamentally different" from the CSM to avoid duplication of effort. Moreover, he insisted, no program would work unless planners could "get to the people—the poor and the workers" and asked why they had not been invited to Bristol. Despite his estrangement from West, Horton joined with him to push CAD toward deeper engagement with grass-roots organizers while endorsing the experiment at Pipestem, which seemed the fulfillment of their long-delayed dream of multiple folk schools throughout the South.[10]

Plagued by doubts, West approached the Charleston meeting with a personal agenda. Four days before the session he wrote to Carl Braden to express his conviction that any program for the organization of Appalachia's poor must have a strong educational component. Convinced that unions had failed, he argued that the poor "must be stirred to the meaning of values . . . to think about what values [were] really worth centering a life effort on." Certain that the masses had "more wisdom than they are generally given credit for," he proposed a radical education program to elevate the human spirit while helping the poor retain their distinctiveness without accepting middle-class values.[11]

True to his word, he told the Charleston delegates that the primary problem lay in "awakening the interest of the poor" and mobilizing their support for the CAD agenda. When some participants doubted the political feasibility of public ownership, West responded that innovation was essential if poverty were to be eradicated. After extensive discussion he moved for the adoption of the name Congress for Appalachian Development, which was accepted on unanimous vote. Persuaded that the organization held potential for meaningful economic change, West also agreed to serve as one of five incorporators, once formal articles were drawn up by West Virginia state senator Paul Kaufman (West's name soon disappeared from the list). The body pledged to launch new educational programs, build communications skills, and speak for the millions in Appalachia who had "missed connections as our nation has moved from the industrial revolution into the space age." In words reminiscent of West's mantra, the congress promised to "motivate the mountaineer and re-instill the independence of which he once prided himself." Just as the CIO had spoken for labor in the 1930s, CAD would become the voice of Appalachia and expand the buying power of a "resource-rich, but poverty-stricken Appalachian region."[12]

The decision to omit West's name from the board of directors named in January at Abingdon, Virginia, although politically expedient, angered Harry Caudill, who wrote to Don to promise that the error would be rectified. After West left the Charleston meeting, Caudill argued that he more than anyone else had been the "inspirer" of the "whole movement" through the advocacy efforts of *Appalachian South*. By February 1967 West had reluctantly accepted a position on the board, not wishing to be seen as a "slacker." Still uncomfortable with the group's middle-class orientation, he told Horton that CAD was "overloaded with experts" but might just succeed if they could get some "common folk" involved. He agreed to serve because "for the first time it look[ed] like something real [was] under way, something that [would] attract support."[13]

West wasted little time in advancing his own agenda. First, he devoted the next issue of *Appalachian South* to CAD. His front-page editorial portrayed it as a body ready to "use the tools of a democratic society" to "meet the challenge of an age of cybernetics and technology." To West, the organization's significance lay in the willingness of mountain leaders to engage in serious discussion over a response to "rampant corporate greed" based upon "economic planning and public ownership of basic resources."[14] To implement this principle, however, he also insisted that the poor be mobilized along the lines he and Horton advocated. In 1967 West wrote to Caudill, whom he believed to share his views, with a proposal to organize the "one-gallused" farmers and workers upon whose support CAD's future depended. The answer, he thought lay in an alliance with the Bradens and SCEF, an organization committed to grass-roots organizing and capable of engaging the poor in their own communities. West proposed that CAD collaborate with the SCEF's Southern Mountain Project to generate "genuine organization among the poor."[15]

Meanwhile, West worked to engage the SCEF in the activities of CAD. Since Charleston, he had badgered Carl Braden with concerns about the fledgling group's middle-class character as well as his determination to move the organization toward grass-roots activity among the poor. Although he continued to hope that the Southern Mountain Project would encourage young volunteers to concentrate on troubled mountain communities, he growled about the physical appearance and demeanor of workers previously sent into the mountains: "Some see it as a chance to flout custom and take every opportunity to shock by showing how non-conforming they are. Such inevitably alienate and destroy poor people's unity potential." In a letter to the Bradens, he noted that to some young radicals, CAD's middle-class membership made it irrelevant to the solution of regional problems. Far from it, he argued, the body was moving toward engagement with the poor, a trend that already aroused the suspicion of conservatives in the Council for the Southern Mountains. West's position was that all progressive forces must cooperate in the fight against corporate power and external control, which meant the SCEF and CAD must be allied in a drive to raise the economic and political consciousness of Appalachia's have-nots.[16]

Hoping to solidify that relationship, West solicited Anne Braden's endorsement of CAD and urged Caudill to pursue collaboration, especially since the SCEF's grass-roots focus complemented CAD's troublesome middle-class composition. He proposed that Anne and Carl attend the next board meeting to explore avenues of cooperation in organizing mountain communities. In her tardy response, an overworked Anne Braden expressed exasperation over Don's tendency to be somewhat "hyper-critical of the human weaknesses" in all active people but accepted his plan for her to attend CAD's board meeting.[17] The Bradens missed the meeting, but Bob Zellner of the SCEF spoke to CAD and made a positive impression, thus opening an avenue for an alliance. Meanwhile, Braden informed Caudill that she had been following CAD's progress and that the SCEF was ready to cooperate in any way with the new organization.[18]

While Gordon Ebersole, Harry Caudill, and others worked with federal agencies as well as UAW and other union groups to generate financial support, the CAD board struggled unsuccessfully to broaden the organization and mobilize the elusive "one-gallus" folk whom West and Horton thought essential to any movement toward public ownership. Their efforts were doomed to failure because establishment organizations like the Area Redevelopment Administration, Appalachian Regional Commission, and Council for the Southern Mountains distanced themselves from the radical ideas circulating in the mountain colonies. Nor did the hoped-for grass-roots activism materialize, in part due to a top-down organizational structure that undercut local initiative. At its March meeting, under pressure from West, Horton, and the Rev. Richard Austin, a Presbyterian social activist, the CAD board laid plans to rescue the floundering organization by holding an Appalachian People's Congress, which would meet during the summer months. Even that initiative was hampered by internal differences evident in the contrast between the Ebersole-Caudill hopes for an array of "speakers of outstanding experience" and the West-Austin emphasis on a more open expression of grass-roots concerns. In the end, the body issued a call to a congress "so that the people may speak out on their needs" and develop a program for regional development through "participatory democracy."[19]

The idea of the People's Congress, despite West's hopes, was stillborn. At the first planning session, conferees agreed that they lacked sufficient representation from indigenous community action groups to issue a credible call to congress and instead urged interested organizations to do so on a state basis should they be so inclined. Some participants, including the Appalachian Volunteers, CAD, and CSM, planned for a summer congress in Frakes, Kentucky, but financial support was nowhere to be found and state level interest lagged. Although he still hoped the event could be salvaged, by July even Caudill sensed that CAD was at a "crossroad" and its survival in doubt. By August it was obvious that the congress would not meet, but that failure did not discourage diehards from opening discussion of the best way to resurrect the idea the following year. Under the leadership of Austin and the Appalachian Volunteers' Milton Ogle, CAD again proposed a summer gathering in 1968 but only if it was the product of grass-roots planning along lines long urged by West, Horton, and Austin.[20]

West recognized that there was "some discouragement" concerning CAD's future but reminded the Caudills that they "[could] not expect to move Rome in a day." Still enthusiastic about the idea of a People's Congress, West told the CAD board in October that the West Virginia state congress had been the "most significant meeting in Appalachia in modern times."[21] Despite the optimism, the People's Congress was an idea whose time had passed. The same could be said for CAD, which limped along for a few years in search of financial backing that was not to be found. While it had raised the public power issue in a compelling fashion, won a few minor victories, and opened a conversation on effective resource management, it never became the militant people's movement envisioned by West. However, as David Whisnant observed in 1972, CAD offered the "most hopeful program" for Appalachia to date, largely because it cut to the heart of the regional problem: "public ownership of public wealth, and its development for the public good."[22] These words echoed sentiments central to Don West's long-held vision of social organization and production for use.

Although the promise of CAD captured West's imagination, his majo concern after 1965 was to establish the Folklife Center and explore funding mechanisms that would sustain a program largely financed by personal savings and Connie's continued income-earning capacity. Almost immediately it became obvious that a rationale for tax exemption would be critical to Pipestem's future. Consequently, it made perfect sense to link the educational program with the social goals always present in West's religious commitment to the "revolutionary Jesus" and the "religion of man." The absence of a clear denominational tie presented an awkward logistical problem, at least until Don encountered the Universal Christian Church, a new group headquartered in Baltimore and coordinated by the Rev. Marlin Ballard of that city.

Well out of the religious mainstream, this body was decidedly short on theological underpinnings and long on humanistic social concern. The church's doctrine, wholly compatible with West's religious views, was essentially "nonsectarian" and committed to creating a "world fellowship" based on Christian brotherhood, tolerance, and charity. Avowedly opposed to proselytizing, the group embraced the "warm human love and concern" taught and practiced by a Jesus whose promotion of "peace and brotherly feeling" was "basic to being human." Noting that those who "actually live the spirit of Jesus" sometimes turn against "institutionalized faith," West eagerly embraced a church that had "no ambition to convert others" but worked to strengthen the faith of its members.[23] In 1967 this small, intensely humanistic religious community ordained Don West the "Bishop of Pipestem and Southern Appalachia" and, according to Horton, "sponsored" his new educational program. Not incidentally, it also provided the basis for the Folklife Center's sorely needed tax exemption.[24]

West's adherence to the Universal Christian Church underscored the distance he had traveled in his personal religious odyssey since his youthful exposure to the practical faith of Larkin Chastain and Alva Taylor's living Social Gospel. By the time he relocated in West Virginia, West had abandoned traditional Christian religion for his own brand of humanistic commitment to follow the path trod by the man, Jesus, whose life was a model of charity, social concern, and revolutionary fire. Most of West's friends recall his unorthodox beliefs as devoid of references to the divinity of Jesus or God. Many saw him as a proponent of self-help along the path to a better world in the here and now. Late in life in a private moment he frankly acknowledged to his daughter Hedy that he had become, for all practical purposes, an atheist who adhered to personal moral precepts influenced by early religious teachings, family instruction, intellectual exercise, and his personal perception of Jesus. Some observers have argued that, for West, the moral teachings of the early Marx and a lifelong commitment to socialism essentially replaced the homespun Christianity of his childhood. None of that prevented him from employing religion and religious institutions in efforts to validate mountain culture and liberate farmers, workers, and minorities from the poverty and injustice that was their lot. He understood mountain people and their commitment to personal, emotional religion and respected their religious practices and beliefs. Consequently, he was welcome as a preacher in local churches, effective in his own chapel, comfortable with the use of Jesus as a model in his teaching, and inspirational as a speaker.[25] Few students and colleagues would deny that West's commanding presence and charisma were capable of producing a life-changing experience, nor that the message, although secular and militant, owed much to the religious roots of his lifetime encounter with Jesus. It was Don's remarkable power to influence people that sustained the Folklife Center in its formative years.

With $30,000 invested and a commitment to experiential education, West hoped to make his lifelong dream a reality. Collecting farm machinery, constructing buildings, founding a library, and launching a publication program, he readied the Folklife Center for the active programming that began in 1968. In that year, when Connie retired to join Don at the center, the first summer camp brought fifty-five students to Pipestem for a tuition-free program geared to the needs of children at risk and dropouts. Its goal was to facilitate reentry into the academic system while cultivating sound values usable in turbulent times. As a follow-up, the Wests also held the First Annual Appalachian South Folk Festival, which blended traditional music, mountain culture, and the grass-roots dimension of the ill-fated People's Congress. Over the years, the Folk Festival evolved into a major event that attracted not only renowned performers such as Pete Seeger, Merle Travis, and Hedy West but also the finest regional performers of traditional Appalachian music. In 1970 the folk music scholar-activist Archie Green kept a log of the event, which he described as "unstructured" and "elastic," characterized by a high degree of "spontaneity." More than a series of musical performances, the festival combined political engagement, social activism, nondenominational religious commitment, and, for Green, a "get-acquainted-with-the Appalachian movement" experience.[26]

From the late 1960s on, the ASFC program expanded to incorporate citizenship training, cultural history, volunteer activity for religious groups, community organizing, outreach education, and sociopolitical activism. Focusing on its host communities, West soon became local coordinator for the worldwide Heifer Project, which gave $200,000 worth of livestock to needy families in West Virginia, Virginia, and Georgia. Although he understood that the project would not "solve poor people's need," he thought it would "build understanding of the need to cooperate, work together, have a little more faith in fellow worker-poor people's capacity to be concerned for a bit more than the purely selfish." Above all, Pipestem was dedicated to awakening pride in culture among the children of the Appalachian poor by providing an educational environment that encouraged self-discovery through experience. The program focused on cultural preservation, practical education, and academic rescue but always contained a strong social justice component that challenged students of all ages to embrace brotherhood. In that sense, West's goal was to "train revolutionaries." A revolutionary, Don maintained, is "one who wants to change ugly conditions to more positive humane conditions" and promote a "turnover from the kind of regime that may be rotten and corrupt."[27] Though muted, that objective mirrored West's lifelong dedication to political, economic, and social change on a socialist model informed by a Marxist analysis of American capitalism and the toll it exacted from the poor. At the Folklife Center, he hoped to not only raise participant consciousness of Appalachian culture and corporate exploitation of mountain people and their resources but also to encourage development of the necessary will to change circumstances through direct action.[28]

Although the revolutionary implications of West's objectives were subtle, the program and his history of activism soon drew the attention of local critics. He maintained cordial relations with neighbors, but there was always an undercurrent of discontent over the activities at the ASFC. Especially damaging was the uninformed reaction of the *Princeton Times* and its young editor David Pedneau, who launched a barrage of critical editorials attacking the Folklife Center as a "hippie camp" likely to became a regional center for "activism and leftist teaching." West recalled critics' descriptions of a "free love colony" and an outright "Communist cell," neither of which was accurate.[29]

The allegations were sufficient to engage the attention of both senators Jennings Randolph and Robert Byrd, who called on the FBI to supply evidence of any radical activity at the Folklife Center. None was forthcoming, but Randolph made a friendly investigative visit to Pipestem and Byrd learned that the center had never been cited as subversive by the Senate Internal Security Subcommittee.[30] Although FBI watchdogs monitored West's activities into the 1970s the search for subversive activity was fruitless.

The paucity of hard evidence did not deter local patriots, who continued to hound West and the Pipestem program. In Summers County, the ad hoc Citizens Committee for the Prevention of Anti-American Infiltration into Summers County reprinted the *Times* attack as a paid advertisement. In Nitro, the *Kanahwa County Leader* charged that West was involved in "more dirt than farming." Not to be outdone, Charleston right-wingers established a "Truth about Civil Turmoil" Committee (TACT) that entertained Donald L.

Jackson, a member of Congress from California, who served on the House Un-American Activities Committee (HUAC), for an evening of anticommunist revel. Led by investment broker Herbert W. Stone, TACT made exposing Don West's radical past its primary goal and speculated that West hoped to persuade the young to "commit their lives to the Communist conspiracy." Moreover, by this time both West and Horton had become "popular subjects of insinuations at the Kentucky Un-American Activities hearings" held in Pikeville during the same week.[31]

These assaults induced West to again deny that he had ever been a member of the Communist Party, an understandable but disingenuous response to the relentless attacks. In Charleston, he told a Unitarian Church convention that he was "annoyed" at being forced to issue such denials. Boldly standing on his record of lifelong social activism, he pled guilty to premature social concern and literary exposure of poverty. When approached by attorneys proposing a libel suit against the *Princeton Times*, West refused. Nor would he waste his energy defending himself: "If my life can't speak for me, then I think my tongue's a pretty feeble instrument to defend myself with."[32]

The specter of subversion fueled the opposition, but even more alarming to some observers was the image of cultural radicalism conveyed by the free-spirited, long-haired inhabitants of the 1960s' counterculture, many of whom found their way to Pipestem, especially during the folk festivals. Several of West's supporters recalled that the "hippie" types who often gathered at the Folklife Center enraged local residents, giving the ASFC what Don Rasmussen adjudged the "worst possible local publicity he could have gotten." Included in the outsiders who came to Appalachia were "movement people" who committed themselves to community organizing among the poor. About them, West was somewhat conflicted in that he respected their idealism but resented their condescension and disapproved of their tendency to offend local residents with their dress, habits, and moral relativism. He came to feel that the youthful radicals of the 1960s were "infantile" in that their effort to appear different from mainstream Americans only created a "barrier" that hampered "communication with common people." In a letter to Claude Williams he dismissed the youth "stuff" that only "turn[ed] people off rather than building unity for struggle." By 1971 his view of "student invasions" had grown "quite negative," and he came to resent the "affluent Yankee kids" whose presence tended to "destroy our native mountain culture" and "hinder our development of a self-identity." In the final analysis, Don concluded that the New Left included too many middle-class radicals who wanted to make a revolution, but who, without any sense of history, had "written off labor and the working man as hopeless." Many of West's acquaintances remember vividly his derisive dismissal of those who "came in and sowed their Appalachian wild oats and returned to go about their fathers' businesses."[33]

The presence of cultural dissenters and the image of political radicalism hampered public relations, but West soon became a respected figure in Summers County and beyond. In part due to CAD lobbying in Washington and a subsequent meeting with West, Eloise Cohen, wife of Secretary of Health, Education, and Welfare Wilbur J. Cohen, became an early supporter of the ASFC and worked to find financial support for the project. Moreover, when local vigilantes invaded the center the *Charleston Gazette*, a reliable liberal newspaper, attacked his detractors as "beneath contempt." At this time a large committee of supporters from West Virginia political and social action groups embraced the Folklife Center and West's attempt to assist mountain people, educate the children of the poor, amd preserve mountain culture. Sparked by West Virginia AFL-CIO leader Jim Williams, the committee called upon citizens to reject the *Princeton Times*'s charges of subversion and declare support for West. The West Virginia SDS also criticized vigilante intimidation and urged members to offer volunteer support.[34]

As the years passed West became a local dignitary, and support for the Folklife Center overcame the early opposition. Moreover, a rash of favorable publicity helped legitimize the Pipestem program, including a 1972 feature spread in *National Geographic* lauding West's determination to instill in mountain children pride in culture. He was especially successful in gaining acceptance from Summers County community leaders and his immediate neighbors although suspicions lingered among those who had less contact with the ASFC. As a result of a calculated decision to avoid domination by intellectuals, the center's governing body was composed of local citizens, including a committed physician, a disabled miner, a neighboring farmer, a feisty railroad conductor, and a black female activist from the 1950s. As a whole, they were a far cry from the "button down non-profit types" often encountered in the public service organizations of the era. An undercurrent of suspicion was always present, but most residents of Summers County and other West Virginia communities came to see the value of the ASFC as a force for education, cultural conservation, economic change, and promoting regional identity. Even his early critics, such as Pedneau and the *Princeton Times*, changed their outlook as the Pipestem program was better understood. Once the leader of the opposition, Pedneau became one of Don's staunchest supporters. Finally, for many young people who came to the Folklife Center, both the educational program and exposure to West's charismatic presence was a life-altering experience. Through work with the Appalachian poor, West probably had a greater impact on mining families during the Pipestem years than he had during his organizing years in Wilder and Bell Counties.[35]

Not only did West prepare the children of miners for an uncertain economic future but he also encouraged their parents to support collective action that promised economic liberation in the present. Although he was not an engaged labor activist at this time, he was friendly with Jock and Chip Yablonski and supported Miners for Democracy in its challenge to Tony Boyle and the UMWA establishment. In a letter to *Miner's Voice*, West attacked John L. Lewis for building a "totalitarian" union machine that enabled him to choose Boyle, who consistently brokered "sweetheart contracts" with operators and employed violence after the Lewis fashion. Likewise, he faulted Boyle for collaborating with red-baiters in management who hoped to weaken union solidarity. His sense of history made West an enthusiastic supporter of Arnold Miller and the rebels who overthrew the Boyle administration in 1972. Endorsement for Miller as well as an interest in the health of miners and safety reform drew him into a close relationship with Donald Rasmussen, a fierce fighter for miners disabled by exposure to coal dust. Rasmussen, a Beckley physician who worked tirelessly for the enactment of the Coal Mine Health and Safety Act and was a pioneer in silicosis diagnosis, harbored attitudes toward workers consistent with Don's. Consequently, he was often invited to speak at the Folklife Center and eventually became the president of its board. He later observed that because West supported labor organizing, he was at all times "very protective of the union as an institution."[36]

Although West was keenly interested in Miners for Democracy, most of his energies were devoted to Pipestem's educational mission, which included both farming and teaching. Although often joined by student interns and guest teachers, including Hosea Hudson, Pete Seeger, Willard Uphaus, P. J. Laska, Don Rasmussen, Ann, and Connie, Don West was always the featured attraction. By all accounts he was a gifted teacher who commanded the attention of any audience he addressed. To many, what made his classes so powerful was his emphasis on the integrity of mountain culture, which penetrated his teaching of Appalachian history, economic development, and artistic and musical heritage. Summarizing this unique appeal, Yvonne Farley, a former student and Pipestem worker, remembered that West "made contact with your intellectual and cultural past. He had done it all—he was political, artistic, and intellectual; the real thing . . . an authentic revolutionary." Others, like young Mildred Shackleford, recalled individualized education, courses in which Don encouraged students to think independently about history and culture, engage in field experience, and arrive at their own conclusions. To Margie Hutchens West's greatest contribution to her learning experience was the way in which he modeled service to others; she saw him as "loving, caring, hardworking, gentle, quiet, solid, strong in character, attentive, at ease, calm, thoughtful

. . . a model of a spiritual man." Even more telling was the experience of a Pentecostal preacher who learned a lesson in life from Don as a student in Appalachian activist Helen Lewis's class. After listening to West's account of mountain history, abolitionism, and personal experiences as an organizer of the poor, she broke out in tears. Married to a mountaineer, she had considered mountain people slow and dull, but he showed her another side of Appalachian culture. Don's impact was evident in the simple words she spoke to him: "You have changed my life; you have changed my mind."[37]

Others who came to appreciate Don West's power as an educator included the academics and students affiliated with Antioch College's Antioch Appalachia Program, a college-level "contemporary folk school" based in part on West's ideas. The leading figure in Antioch's Beckley Center was Bob Snyder, who became acquainted with West through contacts with students at Beckley. Later, the Beckley Center was instrumental in Don's appointment to the board of Antioch College in Yellow Springs, Ohio. At Snyder's invitation, West taught courses for Antioch in both Beckley and Huntington, where he advanced his unique perspective on Appalachian history. Snyder often arranged for Antioch students to work and study at the Folklife Center, and on more than one occasion they directed the ASFC summer camp program. For some, like sixteen-year-old dropout Vickie Shackleford, the Antioch program's flexibility, including its Pipestem component, provided a new lease on academic life after years of aimless wandering. Don's involvement in her education, as well as her cousin Mildred's presence, helped her to find herself; both had respect for West as a teacher who was, in Mildred's words, a "rare person of value." Indeed, most Antioch students "held him in awe" as a "towering figure" who had made "great sacrifices" in the civil rights and labor movements.[38]

The Antioch connection also brought Don into contact with a group of young writers, the "Soupbean Poets" affiliated with the college's strong creative writing program. Formed in 1975, the writers' collective included P. J. Laska, Bob Henry Baber, Gail Amburgey, Pauletta Hansel, Don Williams, Mary Joan Coleman, and David Chaffins, all of whom produced poetry focusing on the region. It was natural for him to become an inspiration for the group, whose angry works emphasized the fight against outside colonization, a battle long waged by Don West. At Pipestem, West read poetry with the group in performance sessions that Laska and other artists remembered as "profoundly moving." Laska, who came to Beckley in 1974 to teach in the Antioch program, later concluded that West's "radicalizing legacy" to the Soupbean Poets was expressed in their protest poetry, which decried the exploitation of mountain people and their "past humiliation and demonization . . . in literature and the mass media."[39]

By the 1970s, West had become "more and more amused" by the new interest in Appalachian studies at places like Antioch and Berea College, which in 1971 finally created a Department of Appalachian Studies. What most irritated him was the tardiness of the discovery that Appalachia "does have a cultural heritage." Nonetheless, he later expressed approval of the "proliferating numbers of institutions . . . putting in Appalachian Studies courses." West understood that this focus, although late in coming, was needed in view of distortions evident in the modern media, which had solidified what the ASFC deplored as the "poor national image of the southern mountaineer."[40]

One important vehicle for reshaping that image was the Appalachian Movement Press, founded in 1969 with Don's assistance by student activists Tom Woodruff and Danny Stewart as an experiment in nontraditional media with a radical mission to inform readers on issues of concern to mountain people. Based in Huntington, the press was an important outlet for pamphlet literature and underground material not likely to find a mainstream publisher in the 1970s. Because he frequently published with the Movement Press until it closed in 1982, some suggest that the operation should have been called the "Don West Press." Indeed, it issued some of West's strongest pamphlet writings as well as the more ambitious collection of his works spanning a productive forty years, *O Mountaineers!* Although Woodruff maintained that West provided "spirit and moral support," others recall him having mixed emotions about the venture. John Crawford, a book dealer and leftist publisher, remembered Don's misgivings about the "hippie printers" of Huntington whose goals he embraced despite a countercultural lifestyle that sometimes concerned him. Mixed feelings on lifestyle issues aside, West was a strong supporter of the press project and took pride in "helping [it] to get under way."[41]

While West immersed himself in various publishing projects, consciousness-raising group activities, and performance readings, he was increasingly forced to expend his energies on the mundane details of fund-raising to keep Pipestem afloat. With a substantial personal investment of $75,000 in facilities by 1971, Don and Connie waged a never-ending battle to provide scholarships, maintain facilities, and operate the program. In the early years the SCEF helped with subsidies of $100 to $200 per month as well as assistance in recruiting volunteers, but by mid-1967 it, too, was running out of money. Similarly, proceeds from some of Hedy's concerts went to support the Folklife Center, as did Don's Antioch salary and proceeds from sales of his writing and Connie's works. Sporadic income and volunteer assistance also came from liberal churches and religious groups that often used Pipestem for workshop sessions. Likewise, occasional grants from the Commission on Religion in Appalachia (CORA) provided stop-gap funding.[42] Although West was fully aware of potential support through the Office of Economic Opportunity, he steadfastly declined to apply for public funds. In a 1975 interview he ridiculed the federal poverty program, noting that in the 1960s "it was discovered that we had poverty down there," a revelation to politicians but old news to the people of Appalachia. Not only was he leery of government controls, but he "didn't want to get that kind of money."[43]

Despite modest external support, it was clear that some sort of sustained financing was essential to the long-term stability of the program. One promising source was the Rockefeller Foundation, which had long demonstrated interest in Appalachian culture and the folk school idea. After a tip from Dave Morris, organizer of an old-time music festival in his own right, West approached the foundation with a proposal for support of both the summer music program and the larger educational mission of the ASFC. Fortified by reference letters from the Appalachian Regional Commission, several United Church of Christ leaders, Don Rasmussen, and assorted academics, he secured a grant of $14,200 to cover the 1971 summer festival and a related workshop. Suppressing resentment against the Rockefeller empire, West quickly followed up by landing a $25,000 grant for each of the next two years, one-third of Pipestem's annual budget.[44]

By early 1974 the program was on a relatively firm footing. What promised stability was the steady income provided by speaking fees, poetry readings, and fund-raising proceeds, most of it generated by West's annual pilgrimage to the churches and college campuses of New York, New England, and the Midwest where there was ongoing interest in his literary work and educational innovations. A key figure in arranging these appearances was a young University of Connecticut graduate student, Warren Doyle, who met Don in 1971 when taking a group of American Friends Service Committee student volunteers to the Folklife Center for the first of many summer work-study projects. From 1974 on Doyle coordinated Don's fund-raising tours, and in 1981 he assumed new responsibility as associate director of the ASFC program. Like so many other young people who encountered Don West, Doyle was deeply impressed with his mentor, who commanded respect and captured his loyalty.[45]

Neither Doyle's fund-raising nor Rockefeller money, however, could prevent the Folklife Center's most serious setback, which came in January 1974 when a fire destroyed the main activities building, including the dining hall, kitchen, museum, oil paintings, office supplies, and records. All were uninsured. Not to be deterred, the center called on its many friends, and their response demonstrated a "spirit of concern" that enabled the program to recover. Countless volunteers and church organizations aided in the rebuilding process, donated supplies, or contributed financially to a restoration effort that enabled Don and Connie to call 1974 a "good year." The achievement was immense, but it stretched resources to the limit. Although West reported to the Rockefeller Foundation in March 1975 that facilities had been rebuilt and the center was free of debt, there was little cash on hand.[46]

Despite the ASFC's dire straits, however, Rockefeller priorities had shifted from the arts, which meant a renewed struggle to keep the program alive. The result was increased emphasis on direct mail fund-raising and intensification of West's fall and winter workload due to the pressure of performance and speaking engagements. By 1978 he reported to his old friend George Weissman that the Folklife Center was able to "get along" although the search for the elusive major grant to replace the Rockefeller money never succeeded. The reason, Don thought, was that big foundations "[knew] where they put their money" to "make sure it [was] in safe places." Similarly, he complained to Claude Williams that he constantly heard of grants available but it was "hard as heck for us to get [one]."[47]

West built a good working relationship with the community and also managed to maintain loose ties with radical groups as well as some of his old friends from party circles. There was an existing complex of leftist activists in West Virginia, a network Yvonne Farley remembers as "an Appalachian intifada" that included the Appalachian Movement Press, Council on Southern Mountains, UMWA activists, Miners for Democracy, SDS, Socialist Workers Party, Revolutionary Communist Party (RCP), Greens, and the mainstream CP. West's main contact with the CP was George Meyers, the Party's labor secretary, who was a regular visitor to the West Virginia coalfields and occasional guest at Pipestem. Meyers, like West, had reservations about the New Left, especially the small radical splinter groups such as the RCP and the Miners Right to Strike Committee, organizations he denounced as composed of petit bourgeois radicals who thought they could "solve everything overnight," which gave the Party a bad name. West shared his concern over RCP provocateurs and "counterrevolutionaries" who were "meddling around in the UMWA and giving Arnold Miller a hard time." Fomenting wildcat strikes, they seemed to spend more time attacking Miller than the corporations, which spelled trouble for Miller, whom Don saw as the best hope for labor reform.[48]

Consistent with his public stance since the 1940s, West maintained that he was not a Communist Party member although he asserted that many of the finest people he knew belonged to the Party. As late as 1985, George Meyers told CP member and radical publisher John Crawford that during his regular visits to Don, he received "verbal reports" on events in West Virginia and collected party dues. Meyers acknowledged that West's involvement had been less active than it once had been, due in part to his desire for a low profile and in part to failing health. West preferred to think of himself as a free-lance, grass-roots organizer because open party membership was "too much of a risk, considering his situation and his history." In short, his effective interaction with workers and nonracist activism reflected his own socioeconomic analysis and personal commitment to the poor more than partisan commitment. Meyers's assessment of West's work suggested that "in no way was Don taking direction from anyone about his activities." After all, no one anywhere knew as much as Don West about how to organize southerners; anyone who tried to instruct him would quickly discover that he was too independent to accept external guidance. Comfortable with public denials of party membership, West delighted in confounding those who attempted to pin him down on the issue. When an irksome Anthony P. Dunbar interviewed him for *Against the Grain*, Don sarcastically consoled him by "telling him that he was not alone in not being able to establish [his] CP membership." To West, Dunbar was just one of those spineless social democrats who were "so often the worst kind of red-baiters."[49] In the final analysis, the narrower membership issue is less significant than his instinctive willingness to work with all persons and groups willing to commit to the struggle for economic and social justice, which for West followed from his own brand of native-born American radicalism, an Appalachian application of Marxist analysis, and a nonsectarian religious commitment to follow the path of the revolutionary Jesus.

It was less the grass-roots organizer than the "natural teacher" with an unshakeable commitment to the poor that drew Warren Doyle into West's orbit. He later wrote to West of his "respect and admiration" for West's "life, ideals, and actions," which inspired him to commit his own life to the "struggle for social justice and human decency." In 1979, after Doyle had worked many years with the summer camp program, Don proposed that he become ASFC director upon his own retirement, an unexpected offer that Doyle could not accept until after he completed graduate training. Instead, he served for seventeen months as associate director while completing the Ph.D., working very closely with Don in 1981 and 1982. About to assume the directorship, Doyle embraced the Folklife Center mission in eloquent terms: "I believe in the proud cultural heritage of the Southern Appalachian mountains and the need for its young people to know and understand it. I believe in the role of education and the uniting of common people to cooperatively influence a more just and humane future. I believe that people must study their past to be better able to judge their present and, if they find it lacking, to use this knowledge to shape a better tomorrow." With those words Doyle accepted the new responsibility as the "greatest honor" of his young life. Vowing to fulfill the ASFC's mission, he acknowledged the work that had gone before and pledged to cultivate the soil of Pipestem so others might "experience the inspirational and bountiful harvest of Don and Connie West bursting out."[50]

For the Wests, time was running short. By 1983 Connie was showing signs of fatigue from the ravages of the recurring cancer that had plagued her since the early 1960s. Although she demonstrated a remarkably resilient spirit and continued her art work unabated, her mental acuity began a slow process of deterioration. Most observers remember a multitude of minor squabbles and a tendency for Connie to withdraw from some of Pipestem's daily activities. The financial rock on which Don's enterprise had been built, she had never taken kindly to her husband's condescension in dealing with her concerns and even her art, which he sometimes discounted as bourgeois in character (although late in life he did express pride in her work). Don retained intellectual clarity longer, but he, too, was subject to the handicaps imposed by advancing age and repeated surgeries.[51]

In the late 1970s and early 1980s St. Petersburg became the Wests' winter quarters, although Don returned periodically to deal with the Folklife Center's problems. The couple was growing old, and even Don recognized that the success of the program would soon depend on the infusion of younger blood. On January 1, 1983, Warren Doyle assumed his administrative duties at Pipestem. For Don, it was time to let go.

fourteen

Literary Maturity: An Artist in Full

As Don West prepared for early retirement in 1965 he confidently anticipated the opportunity to reinvest time in the literary work neglected during his last years of teaching. While Connie labored to provide necessary income, Don laid ambitious plans for *Appalachian South*, the long-delayed Appalachian history project, and committed poetry that would inspire mountain people and extol their culture. Seeking to reinvigorate himself intellectually, he reflected on the mainstream academic environment that had in some ways been a disappointment. West expressed deep disillusionment with an education system that displayed cowardice in confronting threats to intellectual freedom and ignored "serious questions about the economic forces that dominate the culture."[1]

During the next phase of his literary career, West's work refocused on validating and preserving the Appalachian culture he loved. Incensed by accelerating economic exploitation and cultural imperialism, he dedicated his educational activities and writing to a wider understanding of mountain history and culture as well as the constant struggle to free his people from economic bondage and poverty of spirit. The result was the climax of West's life as a Gramscian "organic intellectual" whose familiarity with working-class life enabled him to participate in the construction of what David Duke terms a "nonpaternalistic counter-hegemony against the dominating elite."[2] By writing and performing "people's poetry," by promoting varied outlets for artists and intellectuals who challenged the power structure, and by polishing his skills as underground pamphleteer, West became the living symbol of an intellectual renaissance evident in Appalachian culture from the 1960s to the 1980s. Not long after his arrival in West Virginia, West made *Appalachian South* the mouthpiece for a nascent culture of resistance in the southern mountains. Proud of his creation, he confidently consulted his brother-in-law Mike Ross for an evaluation of the new journal. He could not have been prepared for the unexpected verdict rendered by so sympathetic a supporter. Although he saw many virtues in the magazine, Ross chose to comment on several problems that seemed likely to prevent its survival. To Ross, the central defect in the first few issues was a "sterile leftism" found in several articles that were "unfair and partisan," burdened as they were with "sloganizing and verbiage." Ross also argued that the magazine tended to separate the region from the United States by placing rural and urban America at odds. The result, he thought, was an element of "cliqueishness" and a "personalistic" character complicated by a "sanctimonious, pietistic, and holier-than-thou approach." The most brutal cut, however, was Ross's charge that *Appalachian South* contained "leftist romanticism about the mountaineer which emphasizes only his virtues." Failure to note the problems of illiteracy, political apathy, prejudice, provincialism, and Appalachia's diverse opinions on race, Ross argued, created an imbalance that weakened the magazine with all but regional chauvinists. The criticisms came from a supporter who thought that, if properly edited, the magazine might well become a *"major voice* for progress in the region for years to come."[3]

West, on the contrary, saw the venture as an effort to correct an imbalance rooted in a long history of stereotyping and exploitation during which Appalachia had been "missionarized, researched, studied, surveyed, romanticized, dramatized, hillbillyized, Dogpatched, and povertyized again." Given that perception of cultural imperialism and disrespect, Don felt no need for the sophisticated balancing act that Ross proposed; rather, it was time for a revolutionary assertion of identity. Through his writings in the Pipestem years, West mounted a spirited challenge to outsiders who had come to exploit, instruct, and denigrate mountain people.[4] If he overcompensated, as surely he did, the new imbalance seemed perfectly justified as a necessary response to the assault against Appalachian culture.

The newest weapon in West's intellectual arsenal was to be found in the essay and pamphlet literature that flowed from *Appalachian South* and the Appalachian Movement Press in the late 1960s and 1970s. Following the path of the great radical agitators of the American past, West made his argument in persuasive short essays that addressed mountain history, regional culture, and the political issues that dominated the era once the federal government rediscovered Appalachian poverty. Returning to one of his key themes in 1967, he argued for radical action in "Jesus, the Quiet Son of Man" and stressed the "revolutionary quality of love in action." Other pamphlets, including *Freedom on the Mountains, Southern Mountain Folk Tradition and the Folksong "Stars" Syndrome,* and *People's Cultural Heritage in Appalachia,* elaborated on Appalachian history and culture, with emphasis on the nonracist and democratic element in the mountaineer's cultural heritage. West railed against the hijacking of mountain culture by the "folksong stars cult," a vulgar Madison Avenue creation that robbed the people's music of social and cultural meaning and drained it of "steadfast loyalty to the people's cause." Likewise, he stressed a labor movement rooted in the mountain spirit that embraced the union as "militant, democratic, with rank and file participation in the decision-making process." This mountaineer spirit, grounded in history, fueled the successful resistance to Tony Boyle and the bureaucracy of the United Mine Workers of America. It was also directly related, he argued, to the antislavery tradition of the southern mountains, a cultural heritage "differing sharply from that of the old slaveholding South."[5]

Critical to employing pamphlets as expressions of cultural pride was the flowering of the Appalachian Movement Press, which West helped start in late 1969. Tom Woodruff and Danny Stewart conceived of the press as a tool to guarantee them freedom to expose Appalachia's colonial status and celebrate its history of struggle against external control. Without resources, Woodruff recalled, they went to West, who gave them "what he had . . . the Appalachian spirit . . . of self-reliance and independence, a spirit of freedom and democracy." Across the generations, West inspired the young radicals as the very "epitome of that spirit."[6]

Related to his observations on mountain culture was West's suspicion of intruders and growing cynicism concerning the poverty warriors who came to save Appalachia. Increasingly skeptical about capitalism's capacity to promote social justice and relieve economic oppression, West turned against the federal antipoverty program and volunteers who swarmed into the region in the 1960s to work with the poor. The definitive statement of his resentment came with the publication of a biting critique of federal intervention, *Romantic Appalachia; or, Poverty Pays If You Ain't Poor,* which appeared in the alternative press publication *West Virginia Hillbilly* in 1969. Later reprinted in expanded form by Appalachian Movement Press, the essay ridicules the rediscovery of Appalachian poverty, which stimulated hope but ignored the colonial status responsible for the region's economic subjugation. Dismissing missionaries, Volunteers in Service to America (VISTA), the Community Action Program (CAP), Appalachian Volunteers (AV), and even the Southern Conference Educational Fund as transitory do-gooders, West argued that the War on Poverty was "never intended to end poverty." Doing so was impossible without a sweeping restructure of private ownership and production for profit. Part and parcel of this attack was a swipe at the middle-class youths who came to sow "radical wild oats" before resuming comfortable lives. Even more reviled were poverty consultants who benefited from lucrative Office of Economic Opportunity grants while failing to organize the poor as they trained poverty warriors for doomed programs. To West, the lesson was clear: Native mountaineers must organize to save themselves and develop their own self-identities. Outsiders could not alleviate conditions unless mountain people made their own stand in their own interest. Similarly, West argued in "Poverty War Pennies and Baby Sitters" that the War on Poverty led to a "dulled national conscience" that actually made the organization of the poor more difficult.[7] His charges drew a vigorous response from VISTA and AV workers who quarreled with the assertion that they had been "slumming" and functioning as unwitting babysitters. The essays marked Don's increasing estrangement from government programs and ambivalence toward youthful radicals.

West's prolific output of pamphlet literature was soon matched by renewal of his commitment to poetry, which was the product of engagement in the Antioch Appalachia Program, interaction with the Soupbean Poets, and active involvement in performance poetry. Returning to the poetry circuit in the late 1960s due to the pressing financial needs at Pipestem, West refocused his creative life, thus expanding his cultural production significantly. As the performance poet he had always been, he now drew widespread attention as a public proponent of people's art. As P. J. Laska has shown, literary works have their fullest impact in the live performance, and it was in that venue that West's "poetic power and appeal" was most evident. Before an audience he came alive in expressing his persona as the quintessential people's poet.[8]

Although he never lost the firm conviction that "human nature potentially can be very beautiful and very lovable and very peaceful," there was an element of radical bitterness in some of the work West produced in the latter stages of his career. More and more exasperated by intrusions from relief administrators, dewy-eyed volunteers, missionaries, folk music collectors, and corporate exploiters, he indicted the colonizers in language simple and clear. In "Appalachian Blues" he attacks cultural imperialists who "come to study us / to see what is wrong with us, to see that we are poor" as well as the "do-gooders, missionaries of numerous persuasions" and parasitic ballad hunters, those "Columbuses discovering Appalachia.'"[9] This poem, which closes *O Mountaineers!* (1974), the culmination of forty years of people's poetry, brings West's critique of corporate control and Appalachia's colonial status full circle. As Willard Uphaus observed in a friendly review of the book, West never disguised his meaning, preferring to "sensitize the heart of the reader to the hardships, the physical and spiritual hurts, and the unfulfilled dreams of the repressed."[10] As he entered the twilight of his career it was clear he had grown more radical than ever in speaking for dispossessed and alienated mountain people.

It was this outspoken defiance of the exploiters that drew a new generation of literary radicals to West's side. As Alan Wald has observed, West was unusual among Old Left literary artists in that many of the themes in his work crossed generational lines to express post–1960s' "radical cultural concerns": denunciation of corporate exploitation of colonial Appalachia and a liberation theology that depicted Jesus as an anticapitalist revolutionary. Even West's iconic stature as people's poet and natural proletarian artist was distinctive. In West Virginia, his heroic image was central to the coalescence of the Soupbean Poets. Not only did he help "legitimize" Antioch College's Appalachian Program but he was also a living example of a poet "grounding himself in the mountain culture and calling people to terms artistically." For Bob Snyder, also a poet, West provided the clearest role model, someone who "laid out the basic directions" that the Soupbean Poets and the Appalachian Writers Cooperative ultimately adopted. Laska recalled West's impact as stronger on stance than style. His was a "radicalizing legacy" that took the form of protest poetry that was "radical and angry—and sometimes splenetic." West's influence could be seen in other poets' commitments to "writing about mountain people, culture, and experience, the refusal to be moved or to accept exploitation." Most were leftists, and "everybody was political."[11]

By all accounts, West's readings were profoundly moving because of his charismatic presence on the platform as well as the simple, direct impact of words that concealed little. West later summarized his literary purpose as the establishment of an emotional connection that would "sensitize" the poet's time and place to the deep hurt and hopes and needs and yearnings of just plain ordinary human beings."[12] Didactic though they were, his verses connected with readers and listeners, tutored and untutored alike, who acquired his work in numbers that confounded the literary establishment that so studiously ignored his success. In the introduction to *The Road Is Rocky* (the reprinted preface to *A Time for Anger* in 1970), West's old friend from Meansville in South Georgia, Roy Smith, dismissed poets who wrote "little petty-fogging nothings for each other" but failed to see why workers read West's poetry in large numbers. Similar observations were recorded by Warren Doyle, who was transfixed by the aura of dignity that won Don the respect of audiences, whether in Appalachia or academe. For Doyle, the poetry and the presence "transcended politics" although he certainly understood the radical content in West's words.[13] As the critic Michael Henson noted, however, the key dimension of his literary success was his power as a "teaching poet" capable of raising the thorny issues of race and class oppression in modern America, problems that are unavoidably political.[14]

Throughout the final years of his creative life West spoke truth to audiences that hungered for honesty. More and more, his work focused on preserving and transmitting Appalachian culture to present and future generations. In *O Mountaineers!* (his most ambitious work in the late stages of his career), West's folk poetry took on a militant, confrontational, character as he strove to shield mountain people from cultural vulnerability in the face of the powerful metropolitan forces that enveloped them and thus imperiled the survival of hallowed customs and traditions.[15] There is an element of finality in this collection that reveals awareness of his creative effectiveness nearing an end. "Automated Miner," for example, provides a glimpse of the quiet despair of a displaced worker who

> Said twenty years a miner
> That's all I know.
> No job, no home,
> No place to go.

Similarly, there is doubt in the penetrating and personal verses of "For These Sad Ashes," a reflection on the fire that destroyed his library:

> Mourn these days
> While men must mourn
> Confused, in alienation.
> Mourn, but not alone, . . .[16]

Yet defiance and hope stand side by side with despair in *O Mountaineers!* It is a militancy most sharply delineated in the confrontational lines of "Appalachian Blues":

> Down here in Appalachia,
> government designated "poverty area,"
> blue thoughts stagger
> up the valley
> whisper on mountain fogs—.

These words precede angry comments hurled at predatory outsiders feeding on Appalachia's wounded body at a counter-revolutionary repast. But in unity is potential to be found in the promise of organization. In "There'll B a Tomorrow," which is dedicated to the Cabin Creek unionists Clifton and Mary Bryant, West concludes:

> . . . there may be a tomorrow
> On Cabin Creek
> a clean tomorrow,
> child of hope and hurt and solidarity.

And for Don West the artist there was a future as well. Foretold by "Obituary for Despair," written after a period of creative inactivity: For the poet "the silence breaks / we sing again."[17]

O Mountaineers! came twenty-three years after West's last major work and culminated his lifelong drive to write and speak to and for working people. In a reprinted introduction, Aubrey Williams noted that because of Don's "kinship with all the people" he wrote about "us" rather than "them." Williams observed that West so completely took on their struggles, hopes, hurts, and frustrations that "he becomes them." Don West, Williams observed, was a "natural," destined to be regarded one day as "one of the true poets America has produced." The authenticity of his works was evident because "his words [were] backed by his living."[18]

A logical extension of the deep democratic streak in West's life and work was the militant egalitarianism of his approach to the release of his last major publication, *In a Land of Plenty*, in 1982. From its first page it is clear that the book is community property rather than an expression of bourgeois acquisitiveness. West pointedly asserts that no copyright is to prevent the widest possible access to his words, which are intended to instruct readers on the shortcomings of capitalism and the potential benefits of a cooperative society. Moreover, the introductions by workers confirm West's intention of addressing a working-class audience rather than the academics who disregarded his work. Consequently, West's reprinted introduction to *Clods of Southern Earth* reminds a new generation of readers that his poetry is theirs to possess. As he later told a sympathetic interviewer, his poetry avoids abstraction in favor of clear communication. If the words fail to connect with the reader, he argued, what good is it for anybody?"[19]

Published by West End Press, a small but active left-wing house based in Minneapolis, *In a Land of Plenty* represents West's studied perception of his work over the previous fifty years. Specializing in progressive literature, the press was headed by West's friend and admirer John Crawford, who was convinced that a substantial audience still existed for his poetry. A formerly active Communist Party member, he was well aware of Don West, whom he regarded as one the literary world's "best living examples of oral culture." Crawford, who met West at Pipestem in 1980, considered him to be a legendary movement figure and one of the great civil rights leaders of the century rather than an intellectual. His estimate of the potential in West's poetry was based on familiarity with his work as well as the marketing savvy of a publisher well acquainted with the small but intellectually voracious radical audience of the early 1980s. Confident of success, West End declared pride in publishing the work of a lifetime "humanitarian and social activist."[20]

Like his earlier works, the volume is rooted in West's identification with the dispossessed and oppressed, whose sacrifices are underscored throughout. Himself a child of poverty who overcame through will, West was relentless in his drive to reveal the truth of exploitation. Even the book's title, a wry comment on the hollowness of the American dream for the underclass, is uplifting rather than pessimistic, an expression of Don's conviction that the day of the common man would come. After a lifetime of constant challenge he was still able to celebrate an "earth with love and strife," which for him were the essences of living.[21]

Love and strife. Collaboration and conflict. Hope and despair. At the end of his creative life West returned to the themes that had filled his verse from the beginning. Among the poems included in the reprint edition (1985) are several pieces that echo a lifetime of ambivalence. In "The Question Mark," West wonders why blind obedience prevails in the face of social injustice:

Why not scrape away
scales of prejudice
and see—
see who fastens them there?

Bitterly, he adds a critique of poverty with a graphic portrayal of hungry children:

With bellies potted,
Sadness in their eyes,
But cheer up, Brother
It's free enterprise!

Confronted with the contradictions of capitalism, he also questions the validity of religious faith in the biting "I Dare Not Say I Love the Lord":

I saw a Negro lynched one time
By men who talk that way,

And saw a union miner killed
One sunny Sabbath day![22]

West offers his final solution to the problem of class in "Away Down South," which posits a course of action for the poor, whether black or white:

If you must fight—
And fight you must—
Unite against
The upper crust.
What hurts the poor
Hurts white and black,
Unite to throw
Them off your back.[23]

Written in 1963, this poem addresses the civil rights struggle of that era, but it is classic West, the West of old for whom class trumped race in the final struggle.

Although continuing anger and militancy reveals the resilience of West's radical convictions, the volume ends on a note of hope. His tribute to the Bryants, "There'll Be a Tomorrow," acknowledged the destruction brought to the Cabin Creek community by rapacious capital, which created a "today swallowed in poverty's greedy gullet." Despite the pain and suffering everywhere present in "ghost town mining camps," West could still look to the future, a "clean tomorrow" for Cabin Creek.[24] In the face of mounting evidence to the contrary, West managed to remain optimistic as he entered the final decade of an eventful life.

The response to *In a Land of Plenty* confirmed Crawford's estimate of the audience for West's work. A sold-out first edition prompted him to issue a second edition in 1985, which also found a market, resulting in brisk sales of six thousand copies for poetic works beyond the academic fringe. The historian David Roediger found in the volume not only socially committed literature but also a primer in Appalachian history. Predictably, *The People's Daily World* also found much to admire in the book and reminded readers of West's long record of challenging the "power of oppression" in the American South. Even the more nuanced review of Richard Marius in *Appalachian Journal* asserted that West's "passion flame[d] over the Appalachians like some fiery dawn, throwing its red light down into the hollows and across the ridges, burning at the mists and bringing in the morning in a dazzling incandescence." Yet his work was "relentlessly didactic," capable of numbing through repetition. Marius also detected an element of romanticism that sugar-coated Appalachian realities.

Regional literary art, he insisted, cannot flourish until writers abandon the notion that Appalachian people are in some sense *"better* than others." In the final analysis, however, Marius found it impossible to dismiss West, who may not have produced "great art" but had certainly "made a great life for himself and for others . . . an achievement that no one [could] scorn."[25]

It was West's life with the people that grounded the work contained in *In a Land of Plenty.* Intentionally downplaying his intellectual achievements, West crafted an image of the poet organically connected with the masses of working people. The book, like his life, reflects a "moral choice" to become a folk poet, and it was this conscious decision that gave West credibility with his popular following despite the disinterest of the literary elite. The plain and direct language found in his best work, framed in "conscious opposition to the modernist tradition," is the hallmark of West the protest writer.[26] It is worthy of a people's poet committed to revolutionary change, the cooperative commonwealth, and the celebration of Appalachian cultural heritage. As Mike Henson observed in *The Guardian Book Review,* the challenge in Don West's work was never in "sorting out the tricks in language in the poems," for there are none to be found. His "naked words that have no subtle meaning" challenge readers to live "thoroughly engaged with the pain and struggle of others."[27]

West's transparent commitment to celebrating mountain culture dominated his literary production in his last years, but the well-worn plan for a book-length study of the Appalachian antislavery tradition never reached fruition. One unverified account holds that the unfinished historical manuscript mysteriously disappeared from West's files in Pipestem, only to reappear after his death under another writer's authorship. What was certain was his desire to record his lifetime experience in the resistance for the edification of future generations. In 1986 Don told his old comrade George Meyers that he was hard at work on an autobiographical study featuring the "many plain folk [he had known] who were and are of heroic proportions and quality." He thought that an autobiography would enable him to tell the story of a life lived "very close to the raw edge."[28] Although he chose to publish portions of that work separately, West never completed the project. By the early 1980s Don's energy began to give way. His mind remained sharp, but declining health increasingly limited his creative work and physical activities. West was acutely conscious that time was running out.

fifteen

Letting Go: Journey's End, 1983–92

By the time Warren Doyle assumed the directorship of the Folklife Center in early 1983, West's public image had undergone a dramatic change due to Pipestem's many successes and the gradual acceptance of Don as a figure of heroic proportions. As early as 1977, the *Charleston Gazette* observed that "common sense and rugged honesty" had persuaded most West Virginians that "they had nothing to fear and much to learn" from their new neighbor about their heritage. Five years later, Cong. Cleve Benedict of West Virginia formally acknowledged West's contribution to the preservation of Appalachian heritage as a spokesperson for "an historic, eventful, and richly significant culture." Similarly, West Virginia commissioner of public welfare Leon Ginsburg expressed admiration for Don and Connie as providers of multiple benefits to the state's citizens. Added to these tributes were the multiple awards bestowed upon the one-time pariah, including installation in Lincoln Memorial University's Hall of Fame; receipt of the Berea College Service Award; and, in 1987, recognition of his outstanding contribution to Appalachian literature with the Appalachian Writers Association Award.[1] Don West had become a regional institution.

While the official plaudits came in, countless personal observations also testified to West's profound impact on people who interacted with him, learned from him, and drew inspiration from the model he provided. Most of his associates at Antioch Appalachia and Pipestem admired his affirmation of

Appalachian culture, advocacy of the cooperative ideal, faith in reason, and unabashed progressivism. As the poet P. J. Laska observed, the principles he embraced remained as a living legacy of a "true teacher." In this vein, Warren Doyle remembered Don as a "man you came to love and respect," who seemed almost "Christlike" in bearing. Deeply impressed with West's independence, George Brosi still regards him as the "last American cowboy." Most would endorse the conclusion of Doyle's successor David Stanley: "Some day Don West will be considered one of the great leaders of the American civil rights and labor movements."[2]

Despite the posthumous plaudits, some of the conflicts sparked by West's long years as an agitator were never resolved. The many long years never healed the wound opened by the split with Myles Horton, which was rooted in the disruptive circumstances surrounding Don's hasty departure from Highlander in 1933. Although the two communicated in writing and met on a few occasions, their personal relationship remained fraught with tension. Even more fractious was the open warfare between West and his one-time confidant Jesse Stuart. West refused to let Stuart forget the infamous incident in 1935 when Don appealed for help from a Pineville, Kentucky, jail, only to be ignored by his friend. As late as the mid-1970s, Stuart remained angry about West's scathing review of *Taps for Private Tussie*, not to mention the gaping chasm that separated them on political issues.[3]

It is equally true that West's long political history fueled low-level disapproval among West Virginia's diehard conservatives. Among workers and farmers, however, there was never any doubt about the favorable popular reception of the Folklife Center, whose leader celebrated their culture and contributed to the community in numerous ways. The Heifer Project, library, cultural festivals, labor forums, children's camps, and other outreach programs counted for more than the fading memory of youthful radicalism.

West's retirement did not completely relieve him of fund-raising responsibilities, which he shouldered gladly in the effort to keep his dream alive at Pipestem. The speaking tours continued, and the search for grant support went on unabated, resulting in occasional successes with northern and northeastern church groups. Another source of funding was the regional Commission on Religion in Appalachia, which sometimes conferred small grants for dropout programs and other Pipestem activities. When Doyle became director in 1983, Don and Connie wrote to their long-term supporters to endorse the new regime and encourage them to transfer their financial loyalties to the new leadership.[4]

Although West hoped to resume writing it was not long before he became engaged in another project that came to mean a great deal to him. By

May 1983 the nuclear freeze movement had drawn his attention, and, always an internationalist, he hoped to advance the cause, starting with the use of Pipestem for a planning meeting in June. The movement was important, he thought, as a "little bit" that would cause people to "question [an] existing evil." In his view, the nuclear freeze movement constituted the first step in abolishing nuclear weapons.[5] It also lent urgency to a related plan for an Appalachian peace delegation to the Soviet Union, an initiative Don had nurtured since 1982 when he urged his cohort, the Rev. Martin Ballard of Baltimore, to make the Universal Christian Church a sponsor for the trip. By the time the freeze movement took hold in West Virginia in 1983 he was well on the way to raising the $10,000 required to fund a friendship tour. The trip was, in every sense, Don West's project.[6]

West's vision for the trip focused on a mixed delegation dominated by working people who were to communicate directly with workers from similar backgrounds in the USSR. He hoped to "promote peace through understanding of the common people," an approach that studiously avoided politicians. West was intent on informing his hosts of Appalachia's long struggle against slavery and oppression while assuring them that the common folk of the United States loved peace and renounced nuclear warfare against the people of the Soviet Union.[7]

Eventually, seventeen Appalachian ambassadors, including Connie, Ann and two of her children, David Stanley, Bill Blizzard, a few North Georgia residents, a teacher, a miner's wife, and other assorted working people, made the trip in December 1983. At least a few were secret members of the CP, and the tour created a ripple of local controversy. The overall reaction, however, was sufficiently diverse to legitimize the venture. The pilgrims were eager to learn, but it soon became clear that West saw the tour as an opportunity to not only promote international understanding but also advance their political consciousness. The guide, Olga, was courteous and friendly, but other Soviet contacts—and sometimes Don—took the opportunity to proselytize about Moscow's peaceful intentions and the positive aspects of communist society. The propaganda was not always subtle, nor was West's sympathy for the Communist Party. One participant recalled that Don, who "had not yet given up on the Soviet Union," was definitely "out" so far as his CP ties were concerned. His goal became clear when at the Donetz coal mining district he asked at least one delegation member to join the CP, perhaps as a secret member. He seemed disappointed when the designated convert declined. Although the two remained friendly, their relationship was never again quite as close as it had been before Don took the potential recruit into his confidence in this most personal of ways.[8]

Once back in West Virginia, West worked to spread the message of peace and harmony that the tour managers had projected. He described the church celebrations, factory tours, mine visits, museum attractions, and impressive monuments to the World War II dead. The delegation, he asserted, "marveled at the remarkable reconstruction" after the "ghastly devastation" perpetrated by the "Hitler hordes." Equally significant, West thought, was the free medical care and universal education available in the Soviet Union. But most important was the personal understanding achieved between the visitors and their Soviet friends, including the outgoing Olga, who had made the tour a joyful success. At the farewell dinner in Moscow she proclaimed that she had "for years been dreaming of having an American delegation like this Appalachian group, but never before" had her hopes been so fully realized.[9]

Basking in the euphoria that followed the tour, West drove home the important political message he sought to communicate: The working people of the Soviet Union only wanted peaceful coexistence with the United States. West argued that throughout the trip, the most common sentiment expressed was the "desire for peace" and deep concern over more than three hundred American military bases armed with first-strike missiles that could well lead to "world destruction." President Ronald Reagan's nuclear buildup, he insisted, created a "new doctrine making terrorism state policy."[10] In short, West deployed the trip as a useful complement to the growing nuclear freeze movement in the United States.

The friendship tour was an important milestone for West on the path to international understanding, and it also marked the apex of his career as an activist on behalf of the common folk of Appalachia and humanity in general. His health had been failing since the early 1980s, and Connie had entered another stage in the long process of physical decline. As much as he would have preferred to play a central role at Pipestem, he could no longer bear the strain. Starting in the mid-1970s the Wests wintered in St. Petersburg, where the Florida climate was kinder to aging bodies; Don traveled alone to handle business at Pipestem and lecture. Although he dreamed of an eventual return to Georgia, he gave that up as unrealistic as he grew older and weaker. Finally, determined to retire in a community of Appalachian workers, he selected the drab, declining mining community of Cabin Creek, West Virginia, a decision Connie was unsuccessful in fighting. To Don, it made perfect sense because it reunited him with the people he embraced and reminded him of his history of activism among miners. In Cabin Creek he found a landscape he could trust where prosperity had not changed the environment and the community reminded him of his youthful surroundings.[11] Cabin Creek was a return to first priorities: the legacy of struggle, the coal wars of old, and the people he loved and for whom he had fought. Not incidentally, it was also close to Charleston, where daughter Ann and her family resided.

By this time Don had undergone a prostate operation and was soon to endure triple-bypass surgery; Connie coped with the ravages of recurrent cancer and finally the creeping devastation of advancing Alzheimer's Disease. Despite the physical ailments that plagued her, however, she proved remarkably resilient and maintained an optimistic outlook until late in life. Although not actively involved in the day-to-day operations of the Folklife Center, she maintained a productive creative life as a working artist and mounted occasional exhibits in both West Virginia and St. Petersburg. Although Don disapproved of "bourgeois abstraction" and clearly favored a more heroic people's art, he spoke with some pride of her work in later years, perhaps remorseful but more likely in recognition of its practical value in fund-raising and promoting useful impressions of Appalachian character.[12]

Beneath the surface of a collaborative relationship the Wests carried on a long-standing, low-level conflict over Connie's art. It was not until late in life that he fully accommodated himself to her work—at least in disclosures made for public consumption. In moments of candor, however, he asserted that "art is for after the revolution." Although the two bickered over innumerable issues, Don retreated into a paternalistic tolerance of his wife's increasingly erratic behavior but sometimes grew impatient with her. Both experienced mounting health problems, but Don retained mental clarity longer than Connie, whose powers of concentration weakened in the late 1980s.[13] Before long she sank into dementia, in effect marking a sad end to a tumultuous lifetime partnership.

Meanwhile, the Folklife Center struggled for survival under Doyle's leadership. The summer festivals and children's programs now drew shrinking audiences despite inspired teaching sessions by many of the old standbys like Hosea Hudson, Pete Seeger, Mike Ross, and George Meyers who reminded youthful listeners of struggles long gone. Don's mentor and Florida neighbor Willard Uphaus was also an occasional guest. Hudson, whose "beautiful singing" and "wonderful tales" still had the capacity to inspire, was perhaps the program's most respected teacher. In 1984, for example, one young visitor, Carrie Nobel, wrote to thank him for the nontraditional American history he taught that had helped her realize how much she had to learn.[14]

With the passing years, the moral outrage West had felt in his early years intensified. These concerns found expression in his poetry readings, which more and more reflected pained consciousness of his mortality as well as grudging realization that the goals he set for changing the American economic and political system would not be achieved in his lifetime. Disappointed by the pace of social change, West refused to give up and, as his energy faded, grew increasingly angry at the fates. Consequently, as many observers have noted, his brusque manner often frightened or alienated the uninitiated. He was still psychologically incapable of loosening his personal attachment to and control of the Folklife Center, and by 1985 his micromanagement spelled disaster for the earnest and hardworking Warren Doyle, who turned out to be the wrong man in the wrong place at the wrong time.[15]

In October 1984, Carrie Nobel reported to Hosea Hudson that around the end of August, "things went kind of crazy" at the Folklife Center, where the board "turned against Warren for no good reason." Accounts of the change vary from the bland assertion that Doyle's leadership "did not work out" to speculation that Warren, although a dedicated worker, was still "an outsider." His successor David Stanley, however, was a "product of Appalachian culture." Stanley recalled that although Doyle "loved Don beyond measure," West "treated him about as bad as he could treat anybody." Some observers allege that family intervention and concerns over Pipestem land ownership forced the change, but it is equally plausible that Don's tight postretirement control of the center's program influenced Doyle's departure. Despite his protestations to the contrary, it was West who engineered the change and recommended that the board appoint Stanley, a graduate of Antioch Appalachia whom he thought a "good man to take [the] place." West later confided to his friend, the Georgia attorney Lowell Kirby, that in his view Doyle had not been doing much at Pipestem other than work with Appalachian Trail walkers.[16] Available evidence, however, supports a more complex interpretation of the change and emphasizes Don's vision of the Folklife Center's future.

Whatever the explanation, it is clear that the decision to remove Warren Doyle upset many of Pipestem's strongest supporters. Most, like Stanley, remembered Doyle's deep admiration for West and dedicated efforts to carry on his work. Stanley suspected "underhanded manipulations by Don and some of the board," which led to Doyle's questionable dismissal. Board president Don Rasmussen, who had great respect for Don, asserted that West had "some intolerances" of his own, especially pertaining to non-Appalachians. There was, Rasmussen remembered, "some bitterness against Don within the board" over the Doyle dismissal, and tension existed between Don and the new board following the decision.[17]

The change of leadership reflected the extent to which West was constitutionally unable to divorce himself from the day-to-day operation of the Folklife Center. Although Don promised Ann that he was "not going to worry too much" about the center, Rasmussen and Stanley agreed that the board was essentially a "figurehead board" that usually followed Don's lead. The program entered a period of decline in the late 1980s, in part because of

West's inability to relinquish control and in part because of his slow recovery following heart surgery. Insufficient financial resources combined with ongoing personal conflicts to limit the center's effectiveness as Don became increasingly weaker. Broken physically, he was "so serious about the Center and his goals" that he was "always watching and intervening in the program." Repeating a pattern observable throughout his career, West eventually became embroiled in a personal conflict with David Stanley over the disposition of Pipestem property and a rumor of plans afoot to sell the center to Highlander. After David Muse, a conservative anticommunist, purchased West's house, he convinced Don of Stanley's "evil intent," which led to "harsh words" when Stanley opposed Muse's appointment to the board. Certain that Muse was working "against the program," Stanley left the position of director in protest. Rasmussem decided to leave the board as well. To Ann, Stanley's departure was due to "burnout," which, she asserted, he acknowledged at a board meeting in May 1987. Like Doyle, he was a loyal and enthusiastic admirer of West, as well as West's contribution to Appalachian cultural awareness and service to the poor. Consequently, he, like Doyle was deeply hurt by the conflict. The disagreement, Stanley recalled, "broke [his] heart."[18]

While the Pipestem program limped along under Doyle and Stanley's leadership after 1983, West renewed old acquaintances and reaffirmed his commitment to the Left and faith in a collectivist future. Dividing time between St. Petersburg, Cabin Creek, and Pipestem, with another trip to the Soviet Union in 1986, he continued to criticize capitalism. Indeed, the split with Doyle may have been related to Don's unforgiving assault on an economic system that beggared the Appalachian poor. As early as 1983 he worried that Doyle might "think the profit system [could] be reformed and made to serve the people," a hope West rejected. Reminding Doyle that the War on Poverty had promised an end to poverty under the profit system, Don restated his conviction that the only answer was a "system for human needs production and distribution . . . based on cooperation and human welfare."[19]

Throughout the 1980s West maintained contact with his old party comrade George Meyers, who occasionally visited Cabin Creek to share with Don his belief in a communist future. In the mid-1980s, Meyers appeared regularly, several times a year, to monitor political and social developments in West Virginia. By that time, Don was not active in party affairs because of failing health and the necessity for maintaining a low profile because of his connection with the Folklife Center. He did, however, discreetly suggest that some of his close acquaintances talk to others about possible CP membership. After 1986 the two radical warhorses became less certain of the collectivist future as simmering tensions within the Soviet Union began to spill over into the public arena. Early in the era of Mikhail Gorbachev, West had a sobering experience during his follow-up trip to the Soviet Union, taken in 1986 with the intention of restoring the Wests' failing health. In a letter to Meyers, he complained that their guide in the resort area of Sochi was not a CP member, nor was she friendly. When Don asked that she arrange for them to meet with "some politically developed person," she failed to follow up, which was a "bitter experience" for a man who had been "in struggle and in support of the Left" since his teenage years. Worse yet, medical facilities were primitive, and Don returned to the United States "in worse condition healthwise than when [he] left."[20]

Despite disappointment with the limited progress he had seen, he read one Gorbachev report to the Central Committee that he thought "surprisingly excellent" and helpful in "understanding what happened in the USSR." Convinced that the new Soviet leader had "something on the ball," he was also critical of CP members who had party jobs but did "damned little." Although he expressed "hope and faith in men like Gorbachev," he speculated to Connie that he might well be "another short term strongman." Three months later, he observed Soviet youth protests with some concern, noting that he "would not be surprised if the new leader [had] opposition." By 1991 he was more convinced than ever that Gorbachev was likely to be one of the "short term heroes."[21]

As the Soviet Union broke apart West began to entertain doubts concerning the future of the Soviet experiment. In September 1991 he asked Meyers, "What in the world has happened—over there?" Although he tried to "keep hope alive" from Cabin Creek, he admitted to being "sort of bumfuzzled" by the dissolution of the Marxist utopia to which he had always looked for inspiration. In early 1992 he questioned Meyers's adherence to the CP and wondered what was "going to be the current development, loyalty speaking." Near the end of his life he also expressed doubts about trends in the Soviet Union to his daughter Hedy, whose oblique response was intended to spare him unnecessary anxiety. She merely observed that "they were probably corrupt."[22]

West entertained such questions but remained a believer in the Marxist prophecy to the very end. In correspondence with Meyers he never recanted his lifelong beliefs. He did acknowledge that the CP "looks like a mess some times" but could not allow himself to contemplate the possibility of failure. Asked by historian Victoria Byerly to reflect on his lifetime of activism and struggle on behalf of the poor, West responded firmly, "I have always believed that Jesus was a revolutionary who gave his life to the poor . . . I have tried to live my life according to the teachings of Jesus. I believed in everything the Communists were doing that I was involved with. I still do and I *make no apologies.*"[23]

For Don West there was no compromise with social evil, nor could he completely abandon the political ideology that had guided his adult life. Hedy West asserted that he "believed too deeply" and held to those convictions too long. When others deserted the Party his response was that they "never really did understand Marxism."[24] Always an internationalist, he steadfastly believed that the revolution would come, at least until the breakup of the Soviet Union planted the seeds of uncertainty at the very end of his life.

West's career provides a textbook case in native-born American radicalism that grew out of local conditions and abuses, especially the inequities so evident in the South of the depression era. Like many contemporaries in the Party of the 1930s, he was persuaded that there would be an "American way to socialism." It was poverty and racism that stimulated his original conversion to Marxism and the militant activism of the Communist Party that persuaded him to move sharply to the Left in 1933. West never looked back. After 1945, when the onset of the cold war and the Smith Act prosecutions fatally weakened the American CP as an instrument of social change, West distanced himself from overt party activity without abandoning hope for the Soviet Union as the People's Utopia. One former party member and West associate observed that by the 1980s "the rank-and-file member was perfectly capable of living in blissful ignorance of any collusion with the Soviets," and "someone like Don would only have known a few Soviets through personal meetings." Perhaps so, but the record indicates that at least in the years before World War II he was acutely aware of policy emanating from the "center." Moreover, his struggle with the "vanguard" during the Progressive Party campaign is well documented. Finally, in 1992 he did suggest to Meyers that the American Communist Party "takes its direction from others seemingly."[25] Later in life he was closer to the periphery than the center, and the interests of Appalachia and its exploited people were the driving force behind his tireless work as an educator, organizer, and people's poet.

This interpretation of West's perspective as a party sympathizer is consistent with his lifelong willingness to work with any groups or individuals committed to the fight for economic, social, and racial justice. It also lends credence to his daughter Ann's conviction that her father, although a Marxist, was in essence a "socialist" who thought a people's revolution was certain to occur. She confirms his stubborn adherence to these political beliefs to the end of his life, as well as his fierce desire to "fight for poor people and the downtrodden."[26] That account of West's public activism on behalf of Appalachian youth, racial accommodation, and service to the poor, a view held by many of his advocates, is perfectly compatible with Don's low-key, essentially underground party life from the 1940s on.

By 1989 the Wests' daily existence had become a major physical challenge. In 1987 Connie underwent additional surgery for the cancer that relentlessly assaulted her aging body. Two years later, West wrote to George Meyers that their health had not improved and that he could "barely stand up." As Connie's mind slowly slipped away, Don was robbed of the companion who had shared the burdens of common struggle with him for some sixty years. In a moment of introspection he told Hedy in 1990 that "in spite of all the ways I may have caused her pain I do appreciate her willingness to share and bear the hard trail we've known." For Don, it was a rare acknowledgment of Connie's contribution to their partnership. After her dementia became unmanageable she was hospitalized, and she died in the spring of 1990. Connie's death left a void, and Don had not anticipated the sadness it induced "till it happen[ed]." A year later he summarized his own physical dilemma in a cryptic note to Meyers: "My health is shot. Most of the time cannot walk. Live here on Cabin Creek alone. Have always tried to keep hope alive."[27]

In the last year of his life his main contacts with the outside world were Ann, who visited on a regular basis; Linda Meade, a labor activist who spent time with him at his Cabin Creek home; Cliff Bryant, a neighbor who had gone through the coal wars of old; and his faithful comrade George Meyers, who never forgot him when he was alone. Isolated and increasingly uncommunicative after Connie's death, West did not usually welcome visitors, and some were driven away as a result of his apparent bitterness.[28] Resigned to physical debility, puzzled by the fate of the Soviet Union, and exhausted by the strain of living, Don West died at the Charleston Area Medical Center on September 29, 1992. A hard journey in search of social justice was at an end.

The tributes to West tended toward simplicity and frankness. The *New York Times*, while covering his lifelong history of activism, curtly observed his authorship of poetry that "had been read widely in the South." More interested in his contributions to Appalachia, the *Charleston Gazette* cited Anne Braden's recollection of West's "great belief in the progressive traditions of the Southern mountaineer" and his lifetime of work to "bring black and white working class people together." Concentrating more narrowly on his Georgia experiences the *Atlanta Journal-Constitution* also went into his career, noting his clashes with both the House Un-American Activities Committee and Ralph McGill and quoting West's assertion that he had been "run out of Georgia." Even more focused on his career as a social activist, *People's Daily World* memorialized the "poet laureate of Appalachia who celebrated the hard toil and militant struggles of black and white coal miners, textile workers, and farmers." The CP organ also cited his dictum that a literary artist is "never neutral" and that "challenging the status quo" is "the people's poet's responsibility."[29]

When West Virginia labor activists gathered at Pipestem the following May for a worker's memorial solidarity concert, the event included a remembrance of Don West as a people's poet and worker advocate. Advance publicity quoted Yvonne Farley on West's split identity as poet and activist, as well as his preference for the downtrodden. As he parceled out chicken at Pipestem dinners, she recalled, "The harder your life was, the bigger the piece of chicken you got. He always distributed chicken by class." David Stanley remembered his steadfast support for workers and belief that "poor people aren't poor by choice, but are victims of a society that neglected them." And Bob Henry Baber, a poet and faculty member at Concord College, noted the disdain for West's works among academic and literary scholars who found his works "dogmatic and preachy."[30]

It was Baber who best captured the subtlety and contradictions found in Don West's life and work. The product of a "tough life," he asserted, West was "strong-willed and at times dictatorial," yet no one fought harder for "justice for coal miners and sharecroppers" and the principle of "blacks and whites working together." In an appreciation of West's life and work published in *Appalachian Heritage*, Baber acknowledged his flaws. Sometimes "headstrong" and "stubborn," he "strove for control at the Center, sometimes at the very peril of the institution he and his wife Connie created." Yet his image and example "created a lasting impression upon those of us who wished to think of ourselves as true Appalachians." And in an authentic regional voice, he wrote political poetry that stood firmly in the camp of the working class. Don West, Baber argued, was many men—"a rebel, hillbilly, radical, labor organizer, fierce individualist, preacher, and perhaps most important of all a poet." For Baber, and for many who respected West and shared his goals, "a part of Appalachia's conscience [had] died."[31] The void his passing created has not yet been filled.

— —

What is the measure of a man who gave his life to the cause of social justice, racial unity, economic equality, and cultural conservation but who, in the pursuit of his dream, embraced a Marxist analysis of social relations that colored his entire career and, until almost his dying day, nurtured a belief that an international people's revolution lay ahead? How does a scholar assess a writer who subordinated art to politics but produced moving poetry that cried out against injustice and expressed the deep pain of forgotten farmers and workers who created wealth and whose labor made the growth of the economy possible in an industrializing America? What of the educator who instilled cultural pride in the children of the poor while communicating a sharp critique of the economic system that exploited their families? How does a critical observer judge a stern and dictatorial leader who inspired devotion among acolytes who were themselves independent people of principle? And is it possible to reconcile the contradiction inherent in the collectivist convictions of an unreconstructed individualist? To understand Don West is to embrace the paradoxical dimensions of a richly complex character whose life and work continue to speak not only to Appalachian activists but also to working people and humanists irrespective of locale.

In order to evaluate West's life and work it is important to consult students of all ages who absorbed his message and whose lives were affected by his teaching, writing, and model of activism. It is among them that his influence has had its most lasting effect. The impact of his presence was evident in the recollection of Mildred Shackleford, one of his finest students, who regarded her mentor as a powerful instructor who taught her "to be sure that what you are doing is right, then do it."[32] Another student, Margie Hutchens, considered West "a great person, strong, and determined about real life" who provided mountain children stability, nurture, and learning "with great respect for God and His creation." For Hutchens, Pipestem "definitely had a Judeo-Christian foundation: . . . Mr. West was truly a model of Jesus . . . loving, caring, hardworking, gentle, quiet, solid, strong in character, attentive, at ease, calm, thoughtful, interested in each individual . . . sensitive to what life is really about—seeing the inner depths of people and responding with compassion. . . . He had a powerful influence on my life and continues to be a 'counselor' and role model, in continual life."[33] These two reactions demonstrate the complexity and contradictory aspects of West's persona. Both Shackleford and Hutchens were deeply impressed, yet one absorbed a secular message while the other drew a spiritual lesson from her experience at the Folklife Center. Both were sensitive learners who responded to West as a model for living, Shackleford as an activist and Hutchens as a religious leader and counselor.

For others, poetry was the central feature of West's impact. Peter Laska, one of West's students and a professional colleague, recalled his prose and poetry as affirming the belief that men and women can "overcome [their] human weaknesses and transform reality for the benefit of all people without regard for color, creed, or ethnicity." For Laska, West was a radicalizing influence, and his work and model reoriented the militant stance taken by regional poets. Similarly, Bob Henry Baber, inspired by Don's conviction that poetry constituted political action, made his courage and fortitude the yardstick by which Appalachian artists might measure themselves. For Warren Doyle, the political content of his work was clear, but its more deeply humane character transcended partisanship to reach a new level of human understanding.[34]

Any judgment of Don West's career cannot overlook the profound signifi-cance of a people's poet read by unprecedented numbers of working Americans outside the academy. As Michael Henson has shown, his cardinal sin and greatest virtue was that his verse was accessible and spoke hard truths about the injuries of class and the potential in revolution.

Other West associates were drawn to his side by Don's abiding humanism and long history of social and political activism on behalf of the exploited peo-ple of Appalachia. Both Doyle and Stanley were transfixed by West's abiding commitment to the larger cause of humanity. His testimony on Appalachian culture, more than any other aspect of his work, "hit home" with Stanley, who remembered West as "an important political person" and a "major influence" on his own life.[35]

Many of West's students were first attracted by his classroom charisma. As Yvonne Farley asserts, "You knew Don as a good teacher" who had "done it all himself—he was political, artistic, and intellectual; the real thing." But Farley was also deeply impressed with the way he could connect students with their Appalachian past. Taking a sympathetic but more measured stance, Highlander's Helen Lewis acknowledged West's importance as a revered Ap-palachian activist but pointedly noted that in his writing and characterization of his own political history, he became a "historical revisionist."[36] For Lewis, West's political radicalism was a vital part of his story, as was his tendency to profess a rather selective view of Appalachian history that ignored some of the flaws of regional history and culture.

West's "cultural chauvinism" and personal history were, in fact, at the heart of a dilemma many Pipestem volunteers confronted, especially those who came from beyond the mountains. The contradictory dimensions of his character were captured in the ambivalence of Antioch College student Merry Tucker, a twenty-year-old worker who came to the Folklife Center filled with energy and admiration for Don. In May 1967 she told Anne Braden that she had "never met a finer man than Don, nor a man that [she respected] as much in any way." Personally committed to work for social change, Tucker was espe-cially impressed by West's persuasive style. "Unlike most of the radicals with whom I've had any contact," she observed, "Don doesn't spend all his time shouting revolutionary phrases to other radicals who are already convinced. Obviously, these people are not going to have any effect and, on the contrary, may do a lot of damage by alienating the people we must influence. He has an organizing ability that I've never seen before . . . it appears that he's just listening and not propagandizing at all."[37]

That letter, written early in Tucker's stay at Pipestem, reflected her first impressions of West's approach to organizing. Within six months, she had rethought her initial assessment. It eventually became clear that as an outsider she was not to be part of the inner circle; moreover, tension developed when she refused to accept the traditional woman's role. After Connie's arrival, Don either ignored Merry or criticized her work. From her perspective, West was driven by a combination of male chauvinism and cultural chauvinism, perhaps complicated by the paranoia born of years of persecution, which prevented him from placing trust in anyone.[38] Tucker's observations captured the complexity of Don West, a man who was always an amalgam of generous, democratic impulses and authoritarian tendencies, and an inspirational leader capable of alienating his most loyal adherents.

That combination of selflessness, generosity, and self-righteousness represented one of the key themes in his long career, and West left many psychological casualties and broken friendships along the way. His tendency to burn bridges at every turn resulted in a pattern of damaged relationships that tested the friendship of and sometimes alienated collaborators, including Myles Horton, James A. Dombrowski, Warren Doyle, David Stanley, Jesse Stuart, the Georgia liberals, and an assortment of Communist Party figures who vainly attempted to force discipline on him. Even sympathetic friends such as the Bradens, Claude Williams, Don Rasmussen, David Stanley, Warren Doyle, and Yvonne Farley experienced the sharp edge of West's combative side. Like many charismatic leaders, he could be edgy as well as a warm confidant. Most Appalachian activists came to terms with the provocative side of West's character, aware as they were of his extensive contributions to regional cultural revival and pride in mountain heritage.

For modern readers and students of Appalachian history and culture, Don West stands as a figure whose life destroyed stereotypes that for generations misinformed our understanding of the South. He was a literary artist with roots in the simple yet rich mountain culture passing from the scene as he came to maturity. A poet, musician, journalist, essayist, scholar, and educator, his knowledge and refinement do not conform to the flawed image of the uncultured hillbilly. Although he was proud to be called "cracker" and "hillbilly," his literary accomplishments underscored the potential for intellectual achievement present in every human being. They also reflected an accumulation of the folk wisdom inherent in mountain culture and passed on by family and friends. Paradoxically, a long-standing suspicion of the "outsider" that made him a reluctant collaborator in a variety of situations marred West's literary celebration of mountaineer character and individualism.

Beyond West's career as a writer and scholar, however, his life was significant in another profound way in that his highly developed social conscience demonstrated the diversity of southern history, especially in the story of the Appalachian South. Rooted in the lessons taught by Kim Mulkey and Lillie West was an abiding belief in human equality that transcended racial barriers. Don West's firm commitment to the principle of racial reconciliation constituted one of the key themes in a long fight against social injustice that took many forms over time. His adherence to this idea reveals another south far different from the bucolic rural paradise imagined by the Nashville Agrarians. West's career forces us to rethink outmoded assumptions of a monolithic south fatally wounded by racism and atavistic folkways and acknowledge a counterheritage of resistance that bucked the traditions of caste and exclusion.

The backbone of West's alternative south was to be found in the natural virtue that was the birthright of the urban and rural working class. A proud product of a hardworking but cash-strapped mountain family, Don West grew up among people who personified self-reliance but committed themselves to mutual dependence as part of the community of humankind. His youthful experiences taught equality and respect for others as well as the earth that sustained them. Long after his departure from the mountains of North Georgia, West's faith in the capacity of the poor to overcome greed and competition to build an economically just, nonracist society remained solid. That human potential was the rock upon which his new south was to be built.

On many occasions West's vision of a better future for southern workers was sorely tested. Harassed, driven away, burned out, and often reviled for his beliefs and actions, he doggedly pursued his dream until Pipestem finally enabled him to create a learning environment tailor-made for the inculcation of cultural pride and historical understanding. A by-product of his activist years was low-level paranoia that prevented him from placing complete trust in even his closest associates. It was this history of struggle that produced a personal demeanor that many observers perceived as hostility or anger. External appearances aside, it is impossible to examine his career without acknowledging the courage and determination with which West relentlessly pursued his social, political, and educational objectives in the face of exceptional adversity.

The conviction that enabled West to persevere lay in his unshakeable confidence in the coming revolution he saw on the horizon, at least until the last years of his life. A committed internationalist, he viewed the American working-class struggle within the larger context of a transnational movement that would one day usher in a better day for humanity in a workers' utopia. West's faith in the ultimately successful class struggle was rooted in his youthful conversion to a Marxist philosophy that replaced the more traditional religion of his adolescence. Blending the economic and social determinism of Marx with a uniquely personal interpretation of revolutionary Christianity focused on the comrade Jesus as the prophetic son of man, West spent a lifetime organizing for the betterment of the human condition in the here and now.

Although some have argued that he embraced Marxist philosophy too fervently, the life he built and the literary record he amassed marked West as an extraordinary historical figure who influenced all who crossed his path. Most who came to know him in his adopted West Virginia home considered him a charismatic and inspirational leader whose model of faithfulness to himself and the values he espoused continued to shape Appalachian literature and cultural life after his death. Even critics acknowledged the uncompromising integrity that was the hallmark of his public life. If he believed too deeply, he acted passionately and courageously on his convictions, often at great personal risk. In his contribution to literature, cultural awareness, educational access, and the advance of social justice, Don West reached for a future that still struggles to be born.

About the Notes

The first citation in the notes that follow relates to the final assertion in the text to which the note refers. Subsequent citations, in reverse order, are linked to previous points in the same paragraph. In some cases, multiple citations provide additional evidence on a single assertion.

During the research and writing of this book I had access to some of Don West's papers and the Hedy West papers at the residence of the late Hedy West. Subsequently, Talitha West arranged for the transfer of these papers to the Hargrett Rare Books and Manuscripts Library at the University of Georgia in Athens.

At the time of publication, the Don West papers in Hedy West's files and Hedy West's papers remained a completely unprocessed collection. Their organization reflected Hedy West's personal filing system, and some of Don West's papers were completely unorganized. As a result, there may be some inconsistency in citations once the Hargrett Rare Books and Manuscripts Library has completely processed the collections.

Finally, readers should be aware of a change in the location of the manuscript collections, pamphlet files, and other primary source material once held by the Reference Center for Marxist Studies (RCMS) in New York. In 2007 the archives of the Communist Party of the United States, originally held at the Party offices, were transferred to the Tamiment Library in the Elmer Bobst Library at New York University. RCMS materials will eventually be organized according to the Tamiment processing system.

Notes

Prologue

1. Sullivan quoted in James, "A Radical of Long Standing"; see also Henson, "'Naked Words That Have No Subtle Meaning,': Poetry and Teaching in the Writings of Don West," n.d., *Speak Now Against the Day* files, John Egerton Papers, Special Collections, Vanderbilt University; author interviews with Hedy West, March 10, 2004, Narberth, Pa., Frank T. Adams, Nov. 3, 2004, Asheville, N.C., and David Stanley, Aug. 7, 2004, Beckley, W.V., transcripts in author's possession.

2. Among the more recent analyses of West's literary work are Biggers, "The Fugitive of Southern Appalachian Literature," 159–80; Green, "Working Truth Inside Out," 383–406; and Rubin, "Voice of the Cracker," 205–22; see also Duke, *Writers and Miners*, 44–66; Wald, *Exiles from a Future Time*, esp. 28–33; Smethurst, *The New Red Negro*; and Nelson, *Repression and Recovery*, 166, 306–7. West's work is also explored in two dissertations: Green, "The Social Life of Poetry"; and Byerly, "'What Shall a Poet Sing?'"

3. Don West to Byron Herbert Reece, March 17, 1941, box 21, Byron Herbert Reece Papers, Hargrett Rare Books and Manuscript Library, University of Georgia Libraries, Athens.

4. Kelley, *Hammer and Hoe*; Solomon, *The Cry Was Unity*; Craig, *Religion and Radical Politics*; Egerton, *Speak Now Against the Day*; Dunbar, *Against the Grain*.

Chapter 1: Shaping a Value System: Family, the Mountains, and the Wider World, 1906–26

1. Drake, *A History of Appalachia*, ix; Williams, *Appalachia*, 16–17. The destructive impact of industrial capitalism on mountain culture and the "politics of culture" practiced by the missionary schools of the early twentieth century is discussed in Whisnant, *All That Is Native and Fine*, esp. 7–8; see also Kirby, *Rural Worlds Lost*, 223–25. For comment on the concept of "Appalachia" as the product of the northern intellectual imagination, see Shapiro, *Appalachia on Our Minds*. There has been considerable debate among modern historians over the issue of slavery in Appalachia and the harshness of the Peculiar Institution in the mountain South. The prevailing view once held that slavery in the Appalachian South was a relatively benign

institution and that slaves were scarce in the region. Since the late 1980s, however, scholars have begun to emphasize the diversity of the slave experience in the mountains. John Inscoe, for example, has noted in *Mountain Masters* that slavery was vital to the growth of some Appalachian economies. Similarly, Inscoe and Gordon B. McKinney have shown in *The Heart of Confederate Appalachia* (esp. 231) that there were many mountain experiences with slavery and that in some areas it was a stable institution. More strident is Wilma Dunaway (*Slavery in the American Mountain South*, 241), who launches a frontal challenge to the predominant interpretation, emphasizing the sweep and harshness of slavery in many mountain districts. Locating Appalachian slavery within a dynamic international economy, she insists that the "old stereotypes about Appalachian exceptionalism do not hold."

2. Alex Baskin interview with Don West, Feb. 5, 1975, Stony Brook, N.Y.

3. Author interview with Hedy West, March 10–11, 2004, Narberth, Pa.; Hedy West interview with Lillie Mulkey West, Feb. 1976, Blairsville, Ga., Hedy West Papers, Athens, Ga.; Alex Baskin interview with Don West; Byerly, "'What Shall a Poet Sing?'" 30–32. The preceding discussion of the northern Georgia mountains' ethnic and racial composition, as well as the importance of community, neighborliness, and hospitality in the area, is based on the extensive recollections of Lillie Mulkey West that are now held in the Hedy West Papers. For further insight on mountain history and tradition as influences on family attitudes concerning racial equality, see Hedy West interview with Lillie Mulkey West; Sue Thrasher interview with Don West, July 10, 1974, Highlander Research and Education Center Archives, New Market, Tenn.; and Alex Baskin interview with Don West.

4. Hedy West interview with Lillie Mulkey West; Hunt, *The Mulkeys of America*, 729–30; Sue Thrasher interview with Don West; Alex Baskin interview with Don West; Byerly, "'What Shall a Poet Sing?'" 36.

5. Confirmation of debate over the Civil War in Gilmer County may be found in Ward, *The Annals of Upper Georgia*, 607–11.

6. Sue Thrasher interview with Don West.

7. For discussion of Appalachian religious tradition see McCauley, *Appalachian Mountain Religion;* comment on evangelicalism in the nineteenth century, including the conversion experience and commitment to the Social Gospel, appears on 21, 341–42, and 101. The connection between prophetic religion in the twentieth-century South and the evangelical tradition is discussed in Craig, *Religion and Radical Politics* (esp. ch. 4). Chastain's pastoral style is mentioned in the Hedy West interview with Lillie Mulkey West; see also Byerly, "'What Shall a Poet Sing?'" 28. This interpretation of West's humanism and it origins is based in part on extensive correspondence and conversations with Hedy West, who gave extensive critical thought to her father's religious beliefs. Author interview with Hedy West, March 10–11, 2004; see also author interviews with Yvonne Farley, March 13, 2004, St. Albans, W.V.; Mildred Shackleford, June 22, 2004, New Market, Tenn., and P. J. Laska, March 12, 2004, Beckley, W.V., transcripts in author's possession.

8. West, "No Fiddle in My Home," 2, 3, 5–6.

9. Alex Baskin interview with Don West; Sue Thrasher interview with Don West.

10. Ibid.

11. Jacqueline Hall and Ray Faherty interview with Don West, Jan. 22, 1975, interview E-16, Southern Oral History Collection, Southern Historical Collection, Wilson Library, University of North Carolina, Chapel Hill. The family's removal to the lowlands is mentioned in West, *No Lonesome Road*, xiv–xv.

12. Hedy West interview with Lillie Mulkey West; Alex Baskin interview with Don West; Sue Thrasher interview with Don West.

13. Whisnant, *All That Is Native and Fine*, 263–64; see also chapter 1. Although Whisnant focuses on cultural intervention at Kentucky's Hindman Settlement School, the insights in his work are applicable to the impact of the Berry School program on the cultural awareness of the children it served. The origins and objectives of the Berry program are discussed in Byerly, "'What Shall a Poet Sing?'" 47–48; see also Guthrie, "Education and the Evolution of the South"; and Dickey and Mathis, unpublished manuscript History of Berry Schools, Berry College Archives, Memorial Library, Mount Berry, Ga.

14. Alex Baskin interview with Don West; Sue Thrasher interview with Don West; Byerly, "'What Shall a Poet Sing?'" 49.

15. Quoted in Byerly, "'What Shall a Poet Sing?'" 50; see also Alex Baskin interview with Don West, Sue Thrasher interview with Don West, and Jacqueline Hall and Ray Faherty interview with Don West; West, *No Lonesome Road*, xv; Dunbar, *Against the Grain*, 29–30.

16. Sue Thrasher interview with Don West; Jacqueline Hall and Ray Faherty interview with Don West; see also Wiggenton interview of Don West in *Refuse to Stand Silently By*, 69.

17. Alex Baskin interview with Don West; Sue Thrasher interview with Don West; Jacqueline Hall and Ray Faherty interview with Don West.

18. Jacqueline Hall and Ray Faherty interview with Don West; Sue Thrasher interview with Don West.

19. Minutes of Berry Faculty, April 19, 1926, Mt. Berry, series 2: 411, G. Leland Green Papers, Berry College Archives, Memorial Library, Mount Berry, Ga.

20. Alex Baskin interview with Don West; Jacqueline Hall and Ray Faherty interview with Don West.

21. Sue Thrasher interview with Don West; Jacqueline Hall and Ray Faherty interview with Don West; Alex Baskin interview with Don West; George Brosi Notes, Jeff Biggers Papers, Don West Collection, Hargrett Rare Books and Manuscripts Library, University of Georgia Libraries, Athens; Byerly, "'What Shall a Poet Sing?'" 50.

22. G. Leland Green to J. O. West, July 20, 1926, and G. Leland Green to G. B. King, July 24, 1926, W file and G file, G. Leland Green Papers; Jesse Stuart, "Portrait of a Mountain Boy," in the *Cumberland Empire*, ca. 1932, box 76, Highlander Research and Education Center Papers, Archives and Manuscripts Division, Wisconsin Historical Society, Madison.

23. Martha Berry to Emily V. Hammond, Oct. 6, 1933, and to Mrs. Henry Ford, Oct. 7, 1933, both in subject file correspondence, "Don West Matter," Martha Berry Papers, Berry College Archives; G. Leland Green to Edwin White, Aug. 12, 1926, G file, G. Leland Green Papers; Green to J. O. West, July 20, 1926, and to Don West, Aug. 3, 1926, Don West to G. Leland Green, July 31, 1926, and Elsie West to G. Leland Green, Aug. 6, 1926, all in West-Westbrooke file, G. Leland Green Correspondence, Office of the President, G. Leland Green Papers. Green later made explicit reference to "the three students who left school as a *protest* against the removal of Mr. Gurley." Minutes, Regular Meeting, Executive Committee, The Berry Schools, Aug. 11, 1926, Faculty Meetings file, 1926, G. Leland Green Papers.

24. Hedy West interview with Don West, Don West Papers, Athens, Ga.; G. Leland Green to George Lister Carlisle Jr., July 19, 1926, C file, G. Leland Green Papers. Gurley's

acknowledgement of indiscreet behavior is discussed in G. Leland Green to Edwin White, Aug. 12, 1926.

25. Alex Baskin interview with Don West; Sue Thrasher interview with Don West; Byerly, "'What Shall a Poet Sing?'" 51.

26. Alex Baskin interview with Don West; Sue Thrasher interview with Don West; Jacqueline Hall and Roy Faherty interview with Don West; "Entrance Credits," Don West Transcript, Berry School, Registrar's Office, Lincoln Memorial University; Byerly, "'What Shall a Poet Sing?'" 51.

Chapter 2: Expanded Horizons: Lincoln Memorial University as Seedbed of Creativity, 1926–29

1. Byerly, "'What Shall a Poet Sing?'" 53; *Mountain Herald*, Jan. 1927; Sue Thrasher interview with Don West, July 10, 1974, Highlander Research and Education Center Archives, New Market, Tenn.

2. Jacqueline Hall and Ray Faherty interview with Don West, Jan. 22, 1975, interview E-16, Southern Oral History Collection, Southern Historical Collection (SOHC-SHC), Wilson Library, University of North Carolina, Chapel Hill; Hedy West interview with Don West, Don West Papers, Hargrett Rare Books and Manuscripts Library, University of Georgia Libraries, Athens.

3. *Mountain Herald*, Dec. 1926, May 1928, and *Railsplitter*, 1927, 104, all in Lincoln Memorial University (LMU) Archives, Harrogate, Tenn.; Alex Baskin interview with Don West, Feb. 5, 1975, Stony Brook, N.Y.; Jacqueline Hall and Ray Faherty interview with Don West; Don West Transcript, Berry School, Registrar's Office, Lincoln Memorial University; Donald Lee West, "Uniform Transfer Blank for Tennessee Colleges," Don West Papers; Stuart, *Beyond Dark Hills*, 187; see also Stuart, *To Teach, to Love*, 85; and Byerly, "'What Shall a Poet Sing?'" 54–55.

4. Alex Baskin interview with Don West.

5. *The Blue and the Gray*, March 1928, *Mountain Herald*, Nov. 1927, Autumn 1928, and *Rail Splitter*, 1927, all in LMU Archives.

6. Stuart, *Beyond Dark Hills*, 186–87; Alex Baskin interview with Don West; Sue Thrasher interview with Don West; Richardson, *Jesse*, 129.

7. Sue Thrasher interview with Don West; Sullivan, "Don West, Poet and Preacher," 56; Stuart, *Beyond Dark Hills*, 218; West, *No Lonesome Road*, xvi; Byerly, "'What Shall a Poet Sing?'" 56.

8. Don West, "Harry Harrison Kroll: An Essay," *Appalachian Mountain Books*, 2 (1986) in West, *No Lonesome Road*, 18–20; Stuart, *Beyond Dark Hills*, 218; Stuart, *To Teach, to Love*, 115.

9. West, "Harry Harrison Kroll," 21; see also Sue Thrasher interview with Don West.

10. Stuart, *Beyond Dark Hills*, 218; Stuart, *To Teach, to Love*, 118; Sue Thrasher interview with Don West; Byerly, "'What Shall a Poet Sing?'" 67; see also Richard Saunders, draft biography of Harry Harrison Kroll, Special Collections, Paul Meek Library, University of Tennessee–Martin; J. H. Moore, "Reminiscences," LMU Archives.

11. Jesse Stuart, "Portrait of a Mountain Boy," 37, in the *Cumberland Empire*, ca. 1932, box 76, Highlander Research and Education Center Papers, Archives and Manuscripts Division, Wisconsin Historical Society, Madison; *Rail Splitter*, 1928, 104; *Rail Splitter*, 1930, 114; Don West Transcript; Stuart, *Beyond Dark Hills*, 186; *Mountain Herald*, Autumn, 1928; West, *No Lonesome Road*, xv.

12. *The Blue and the Grey*, March 1928, March 12, 1929; *Mountain Herald*, Autumn 1928, Winter 1929, all in LMU Archives.

13. Byerly, "'What Shall a Poet Sing?'" 61.

14. Hedy West interview with Don West; Alex Baskin interview with Don West.

15. West to Mother, April 9, March 1, 1928; West to Bud (Charlie), April 14, 1928, all in Don West Papers; Alex Baskin interview with Don West; Hedy West interview with Don West; Byerly, "'What Shall a Poet Sing?'" 62.

16. Hedy West interview with Don West; Wiggenton interview with Don West in *Refuse to Stand Silently By*, 70–71; Alex Baskin interview with Don West; *Mountain Herald*, April–May 1919, LMU Archives.

17. Alex Baskin interview with Don West; Sue Thrasher interview with Don West; Hedy West interview with Don West; Stuart, "Portrait of a Mountain Boy," 37; Byerly, "'What Shall a Poet Sing?'" 64.

18. Quoted in Stuart, "Portrait of a Mountain Boy," 37; Byerly, "'What Shall a Poet Sing?'" 65; Alex Baskin interview with Don West; Stuart, *Beyond Dark Hills*, 217; C. P. Williams to Stuart, Jan. 16, 1933, Jesse Stuart Foundation, Ashland, Ky.; Hedy West interview with Don West.

19. Stuart, *Beyond Dark Hills*, 216–17; Williams to Stuart, Jan. 16, 1933; Alex Baskin interview with Don West; Hedy West interview with Don West.

20. Stuart, *Beyond Dark Hills*, 217; Williams to Stuart, Jan. 16, 1933; Alex Baskin interview with Don West; Jesse Stuart to Donald Davidson, Dec. 4, 1933, box 12, Donald Davidson Papers, Special Collections and University Archives, Vanderbilt University Library, Nashville; Hedy West interview with Don West; Don West, "Talk by Don West," Jan. 21, 1975, interview E-15, SOHC-SHC; Richardson, *Jesse*, 88.

21. Alex Baskin interview with Don West; Wiggenton interview with Don West in *Refuse to Stand Silently By*, 70; West, "Talk by Don West."

22. Don West to Mama and Father, Nov. 6, 1929, Don West Papers; Jacqueline Hall and Ray Faherty interview with Don West; Sue Thrasher interview with Don West; Alex Baskin interview with Don West.

Chapter 3: Social Gospel and Educational Mission: The Turning Point, 1930–33

1. Alex Baskin interview with Don West, Feb. 5, 1975, Stony Brook, N.Y.; Stuart, *Beyond Dark Hills*, 282–83. For the Southern Agrarians' declaration of intellectual independence see *I'll Take My Stand*, ed. Davidson et al.

2. Jesse Stuart, "Portrait of a Mountain Boy," 38, in the *Cumberland Empire*, ca. 1932, box 76, Highlander Research and Education Papers (Highlander Papers), Archives and Manuscripts Division, Wisconsin Historical Society, Madison; Stuart, *Beyond Dark Hills*, 283; Stuart to Dr. Hensley Woodridge, Oct. 6, 1958, Jesse Stuart Papers, Pogue Library Special Collections, Murray State University, copy in private collection of David Palmore, Erlanger, Ky. I gratefully acknowledge the Jesse Stuart Foundation and Teresa L. Reynolds for granting permission to quote from the Stuart, Still, and West correspondence, some of it housed at Morehead State University and Murray State University. Stuart material is used by permission of the Jesse Stuart Foundation, Ashland, Ky., and citations will reference the appropriate repository. See also Jacqueline Hall and Ray Faherty interview with Don West, Jan. 22, 1975, interview E-16, Southern Oral History Collection, Southern Historical Collection (SOHC-SHC), Wilson Library, University of North Carolina, Chapel Hill;

Alex Baskin interview with Don West; Hedy West interview with Don West, Don West Papers, Hargrett Rare Books and Manuscripts Library, University of Georgia Libraries, Athens; Herndon and Brosi, *Jesse Stuart*, 3; Richardson, *Jesse*, 128; and Stuart, *To Teach, to Love*, 141.

3. Jacqueline Hall and Ray Faherty interview with Don West; Alex Baskin interview with Don West; Sue Thrasher interview with Don West, July 10, 1974, Highlander Research and Education Center Archives, New Market, Tenn.; Hedy West interview with Don West; Wiggenton interview with Don West in *Refuse to Stand Silently By*, 71. For discussion of Taylor's ideas and influence, see Whisnant, *Modernizing the Mountaineer*, 14–17; Craig, *Religion and Radical Politics*, 134, 145; Dunbar, *Against the Grain*, 28–29; and Egerton, *Speak Now Against the Day*, 77–78; see also Harbison, "The Social Gospel Career of Alva W. Taylor," 370, 372, 410; and Byerly, "'What Shall a Poet Sing?'" 70–71.

4. Williams, *Appalachia*, 314; Drake, *A History of Appalachia*, 194–95.

5. West to James Still, Oct. 26, 1930, box 15.4, Don West file, James Still Papers, Special Collections, Morehead State University, Morehead, Ky.

6. Ibid; for discussion of the Danish folk school model for the education of Appalachian mountain people, see Whisnant, *All That Is Native and Fine*, 133–36, and Shapiro, *Appalachia on Our Minds*, esp. 231–42

7. Don West, "Knott County, Kentucky: A Study," thesis, Vanderbilt University School of Religion, 1932, 88; West, *No Lonesome Road*, xvii; West to Still, Nov. 29, Dec. 23, 1930, box 15.4, Don West file, James Still Papers.

8. West to Still, Oct. 26, 1930; see also West to Still, Dec. 23 and Nov. 29, 1930, all in box 15.4, Don West file, James Still Papers.

9. West to Still, March 7, 1931, box 7.7, Don West file, James Still Papers; Sue Thrasher interview with Don West; Alex Baskin interview with Don West; Wiggenton interview with Don West in *Refuse to Stand Silently By*, 72; Stuart, "Portrait of a Mountain Boy," 38.

10. Whisnant, *All That Is Native and Fine*, 162; Byerly, "'What Shall a Poet Sing?'" 83–84.

11. West, *No Lonesome Road*, xviii; West quoted in Alex Baskin interview with Don West; Whisnant, *All That Is Native and Fine*, 128.

12. *Berry Alumni Quarterly*, ca. Jan. 1932, 11, Don West file, G. Leland Green Papers, Berry College Archives, Memorial Library, Mount Berry, Ga.; *Vanderbilt Alumnus*, Feb. 1932, 116; Stuart, "Portrait of a Mountain Boy," 38; Alex Baskin interview with Don West.

13. *Berry Alumni Quarterly*, April 1932, Don West file, G. Leland Green Papers; West to Still, May 13, 1932, box 15.4, Don West file, James Still Papers; Dickey and Mathis, *Berry College*, 66.

14. "Program: Fifty-Seventh Commencement," June 8, 1932, Vanderbilt Archives; West to Still, May 13, 1932; Byerly, "'What Shall a Poet Sing?'" 72; Harbison, "The Social Gospel Career of Alva W. Taylor," 370.

15. McCauley, *Appalachian Mountain Religion*, 7, 342; Byerly, "'What Shall a Poet Sing?'" 74–75.

16. For full discussion of Williams, Kester, and Rogers in their Vanderbilt years, see Craig, *Religion and Radical Politics*, 134, 145–46; Egerton, *Speak Now Against the Day*, 77–78; Dunbar, *Against the Grain*, 29–33; Naison, "Claude and Joyce Williams," 3; Martin, *Howard Kester and the Struggle for Social Justice*; Harbison, "The Social Gospel Career of Alva W. Taylor," 370–71; Belfrage, *A Faith to Free the People*; and Byerly, "'What Shall a Poet Sing?'" 75–78.

17. Sue Thrasher interview with Don West; Jacqueline Hall and Ray Faherty interview

with Don West; Wiggenton interview with Don West in *Refuse to Stand Silently By*, 71. Acting on his mentor's advice, West turned up in Greenville, S.C., in 1930, where he volunteered to organize millworkers into the National Textile Workers Union (NTWU). Preferring not to "waste time doing nothing," he told union organizers that he "wanted to do something useful." Ann Burlak, "Notes," box 32, Don West file, Anne Burlak Timpson Papers, Sophia Smith Collection, Smith College Library, Northhampton, Mass.

18. Duke, *Writers and Miners*, 48. For further discussion of the Wilder strike see Dunbar, *Against the Grain*, 1–15; Craig, *Religion and Radical Politics*, 142–43; Glen, *Highlander*, 22–25; "Trouble in the Tennessee Coal Fields," Dec. 4, 1932, folder 3834, Howard Kester Papers, SOHC-SHC; and Perry, "Labor Struggle at Wilder, Tennessee."

19. Hedy West to Author, April 12 and 22, 2004; author interview with Hedy West, March 10–11, 2004; Hedy West interview with Don West; Jacqueline Hall and Ray Faherty interview with Don West.

20. "Trouble in the Tennessee Coal Fields"; Dunbar, *Against the Grain*, 6; West to Still, Sept. 18, 1932, box 15.4, Don West file, James Still Papers.

21. Kester, Report, Jan. 1933, folder 3834, Howard Kester Papers; Alva Taylor to Jim Myers, Dec. 25, 1932, box 7, Alva W. Taylor Papers, Archives, Disciples of Christ Historical Society, Nashville.

22. Glen, *Highlander*, 15–16.

23. Alice Cobb, interview, May Justus, n.d.; Neil J. O'Connell, "The Religious Origins of the Highlander Folk School," May 5, 1978, box 12, Myles Horton Papers, Archives and Manuscripts Division, Wisconsin Historical Society, Madison; Alanna J. Mozzer, "Lillian W. Johnson—Wellesley Class of 1885," *Graduate Woman* (Nov.–Dec. 1979): 31, and *Foxfire 14* (Summer 1980): 103, both in box 1, May Justus Papers, Special Collections, University of Tennessee, Nashville; May Justus to Frank Adams, May 18, 1975, box 20, Frank T. Adams Papers, Archives and Manuscripts Division, Wisconsin Historical Society, Madison; Alex Baskin interview with Don West; Jacqueline Hall and Ray Faherty interview with Don West. West later maintained that before he met Horton, he and Connie were already living on the Johnson property. Byerly, "'What Shall a Poet Sing?'" 95.

24. D. Blanchard interview with Myles Horton, April 12, 1984, box 2, Myles Horton Papers; Horton, *The Long Haul*, 63; Jacqueline Hall and Ray Faherty interview with Don West; Alex Baskin interview with Don West; Lowell Kirby to Editor, *Atlanta Weekly*, Feb. 22, 1983; West to Byerly, May 28, 1990, Don West Papers; Glen, *Highlander*, 16. The accounts of Highlander's origins vary, but most fail to recognize West's initiative in the acquisition of the Johnson property. The incomplete account of Highlander's origins was perpetuated by Horton's consistent assertions that he was primarily responsible for its establishment. For the conventional story, see Horton, *The Highlander Folk School*; see also Egerton, *Speak Now Against the Day*, 157–58; Dunbar, *Against the Grain*, 44; and Horton, *The Long Haul*, 63. Glen, who recognizes that "it is possible to attribute too much of Highlander's history to a single personality," notes West's preliminary work, as does Byerly. Glen, *Highlander*, 17, 19; Byerly, "'What Shall a Poet Sing?'" 95.

25. Horton, *The Long Haul*, 63; Jacqueline Hall and Ray Faherty interview with Don West; Sue Thrasher interview with Don West; Glen, *Highlander*, 17.

26. Glen, *Highlander*, 20; *Knoxville News-Sentinel*, ca. Oct. 8, 1932, scrapbook 1, Jesse Stuart Papers.

27. "News Reports," *Christian Century*, Sept. 21, 1932, box 5, Alva W. Taylor Papers; Glen, *Highlander*, 17; Harbison, "The Social Gospel Career of Alva W. Taylor," 373. Taylor stayed

in touch with his young followers and urged them to continue reports on the "progress of [their] work." Taylor to Horton, Dec. 6, 1932, box 27, Highlander Papers.

28. Anonymous Student, "Criticism of Highlander Folk School," May 11, 1933, box 1, Highlander Papers; Sue Thrasher interview with Don West. For an example of West's promotional efforts, see enclosure in West to Still, Oct. 1, 1932, "Still Storage" file, James Still Papers, Special Collections, University of Kentucky Library, Lexington.

29. Anonymous Student, "Criticism of Highlander Folk School"; West to Byerly, May 28, 1990; Jacqueline Hall and Ray Faherty interview of Don West; Sue Thrasher interview of Don West.

30. West to *Cumberland Outlook*, Dec. 18, 1932, scrapbook 1, Jesse Stuart Papers; "Grundy Cashier Lambasts [*sic*] Highlander Folk Plan as Dixie Thorn," box 67, Highlander Papers; Sue Thrasher interview of Don West; Anonymous Student, "Criticism of Highlander Folk School"; Glen, *Highlander*, 21; *Cumberland Outlook*, Dec. 15, 1932, record group 4, box 8, Highlander Folk School Collection, Tennessee State Library and Archives, Nashville; Open Letter, May 27, 1932, record group 2, box I-40, Highlander Research and Education Center Archives, New Market, Tenn.

31. Horton to Clarence Senior, Dec. 19, 1932, and West to Socialist Headquarters, Dec. 17, 1932, both roll 26, Socialist Party of the United States Papers, Special Collections (microfilm edition), Duke University; Sue Thrasher interview with Don West; Jacqueline Hall and Ray Faherty interview with Don West.

32. Johnson, "To the Editor of the *Chattanooga Times*," Dec. 8, 1932, and Johnson to Horton, Dec. 8, 1932, both box 16, Highlander Papers; Dunbar, *Against the Grain*, 44-45; Horton, *The Long Haul*, 65.

33. Johnson to Horton, ca. Dec. 1932, Dec. 8, Dec. 12, 1932, all box 16, Highlander Papers; Glen, *Highlander*, 26.

34. Barney Graham to West, Jan. 27, 1933, Don West Papers; West to Kester, Feb 15, 1933, box 1, Howard Kester Papers; Glen, *Highlander*, 24.

35. Dunbar, *Against the Grain*, 8; Alex Baskin interview with Don West; J. B. T. to Thomas, Feb. 23, 1933, box 27, Highlander Papers; Kester to Senior, Feb. 21, 1933, Kester to West, Feb. 21, 1933, and West to Kester, Feb. 15, 1933, all in box 1, Howard Kester Papers; see also Hedy West, "The Davison-Wilder Blues," album notes, folder 20002, Archie Green Papers, Southern Historical Collection (SHC).

36. Alex Baskin interview with Don West; Dunbar, *Against the Grain*, 9-10; Glen, *Highlander*, 24; Duke, *Writers and Miners*, 48.

37. Alex Baskin interview with West; Don West to Hedy West, Jan. 22, 1969, Hedy West Papers; Dunbar, *Against the Grain*, 10; Wiggenton interview with Don West in *Refuse to Stand Silently By*, 71-72; Hedy West, "Lament for Barney Graham," album notes, folder 20002, Archie Green Papers; Byerly, "'What Shall a Poet Sing?'" 107-8.

38. Alex Baskin interview with Don West; Dunbar, *Against the Grain*, 11-14; Glen, *Highlander*, 24-25; Taylor to Jim and Bill, May 18, 1933, and "Cowardly Murder Stains Coal-Mine Strike," *Christian Century*, June 14, 1933, both in box 5, Alva W. Taylor Papers.

39. Dunbar, *Against the Grain*, 14; "Lament for Barney Graham"; Duke, *Writers and Miners*, 49; Glen, *Highlander*, 25; West quotation from Alex Baskin interview with Don West.

40. Sue Thrasher interview with Don West; Horton, "Notes on Jim Dombrowski," box 16, James A. Dombrowski Papers, Archives and Manuscripts Division, Wisconsin Historical Society, Madison; Glen, *Highlander*, 25-26; "Criticism of Highlander Folk School." Dur-

ing her career as social activist and later as CP member Elsie was known by many names, including Johnnye West and Janet or Jeannette Ross or Weaver.

41. "The Peerless Mill Situation," 1933, and "Broadcasting over Station BUNK," Feb. 23, 1933, both box 67, Highlander Papers; Sue Thrasher interview with Don West.

42. "The Highlander Folk School," ca. spring 1933, West to Horton, April 3, 1933, and "Highlander Folk School," ca. May 1933, all in boxes 1, 29, and 12, Highlander Papers; West to John R. Neil, Feb. 15, 1933, box 1, Howard Kester Papers; D. Blanchard interview with Myles Horton; Martin, *Howard Kester and the Struggle for Social Justice*, 49; Taylor to Jerome, March 18, 1933, box 2, Alva W. Taylor Papers; see also Glen, *Highlander*, 29; Adams with Horton, *Unearthing Seeds of Fire*, 44; Horton to Adams, Sept. 6, 1972, box 6, Frank T. Adams Papers; and Adams, *James A. Dombrowski*, 68.

43. "Criticism of Highlander Folk School"; West to Horton, May 12, 1933, both in box 15, Highlander Papers; Egerton, *Speak Now Against the Day*, 159; D. Blanchard interview with Myles Horton; West to Byerly, May 28, 1990; Glen, *Highlander*, 26.

44. There is some evidence that Horton was uncomfortable in the presence of aggressive female activists. Author interview with Frank T. Adams, Nov. 3, 2004, Asheville, N.C.; Ditto (James A. Dombrowski) to Plato (Myles Horton), May 20, 1933, West to Horton, May 12, 1933, and "Criticism of Highlander Folk School," all in boxes 15 and 1, Highlander Papers; Sue Thrasher interview with Don West; see also Byerly, "'What Shall a Poet Sing?'" 114; and Adams, *James A. Dombrowski*, 68.

45. West to Horton, May 12, 1933. By this time Johnnye had become interested in the Communist Party, and Don was moving toward membership. Janet Ross, "Autobiography," fond 495, opis 261, delo 5188, Records of Communist International, Russian State Archive of Social and Political History, Moscow; see also Klehr et al., *Secret World of American Communism*, 287. For Horton's account of West's departure, see D. Blanchard interview with Myles Horton; Horton, *The Long Haul*, 66. Late in life, a still resentful Don West claimed that "it didn't take long to determine that Horton was a Red-baiter," a questionable assertion that nonetheless documented the ideological gap between the two collaborators. West to Byerly, May 28, 1990.

Chapter 4: Radicalization: Baptism of Fire, 1933–34

1. Byerly, "'What Shall a Poet Sing?'" 168; Sue Thrasher interview with Don West, July 10, 1974, Highlander Research and Education Center Archives, New Market, Tenn.; Alex Baskin interview with Don West, Feb. 5, 1975, Stony Brook, N.Y.; Jacqueline Hall and Ray Faherty interview with Don West, Jan. 22, 1975, interview E-16, Southern Oral History Collection, Southern Historical Collection (SOHC-SHC), Wilson Library, University of North Carolina, Chapel Hill; Kelley, *Hammer and Hoe*, 25–26; Klehr, *The Heyday of American Communism*, 258–59.

2. Sue Thrasher interview with Don West; Alex Baskin interview with Don West; Jacqueline Hall and Ray Faherty interview with Don West; Theodore Rosengarten, "South-by-Northeast: The Journey of C. Vann Woodward," box 16, C. Vann Woodward Papers, Manuscripts and Archives, Yale University Library, New Haven; Martin, *The Angelo Herndon Case*, 75–78, 110; interview with C. Vann Woodward, Jan. 12, 1991, interview A-341, SOHC-SHC; *Atlanta Daily World*, Jan. 29, 31, 1933; Glenn Rainey to Pete, March 27, 1933, and Citizens Meeting on the Angelo Herndon Case," May 1933, both box 2, Glenn Rainey Papers, Special Collections, Emory University (SC-EU), Atlanta; *The Daily Worker*, Jan. 29,

Feb. 3, 1933; Mary Raoul Millis to Ethel Davis, May 21, 1933, box 17, Mary Raoul Millis Papers, SC-EU; Solomon, *The Cry Was Unity*, 221.

3. *The Daily Worker*, June 11, 1934; West, "Georgia Wants Me—Dead or Alive," *The New Masses*, June 26, 1934; Byerly, "'What Shall a Poet Sing?'" 115–18; West, *No Lonesome Road*, xx; Wald, *Exiles from a Future Time*, 29; "Provisional Committee for Freedom, Angelo Herndon Formed," March 18, 1933, reel 18 (microfilm edition), International Labor Defense (ILD) Papers, Schomburg Center for Research of Black Culture, New York; Benjamin J. Davis to W. W. Alexander, Sept. 9, 1933, reel 7 (microfilm edition), Commission on Interracial Cooperation (CIC) Papers, Special Collections, Atlanta University Center; Davis, *Communist Councilman from Harlem*, 85.

4. Jacqueline Hall and Ray Faherty interview with Don West.

5. "Report of the Atlanta Section," July 22, 1933, fond 515, opis 1, delo 3311, reel 255, Records of the CPUSA, Russian State Archive of Social and Political History (RGASPI), Moscow; provisional committee quoted in Davis to Alexander, Sept. 9, 1933, reel 7, CIC Papers; Sue Thrasher interview with Don West; Alex Baskin interview with Don West; Wiggenton interview with Don West in *Refuse to Stand Silently By*, 79–80; "Provisional Committee for Freedom, Angelo Herndon Formed." The provisional committee's activities are discussed in Lorence, "Mobilizing the Reserve Army," 73–74.

6. "Report of the Atlanta Section," July 22, 1933. Herndon's replacement as CP unemployed organizer in Atlanta was Clyde Johnson, whose reputation as both student and labor organizer in Rome preceded him. Johnson, "Recollections of the Sharecropper's Union," Jan. 20, 1978, file 4642, box 2, Clyde Johnson Papers, SOHC-SHC.

7. Nat Ross to Secretariat, June 27, 1933, and Unidentified Organizer to Secretariat, June 6, 1933, reels 309, 255, fond 515, opis 1, delos 4407 and 3311, RGASPI; see also Janet Ross, "Autobiography," fond 495, opis 261, delo 5188, RGASPI. For evidence of the Herndon case's value in party organizing among Atlanta's African Americans see Benjamin Davis Jr., manuscript fragment, box 1, Benjamin Davis Jr. Papers, Reference Center for Marxist Studies (RCMS), New York.

8. Horton to Thomas, April 24, 1933, Thomas to Horton, Sept. 19, 1933, West to Senior, June 1, 1933, and "Southern Folk School and Libraries," 1933, all in boxes 27, 29, Highlander Research and Education Center Papers (Highlander Papers), Archives and Manuscripts Division, Wisconsin Historical Society, Madison; see also Don West Scrapbook, Ann West Williams Collection, Charleston, W.V.; Kester to Horton, March 22, 27, and 29, 1933, file 69, record group 2–I, Myles Horton series, Highlander Research and Education Center Archives; "The Highlander Folk School," n.d., encl. March 24, 1933, folder 1819, Frank Porter Graham Papers, SOHC-SHC. West's pre-Herndon educational activities in Georgia are fully discussed in West to Still, March 16, 1933, "Still Storage" file, James Still Papers, Special Collections, University of Kentucky Library, Lexington.

9. The following are all in boxes 29 and 76, Highlander Papers: Mabel Adams West, "Southern Folk Schools and Libraries," *Cumberland Empire*, ca. Nov. 1933; Don West and Clyde Johnson to Dear Friend," Dec. 1933; "To Friends of Underprivileged Southern Toilers," ca. Nov. 1933; and West to Horton, Dec. 16, 1933.

10. Dunbar, *Against the Grain*, 53–55; Alex Baskin interview with Don West; Sue Thrasher interview with Don West; Johnson, "Recollections of the Sharecropper's Union"; West to Tony, Feb. 6, 1979, Don West Scrapbook, Ann West Williams Collection, Charleston, W.V.; Kelley, *Hammer and Hoe*, 63; see also "Report on National Students League," ca. Oct. 1933, subject file correspondence, "Don West Matter," Martha Berry Papers, Berry College

Archives, Memorial Library, Mount Berry, Ga.; "National Student League," Feb. 11, 1941, Atlanta, Feb. 11, 1941, FBI Report 61-7497-72, in box 43, Harvey Klehr Papers, SC-EU.

11. "Protest Injustice to Berry Students," ca. Aug. 1933, boxes 29, 321, Highlander Papers; Johnson, "Recollections of the Sharecropper's Union"; Alex Baskin interview of Don West; "Donald L. West," Louisville, Ky., Jan. 20, 1942, FBI Report, file 100-20396-5x, obtained under a Freedom of Information Act (FOIA) request; Walker Martin, "To the Students from Whom I Have Received Protest Letters of Berry High School for Boys and Berry College," ca. Oct. 1933, subject file correspondence, "Don West Matter," Martha Berry Papers, Berry College Archives; Guthrie, "Education for the Evolution of the South," 87–88; Dickey and Mathews, *Berry College*, 66–67.

12. The following are all in subject file correspondence, "Don West Matter," Martha Berry Papers: Walker Martin to Matson, Oct. 7, 1933, Martin to Merle, Dec. 17, 1932, Martin to Martha Berry, Oct. 9, 1933, *The New Republic*, Oct. 4, 1933, David Lee to Grady Hamrick, Oct. 5, 1933, Serril Gerber to Hamrick, Oct. 5, 1933, Jack Lee to Hamrick, Oct. 4, 1933, W. E. Washburn to Hamrick, Oct. 5, 1933, Al Lehman and Lucien Koch to Martha Berry, Oct. 6, 1933, and Edith Washburn to Berry, Oct. 5, 1933; see also Guthrie, "Education for the Evolution of the South," 91; Dickey and Mathews, *Berry College*, 13–14; and Dunbar, *Against the Grain*, 54.

13. Stuart to Still, Dec. 3, 1933, box 14.3, Don West file, James Still Papers, Special Collections, Morehead State University, Morehead, Ky.; Stuart to Donald Davidson, Dec. 4, 1933, box 12, Donald Davidson Papers, Special Collections and University Archives, Vanderbilt University Library, Nashville, Tenn.; "Protest of Berry Students against False Propaganda Being Spread by Don West and Others," *The New Republic*, n.d., and *Mt. Berry News*, Oct. 25, 1933, all in subject file correspondence, "Don West Matter," Martha Berry Papers; Holman, "Berry Schools Students Foil Attempts to Foment Strike"; Alex Baskin interview with Don West. The closest student of the Berry strike, Carol Guthrie, concludes that Berry's response to the strike was an overreaction "out of proportion" to the challenge it represented ("Education for the Evolution of the South," 92–93, 101–2). See also Dunbar, *Against the Grain*, 54.

14. Alex Baskin interview with Don West; Basso, "About the Berry Schools" (for full discussion of Basso's conclusions, see Guthrie, "Education for the Evolution of the South," 99–100); Taylor to Paul, Oct. 16, 1933, box 2, Alva W. Taylor Papers, Archives, Disciples of Christ Historical Society, Nashville; Taylor to Horton, Nov. 11 and Oct. 17, 1933, and West to Horton, Dec. 16, 1933, boxes 27, 29, Highlander Papers; Berry to Emily V. Hammond, Oct. 6, 1933, subject file correspondence, "Don West Matter," Martha Berry Papers; Dickey and Mathews, *Berry College*, 67–68.

15. The following are in Miles Horton series, record group 2–I, file 69 and record group 2–I, file 113, Don West file, Highlander Papers. For Kestyer's cautionary note, see Kester to Horton, ca. Nov. 1933. Horton's criticism of Berry's denials may be found in Horton to Bliven, Nov. 1, 1933; see also West to Horton, ca. Oct. 1933, Horton to Alexander, Oct. 19, 1933, Alexander to Taylor, Oct. 11, 1933, Alexander to Horton, Oct. 11, 1933, and G. Leland Green to Sherwood Eddy, Oct. 9, 1933. See also Taylor to Horton, Nov. 11, 1933, box 2, Taylor Papers. Highlander's statement of support is found in Horton to Alexander, Nov. 11, 1933, subject matter correspondence, "Don West Matter," Martha Berry Papers; Guthrie, "Education for the Evolution of the South," 95; and George Wesley to Bliven, Oct. 31, 1933, Don West Scrapbook, Ann West Williams Collection, Charleston, W.V.

16. "Memorandum," ca. May 1933, fond 515, opis 1, delo 2929, reel 225, RGASPI; Johnson, "Recollections of the Sharecropper's Union."

17. Jacqueline Hall and Ray Faherty interview with Don West; Ross to Secretariat, June 27, 1933, fond 515, opis 1, delo 3311, reel 255, RGASPI.

18. Jacqueline Hall and Ray Faherty interview with Don West; Alex Baskin interview with Don West; "Donald L. West," Atlanta, file 100-20396, FBI Report 100-559.

19. Wiggenton interview with Don West in *Refuse to Stand Silently By*, 80; Jacqueline Hall and Ray Faherty interview with Don West; Martin, *Angelo Herndom and Southern Justice*, 112; interview with Nannie Washburn, box 39, Living Atlanta Collection, Atlanta History Center; Kuhn and Joye, eds., *Living Atlanta*, 202–3, 286–87; Daisy Lampkin to Roy Wilkins, Feb. 4, 1933, pt. 1, box G-44, NAACP Papers, Manuscripts Division, Library of Congress, Washington, D.C.; Byerly, "'What Shall a Poet Sing?'" 164, 178; Dunbar, *Against the Grain*, 58. The breadth of the national Herndon defense committee is evident in Sasha Small, "Hell in Georgia: What Angelo Herndon Faces!" n.d., 12–13, and Angelo Herndon, "You Cannot Kill the Working Class," ca. 1934, 29–30, both RCMS; see also Davis, *Communist Councilman from Harlem*, ch. 5.

20. Sue Thrasher interview with Don West; Jacqueline Hall and Ray Faherty interview with Don West; Martin, *Angelo Herndon and Southern Justice*, 85; Lorence, "Mobilizing the Reserve Army," 73.

21. Wiggenton interview with Don West in *Refuse to Stand Silently By*, 81–82; Jacqueline Hall and Ray Fahety interview with Don West.

22. This account of West's early relationship with Hosea Hudson is based in part on Painter, *The Narrative of Hosea Hudson*, 204–5, 214–23; Nell Painter interview of Hosea Hudson, folder 4007, E-1, SOHC-SHC; and Painter to Hosea Hudson, Aug. 1981, box 1, Hosea Hudson Papers, RCMS; see also Jacqueline Hall and Ray Faherty interview with Don West; and Kelley, *Hammer and Hoe*, 95.

23. Martin, *Angelo Herndon and Southern Justice*, 110–12; Byerly, "'What Shall a Poet Sing?'" 180–84.

24. Both Branch and Washburn were active members of the Herndon defense committee. Washburn, husband of activist textile worker Nannie Leah Washburn, was a veteran radical who was among the advisors to the Southern Folk School and Libraries. Branch was one of many black clergy who took risks in defense of Angelo Herndon. For details on the escalation of the Red Scare during the Hudson raids of May 1934, see West, "The Atlanta Situation and the Recent Herndon Decision," June 24, 1934, reel 112, American Civil Liberties Union (ACLU) Papers (microfilm edition), Seeley G. Mudd Manuscript Library, Princeton University; West, "Georgia Wants Me—Dead or Alive"; "Wisdom, Justice, and Moderation: The Case of Angelo Herndon," 9–10, ca. 1935, Joint Committee to Aid the Herndon Defense, RCMS; John Howard Lawson, "Southern Exposure," n.d., and "A Southern Welcome," Nov. 1934, boxes 6, 98, John Howard Lawson Papers, Special Collections, Southern Illinois University, Carbondale; Wiggenton interview with Don West in *Refuse to Stand Silently By*, 81–82; Solomon, *The Cry Was Unity*, 248; Byerly, "'What Shall a Poet Sing?'" 186–87; and Martin, *Angelo Herndon and Southern Justice*, 110–11.

25. Martin, *Angelo Herndon and Southern Justice*, 111, 113; Millis to Roger Baldwin, Nov. 21, 1931, box 17, Mary Raoul Millis Papers; West, "The Atlanta Situation and the Recent Herndon Decision," June 24, 1934, and Morrison to West, May 29, 1934, both in reel 112, ACLU Papers; Morrison to E. H. Hoge, Nov. 25, 1931, file I-N, E. H. Hoge files, Berry College Archives.

26. Jacqueline Hall and Ray Faherty interview with Don West; Alex Baskin interview with

Don West; Martin, *Angelo Herndon and Southern Justice*, 112–13. For insight on Morrison's treachery, see Morrison to West, May 29, 1934, reel 112, ACLU Papers.

27. *The Daily Worker*, ca. May 1934, June 11, 1934; Wiggenton interview with Don West in *Refuse to Stand Silently By*, 82; West, "Georgia Wants Me—Dead or Alive"; see also West, "The Atlanta Situation and Recent Herndon Decision," June 24, 1934.

28. West, "Georgia Wants Me—Dead or Alive" and "Georgia Officials Ape Hitler Terror," *The Daily Worker*, ca. July 1934, box 2, Solomon Papers, Tamiment Library, New York; Martin, *Angelo Herndon and Southern Justice*, 112; Wiggenton interview with Don West in *Refuse to Stand Silently By*, 82.

29. West, "Georgia Wants Me—Dead or Alive"; *The Daily Worker*, June 11, 19, 1934; *The New Masses*, June 5, 12, 1934.

30. Byerly, "'What Shall a Poet Sing?'" 131; Hedy West interview with Lillie Mulkey West, Feb. 1976, Blairsville, Ga., Hedy West Papers, author interview with Ann West Williams, Aug. 8, 2004, Charleston, W.V.

31. This analysis is based in part on author interviews with Hedy West, March 10–11, 2004, Narberth, Pa., Ann West Williams, and Yvonne Farley, March 13, 2004, St. Albans, W.V.

32. Author interviews with Hedy West and Ann West Williams. For discussion of the Party's stance on the "woman question" see Hill, "Re-evaluating the CPUSA's Answer to the Woman Question"; Baxandall, "The Question Seldom Asked," 151–59; Gosse, "To Organize in Every Neighborhood"; and Zehavi, "Passionate Commitments," 542.

33. Hedy West interview with Lillie Mulkey West; author interviews with Hedy West and Ann West Williams. For further discussion of the Wests' marriage, sexual division of labor, and concept of family see Byerly, "'What Shall a Poet Sing?'" 133–37.

34. Berry to Mrs. Henry Ford, Oct. 7, 1933, and to Mrs. Emily V. Hammond, Oct. 16, 1933, both in subject file correspondence, "Don West Matter," Martha Berry Papers; Aubrey Williams, "Introduction," June 6, 1964, box 64, Carl and Anne Braden Papers, Archives and Manuscripts, Wisconsin Historical Society (WHS), Madison.

35. Taylor to Berry, Oct. 16, 1933, and to Alexander, Oct. 16, 1933, both in subject file correspondence, "Don West Matter," Martha Berry Papers.

36. For comment on West's physical and personal presence, see Byerly, "'What Shall a Poet Sing?'" 189–90.

Chapter 5: On the Road: Party Activism and Organizational Work, 1934–37

1. Paul Crouch to Organization Committee, CC, Aug. 19, 1934, and Crouch to Earl Browder, July 14, 1934, both fond 515, opis 1, delo 3625, reel 281, Records of the CPUSA, Russian State Archive of Social and Political History (RGASPI), Moscow.

2. Janet Ross, "Autobiography" and "Reference," both fond 495, opis 261, delo 5188, Records of the Communist International, RGASPI; Byerly, "'What Shall a Poet Sing?'" 200; see also Kelley, *Hammer and Hoe*, 126.

3. Crouch to Organization Committee, CC, Aug. 19, 1934; Crouch, "Brief History of the Communist Movement in North and South Carolina," n.d., box 1, Paul Crouch Papers, Hoover Institution on War, Revolution, and Peace, Stanford.

4. Flying squadrons were well-organized groups of striking unionists who traveled through the southern countryside in automobiles and trucks, moving from plant to plant, where they exhorted working millhands to lay down their tools and close the plants. These mobile

unionists were so effective that mill closings threatened to shut down the entire textile industry in early September 1934. Sue Thrasher interview with Don West, July 10, 1974, Highlander Research and Education Center Archives, New Market, Tenn.; Jacqueline Hall and Ray Faherty interview with Don West, Jan. 22, 1975, interview E-16, Southern Oral History Collection, Southern Historical Collection (SOHC-SHC), Wilson Library, University of North Carolina, Chapel Hill; Wiggenton interview with Don West in *Refuse to Stand Silently By*, 81–82; Woodward to Rainey, Sept. 24, 1934, box 7, Glenn Rainey Papers, Special Collections, Emory University (SC-EU), Atlanta; Walt Pickard, "The Burlington Dynamite Plot," North Carolina Collection, Wilson Library, University of North Carolina, Chapel Hill; J. Spencer Love to Si, Sept. 16, 1934, folder 4240, James Spencer Love Papers, Southern Historical Collection (SHC). For discussion of the textile strike in Burlington and West's role in these events, see Salmond, *The General Textile Strike of 1934*, 223–25; see also Salmond, "The Burlington Dynamite Plot," esp. 422–30; Dunbar, *Against the Grain*, 138–41; Hall et al., *Like a Family*, 342–44; Irons, *Testing the New Deal*, esp. ch. 9; and Hodges, *New Deal Labor Policy and the Southern Cotton Textile Industry*, esp. ch. 7. An optimistic communist analysis of the outcome may be found in Myra Page, "The South Talks Re-Strike," Sept. 1934, folder 5143, Myra Page Papers, SHC.

5. "National Party Textile Conference," Oct. 6, 1934, fond 515, opis 1, delo 3424, reel 265, RGASPI.

6. Quoted in Salmond, *The General Textile Strike of 1934*, 215; see also Dunbar, *Against the Grain*, 138–39. In fact, at union meetings, West claimed that the mill owners had sent spies to infiltrate the local by pushing the idea of sabotage at the mill. In response to these provocations, union leader Walt Pickard had consistently argued against violence. Byerly, "'What Shall a Poet Sing?'" 206. A contrasting view was advanced by Crouch ("Brief History of the Communist Movement in North and South Carolina"), who after leaving the CP maintained that the accused were guilty as charged. Because he was by this time functioning as a government witness, the veracity of this allegation remains in doubt.

7. For the ILD's account of the conspiracy cases and the court's handling of the defendants, see Jim Weaver, "The Burlington Six 'Dynamite' Case: A Summary," ca. Dec. 1934, folder 3693, Paul Eliot Green Papers, SHC. A full discussion of the court proceedings may be found in Salmond, *The General Textile Strike of 1934*, 216–22; see also Pickard, "The Burlington Dynamite Plot." West's initiative is discussed in Jacqueline Hall and Ray Faherty interview with Don West; see also Dunbar, *Against the Grain*, 140. For evidence of the defense committee's influence on public opinion, see Crouch, "Brief History of the Communist Movement in North and South Carolina."

8. "Re: The Burlington Dynamite Case," Dec. 26, 1934, Pickard to Fellow Worker (Bertha Gurley), Dec. 31, 1934, and "Justice in Chains," ca. Dec. 1934, all filed with Jacqueline Hall and Ray Faherty interview of Don West; Ross to Kester, Nov. 30, 1934, folder 3834, Howard Kester Papers, SHC; Dunbar, *Against the Grain*, 139.

9. Pickard to Brothers, ca. Dec. 1934, and "To: Thomas F. McMahon," ca. Dec. 1934, both fond 515, opis 1, delo 3919, reel 300, RGASPI.

10. Pickard, "The Burlington Dynamite Plot," 23, see also 17–19, 1; Salmond, *The General Textile Strike of 1934*, 229; Jacqueline Hall and Ray Faherty interview of Don West; "Dear Presh," memorandum, n.d., Hedy West Papers, Athens, Ga.

11. Weaver to Crouch, Dec. 28, 1934, fond 515, opis 1, delo 3625, reel 281, RGASPI; Dunbar, *Against the Grain*, 140. Although Dunbar suggests that West was being supported by sympathetic local citizens, other evidence indicates that the CP Southern Committee

was providing a subsidy of $8 per week for trade union organizing. "Section of Letter from Jim Weaver to Paul Crouch Regarding Comrade David Clark," ca. Nov. 24, 1931, fond 515, opis 1, delo 3625, reel 281, RGASPI.

12. "Notes: Workers' Defense Committee, Burlington, N.C.," Jan. 10, 1935, folder 3693, Paul Eliot Green Papers; West quoted in Weaver to John Anderson, Jan. 10, 1934 [sic 1935], and "Re: Burlington Dynamite Case," Dec. 31, 1934, both filed with Jacqueline Hall and Ray Faherty interview of Don West; interviews with Paul Eliot Green, William Terry Couch, and Olive Stone, all in folder 4007, SOHC-SHC; Crouch, "Brief History of the Communist Movement in North and South Carolina"; Sue Thrasher interview with Don West.

13. Interview with Paul Eliot Green; "Re: Burlington Dynamite Case"; West quoted in West to Linda Williams, Dec. 21, 1984, Don West Papers, Si to B, Jan. 22, 1935, folder 4240, James Spencer Love Papers. Green's activism in the defense is discussed in Roper, *Paul Green*, 152–54.

14. Minutes, Burlington Defense Committee, ca. Jan. 1935, folder 3693, Paul Eliot Green Papers. For further evidence of tension over the presence of radicals within the defense committee, see interview with William Terry Couch and Paul Eliot Green.

15. Love to Si, Jan. 21 and 25, folder 4240, James Spencer Love Papers; Salmond, *The General Textile Strike of 1934*, 224, 227.

16. Weaver to Anderson, Jan. 10, 1934 [sic 1935]; Salmond, *The General Textile Strike of 1934*, 224.

17. West to Crouch, Feb. 18 and 20, 1935, fond 515, opis 1, delo 3882, reel 298, RGASPI; Byerly, "'What Shall a Poet Sing?'" 211.

18. ILD, "Immediate Release," Feb. 1, 1935, folder 3693, Paul Eliot Green Papers.

19. Salmond, *The General Textile Strike of 1934*, 230–32.

20. Weaver to Crouch, Feb. 18, 1935, fond 515, opis 1, delo 3625, reel 281, RGASPI; and (all entry 402, boxes 19, 62, record group 9, National Archives [NA]): Homer J. Brown, "Preliminary Report of Commissioner of Conciliation," April 19, 1934; Brown to Samuel R. McClurd, April 19, 1935; and Lynn B. Williamson, "Statement of What Occurred at the E. M. Holt Plaid Mills during the Recent General Strike," Oct. 4, 1934.

21. L. M. Austin to Weaver, March 12, 1935, Weaver to Earl Browder, March 15, 1935, Weaver to James Ford, April 5, 1935, and Weaver to Crouch, Feb. 20, 1935, all fond 515, opis 1, delo 3882, reel 298, RGASPI; Crouch, "Brief History of the Communist Movement in North and South Carolina."

22. United Textile Workers of America, Local Union No. 1777, "To Whom It May Concern," March 2, 1935, box 1867, AFL-CIO Region 8 Papers, Southern Labor Archives (SLA), Special Collections, Georgia State University, Atlanta; Weaver to Ford, April 5, 1935, fond 515, opis 1, delo 3882, reel 298, RGASPI.

23. Minutes, All Southern Conference for Civil and Trade Union Rights, fond 515, opis 1, delo 3951, reel 301, RGASPI; Dombrowski to My Friend, Feb. 4, 1935, and "Call for the All-Southern Conference for Civil and Trade Union Rights," both box 31, Highlander Research and Education Papers (Highlander Papers), Archives and Manuscripts Division, Wisconsin Historical Society, Madison. For discussion of the All-Southern Conference as a united front effort, see Adams, *James A. Dombrowski*, 89–94, and Adams, *Unearthing Seeds of Fire*, 93–97.

24. Crouch to Organizing Committee, Central Committee, June 10, 1935, fond 515, opis, delo 3882, reel 298, RGASPI.

25. Weaver to Jim Crews, April 12, 1935, and "Organizational Problems in District 16," ca. summer 1935, both fond 515, opis 1, delo 3882, reel 298, RGASPI.

26. Crouch to Organizing Commission, Central Committee, June 10, 1935, and West to F. Brown, June 3, 1935, both fond 515, opis 1, delo 3882, RGASPI.

27. Joe Hart to F. Brown, Aug. 14, 1935, Allen Johnson to Organizing Commission, Central Committee, Aug. 15, 1935, and J. A. Weaver, "Leonard J. Green Helps Mill Owners against Burlington Defense," all fond 515, opis 1, delo 3882, reel 298, RGASPI. For West's diatribe see also *Burlington Times-News*, Aug. 3, 1935, folder 3693, Paul Eliot Green Papers; and Salmond, *The General Textile Strike of 1934*, 223.

28. Johnson to Organizing Commission, Central Committtee, Aug. 15, 1935; Hart to Brown, Aug. 14, 1935.

29. *Burlington Times-News*, Aug. 12, 1935.

30. Clarence Senior to Kester, Sept. 12, 1935, Jack Fies to Thomas, Aug. 26, 1935, Kester to Senior, Aug. 24, 1935, and Kester to West, Aug. 24, 1935, all in box 1, folder 3834, Howard Kester Papers; Crouch to Trade Union Commission, Central Committee, Jan. 20, 1936, fond 515, opis 1, delo 4028, reel 304, RGASPI.

31. Dunbar, *Against the Grain*, 141–42; Byerly, "'What Shall a Poet Sing?'" 213; Salmond, "The Burlington Bomb Plot," 422; Salmond, *The General Textile Strike of 1934*, 223.

32. Weaver to Joe, ca. July 1935, Crouch to Organizing Committee, Central Committee, June 27, 1935, and Crouch to Central Committee, Sept. 25, 1935, all fond 515, opis 1, delo 3882, reel 298, RGASPI; Crouch, "Brief History of the Communist Movement in North and South Carolina"; Kelley, *Hammer and Hoe*, 126.

33. Garland to Political Buro, March 13, 1935, and Organizing Commission and Central Committee to Garland, March 25, 1935, both in fond 515, opis 1, delo 3764, reel 292, RGASPI; Alex Baskin interview with Don West, Feb. 5, 1975, Stony Brook, N.Y.; Duke, *Writers and Miners*, 51. There is some evidence that Garland, although a dedicated Marxist, chafed under party discipline. See "Jim Garland Notes" with Archie Green interview, March 31, 1961, box 19, Archie Green Papers.

34. West to Comrades, Sept. 18, 1935, Garland to Comrade, Sept. 17, 1935, and West to Brown, Aug. 8, 1935, all fond 515, opis 1, delos 3898 and 3882, reel 298, RGASPI.

35. West to Friends, Oct. 8, 1935, George Hart to Comrades, Sept. 21, 1935, and D.O. 23 to Comrade, Oct. 18, 1935, all fond 515, opis 1, delo 3898, reel 298, RGASPI; Sue Thrasher interview with Don West; Alex Baskin interview with Don West; Duke, *Writers and Miners*, 52. For full coverage of the Kentucky coal field wars see Hevener, *Which Side Are You On?* see also Duke, *Writers and Miners*, 28–45.

36. "Donald Lee West," Sept. 22, 1942, FBI Report 100-20396-23; Alex Baskin interview with Don West; Sue Thrasher interview with Don West; West to Linda Williams, Dec. 21, 1984, Don West Papers; West to Comrade, Oct. 16, 1935, fond 515, opis 1, delo 3899, reel 298, RGASPI; Duke, *Writers and Miners*, 52.

37. Wiggenton interview with Don West in *Refuse to Stand Silently By*, 88; D.O. 23 to Comrade, Oct. 18, 1935, fond 515, opis 1, delo 3998, reel 298, RGASPI.

38. Jacqueline Hall and Ray Faherty interview with Don West; Alex Baskin interview with West; Wiggenton interview with Don West in *Refuse to Stand Silently By*, 88; West to Linda Williams, Dec. 21, 1984, Don West Papers; George Brosi Notes, Jeff Biggers Papers, Don West Collection; Dunbar, *Against the Grain*, 142–43; Duke, *Writers and Miners*, 52.

39. Sue Thrasher interview with Don West; author interview with Ann West Williams, Aug. 8, 2004, Charleston, W.V. West to Charlotte Moscowitz, Oct. 27 and 28, 1935, folder

5143, Myra Page Papers; *Commonwealth College Fortnightly*, Nov. 15, 1935, Feb. 15, 1936, box 3, Raymond and Charlotte Moscowitz-Koch Collection, Walter P. Reuther Library, Archives of Labor and Urban Affairs (ALUA), Wayne State University, Detroit. For discussion of Commonwealth College and its role in the labor movement in the 1930s, see Cobb, *Radical Education in the Rural South*, esp. chs. 6 and 7.

40. West to Tony, Feb. 6, 1979, Don West Scrapbook, Ann West Williams Collection, Charleston, W.V.; Stuart to Still, Nov. 13, 1935, box 15.4, Don West file, James Still Papers, Special Collections, Morehead State University, Morehead, Ky.; Alex Baskin interview of Don West; West, *No Lonesome Road*, xxv. In January 1936 an angry Stuart wrote derisively of the "Donnie-religion of stirring up strife," and not long thereafter he asserted that Don had "gone haywire" and was "still seeing things through Communist colored glasses." Stuart to Still, Jan. 30 and May 26, 1936, box 15.4, James Still Papers. The estrangement was confirmed in May 1937 when West and Stuart nearly came to blows as a result of Don's visit to Jesse during a break from his organizing work. Stuart told his mentor Donald Davidson that "the Communists were backing Don" and that he (Stuart) could simply "not tolerate this stuff." Stuart to Davidson, May 5, 1937, box 12, Donald Davidson Papers, Special Collections and University Archives, Vanderbilt University Library, Nashville, Tenn.

41. Alex Baskin interview with West; George Brosi Notes. The origins and development of the Workers Alliance of America is discussed in Leibman, "The Workers Alliance of America"; Klehr, *The Heyday of American Communism*; Piven and Cloward, *Poor Peoples Movements*; Lorence, *Organizing the Unemployed*; Rosenzweig, "Radicals and the Jobless"; Rosenzweig, "Organizing the Unemployed"; Rosenzweig, "Socialism in Our Time"; and Leab, "United We Eat."

42. District Organizer, Dist. 23, CPUSA, to Arthur S. Kling, Feb. 20, 21, 1936, and National Unemployed Fraction to All District Organizers, Feb. 12, 1936, fond 515, opis 1, delos 4035 and 4047, reel 305, RGASPI.

43. Arnold Johnson to Benjamin, March 9, April 1, 2, 1936, and "Financial" file, 1934–36, all in box 2, Herbert Benjamin Papers, Manuscript Division, Library of Congress, Washington, D.C.

44. Allen McElfresh and Giles Cooper, "They Fought Hunger! The Story of the Kentucky Workers Alliance during the 1930s," box 34, Mike Ross Papers, SLA; see also page 90 of the duplicate copy in Special Collections, University of Kentucky Library, Lexington; author interview with Mildred Shackleford, June 22, 2004, New Market, Tenn.; Mildred Shackleford interview with Allen McElfresh, 1973, Louisville, Ky.; Jacqueline Hall and Ray Faherty interview with Don West.

45. McElfresh and Cooper, "They Fought Hunger!" 87–92; Alex Baskin interview with Don West; Jacqueline Hall and Ray Faherty interview with Don West; Mildred Shackleford interview with Allen McElfresh.

46. Don West, "A Page from an Organizer's Diary," *Commonwealth College Fortnightly*, June 1, 1936, box 3, Raymond and Charlotte Moscowitz-Koch Collection; Jacqueline Hall and Ray Faherty interview with Don West; Sue Thrasher interview with Don West; McElfresh and Cooper, "They Fought Hunger!" 95–96; West, "'My Old Kentucky Home'"; Mildred Shackleford interview with Allen McElfresh; "Organize! For Jobs and a Living Wage on WPA," box 29, Highlander Papers; "What Does the Kentucky Workers Alliance Want?" in West, "Songs for Southern Workers" (mimeo), box 21, Mike Ross Papers, SLA; Dunbar, *Against the Grain*, 143.

47. West to Claude Williams, Jan. 8, 1971, box 15, Claude C. Williams Collection, AL-

HUA; West to Linda Williams, Dec. 21, 1984, Don West Papers; Claude Williams to Mark Naison, ca. 1972, box 4, Cedric Belfrage Papers, Tamiment Collection, Elmer Holmes Bobst Library, New York University; Sue Thrasher interview with Don West.

48. McElfresh and Cooper, "They Fought Hunger!" 103–4; Mildred Shackleford interview with Allen McElfresh.

49. "1936 Reports File," box 2, Herbert Benjamin Papers; *Workers Alliance*, Aug., Sept. 1936.

50. Sue Thrasher interview with Don West; Byerly, "'What Shall a Poet Sing?'" 241.

51. McElfresh and Cooper, "They Fought Hunger!" 120–23; Jacqueline Hall and Ray Faherty interview with Don West; *Southern Worker*, Oct. 1936; Dunbar, *Against the Grain*, 143–44.

52. West to Williams, Jan. 8, 1971; Alex Baskin interview with Don West; Jacqueline Hall and Ray Faherty interview with Don West; West quoted in *People's Press*, Nov. 28, Dec. 5, 1936, Jan. 9, Feb. 20, April 3, 1937; McElfresh and Cooper, "They Fought Hunger!" 131–33; *Southern Worker*, Oct. 1936. On the wage differential see (all in file 641, box 1386 and file 693.1, box 1408, WPA central files, 1935–41, record group 69, NA): Cooper, West, T. C. Cadle, and Frank Daniels to Harry L. Hopkins, July 16, 1937; West to Alben W. Barkley, Aug. 4, 1937; *Alliance News*, ca. July 1937; and Daniels and Cadle to Hopkins, July 27, 1937. For evidence of the significant wage increase granted WPA workers in thirteen southern states, see Aubrey Williams to Lasser, July 1, 1938, and Lasser to Hopkins, June 23, 1938, both in file 040, box 0058, record group 69, NA; see also Wiggenton interview of Don West in *Refuse to Stand Silently By*, 85.

53. "Organize! For Jobs and a Living Wage on WPA"; McElfresh and Cooper, "They Fought Hunger!" 111–15, 133; West, "Build the New South"; West to Herbert Agar, June 22, 1937, Don West Scrapbook; "Donald Lee West," April 3, 1947, FBI file 100-20396-47.

54. McElfresh and Cooper, "They Fought Hunger!" 133; West to Herbert Agar, June 22, 1937; "Memorandum (Re: Don West, also known as Rev. Donald L. West, of Douglasville, Georgia")," and Robert Morris to James Eastland, May 18, 1957, both reference name file "Don West, Committee on Un-American Activities (HUAC) files, record group 233, Records of the U.S. House of Representatives, NA.

55. Alex Baskin interview with Don West; Sue Thrasher interview with Don West; Cooper and McElfresh, "They Fought Hunger!" 104, 107.

56. Cooper and McElfresh, "They Fought Hunger!" 107.

57. Preface to West, *Songs for Southern Workers*; McElfresh and Cooper, "They Fought Hunger!" 134–36; Sue Thrasher interview with Don West; *Southern Worker*, Jan. 1937, see also Dec. 1936, May 1937. The place of Jackson, Garland, and West in the history of labor music and balladry is discussed in Green, *Only a Miner*, 419–23; Malone, *Don't Get above Your Raisin'*, 232; and Romalis, *Pistol Packin' Mama*. For examples of Jackson's original work on behalf of the Workers Alliance, see Jackson, "The Workers Alliance" and "The Hungry and Disgusted Blues," March 1, 10, 1938, vertical files, Labadie Collection, Harlan Hatcher Research Library, University of Michigan, Ann Arbor.

58. Minutes of the Meeting of the Central Control Commission Held 16 May 1939, fond 515, opis 1, delo 4086, RGASPI. This copy of the CCC Minutes was furnished by John Haynes of the Library of Congress and Harvey Klehr of Emory University; the document was translated from the Russian by Timothy Sergay. For discussion of both local and central control commissions and the Communist Party's structured disciplinary procedures, see

Storch, "'The Realities of the Situation'"; see also "Control of How Party Instructions Are Carried Out," 13. For West's account of his decision to leave Kentucky, see Jacqueline Hall and Ray Faherty interview with Don West; Alex Baskin interview with Don West; and Sue Thrasher interview with Don West; see also McElfresh and Cooper, "They Fought Hunger!" 136. Byerly ("'What Shall a Poet Sing?'" 243–44) accepts West's assertion that family responsibilities were important influences on his departure from Kentucky but also suggests that he shared Earl Browder's broader definition of the Democratic Front and the need to work for it in a variety of venues, such as the church. West's sister, Johnnye (Janet Ross), maintained in 1941 that although Don "was not active in the Party because of family difficulties," he remained "at least friendly to the Party." Ross, "Autobiography."

Chapter 6: A Poet in Formation: The Creative Impulse

1. West, *No Lonesome Road*, xxviii; Rubin, "Voice of the Cracker," 207. For discussion of the historical process of exclusion imposed by literary elites, see Nelson, *Repression and Recovery*. A bold proponent of the recovery process is Michael Denning, who provides a broad analysis of modern American cultural transformation that explores the proletarian literature of the 1930s, including its impact and legacy. Altough Denning's work lacks detailed analysis of poetry's place in this movement, his treatment of the "proletarian literary movement" as part of a "class war in literature" is consistent with West's perspective on the potentially revolutionary function of art in society. Denning, *The Cultural Front*, 200–229, esp 213, 217, 228–29.

2. West to Reece, March 28, 1941, box 21, Byron Herbert Reece Papers, Hargrett Rare Books and Manuscript Library, University of Georgia Libraries, Athens.

3. West to Reece, March 17, 1941, box 21, Byron Herbert Reece Papers. Michael Henson argues ("'Naked Words That Have No Subtle Meaning,'" 55) that West violated several widely held assumptions about poetry: that it must be rooted in "literary" sources, that it must be structurally complex, and that it must not speak with moral clarity. For evidence of West's commitment to "people's poetry" and disdain for sterile intellectualism, see West, "Toward a Southern Peoples Literature," *The Call* (1955), Don West Scrapbook, Ann West Williams Collection, Charleston, W.V.

4. Wald, *Exiles from a Future Time*, 28; Stuart, *Beyond Dark Hills*, 186.

5. West, *Crab-Grass*.

6. West, "Bill Dalton's Wife," in *Crab-Grass*, 12.

7. Henson, "'Naked Words That Have No Subtle Meaning,'" 59.

8. West, "Laid Off," in *Crab-Grass*, 40.

9. West, "My People," in *Crab-Grass*, 28.

10. West, "Clodhopper," in *No Lonesome Road*, 130; May Smith, "Crab Grass," *Mountain Life and Work* (July 1932): 16; see also Rubin, "Voice of the Cracker," 207.

11. West, "I've Seen God," in *No Lonesome Road*, 115.

12. West, "Listen, I Am a Communist"; *The Daily Worker*, March 13, 1934; Mike Gold, "Change the World," *The Daily Worker*, Jan. 13, 1934.

13. Duke, *Writers and Miners*, 51; see also Wald, *Exiles from a Future Time*, 33.

14. Denning, *The Cultural Front*, 200–201; West, *No Lonesome Road*, xx–xxiii; Wald, *Exiles from a Future Time*, 33; see also Smethurst, *The New Red Negro*, 6; Nelson, *Repression and Recovery*, 152–59; Nelson, "Poetry Chorus: Dialogic Politics in 1930s Poetry," 55; Joseph Freeman, "Introduction," in Hicks et al., *The New Negro*, 13–14.

15. Smethurst, *The New Red Negro*, 120; West, "Dark Winds," in Hicks et al., *Proletarian Literature in the United States*, 198; West, *No Lonesome Road*, xviii; see also Nelson, *Repression and Recovery*, 102–3.

16. West, "Southern Lullaby," in Hicks et al., *Proletarian Literature in the United States*, 199.

17. Nelson, *Repression and Recovery*, 169–71; West, *No Lonesome Road*, xvii, 212n12. For full discussion of scholarship pertaining to the fugitive poets, see Nelson, *Repression and Recovery*, 306n212; see also Henson, "'Naked Words That Have No Subtle Meaning,'" 59; Singal, *The War Within*; Pells, *Radical Visions and American Dreams*, 103–5; O'Brien, *The Idea of the Modern South*, 117–212; Cobb, *Away Down South*, 116–19; Jackson, *Byron Herbert Reece*, 58–60, 62–63, 71–72.

18. West, "They Take Their Stand (for Some Professional Agrarians)," *The New Masses*, Aug. 27, 1935; West, *No Lonesome Road*, 129–30; see also Nelson, *Repression and Recovery*, 306–7n212.

19. Sullivan, "Don West, Poet and Preacher," 56; Duke, *Writers and Miners*, 52–53; West, *No Lonesome Road*, 133–35. For comment on the straightforward simplicity of the worker-poetry tradition West represented, see Wald, *Exiles from a Future Time*, 28, 30. West's intent to "write it plain" was evident in the introduction to *Crab-Grass*, in which he noted that "too many poets write in the old tradition. Using an obscure and 'subtle' private language, they write only for the little clique of the 'highly literate' elite . . . you want a poem with its roots in the earth; a poem, that may sometimes show reasons for the heartache and sorrow of the plain folks and sometimes point the way ahead" (16). The teaching aspect of poetry is discussed in Henson, "'Naked Words That Have No Subtle Meaning,'" 57–58.

20. See also "Southern Organizer on 'Let Freedom Ring,'" n.d., Hedy West Papers.

21. West, "Miner's Widow," in *No Lonesome Road*, 139; Duke, *Writers and Miners*, 163.

22. West, "Harlan County Coal Digger, 1934," in *No Lonesome Road*, 142–43.

23. Duke, *Writers and Miners*, 165; "Portraits of Harlan, Kentucky," in box 10, Lillian Smith Papers, Special Collections, University of Florida Library, Gainesville.

24. See also West, *No Lonesome Road*, 36–37.

25. Hedy West to Editors, *Mountain Life and Work*, June 17, 1961, box 68, Council of Southern Mountain Papers, Special Collections, Berea College Library, Berea, Ky.; West to Still, Nov. 6, 1936, box 15.4, Don West file, James Still Papers, Special Collections, Morehead State University, Morehead, Ky.

26. Cooper and McElfresh, "They Fought Hunger!" 134; Mildred Shackleford interview with Allen McElfresh, 1973, Louisville, Ky.

27. West, *No Lonesome Road*, xxix; Rubin, "Voice of the Cracker," 210; Byerly, "'What Shall a Poet Sing?'" 252; Cooper and McElfresh, "They Fought Hunger!" 134.

28. Don West, "Songs for Southern Workers" (mimeo), box 21, Mike Ross Papers, Southern Labor Archives (SLA), Special Collections, Georgia State University, Atlanta; West, "Songs for Kentucky Workers: Songs Collected by Don West for the KWA," box 1, Arnold Johnson Papers, Tamiment Collection, Elmer Holmes Bobst Library, New York University; Rubin, "Voice of the Cracker," 210. For evidence of KWA hostility toward George Goodman, see "Resolution," Workers Alliance of America, Paducah, Ky., June 15, 1936, box 115, subject file, Relief, May–June 1936, Albert B. Chandler Papers, Special Collections, University of Kentucky Library, Lexington; Kentucky Workers Alliance (Lexington) to Harry Hopkins, Nov. 5, 1936, file 641, box 1385, WPA Central files, 1935–1944, Kentucky, record group 69, National Archives.

29. Stuart to Still, Sept. 8, 1937, Jan. 30, 1936, and West to Still, Nov. 8, 1936, all in box 15.4, James Still Papers; see also Stuart to Woodbridge, Oct. 6, 1958.

30. "'What Shall a Poet Sing?'" in *Lonesome Road*, 120.

31. West, "Southern Nights," in *No Lonesome Road*, 122–23; see also text version, 1937, box 10, Lillian Smith Papers.

32. Snelling to West, July 30, 1937, box 10, Lillian Smith Papers.

33. "Family Record," Hedy West Papers; author interviews with Hedy West and Ann West Williams; Sue Thrasher interview with Don West, July 10, 1974, Highlander Research and Education Center Archives, New Market, Tenn.; Alex Baskin interview with Don West, Feb. 5, 1975, Stony Brook, N.Y.; West, *No Lonesome Road*, 14.

34. Interview with Jancy Ross Davis, box 95, Mike Ross Papers, SLA.

35. The following are all in box 112, James L. Adams Papers, Special Collections, Arents Library, Syracuse University: H. H. Taylor to Whom It May Concern, June 10, 1933; J. N. Nicholson to Sir, Dec. 6, 1937; Alva W. Taylor to Mr . . . , Oct. 31, 1937; and W. D. Potter to Mr . . . , Dec. 3, 1937.

36. West to Kester, Oct. 28, Nov. 29, 1938, folder 3834, Howard Kester Papers, Southern Historical Collection, Wilson Library, University of North Carolina, Chapel Hill.

Chapter 7: Refuge and Respectability: From the Pulpit to the Classroom 1939–42

1. "Donald Lee West," March 16, 1942, Atlanta, FBI file 100-559; "Donald Lee West," Aug. 3, 1942, Cincinnati, FBI file 100-2820; U.S. Congress, House of Representatives, *Hearings Before the Committee on Un-American Activities*, 81st Cong., 2d sess., July 12, 13, 14, 15, Aug. 8, 1950 (Washington: Government Printing Office, 1950), 2716, 2726; "Memorandum," Morris to Eastland, May 18, 1957, both reference name file "Don West," Committee on Un-American Activities (HUAC) files, record group 233, Records of the U.S. House of Representatives, National Archives (NA); Woods, *Black Struggle, Red Scare*, 109. Although West consistently denied that he was a "card-carrying member" of the Communist Party from 1940 on, it is difficult to determine conclusively whether his assertion was accurate. What is certain is that he never abandoned his belief in Marxism and that he frequently took positions consistent with those of the Party on issues of great importance. The post-1940 membership issue is debatable, but anecdotal accounts strongly suggest that West retained his CP ties and stubbornly held to his political beliefs.

2. Although Kester accepted West's FSC application, he did so with little enthusiasm. Although the organization had no "hero's corner," he dryly suggested that it might be done "for those who consider themselves so almighty different from other Christians." Kester to West, Dec. 11, 1939, and West to Kester, Nov. 27, 1939, both in box 3, Howard Kester Papers, Southern Oral History Collection, Southern Historical Collection (SOHC-SHC), Wilson Library, University of North Carolina, Chapel Hill. For full discussion of the Fellowship of Southern Churchmen and its goals, see *The Southern Churchman*, 1 (Dec. 1937), Fellowship of Southern Churchmen Papers, folder 3479, SHC; and Robert F. Martin, "Religious Radicalism's Critique of the South: The Fellowship of Southern Churchmen, 1934–1957," n.d., box 4, David S. Burgess Collection, Walter P. Reuther Library, Archives of Labor and Urban Affairs (ALUA), Wayne State University, Detroit; see also Craig, *Religion and Radical Politics*, 157; Dunbar, *Against the Grain*, 59–61, 197–98; and Tindall, *The Emergence of the New South*, 634–35.

3. West to Kester, Nov. 27, 1939, and Kester to West, Dec. 11, 1939, both in box 3, How-

ard Kester Papers. The FSC excluded "known communists or fellow travelers" as a matter of policy. "Notes on Tindall's *The Emergence of the New South*," box 15, Frank T. Adams Papers, Archives and Manuscripts Division, Wisconsin Historical Society, Madison.

4. West to Taylor, July 25, 1941, box 4, Alva W. Taylor Papers, Archives, Disciples of Christ Historical Society, Nashville; West to Kester, Dec. 14, 1939, box 3, Howard Kester Papers; Egerton, *Speak Now Against the Day*, 172, 289.

5. Dunbar, *Against the Grain*, 228–29, 247; Byerly, "'What Shall a Poet Sing?'" 244–45; West quoted in Egerton, *Speak Now Against the Day*, 290.

6. West, "Blessed Are the Peace Makers," ca. Dec. 1940, box 76, Highlander Research and Education Papers (Highlander Papers), Archives and Manuscripts Division, Wisconsin Historical Society, Madison; West, "War, Why Do We Have It," ca. 1940, Don West Scrapbook, Ann West Williams Collection, Charleston, W.V. The Communist Party's control of the American Peace Mobilization is discussed by North Carolina communist leader Junius Irving Scales in his memoir *Cause at Heart*, 118. See also "Confidential—USA: The American Peace Mobilization," March 1941, Records of Communist International, Russian State Archive of Social and Political History, Moscow, cited in Haynes and Klehr, "The CPUSA Reports to the Comintern," 36; see also "What Is APM?" folder 4879, Junius Irving Scales Papers, SHC; and "Information from the Files of the Committee on Un-American Activities, U.S. House of Representatives," March 8, 1956, HUAC-SISS files, record group 233, NA.

7. Horton to West, Sept. 16, 1939, and West to Horton, Sept. 14, 1939, both in box 29, Highlander Papers.

8. West to James L. Adams, Aug. 9, 1943; April 22, 1940, and Sept. 4, 1939, all in box 112, J. L. Adams Papers.

9. West to W. E. B. Du Bois, March 23, 1940, reel 52 (microfilm edition), W. E. B. Du Bois Papers, Special Collections, University of Massachusetts Library, Amherst; West to James L. Adams, April 22, 1940, box 112, J. L. Adams Papers.

10. West to Snelling, Sept. 23, 1940, box 10, Lillian Smith Papers, Special Collections, University of Florida Library, Gainesville.

11. "The Awakening Church," ca. summer 1940, and "A Christian Fellowship Message," ca. summer 1940, both in West to Snelling, Sept. 23, 1940, box 10, Lillian Smith Papers; see also Hedy West Papers; Jacqueline Hall and Ray Faherty interview with Don West, Jan. 22, 1975, interview E-16, SOHC-SHC. For discussion of the *Southern News Almanac* and its tie with the Communist Party's Birmingham district office, see Kelly, *Hammer and Hoe*, 196–97; and West, *No Lonesome Road*, xxxi.

12. "The Awakening Church," April 13, 1940, Oct. 10, 1940, box 112, J. L. Adams Papers; box 10, Lillian Smith Papers.

13. "The Awakening Church," ca. summer 1940, in West to Snelling, Sept. 23, 1940, box 10, Lillian Smith Papers.

14. West to Snelling, Sept. 23, 1940.

15. For discussion of Williams and his career as a religious radical, see Belfrage, *A Faith to Free the People*; Naison, "Claude and Joyce Williams: Pilgrims of Justice," 1–13; Craig, *Religion and Radical Politics*, 144–61; Cobb, *Radical Education in the Rural South*, 187–201; and Dunbar, *Against the Grain*, 67–73, 170–75.

16. People's Institute for Applied Religion, "Report to Sponsors and Friends," ca. Jan 15, 1941, box 19, Claude C. Williams Collection, ALUA; Bill Troy and Claude Williams "People's Institute for Applied Religion," ca. 1975, box 4, Cedric Belfrage Papers, Tamiment Collection, Elmer Holmes Bobst Library, New York University; David S. Burgess, "Claude

Williams and the PIAR," 1944, box 6, David S. Burgess Collection; Green, "The Social Life of Poetry," 249; Craig, *Religion and Radical Politics,* 164.

17. Craig, *Religion and Radical Politics,* 165; Green, "The Social Life of Poetry," 250; Troy and Williams, "People's Institute for Applied Religion," 53.

18. Egerton, *Speak Now Against the Day,* 290; West quoted in Williams, PIAR Progress Report, ca. 1941, box 19, Claude C. Williams Collection; Williams quoted in Troy and Williams, "People's Institute for Applied Religion," 53.

19. Information from the Files of the Committee on Un-American Activities, U.S. House of Representatives, March 8, 1956; "Donald Lee West," Jan. 22, 1943, FBI file 100-559; West to Horton, Jan. 25, 1941, and Horton to West, Jan. 21, April 15, 1941, box 31, Highlander Papers.

20. West to Reece, March 17, 1941, box 21, Byron Herbert Reece Papers, Hargrett Rare Books and Manuscript Library, University of Georgia Libraries, Athens; Reece, "I'll Take My Stand," *Union County News,* ca. March 1941, folder BHR-278, Byron Herbert Reece Collection (Reece Collection), Young Harris College Library, Young Harris, Ga.

21. West to Reece, Aug. 4, March 28, 1941, box 21, Byron Herbert Reece Papers; Reece, "I'll Take My Stand," *Union County Citizen,* April 3, 1941, folder BHR-278, Reece Collection.

22. West to Smith, March 28, 1941, box 10, Lillian Smith Papers.

23. Jacqueline Hall and Ray Faherty interview with Don West; author interviews with Hedy West, March 10, 2004, Narberth, Pa., and Ann West Williams, Aug. 8, 2004, Charleston, W.V.; Robert Carmichael to McGill, June 18, 1948, box 54, Ralph McGill Papers, Special Collections, Emory University, Atlanta; see also West, *No Lonesome Road,* xxxi.

24. West to Taylor, July 25, 1941, box 4, Alva W. Taylor Papers.

25. West to Reece, Sept. 8, 1941, box 21, Byron Herbert Reece Papers; West to Taylor, July 25, 1941, box 4, Alva W. Taylor Papers; Jacqueline Hall and Ray Faherty interview with Don West.

26. "To Special Agent in Charge" (Confidential), Dec. 1, 1941, Atlanta, FBI file 100-20396-5; Henderson quoted in Wiggenton interview of Don West in *Refuse to Stand Silently By,* 194–95 and Jacqueline Hall and Ray Faherty interview with Don West; see also Alex Baskin interview with Don West, Feb. 5, 1975, Stony Brook, N.Y.; Dunbar, *Against the Grain,* 211; and West to Reece, Sept. 8, 1941, box 21, Byron Herbert Reece Papers.

Chapter 8: Teacher and Learner: Don West and the Democratic Classroom, 1942–45

1. "Donald Lee West," July 7, Aug. 3, 7, Sept. 22, Nov. 13, 1942, Atlanta, file 100-559, FBI Reports 100-20396-19, 20, 21, 22, and 23.

2. West to Reece, Jan. 18, 1944 and Feb. 12, 1945, both in box 21, Byron Herbert Reece Papers, Hargrett Rare Books and Manuscript Library, University of Georgia Libraries, Athens; Henrietta Buckmaster to Smith, ca. Feb. 2 and May 20, 1943, box 8, Lillian Smith Papers, Special Collections, University of Florida Library, Gainesville; see also Buckmaster, *Deep River,* 479; West, *No Lonesome Road,* xxxii, 213; and author interview with Hedy West, March 10, 2004, Narberth, Pa.

3. "Donald Lee West," Jan. 22, 1943, Atlanta, file 100-559, FBI Report 100-20396-28; quotes from local citizens from John E. Jones, "To Whom It May Concern," June 24, 1948, box 54, Ralph McGill Papers, Special Collections, Emory University (SC-EU), Atlanta; see also Sue Thrasher interview with Don West, July 10, 1974, Highlander Research and

Education Center Archives, New Market, Tenn.; Alex Baskin interview with Don West, Feb. 5, 1975, Stony Brook, N.Y.; and Jacqueline Hall and Ray Faherty interview with Don West, Jan. 22, 1975, interview E-16, Southern Oral History Collection, Southern Historical Collection, Wilson Library, University of North Carolina, Chapel Hill.

4. Quotes from Jones, "To Whom It May Concern"; see also Alex Baskin interview with Don West; "Donald Lee West," Jan. 22, 1943, Atlanta, file 100-559, FBI Report 100-20396-28; and Wiggenton interview of Don West in *Refuse to Stand Silently By*, 195. For comment on John Ernest Jones's support for West, see Heale, *McCarthy's Americans*, 231–32.

5. West, *No Lonesome Road*, xxxi; Griffin Davis, "From the Hills of Georgia," *Reader's Scope* (Jan. 1946), J. E. Jones, "Lula School, Leader of Community Progress," *The American Teacher* (May 1944), and "Plumb to Yonder," *Seventeen* (May 1944), all in box 32, Mike Ross Papers, Southern Labor Archives (SLA), Special Collections, Georgia State University, Atlanta; Jones, "To Whom It May Concern"; Sue Thrasher interview with Don West; Byerly, "'What Shall a Poet Sing?'" 295–96.

6. West to Horton, March 2, 1946, box 29, Highlander Research and Education Papers (Highlander Papers), Archives and Manuscripts Division, Wisconsin Historical Society, Madison; Davis, "From the Hills of Georgia," 42; Dunbar, *Against the Grain*, 212; West to Reece, ca. Feb. 12, 1945, box 21, Byron Herbert Reece Papers; "Donald Lee West," April 1, 1943, file 100-559, FBI Report 100-20396-29; Sue Thrasher interview with Don West; author interview with Guenivere Chapman, Genevieve Duncan, Bobbie and Clyde Moore, Jan. 23, 2004, Lula, Ga.; author interview (telephone) with Ruth Tribble Forestor, June 14, 2004, Waleska, Ga., transcripts in author's possession; Byerly, "'What Shall a Poet Sing?'" 296–97; West, *No Lonesome Road*, 42; author interview with Hedy West; author interview with Ann West Williams, Aug. 8, 2004, Charleston, W.V.

7. "Plumb to Yonder," 139; Jones, "Lula School"; "The Georgia Institute for Educational Service: Statement of Purpose," ca. 1943, box 14, Aubrey Williams Papers, Franklin D. Roosevelt Presidential Library (FDR Library), Hyde Park; Williams to Horton, May 10, 1945, box 31, Highlander Papers; Taylor to Claude Williams, Oct. 1, 1943, box 3, Claude C. Williams Collection, Walter P. Reuther Library, Archives of Labor and Urban Affairs, Wayne State University, Detroit; Alex Baskin interview with Don West; Jacqueline Hall and Ray Faherty interview with Don West; author interviews with Guenivere Chapman, Genevieve Duncan, Bobbie and Clyde Moore, Ruth Tribble Forestor, Hedy West, and Ann West; Dunbar, *Against the Grain*, 212.

8. "Georgia Locals That Have Paid Their Dues for 1944," in Daisy S. Kuwano to Williams, May 10, 1945, box 35, Aubrey Williams Papers; Jones, "To Whom It May Concern"; West to Claude Williams, Feb. 11, 1944, box 3, Claude C. Williams Collection; Davis, "From the Hills of Georgia"; Alex Baskin interview with Don West; Jacqueline Hall and Ray Faherty interview with Don West; author interviews with Hedy West and Ann West Williams; Byerly, "'What Shall a Poet Sing?'" 297.

9. Student recollections in author interviews with Guenivere Chapman, Genevieve Duncan, and Bobbie and Clyde Moore. For the program's classroom component, see West to Henry A. Wallace, May 14, 1943, box 74, Henry A. Wallace Papers, FDR Library. Community campaigns are discussed in Jones, "To Whom It May Concern"; see also Hedy West Diary, Hedy West Papers; and Hedy West to Author, Sept. 18, 2004. West's remarks are from West to Claude Williams, Feb. 16, 1944, box 3, Claude C. Williams Collection; see also Byerly, "'What Shall a Poet Sing?'" 298; Dunbar, *Against the Grain*, 212; and West, *No Lonesome Road*, xxxii.

10. For discussion of the trend toward education with a broadened social mission, see Chirhart, *Torches of Light*, 190–91; "Southern Educational Service," Feb. 1946, and Davis, "From the Hills of Georgia," 45, both in box 32, Mike Ross Papers; see also "The Georgia Institute for Educational Service: Statement of Purpose," Aubrey Williams Papers. One of the first steps taken to broaden community education in Lula was the establishment of a new community library, with a large donation of books from the Wests as the base collection. West to Reece, ca. 1944, box 21, Byron Herbert Reece Papers. In early 1945 West also opened dialogue with Arnold Forster of the Anti-Defamation League, warning against the Georgia Commoner Party, an anti-Semitic organization that urged Gentile political action. West to Arnold Forster, ca. Feb. 1945; Forster to West, Feb. 16, 1945; Charles Emmons to West, Feb. 10, 1945, all in Don West Scrapbook, Ann West Williams Collection, Charleston, W.V.

11. *Monthly Scrapper*, March, April 1944; Davis, "From the Hills of Georgia," 42; Byerly, "'What Shall a Poet Sing?'" 298; Dunbar, *Against the Grain*, 212.

12. West, "By Their Fruits," and "Our Most Precious Possession," in "Education for Victory," Sept. 1944, March 19, 1943, box 1881, AFL-CIO Region 8 Collection, SLA; *Lula Scrapper*, 2d ed., 1943–44; author interviews with Guenivere Chapman, Genevieve Duncan, and Bobbie and Clyde Moore; *Monthly Scrapper*, Jan., Feb., April, Nov. 1944; Dunbar, *Against the Grain*, 212; Byerly, "'What Shall a Poet Sing?'" 298.

13. Reece to Genevieve Stephens, Feb. 6, 1945, and Stephens to Reece, Jan. 29, 1945, box 19, Byron Herbert Reece Papers; *Monthly Scrapper*, Feb. 1945; Genevieve Stephens, Gussie Pool, and Mildred Hunt, "Lula Schools Builds Good Will," *American Unity*, ca. March 1945; see also author interviews with Guenivere Chapman, Genevieve Duncan, and Bobbie and Clyde Moore, and Ruth Tribble Forestor.

14. West to George S. Mitchell, Feb. 25, March 1, 1944, and Mitchell to West, Feb. 28, 1944, all in box 1881, AFL-CIO Region 8 Collection; West to Claude Williams, Feb. 16, 1944, box 3, Claude C. Williams Collection; Josephine Wilkins to West, Jan.25, 1944, box 2, Josephine Wilkins Papers, SC-EU; Hedy West to Author, Sept. 18, 2004.

15. "Seek Your Support," ca. Feb. 1944, and West to Mitchell, March 1, Feb. 28, 1944, all in box 1881, AFL-CIO Region 8 Collection.

16. West to Mitchell, Sept. 18, 1944, box 1881, AFL-CIO Region 8 Collection; West to Langston Hughes, May 12, 1944, Donald L. West file, Julius Rosenwald Fund Papers, Fisk University Archives, Nashville; "A Word from the Teachers," *Monthly Scrapper*, Feb. 1944.

17. West, "Governor Ellis Arnall Challenges State Teachers to Have 'Vision and Courage to Build a Better World," Nov. 11, 1944, Donald L. West file, Julius Rosenwald Fund Papers; Arnall, "Inaugural Address," Jan. 12, 1943, Clayton, Ga., box 208A, Governor's Papers, Georgia State Archives; West to Mitchell, Sept. 18, 1944. For evidence of Arnall's progressive views on race and education in 1944 and 1945, see John Egerton interview with Ellis Arnall, June 25, 1990 (for the Southern Oral History Collection), in box 69, John Egerton Papers, Vanderbilt University Archives, Nashville; see also Heale, *McCarthy's Americans*, 223, 227, and Bartley, *The Creation of Modern Georgia*, 194–95, 197.

18. West to Hughes, Sept. 2, 30, 1943, box 169, Langston Hughes Papers, Yale Collection of American Literature, the Beinicke Rare Book and Manuscript Library, New Haven; see also Rubin, "Voice of the Cracker," 216–17; and Wald, *Exiles from a Future Time*, 30. For further comment on West's deep antipathy toward the distortions of the "hillbilly" image, see the *St. Louis Post-Dispatch*, ca. April 15, 1945, box 76, Highlander Papers; and West, *No Lonesome Road*, xxvi–xxvii. For discussion of the hillbilly stereotype so abhorred by Don West,

see Harkins, *Hillbilly;* Billings, *Back Talk from Appalachia,* esp. 3–20; Williams, *Appalachia,* 197–99, 396–97; and Drake, *A History of Appalachia,* 222–23, 234–36.

19. West to Hughes, Oct. 10, 1943, box 169, Langston Hughes Papers.

20. West to Hughes, May 14, 1944, Donald L. West file, Julius Rosenwald Fund Papers; Hughes to Arna Bontemps, Sept. 1943, in Bontemps and Hughes, *Arna Bontemps–Langston Hughes Letters,* 143; Rubin, "Voice of the Cracker," 216–17.

21. Hedy West Diary, ca. 1972, 36; author interview with Hedy West; author interviews with Guenivere Chapman, Genevieve Duncan, and Bobbie and Clyde Moore, and Ruth Tribble Forestor; Dunbar, *Against the Grain,* 212.

22. Author interviews with Hedy West and Ann West Williams; see also Hedy West Diary and Don West to Presh, Sept. 1, 1967, both in Hedy West Papers; Byerly, "'What Shall a Poet Sing?'" 302; author interviews with Guenivere Chapman, Genevieve Duncan, and Bobbie and Clyde Moore. See also Jones, "To Whom it May Concern," for evidence of West's "access to the society of intellectuals" as well as outside visitors to Lula.

23. West to Claude Williams, May 4, 1945, box 15, Claude C. Williams Collection; Jones, "To Whom It May Concern"; author interviews with Guenivere Chapman, Genevieve Duncan, and Bobbie and Clyde Moore; Hall County Audit Reports, 1944–45, Hall County Board of Education Offices, Gainesville, Ga.

24. Kenneth R. Williams to Edwin R. Embree, Dec. 20, 1944, West to Rosenwald Fund, June 8, 1944, and West to Fred G. Wale, Feb. 4, 1945, all in Donald L. West file, Julius Rosenwald Fund Papers; West, *No Lonesome Road,* xxxii; *Monthly Scrapper,* Dec. 1943.

25. Jane Franseth to Rosenwald Fund and Jones to Rosenwald Fund, n.d., both in Donald L. West file, Julius Rosenwald Fund Papers; West to Reece, Jan. 18, 1944, box 21, Byron Herbert Reece Papers. For student perception of West's commitment to intercultural understanding and racial toleration, see author interviews with Guenivere Chapman, Genevieve Duncan, and Bobbie and Clyde Moore, and Ruth Tribble Forestor; see also Stevens, Pool, and Hunt, "Lula Schools Build Good Will" in Donald L. West file, Julius Rosenwald Fund Papers.

26. Byerly, "'What Shall a Poet Sing?'" 302; West, "Statement of Plan of Work," Dec. 20, 1944, and West to Wale, Feb. 5, April 8, 11, and 17, 1945, all in Donald L. West file, Julius Rosenwald Fund Papers; West to Linda Williams, Dec. 21, 1984, Don West Papers.

27. Davis, "From the Hills of Georgia," 43; "Plumb to Yonder," 144.

28. "RE: Donald Lee West" (Confidential), ca. April 10, 1956, Senate Internal Security Subcommittee files, record group 233, National Archives; FBI Reports, Aug. 3, 1944, Feb. 8, July 20, 1945, all in file 100-550, FBI Reports 100-20396-33, 36, 37; author interviews with Guenivere Chapman, Genevieve Duncan, and Bobbie and Clyde Moore.

29. Author interview with Ruth Tribble Forestor; author interviews with Guenivere Chapman, Genevieve Duncan, and Bobbie and Clyde Moore; "To Whom It May Concern."

30. West to Reece, Dec. 9, 19, 1945, Jan. 3, 1946, all in box 21, Byron Herbert Reece Papers; West to Claude Williams, May 4, April 20, 1945, both in box 15, Claude C. Williams Collection; author interviews with Guenivere Chapman, Genevieve Duncan, and Bobbie and Clyde Moore.

31. Author interviews with Ruth Tribble Forestor and Ann West Williams.

32. "To Whom It May Concern"; author interviews with Guenivere Chapman, Genevieve Duncan, and Bobbie and Clyde Moore, and Ruth Tribble Forestor.

Chapter 9: Literary Achievement and the Academic Life: The Price of Social Engagement, 1945–48

1. Hedy West to Author, Sept. 19, 2004; "Hedy West Is Too Cosmopolitan to be Commercial Folksinger," ca. 1970, box 31, Mike Ross Papers, Southern Labor Archives (SLA), Special Collections, Georgia State University, Atlanta; Cratis Williams, "Hedy West: Songbird of the Appalachians," *Appalachian South* 1 (Summer 1965), 8–11; Byerly, "'What Shall a Poet Sing?'" 301–2; West to Reece, ca. summer 1945, box 21, Byron Herbert Reece Papers, Hargrett Rare Books and Manuscript Library, University of Georgia Libraries, Athens; West, "Statement of Plan of Work," Donald L. West file, Julius Rosenwald Fund Papers, Fisk University Archives, Nashville; West to Claude Williams, June 20, 1945, box 5, Claude C. Williams Collection, Walter P. Reuther Library, Archives of Labor and Urban Affairs, Wayne State University, Detroit; Dunbar, *Against the Grain*, 213.

2. "Meeting of the National Council of PIAR," Dec. 29, 1945, box 18, Claude C. Williams Collection; West to Reece, Nov. 28, Dec. 9, 19, 1945, Jan. 3, 1946, all in box 21, Byron Herbert Reece Papers.

3. Sue Thrasher interview with Don West, July 10, 1974, Highlander Research and Education Center Archives, New Market, Tenn.; *Amalgamated Clothing Worker*, April 10, 1946, West to Horton, April 5, Feb. 25, 1946, boxes 76, 29, Highlander Research and Education Papers (Highlander Papers), Archives and Manuscripts Division, Wisconsin Historical Society, Madison; Claude Williams to Friend, Jan. 25, 1946, and "To All National Board Members," April 8, 1946, both in box 18, Claude C. Williams Collection; Dunbar, *Against the Grain*, 213.

4. "Donald Lee West," March 1, 1946, file 100-559, FBI Report 100-20396-39.

5. The following are all in the Donald L. West file, Julius Rosenwald Fund Papers: Shirley Graham, "Confidential Report on Candidate for Fellowship," Feb. 10, 1946; L. D. Haskew to Division for Fellowships," n.d.; Du Bois to Edwin R. Embree, Jan. 28, Feb. 4, 13, 1946; West to William C. Haygood, Nov. 30, 1945; and West, "Report of Progress and Future Plans," ca. Jan. 1946.

6. Egerton, *Speak Now Against the Day*, 419; Dunbar, *Against the Grain*, 213; Green, "The Social Life of Poetry," 261–64; West, *No Lonesome Road*, xxxii; West to Horton, Feb. 25, April 5, 1946, box 29, Highlander Papers.

7. "Charles Boni and Joseph Gaer Start New Publishing House," *Publishers' Weekly*, Feb. 9, 1946, 1028. For details on the business careers of Charles Boni and Joseph Gaer, see Green, "The Social Life of Poetry," 266–71. For evidence of the publisher's enthusiasm for West's work, see Gaer to Wilkens, Jan. 24, 1946, box 23, Josephine Wilkens Papers, Special Collections, Emory University (SC-EU), Atlanta.

8. Green, "The Social Life of Poetry," 271–72, Williams to Fay Gaer, July 20, 1946, West to Williams, ca. Sept. 1946, and "Something New in the Book World," ca. 1946, all in boxes 6, 16, 19, Claude C. Williams Collection; *Publisher's Weekly*, March 22, 1947, 1726. West later asserted that total sales exceeded a hundred thousand volumes, a remarkable feat for any writer but stunning for a book of poems. Sullivan, "Don West: Poet and Preacher," 56; Green, "The Social Life of Poetry," 226.

9. West, "Introduction," *Clods of Southern Earth*, 12; see also West, "I Love the South," 3.

10. Stuart to Roland Carter, June 19, 1944, "Jesse Stuart—Correspondence with Roland Carter," Digital Library of Appalachia, http://www.aca_dla.org/; "Lost Leader," quoted in Green, "The Social Life of Poetry," 262; West to Reece, Jan. 18, 1944, box 21, Byron

Herbert Reece Papers; West, "*Taps for Private Tussie*," 39; Horton to West, July 13, 1944, box 9, Highlander Papers; Lawrence Bolling to Stuart, 1969, Stuart Papers, Murray State University, in private collection of David Palmore, Erlanger, Ky. For discussion of West's confrontation with Stuart, see Whisnant, "The Folk Hero in Appalachian Struggle History," 33; and Drake, *A History of Appalachia*, 220. Stuart's romanticism is noted in Egerton, *Speak Now Against the Day*, 264–65. For discussion of West's defiant repudiation of the "hillbilly" stereotype see Rubin, "Voice of the Cracker," esp. 214–16.

11. "Clodhopper"; "Voice of the Cracker," *Clods of Southern Earth*, 45; West, *No Lonesome Road*, 144–45; Rubin, "Voice of the Cracker," 207, 217.

12. West, *No Lonesome Road*, xxii, xxxii; Rubin, "Voice of the Cracker," 208.

13. West, "Look Here, America" and "What Shall a Poet Sing?" both in *No Lonesome Road*, 137–38, 120. The didactic dimension of West's work is discussed in Henson, "'Naked Words That Have No Subtle Meaning,'" 57–58.

14. Laska, "Don West—People's Poet"; West, "Introduction," *Clods of Southern Earth*, 1–12; Wald, *Exiles from a Future Time*, 30; see also Green, "Social Life of Poetry," 235.

15. Samuel Sillen, "The Cry for Justice in the South Today," *The Daily Worker*, Aug. 25, 1946; Alex Hite, "Poetry Books are Written by Georgians," *Atlanta Constitution*, Aug. 4, 1946; "*Clods of Southern Earth*," *Mountain Life and Work* (Fall 1946), 26–27; see also "Poetry Books Are Written by Georgians," *Atlanta Constitution*, Aug. 4, 1946, and "Something New in the Book World," ca. fall 1946, box 19, Claude C. Williams Collection. For full discussion of the critical reaction see Green, "Social Life of Poetry," 235–37, 241–42, 244–47; and West, *No Lonesome Road*, xxxii–xxiii.

16. Preece quoted in Green, "The Social Life of Poetry," 236–37; see also Lechlitner, "Overalls Poet"; Burger, "Homespun Poem of the South"; West, *No Lonesome Road*, xxxiii.

17. Quoted in Green, "The Social Life of Poetry," 249 (for Jones's remarks see 248); see also Martin, "West's Poems Raise a Controversy"; Claude Williams to "Teacher," ca. fall 1946, box 54, Ralph McGill Papers, Special Collections, Emory University, Atlanta.

18. Author interview with Hedy West, March 10, 2004, Narberth, Pa.; author interview with Ann West Williams, Aug. 8, 2004, Charleston, W.V.; West to Williams, Sept. 4, 1946, box 15, Claude C. Williams Collection; "Poet Don West, Here on Visit, Will Join Oglethorpe Faculty," ca. summer 1946, Don West file, Atlanta History Center; Byerly, "'What Shall a Poet Sing?'" 302–3.

19. West to Williams, Nov. 18, Sept. 4, 30, 1946, boxes 12, 15, Claude C. Williams Collection; West to Bert Gilden, Oct. 2, Nov. 21, 1946, both in box 7, Bert and Katya Gilden Papers, Special Collections, John Hay Library, Brown University, Providence, R.I.; West to Reece, Oct. 20, 1946, box 21, Byron Herbert Reece Papers; West to Horton, Oct. 23, 1946, box 29, Highlander Papers; "Dear Friend," ca. Jan. 1947, reel 61, W. E. B. Du Bois Papers, Special Collections, University of Massachusetts Library, Amherst; "Lula Author Sued on Libel Charge"; "'Ridiculous,' West Says of Libel Suit."

20. *Winston-Salem Industrial Leader*, Nov. 11, 1946, Don West Scrapbook, Ann West Williams Collection, Charleston, W.V.; "Dear Friend," ca. Jan. 1947, and West to Williams, Nov. 18, 1946, both in box 12, Claude C. Williams Collection; West to Reece, Oct. 20, 1946, box 21, Byron Herbert Reece Papers; "'Ridiculous' West Says of Libel Suit"; see also West to Gilden, March 17, 1947, box 7, Bert and Katya Gilden Papers.

21. Herb Leslie, comments, Appalachian weekend, Craddock Center, Sept. 25, 2004, Blue Ridge, Ga., author's notes; Green, "The Social Life of Poetry," 280–81; Sue Thrasher interview with Don West; "Poet Don West, Here on Visit."

22. Herb Leslie comments; "Announcement of Courses for 1947–1948," Archives, Philip Weltner Library, Oglethorpe University, Atlanta; *Stormy Petrel*, Jan. 24, 1947; West to Gilden, Nov. 21, 1946; Green, "The Social Life of Poetry, 281.

23. *Stormy Petrel*, Nov. 7, 1947; Green, "The Social Life of Poetry," 281.

24. Jacqueline Hall and Ray Faherty interview with Don West, Jan. 22, 1975, interview E-16, Southern Oral History Collection, Southern Historical Collection, Wilson Library, University of North Carolina, Chapel Hill; *Oglethorpe Workshop Echo* 1 (July 1947), Don West Scrapbook, Ann West Williams Collection; "Adult Education," ca. 1947, and "Report to the Faculty and Faculty Council of Enrollment," ca. 1947, MS 2, box 2, Faculty Correspondence folder, Philip Weltner Papers, Philip Weltner Library, Oglethorpe University, Atlanta; Green, "The Social Life of Poetry," 281.

25. "Four Gifts for Man." For an informed analysis of this poem and its significance for Oglethorpe's experiment in liberal education, see Green, "The Social Life of Poetry," 282–84.

26. P. W. to the Faculty, Nov. 7, 1946, box 2, Philip Weltner Papers; Green, "The Social Life of Poetry," 284.

27. West to Williams, Dec. 4, 1946, box 15, Claude C. Williams Collection; see also West to Gilden, Nov. 21, 1946, box 7, Bert and Katya Gilden Papers.

28. Green, "The Social Life of Poetry," 285; Ferguson, *Black Politics in New Deal Atlanta*, 256–57. For full discussion of Columbians see Weisenberger, "The Columbians, Inc," esp. 821–23; and Patrick, "A Nail in the Coffin of Racism"; see also Keeler McCartney to McGill, Dec. 2, 1946, box 3, Ralph McGill Papers.

29. *Stormy Petrel*, Nov. 22, 1946; Green, "The Social Life of Poetry," 285; West to Williams, Sept. 30, 1946, box 15, Claude C. Williams Collection.

30. West to Williams, Dec. 4, 1946, box 15, Claude C. Williams Collection.

31. West to Williams, Nov. 18, Dec. 4, 1946, box 15, Claude C. Williams Collection.

32. The following are all in boxes 5 and 33, SCHW Papers, Trevor Arnett Library Archives, Atlanta University Center: Smith to Clark Foreman, May 9, 1945; Smith to Dombrowski, May 7, 1945; "Report, Committee for Georgia," Jan. 13, 1945; and "Committee for Georgia: Building Together," Jan. 1945. See also Bartley, *The Creation of Modern Georgia*, 211. In boxes 3 and 29, SCHW Papers, Tuskegee Archives and Museums, Tuskegee, Ala., are: "Committee for Georgia," Feb. 28, 1945, Lucy Randolph Mason to Dombrowski, Feb. 22, 1945, and "Report of a Meeting Held at the Chamber of Commerce Auditorium at 2:30 P.M. on Saturday, Jan. 13, 1945," 14–16. See also Mason to Philip Murray, Jan. 14, 1945, roll 63 (microfilm edition), Lucy Randolph Mason Papers in CIO Southern Organizing Drive Papers, Duke University, Durham, N.C. The charges of communist domination in the SCHW were greatly exaggerated; the CP never gained control of the organization. Egerton, *Speak Now Against the Day*, 296–301.

33. West to Dombrowski, Oct. 24, 1945, and Buckmaster to Dombrowski, ca. Oct. 1945, both in box 29, SCHW Papers, Tuskegee. By mid-1946 the Georgia committee was, in the words of liberal firebrand Virginia Durr, "torn and rent and not functioning." Durr to Dombrowski, ca. Sept. 1946, box 17, James A. Dombrowski Papers, Archives and Manuscripts Division, Wisconsin Historical Society, Madison.

34. For discussion of tensions between the SCHW and CIO, including West's efforts to support Mason's initiatives, see Green, "The Social Life of Poetry," esp. 272–75. Mason's enthusiasm for the SCHW as an asset in the CIO's southern organizing drive is discussed in Mason to Murray, Oct. 30, 1944, and Jan. 14, 1945, reel 63, Lucy Randolph Mason Papers.

35. West to Horton, Oct. 23, 30, 1946, and West to Aubrey Williams, Oct. 30, 1946, all in box 29, Highlander Papers; West to Claude Williams, ca. Oct. 1946, box 15, Claude C. Williams Collection; Green, "The Social Life of Poetry," 285–86.

36. West, "Georgia's Crisis," radio speech, Feb. 5, 1947, Don West file, Atlanta History Center. For discussion of the three governors' controversy, see Bartley, *The Creation of Modern Georgia*, 201–5; Tuck, *Beyond Atlanta*, 66–70; Egerton, *Speak Now Against the Day*, 386–89; and Heale, *McCarthy's Americans*, 229–30.

37. Krueger, *And Promises to Keep*, 155, 160; West to Frank C. Bancroft, March 14, 1947, and J. E. P. to Dombrowski, Feb. 15, 1947, boxes 29, 3, SCHW Papers, Tuskegee; Green, "Social Life of Poetry," 288–89.

38. Foreman to Aubrey Williams, April 24, 1947, box 38, Aubrey Williams Papers, Franklin D. Roosevelt Presidential Library, Hyde Park; Minutes of the Meeting of Board of Directors, SCHW, Birmingham, Ala., April 19, 1947, box 5, SCHW Papers, Atlanta; Green, "Social Life of Poetry," 200. Dombrowski's ouster is discussed in Adams, *James A. Dombrowski*, 171–77; see also Foreman to Dombrowski, Dec. 6. 1946, box 17, James A. Dombrowski Papers.

39. West to Williams, Nov. 29, 1946, box 15, Claude C. Williams Collection. For evidence of red-baiting within the Committee for Georgia, see Frank McAllister to Foreman, May 4, 1942, box 17, James A. Dombrowski Papers; and interview, Virginia Durr, Oct. 25, 1978, box 15, Frank T. Adams Papers.

40. West to Williams, Dec. 4, Nov. 29, 1946, box 15, Claude C. Williams Collection. For comment on McGill's anticommunism and the growth of red-baiting, see interview, Virginia Durr; and Durr to Dombrowski, ca. fall 1946, box 17, James A. Dombrowski Papers.

41. Minutes of Meeting of Board of Directors, SCHW, April 19, July 12, 1947, and Edmonia W. Grant to Administrative Committee, Nov. 5, 1947, boxes 1, 5, SCHW Papers, Atlanta; Grant to Administrative Committee, Oct. 30, 1947, box 38, Aubrey Williams Papers; West to Claude Williams, Feb. 11, 1947 (dated 1946 in error), box 15, Claude C. Williams Collection; "File, Fisher," n.d., reel 63, Lucy Randolph Mason Papers; Adams, *James A. Dombrowski*, 157. Fisher's rebuttal to the charges against her may be found in Fisher to Foreman, Dec. 29, 1946, box 17, James A. Dombrowski Papers.

42. The following are all in box 29, SCHW Papers, Tuskegee: Minutes, Atlanta Chapter, SCHW, Oct. 30, 1947; Grant to West, Sept. 20, 30, 1947; West to Grant, Sept. 9, 1947; and Josephine Wilkins to Forman, Oct. 6, 1947; West to Claude Williams, Sept. 20, April 30, 1947, box 15, Claude C. Williams Collection; Salmond, *Miss Lucy of the CIO*, 166; Grant to Administrative Committee, Nov. 5, 1947, box 38, Aubrey Williams Papers; Green, "The Social Life of Poetry," 292.

43. Communist Party of Georgia to "Dear Friend," Jan. 1, 1948, box 150, James C. Davis Papers, SC-EU; Green, "The Social Life of Poetry," 293; Grant to Administrative Committee, Nov. 5, 1947, box 38, Aubrey Williams Papers; *Stormy Petrel*, Nov. 7, 1947; West to Weltner, Oct. 20, 1947, Don West Papers; Grant to Board Members, SCHW, Jan. 23, 1948, box 2, Carl and Anne Braden Papers, Special Collections, Hoskins Library (SC, HL), University of Tennessee, Knoxville; Grant to Rabun, Sept. 30, 1947, box 49, SCHW Papers, Tuskegee.

44. For evidence of a communist role in the SCHW, the Progressive Party, and the Wallace campaign, see Klehr, *The Heyday of American Communism*, 276–78; Kelly, *Hammer and Hoe*, 186–90; Scales, *Cause at Heart*, 186–87; Adams, *James A. Dombrowski*, 128; Egerton, *Speak Now Against the Day*, 457, 458, 528–29; Heale, *McCarthy's Americans*, 230–31; and Woods, *Black Struggle*, 30–31.

45. "RE: Donald L. West," June 16, 1948, McGill to Davis, June 11, 1948 (telegram), and Davis to McGill, June 11, 1948, all in box 54, Ralph McGill Papers; "Information from the Files of the Committee on Un-American Activities," April 13, 1948, box 65, James C. Davis Papers; Heale, *McCarthy's Americans*, 231; Dunbar, *Against the Grain*, 229; Byerly, "'What Shall a Poet Sing?'" 303.

46. West to Williams, Sept. 20, Oct. 16, Nov. 1, 10, 21, 1947, all in box 15, Claude C. Williams Collection; West to Gilden, Dec. 23 and 27, 1946, both in box 7, Bert and Katya Gilden Papers; PIAR, "Greetings, Friends," Dec. 1947, and "Dear Church Member," April 12, 1948, both in box 54, McGill Papers. For comment on the Rev. Archer Torrey's early experiences ministering to an African American congregation in Darien and working with writer Bert Gilden in the same coastal Georgia community, see Ben Torrey, "Tribute to Reuben Archer Torrey III," http://www.jesusabbey.tv/torrey_library/rat3_splash.jsp.

47. "Dear Church Member" and "Did You Know This," April 12, 1948, box 54, Ralph McGill Papers; McGill, "Add Don West's Subversive Associates"; McGill, "Don West Signs Himself a Communist"; McGill, "It Is Now Officially Communist"; McGill, "The Unitarians Have Reason to Fret."

48. Alex Baskin interview with Don West, Feb. 5, 1975, Stony Brook, N.Y.; Jacqueline Hall and Ray Faherty interview of Don West; West to Linda Williams, Dec. 21, 1984, Don West Papers; Dunbar, *Against the Grain*, 229; Egerton, *Speak Now Against the Day*, 374; Byerly, "'What Shall a Poet Sing?'" 305. For full discussion of the Ingram case, see Shadron, "Popular Protest and Legal Authority in Post–World War II Georgia."

49. Harry Raymond, "The Ingrams Shall Not Die!" box 54, Ralph McGill Papers; "Wallace Statement" and "Mass Defense," both in Civil Rights Congress Papers (microfilm ed.), pt. 1, reel 8, Schomburg Center for Research in Black Culture, New York; "Help Save the Ingrams," pt. 2, box C-37, NAACP Papers, Manuscripts Division, Library of Congress, Washington, D.C.; "The 1948 Elections: The People Must Act," and Carolina District of the CPUSA, "Free Mrs. Ingram and Her Two Sons from Georgia Justice," folder 4879, Junius Irving Scales Papers, Southern Historical Collection, Wilson Library, University of North Carolina, Chapel Hill; Charlotte Bass to Walter White, April 5, 1952 and interview, Louise Patterson, April 13, 1988, both in boxes 8, 31, Louise Patterson Papers, SC-EU; Green, "The Social Life of Poetry," 294; Dunbar, *Against the Grain*, 229.

50. Alex Baskin interview with Don West; Jacqueline Hall and Ray Faherty interview with Don West; author interview with Ann West Williams; author interview with Hedy West; West to Weltner, Oct. 20, 1947, Don West Papers; Rainey to Johnnie, April 4, 1948, box 4, Glenn Rainey Papers, SC-EU. For press reports of West's uncertain status see "Oglethorpe Not Ousting Georgia Wallace Backer," unidentified clipping, box 35, Progressive Party Papers, University of Iowa Library, Special Collections, Iowa City; see also McGill to Davis, June 11, 1948, box 65, James C. Davis Papers; *Atlanta Journal*, April 4, 1948, and *Stormy Petrel*, March 17, 1948. Weltner's notes on West are found in "Don West," n.d., MS 2, box 2, Faculty Correspondence file, Philip Weltner Papers, Philip Weltner Library, Oglethorpe University, Atlanta.

51. Torrey to Bert, Homer, Don, Sept. 11, 1947, and Torrey to Gilden, Aug. 25, 1947, both in box 17, Bert and Katya Gilden Papers.

52. "Religious Fervor in Wallace Rally," May 19, 1948, "Call to the Founding Convention of a New People's Party of Georgia," and "Jim Barfoot for Governor," 1948, all in boxes 32, 1, Mike Ross Papers; Jacqueline Hall and Ray Faherty interview with Don West; Alex Baskin interview with Don West; Sue Thrasher interview with Don West; *The Daily Worker* Feb. 29,

May 10, 1948, card file, HUAC-SISS file, record group 233, National Archives; "Activities in Connection with Third Party," in "Donald Lee West," April 6, 1948, file 100-559, FBI Report 100-20396-66; Bro (West) to Bro (Bart Logan), Aug. 19, 1948, Don West Scrapbook, Ann West Williams Collection; "Notes on a Meeting to Discuss the Third Party in the South," ca. Feb. 2, 1948, box 35, Progressive Party Papers; West, "My Dad Died Young," *Union Farmer*, Feb. 1948, folder 4879, Junius Irving Scales Papers. On Pratt, see Flamming, *Creating the Modern South*, 291; Dunbar, *Against the Grain*, 213; and Byerly, "'What Shall a Poet Sing?'" 310–11.

53. Wallace, "How the Poll Tax Hurts the South," "Wallace Shows It Can be Done," ca. 1948, and *These Fifteen Million-Wallace* 1 (July 1948), all in box 1, folder 4879, Junius Irving Scales Papers; Alex Baskin interview with Don West; Jacqueline Hall and Ray Faherty interview with Don West; Palmer Weber to Mr. Gitt, box 35, Progressive Party Papers; Tuck, *Beyond Atlanta*, 83–84. For discussion of the Progressive breakthrough on the race issue in the South, see also "Report by C. B. Baldwin," Nov. 15, 1948, box 29, Anita McCormick Blaine Papers, Archives and Manuscripts Division, Wisconsin Historical Society, Madison; and "Report of the Subcommittee on the Negro Vote to the National Committee of the Progressive Party," Sept. 10, 1948, box 35, Progressive Party Papers.

54. Torrey to Gilden, Aug. 9, 1948, box 17, Bert and Katya Gilden Papers; Scales, *Cause at Heart*, 192–93; "Program, Founding Convention of the North Carolina Progressive Party," Winston-Salem, April 25, 1948, box 2, Junius Irving Scales Papers.

55. Green, "The Social Life of Poetry," 295; Clowse, *Ralph McGill*, 150; Heale, *McCarthy's Americans*, 231; *Atlanta Constitution*, June 18, 24, 27, 28, 1948; Davis to McGill, June 22, 1948, box 65, James C. Davis Papers.

56. Bro (West) to Bro (Logan), Aug. 19, 1948; George Brosi Notes, Jeff Biggers Papers, Don West Collection. Byerly quotes an undated letter containing similar language but maintains that it was addressed to Nat Ross rather than Bart Logan. It is unclear if the two documents are identical. Byerly, "'What Shall a Poet Sing?'" 313. See also Alex Baskin interview with Don West, and Jacqueline Hall and Ray Faherty interview with Don West. At the same approximate moment, Torrey informed Gilden that West was "under persecution by some who are supposed to be his friends." Torrey to Gilden, Aug. 9, 1948, box 17, Bert and Katya Gilden Papers. For detail on Chase's Communist Party background, see Chase to McGill, Oct. 4, 1947; box 3, Ralph McGill Papers; Homer Chase, biographical summary, ca. Oct. 1947, box 63, James C. Davis Papers; Heale, *McCarthy's Americans*, 230.

57. "Text of Speech by Henry Wallace Before Conference of Ministers of the Church of God," Dalton, Ga., Oct. 16, 1948, and "Present at National Committee Meeting," Sept. 10, 1948, both in box 1, Mike Ross Papers; see also box 742, Anita McCormick Blaine Papers; Sue Thrasher interview with Don West; Arnold Goldman to Mr. Gitt, Sept. 26, 1948, and "For Release Week of Oct. 11, 1948," both in box 35, Progressive Party Papers; Torrey to Bert and Katya Gilden, Oct. 16, 1948, box 17, Bert and Katya Gilden Papers; Bro (West) to Bro (Logan), Aug. 19, 1948; Green, "The Social Life of Poetry," 296.

58. McGill, "All Right, Here It Is!"; see also Green, "The Social Life of Poetry," 296–97. West's position was consistent with his candidate's refusal to fully repudiate communist support. Late in the campaign, Wallace asserted that "if the Communists want to help us in our work" he was willing to "do exactly what Jesus advocated with publicans and sinners." Gillmor to *York Gazette* (telegram) ca. Oct. 30, 1948, and Wallace, "Progressives and Marxism," *Sunday Compass*, Oct. 30, 1948, both in boxes 33, 6, Progressive Party Papers.

59. West eventually signed the document. "A Declaration of Civil Rights," Nov. 20,

1948, box 39, Aubrey Williams Papers; *Southern Patriot*, Dec. 1948; Egerton, *Speak Now Against the Day*, 530; see also Adams, *James A. Dombrowski*, 195–96, 201–2; Krueger, 190; and Green, "The Social Life of Poetry," 299. For discussion of Wallace's frustration with the communists, see Schrecker, *Many Are the Crimes*, 36. Both the promise and the failure of the Wallace campaign in the South is discussed in Fosl, *Subversive Southerner*, 100–101, and Egerton, *Speak Now Against the Day*, 491–92, 504–6, 508.

60. Barfoot to C. B. Baldwin, June 29, 1949, reel 46 (microfilm edition), Henry A. Wallace Papers, Special Collections, University of Iowa Library, Iowa City; "News Release," June 29, 1949, and Barfoot to Fellow Georgian, July 6, 1949, both in boxes 54, 4, Ralph McGill Papers; *Atlanta Constitution*, June 29, 1949; West to Gilden, Jan. 15, 1950, box 7, Bert and Katya Gilden Papers; *Macon World*, May 7, 1949.

61. Green, "The Social Life of Poetry," 300; Torrey to Gilden, Oct. 16, 1948, box 17, Bert and Katya Gilden Papers; Byerly, "'What Shall a Poet Sing?'" 319; West, *No Lonesome Road*, xxxiv.

Chapter 10: Before the Storm: Back at the Farm, 1949–54

1. Alex Baskin interview with Don West, Feb. 5, 1975, Stony Brook, N.Y.; West to Linda Williams, Dec. 21, 1984, Don West Papers; "Donald Lee West," April 4, 1950, file 100-559, FBI Report 100-20396-87; author interview with Hedy West, March 10, 2004, Narberth, Pa.; author interview with Ann West Williams, Aug. 8, 2004, Charleston, W.V.; author interview with Janet Ross Davis, Atlanta, Dec. 5, 2003.

2. Don West to Presh, Sept. 7, 1967, Hedy West Papers; Alex Baskin interview with Don West; author interview with Hedy West. For evidence of interpersonal conflict between Don and Connie, see Mere to Don, Oct. 23, 1973, Don West Papers; see also Hedy West Diary, ca. 1972, 3c, Hedy West Papers.

3. West to Reece, Nov. 7, 1949, box 21, Byron Herbert Reece Papers, Hargrett Rare Books and Manuscript Library, University of Georgia Libraries, Athens.

4. Ibid.

5. West to Hughes, April 11, 1951, box 169, Langston Hughes Papers, Yale Collection of American Literature, the Beinicke Rare Book and Manuscript Library, New Haven; West to Gilden, Jan. 15, 1950, box 7, Bert and Katya Gilden Papers, Special Collections, John Hay Library, Brown University, Providence, R.I.; author interview with Ann West Williams. For evidence of the Home Mission Council's social service and organizing work, see AR66, box 1, Harry Koger Papers, Special Collections, Texas Labor History Archives, University of Texas-Arlington. In the period from September 1950 to September 1951, FBI reports invariably concluded that West was not engaged in subversive activity. "Donald Lee West," FBI files 100-559, 100-7192, 100-8851.

6. Koger to Marion Davidson, Aug. 11, 1958, box 6, Claude C. Williams Collection, Walter P. Reuther Library, Archives of Labor and Urban Affairs, Wayne State University, Detroit; *Agricultural Workers Bulletin* (Spring) and (Dec. 1954), and "Dear Friend," mid-Sept. 1960, all in box 1, Koger Papers; "Donald Lee West," May 4, 1951, file 100-559, FBI Report 100-20396-107; Alex Baskin interview of Don West.

7. Byerly, "'What Shall a Poet Sing?'" 330.

8. West, "There's Anger in the Land," in *The Road Is Rocky*, 15–16; author interview with Hedy West; Byerly, "'What Shall a Poet Sing?'" 331–32.

9. West, "Sad, Sad America," in *The Road Is Rocky*, 21–22.

10. West, "I Saw a Hungry Child," "I've Known Hunger," "Ballad of the Migrants," and "If Sometimes Sorrow," all in *The Road Is Rocky*, 25, 29–30, 32–34. For comment on West as a "people's poet," see Roy Smith, "Introduction" in *The Road Is Rocky*, in which Smith christens West the "poet laureate of the South." See also Byron Herbert Reece, Preface in *The Road Is Rocky*; Laska, "Don West—People's Poet"; and Tom Woodruff, Forward in *A Time for Anger*; see also West, *No Lonesome Road*, xxvi–xxviii, xxxv–xxxvi.

11. SAC, San Antonio to Director, Dec. 19, 1951, in "Donald Lee West," Houston, Dec. 4, 1951, file 100-7192, FBI Reports 100-20396-117, 119, and 121.

12. West, "Little Scared One" and "Oh, Pity Those," in *The Road Is Rocky*, 28, 36.

13. Sibley, "Neither Red nor Scout Organizer"; *Atlanta Journal*, Aug. 14, 1952; SAC, Atlanta, to Director, Sept. 11, 19, Nov. 7, 1952, Dec. 22, 1952, Cincinnati, Sept. 25, 1952 (all RE: Security Matter, Donald Lee West), files 100-559, 100-2820, FBI Reports 100-20396-125-129; U.S Congress, House, *Hearings before the House Committee on Un-American Activities*, 81st Cong., 1st sess., 1949, 191, 208; files and Reference Section to Mary Valente, July 7, 1964, HUAC-SISS files, record group 233, National Archives; Jacqueline Hall and Ray Faherty interview with Don West, Jan. 22, 1975, interview E-16, Southern Oral History Collection, Southern Historical Collection, Wilson Library, University of North Carolina, Chapel Hill; Woods, *Black Struggle*, 109; Byerly, "'What Shall a Poet Sing?'" 332.

14. Williams to West, Feb. 12, 1953, and West to Williams, Jan. 15, 1953, both in box 32, Aubrey Williams Papers, Franklin D. Roosevelt Presidential Library, Hyde Park.

15. Author interview with Kenneth West, Sept. 25, 2004, Appalachian Weekend, Craddock Center, Blue Ridge, Ga.; Hedy West to Author, Feb. 16, 2004; Don West to Williams, box 32, Aubrey Williams Papers; Don West to Reece, Feb. 12, 1945, box 21, Byron Herbert Reece Papers; Reece to West, Feb. 14, 1945, Don West Scrapbook, Ann West Williams Collection, Charleston, W.V.; Reece to West, n.d., Don West Papers.

16. Byerly, "'What Shall a Poet Sing?'" 332; West quotation from West to Williams, Jan. 15, 1953, box 32, Aubrey Williams Papers.

17. SAC, Atlanta to Director, March 4, 1954; "Donald Lee West," May 31, 1954, file 100-559, FBI Report 100-20396-135.

18. West to Taylor, Feb. 5, 1954, box 2, Alva W. Taylor Papers, Archives, Disciples of Christ Historical Society, Nashville; "Donald Lee West," May 31, 1954, file 100-559, FBI Report 100-20396-135; Byerly, "'What Shall a Poet Sing?'" 332.

19. Schrecker, *Many Are the Crimes*, 349. For further comment on Matusow's misrepresentations, see Kahn, *The Matusow Affair*; see also Schrecker, *Many Are the Crimes*, 351–52; and Lichtman and Cohen, *Deadly Farce*.

20. Sue Thrasher interview with Don West, July 10, 1974, Highlander Research and Education Center Archives, New Market, Tenn.; Alex Baskin interview with Don West; West to Pete Seeger, Feb. 2, 1979, Don West Scrapbook, Ann West Williams Collection; Flamming, *Creating the Modern South*, 289–90.

Chapter 11: Trouble Brewing: The Great Dalton Red Hunt, 1954–56

1. John G. Ramsay to Victor Reuther, John Edelman, and Boyd Payton, Oct. 12, 1955, box 1563, John G. Ramsay Papers, Southern Labor Archives, Special Collections, Georgia State University, Atlanta; Sue Thrasher interview with Don West, July 10, 1974, Highlander Research and Education Center Archives, New Market, Tenn.; Alex Baskin interview with

Don West, Feb. 5, 1975, Stony Brook, N.Y.; Flamming, *Creating the Modern South*, 290; Dunbar, *Against the Grain*, 245–46.

2. SAC, Atlanta to Director, April 14, 1955, FBI file 100-559, FBI Report 100-20396-139; *The Southerner*, March 1955; West to Taylor, Jan. 25, 1955, box 4, Alva W. Taylor Papers, Archives, Disciples of Christ Historical Society, Nashville; Sue Thrasher interview with Don West; interview with Mike Ross, Aug. 4, 5, 1981, Special Collections, Emory University, Atlanta; West to J. L. Adams, box 112, J. L. Adams Papers, Papers, Special Collections, Arents Library, Syracuse University; Margaret Shannon, "Don West Joins Dalton's Brother Pratt as Preacher, Editor, Right-Hand Man," *Atlanta Journal*, Aug. 29, 1955, Mark Pace Papers (private collection), Dalton, Ga. Flamming suggests that Pratt recruited West, an account consistent with West's recollections, but Shannon's account quotes Pratt's assertion that West had approached him. See also Flamming, *Creating the Modern South*, 290; and Dunbar, *Against the Grain*, 246. It is likely that West suggested an alliance based on their Progressive Party ties and that Pratt responded with an invitation.

3. West to Taylor, Jan. 2, 1955, box 4, Alva W. Taylor Papers; West, "He Pleads the Cause of the Poor," n.d., box 112, J. L. Adams Papers. To other Dalton citizens, West, and even Pratt, were regarded as "outsiders" reluctant to talk about their church and integrate into the wider community. Author interviews, Marcelle White, Dalton Ga., Nov. 4, 2003, and Mark Pace, Dalton, Ga., Dec. 17, 2003.

4. *The Southerner*, April, 1955; Flamming, *Creating the Modern South*, 290; West to Taylor, Feb. 10, 1955, box 4, Alva W. Taylor Papers.

5. Robert A. Freeman to West, July 30, 1982, correspondence file 1, Warren Doyle Papers (private collection), Hays, N.C. Local 1376 is quoted in Flamming, *Creating the Modern South*, 292; see also *The Southerner*, April 1955; Alex Baskin interview of Don West; and Sue Thrasher interview of Don West. The most complete account of the chenille campaign of 1955, including West's role in the effort, may be found in Flamming, *Creating the Modern South*, 290–306.

6. Flamming, *Creating the Modern South*, 291.

7. *The Southerner*, in Flamming, *Creating the Modern South*, 291.

8. Henderson Lanham to Henry C. Ball, April 30, 1955, HUAC to Lanham, May 3, 1955, and Ball to Lanham, April 28, 1955, all in box 36, Henderson Lanham Papers, Richard B. Russell Library for Political Research and Studies, University of Georgia Libraries, Athens; Flamming, *Creating the Modern South*, 292.

9. The following are all in box 1559 of the John G. Ramsay Papers: James O'Shea to West, May 19, 1955, William Pollock to O'Shea, May 13, 17, 1955, Pollock to David Burgess, May 16, 1955, "Statement of David Burgess, Executive Secretary, Georgia State CIO Council," May 10, 1955, C. H. Gillman to Pollock, May 10, 1955, and Burgess to Pollock, May 11, 1955. See also Flamming, *Creating the Modern South*, 292. The anticommunist commitment of both Burgess and the Religion and Labor Foundation are evident in Burgess, "The Future of the Religion and Labor Foundation," n.d., box 1, David S. Burgess Collection, Walter P. Reuther Library, Archives of Labor and Urban Affairs, Wayne State University, Detroit.

10. West to Williams, June 24, 1955, box 32, Aubrey Williams Papers, Franklin D. Roosevelt Presidential Library, Hyde Park; West to O'Shea, May 23, 1955, box 1559, John G. Ramsey Papers; Flamming, *Creating the Modern South*, 292.

11. West to Williams, June 24, 1955; O'Shea to Pollock, May 31, 1955, box 1559, John G. Ramsey Papers; Flamming, *Creating the Modern South*, 292–93.

12. *The Southerner,* Oct. 15, 1955; Sue Thrasher interview with Don West; Alex Baskin interview with Don West; Flamming, *Creating the Modern South,* 293–94; Byerly, "'What Shall a Poet Sing?'" 335.

13. Author interview with Mark Pace; West to Williams, n.d., box 15, Claude C. Williams Collection, Walter P. Reuther Library, Archives of Labor and Urban Affairs, Wayne State University, Detroit; Flamming, *Creating the Modern South,* 294.

14. *Dalton Citizen,* Aug. 25, 1955; *Dalton News,* Aug. 21, 18, 1955. See also Flamming, *Creating the Modern South,* 294–96, for discussion of the campaign against West.

15. West to Reece, ca. Aug. 30, 25, and Sept. 1, 1955, box 21, Byron Herbert Reece Papers, Hargrett Rare Books and Manuscript Library, University of Georgia Libraries, Athens; Shannon, "Don West Joins Dalton's Brother Pratt."

16. Horace to Alton Lawrence, Aug. 31, 1955, box 32, Mike Ross Papers, Southern Labor Archives (SLA), Special Collections, Georgia State University, Atlanta; Flamming, *Creating the Modern South,* 197; Weissman, "Pulpit for Unionism," 149.

17. Horace to Lawrence, Aug. 31, 1955.

18. Quoted in Flamming, *Creating the Modern South,* 298 (see also 297).

19. Flamming, *Creating the Modern South,* 298.

20. Sue Thrasher interview with Don West; Alex Baskin interview with Don West; Byerly, "'What Shall a Poet Sing?'" 335; "Ex-Coal Miner Preacher Helps Union Fight Medieval Georgia," *Labor Daily,* n.d., box 1, George Weissman Papers, Archives and Special Collections, Wisconsin Historical Society, Madison.

21. John G. Ramsey to Rev. S. Wilkes Dendy, Oct. 21, 1955, and TWUA, press release, Sept. 8, 1955, both in box 1563, John G. Ramsey Papers; *Atlanta Journal,* Sept. 9, 1955; Flamming, *Creating the Modern South,* 299.

22. Margaret Howard, Helen Bivins, Isabelle Peters, and Geneva Hughes, affidavits, ca. Sept. 1955; see also TWUA, press releases, Sept. 8, 13, 1955, all in box 1, George Weissman Papers. For press accounts, see box 1563, John G. Ramsey Papers; see also Sue Thrasher interview with Don West; and Alex Baskin interview with Don West.

23. Milton Ellerin to Arthur J. Levin, Sept. 14, 1955, John W. Edelman to Msgr. George G. Higgins, Sept. 9, 1955, and "Mass Meeting," ca. Aug 31, 1955, all in box 1563, John G. Ramsey Papers.

24. Flamming, *Creating the Modern South,* 299; Byerly, "'What Shall a Poet Sing?'" 336; Dunbar, *Against the Grain,* 246.

25. Reece to Elliot, Sept. 17, 1955, E. P. Dutton file, Byron Herbert Reece Collection, Young Harris College Library, Young Harris, Ga.; Reece to West, Sept. 1, 1955, box 21, Byron Herbert Reece Papers.

26. West to Claude C. Williams, Sept. 17, 1955, box 15, Claude C. Williams Papers; West to Aubrey Williams, Sept. 6, 1955, box 32, Aubrey Williams Papers; West to Reece, Sept. 16, 1955, box 21, Byron Herbert Reece Papers. For evidence of the sweeping attack on Aubrey Williams and Alva W. Taylor, see the *Dalton News,* Sept. 18, 1995.

27. Pace to J. Edgar Hoover, Sept. 21, 1955, FBI file 100-20396-142.

28. Mr. Nichols to M. A. Jones, "Subject: Mark Pace," Sept. 29, 1955, FBI file 100-20396-143.

29. SAC, Atlanta to Director, Oct. 11, 1955, and Hoover to Pace (with notation: "Attention, SAC"), Sept. 30, 1955, FBI files 100-20396-144, 145, 147.

30. Director, FBI to SAC, Oct. 11, 1955, FBI to Director, FBI, Oct. 7, 1955, and Pace to Hoover, Oct. 8, 1955, FBI files 100-20396-146, 148; *The Southerner,* Oct. 15, 1955.

31. *Dalton Citizen*, Oct. 20, 1955 (see also Oct. 6, 1955); Flamming, *Creating the Modern South*, 301; Sue Thrasher interview with Don West; author interview with Mark Pace.

32. *Dalton Citizen*, Oct. 20, 1955; Flamming, *Creating the Modern South*, 301; Allston Calhoun Jr., script, Radio Broadcast, March 21–24, 1959, box 8, reel 4, Highlander Folk School Collection, Tennessee State Library and Archives, Nashville.

33. West to Claude C. Williams, Sept. 17, 1955, box 15, Claude C. Williams Papers; *Dalton Citizen*, Nov. 3, 1955; West to Aubrey Williams, Sept. 6, 1955, and Aubrey Williams, "Don West," Sept. 8, 1955, both in box 32, Aubrey Williams Papers; *The Southerner*, Nov. 1955.

34. West to Williams, Sept. 17, Oct. 4, 1955, box 15, Claude C. Williams Papers. For West's assessment of the newspaper's role in the struggle for unionism as a "true voice of the public," see *The Southerner*, Nov. 1955.

35. Williams to West, ca. Oct. 1955, box 15, Claude C. Williams Papers.

36. *Atlanta Constitution*, Dec. 31, 1955; *Dalton Citizen*, Jan. 5, 1956; *Dalton News*, Oct. 23, 1955; Dunbar, *Against the Grain*, 246.

37. *Dalton Citizen*, Jan. 12, 1956, Dec. 29, 1955; author interview with Mark Pace; Flamming, *Creating the Modern South*, 304–5.

38. Lanham to Pratt, Pace, and Mitchell (telegrams), Jan. 16, 1955, all in box 36, Henderson Lanham Papers; *Dalton News*, Jan. 13, 1956; *Atlanta Journal*, Jan. 14, 1956; *Atlanta Constitution*, Jan. 14. 1956; West, "Why I Resigned from the Church of God," n.d., box 1, George Weissman Papers; Alex Baskin interview with Don West; Sue Thrasher interview with Don West; Dunbar, *Against the Grain*, 256–57; author interview with Mark Pace; Freeman to West, July 30, 1982, correspondence file 1, Warren Doyle Papers.

39. "The Oath I Was Ready to Take" and "Why I Resigned from the Church of God," both in box 1, George Weissman Papers; "Resigned Prior to Ouster, West Says; Puts Blame of Pratt's Change of Mind on Mitchell," *Dalton Citizen*, ca. Jan. 15, 1955; Sue Thrasher interview with Don West; Alex Baskin interview with Don West; Dunbar, *Against the Grain*, 247; Flamming, *Creating the Modern South*, 306.

Chapter 12: Economic Struggle: The Ravages of Anticommunism and Years of Exile, 1956–65

1. Author interview with Ann West Williams, Aug. 8, 2004, Charleston, W.V.; author interview with Hedy West, March 10, 2004, Narberth, Penn.

2. John W. Edelman to George Wiseman [*sic*], Nov. 18, 1955, TWUA, Press Release, Nov. 21, 1955, and *Chattanooga Times*, Nov. 5, 1955, all in box 1, George Weissman Papers, Archives and Special Collections, Wisconsin Historical Society, Madison.

3. *The Nation*, Feb. 25, 1956, *The Churchman*, April 15, 1956, *Commentary* (draft), ca. 1956, and West to Weissman, March 22, 1956, all in box 1, George Weissman Papers; Hedy West to Author, July 7, 2004.

4. *The Daily Worker*, March 20, 1956; Freda Brown to Weissman, March 16, 1956, box 1, George Weissman Papers; see also Sue Thrasher interview with Don West, July 10, 1974, Highlander Research and Education Center Archives, New Market, Tenn.

5. *The New Southerner*, April 1956, box 102, Mike Ross Papers, Southern Labor Archives, Special Collections, Georgia State University, Atlanta; West to Weissman, March 26, 27, 1956, "*The New Southerner* for a New South," ca. March 1956, and West, "Why I Resigned

from the Church of God," all in box 1, George Weissman Papers; Byerly, "'What Shall a Poet Sing?'" 337.

6. West to Weissman, April 5, 1956; *Montgomery Advertiser*, ca. April 1, 1956, box 1, George Weissman Papers; see also *The New Southerner*, April 1956, box 102, Mike Ross Papers.

7. West to Weissman, April 5, 15, 1956, box 1, George Weissman Papers.

8. Koinonia Farm, "Newsletter No. 21," May 1, 1959, box 42, National Sharecroppers Fund Collection, Walter P. Reuther Library, Archives of Labor and Urban Affairs, Wayne State University, Detroit; West to Reece, Sept. 17, 1956, box 21, Byron Herbert Reece Papers, Hargrett Rare Books and Manuscript Library, University of Georgia Libraries, Athens; Margaret Shannon, "Don West Joins Dalton's Brother Pratt as Preacher, Editor, Right-Hand Man," *Atlanta Journal*, Aug. 29, 1955, Mark Pace Papers (private collection), Dalton, Ga.; West to Weissman, Feb. 15, 1957, box 1, George Weissman Papers; Koinonia Farm, "Newsletter No. 8," Nov. 23, 1956, box 2, Lillian Smith Papers, Hargrett Rare Books and Special Collections Library, University of Georgia Library, Athens; Harold E. Fey, "Report from Koinonia," *Christian Century*, March 6, 1957, box 3, Carl and Anne Braden Papers, Archives and Manuscripts, Wisconsin Historical Society (WHS), Madison. GBI interest in Koinonia Farm is discussed in Woods, *Black Struggle*, 105.

9. Sue Thrasher interview with Don West; West to Weissman, Feb. 15, Dec. 22, 1957, box 1, George Weissman Papers.

10. Bob Morris to Frank W. Schroeder, May 27, 1957, and Ed and Frank to Dick, April 10, 1956, HUAC-SISS file, record group 233, National Archives (NA); "Communism in the Mid-South: Hearings before the Subcommittee to Investigate the Administration of the Internal Security Act and Other Internal Security Laws, U.S. Congress," 85th Cong., 1st Sess., Senate, Committee on the Judiciary, 25; Durr, *Outside the Magic Circle*, 258; Byerly, "'What Shall a Poet Sing?'" 340.

11. "Communism in the Mid-South," 29–31.

12. Georgia Commission on Education, "Every American Has the Right to Know the Truth," ca. Oct. 1957, box 20, Georgia Commission on Education Papers, Georgia State Archives, Clayton; Methodist Federation for Social Action Civil Rights to James Eastland, Oct. 28, 1957 (telegram), HUAC-SISS files, record group 233, NA. For discussion of the Georgia Commission on Education, see Heale, *McCarthy's Americans*, 247, 249, 250, 256–62; and Woods, *Black Struggle*, 97–98, 105–7.

13. Heale, *McCarthy's Americans*, 258–59; Woods, *Black Struggle*, 105–6; Dunbar, *Against the Grain*, 247–48; West to Williams, Jan. 12, 1958, box 15, Claude C. Williams Collection, Walter P. Reuther Library, Archives of Labor and Urban Affairs, Wayne State University, Detroit.

14. *The Southerner*, ca. Oct. 1957, box 32, Mike Ross Papers.

15. T. V. Williams to Douglas Carlisle, Dec. 3, 1957, and Carlisle to T. V. Williams, Nov. 25, 1957, both in box 25, Georgia Commission on Education Papers. Not far behind Pratt was Ralph McGill and the *Atlanta Constitution*, which gave extensive coverage to the Highlander meeting, so much that it drew a rebuke from Aubrey Williams. Williams to McGill, Dec. 19, 1957, box 21, Carl and Anne Braden Papers, WHS.

16. West to Weissman, Dec. 22, 1957; "'Hill-Billy,' 'Plow-boy,' 'Wool-Hats,' and 'Crackers,'" ca. Dec. 1957, box 1, George Weissman Papers; West to Dombrowski, Dec. 12, 1958, box 63, SCHW Papers, Tuskegee Archives and Museums, Tuskegee, Ala.; "Donald Lee West," March 7, 1958, file 100-559, FBI Report 100-20396-172; Dunbar, *Against the Grain*, 247.

17. West to Williams, Jan. 10, 17, 1958, box 32, Aubrey Williams Papers, Franklin D. Roosevelt Presidential Library, Hyde Park; West to Williams, July 7, 1958, box 63, SCHW Papers, Tuskegee.

18. West to Williams, July 7, 1958, box 63, SCHW Papers, Tuskegee; *Firing Line*, Feb., 1958; HUAC, Press Release, July 11, 1958, box 107, James C. Davis Papers, Special Collections, Emory University, Atlanta.

19. West to Aubrey Williams, July 7, 1958, box 63, SCHW Papers, Tuskegee; West to Linda Williams, Dec. 21, 1984, Hedy West Papers; *Carolina Times*, July 26, 1958; Sue Thrasher interview with Don West; Dunbar, *Against the Grain*, 248.

20. Aubrey Williams to West, July 8, 1958, box 63, SCHW Papers, Tuskegee.

21. *Carolina Times*, July 26, 1958; Williams to James Roosevelt, July 9, 1958 (telegram); "An Open Letter to the U. S. House of Representatives, ca. July, 1958, both in box 32, Aubrey Williams Papers.

22. SAC, Atlanta to Director, Oct. 10, 1958, file 100-559; Report 100-20396-179; Ed and Frank to Dick, April 10, 1956, record group 233, HUAC-SISS files, NA; West to Weissman, Dec. 29, 1958, box 1, George Weissman Papers; West to Linda Williams, Dec. 21, 1984 and West to Brosi, Feb. 24, 1987, both in Don West Papers; Sue Thrasher interview with Don West.

23. West to Weissman, Dec. 29, 1958, box 1, George Weissman Papers; West to Dombrowski, July 30, Sept. 6, Oct. 2, 15, 1958, all in box 63, SCHW Papers, Tuskegee.

24. West to Dombrowski, Oct. 2, 15, 1958, box 63, SCHW Papers, Tuskegee; West to Weissman, Dec. 29, 1958, box 1, George Weissman Papers; Belle Logan to Lillie West, Nov. 12, 1958, Don West Papers.

25. Sue Thrasher interview with Don West; Byerly, "'What Shall a Poet Sing?'" 348; West to Dombrowski, Oct. 15 and 20, 1958, box 63, SCHW Papers, Tuskegee.

26. West to Williams, May 7, 1959, box 15, Claude C. Williams Papers; West to Bert and Family, May 19, 1960, box 7, Bert and Katya Gilden Papers, Special Collections, John Hay Library, Brown University, Providence, R.I.; Byerly, "'What Shall a Poet Sing?'" 358. Although the FBI maintained its regular surveillance of West's movements, informants typically placed him at the Douglasville farm, working to earn a living in the only occupation open to him. The Atlanta office, however, continued to highlight the unsubstantiated allegation, first made at the HUAC hearings, that he had been a contact for Jeffrey White, who had been sent from New York to "colonize" for the Party in the South. "Donald Lee West," Sept. 22, 1959, file 100-559, FBI Report 100-20396-182.

27. West to Claude Williams, May 7, 1959; West, "Antislavery Sentiment (and Activity) in the Appalachian South prior to and during the Civil War: An Evaluation," ca. May 1959, box 15, Claude C. Williams Papers; Aubrey Williams to West, April 14, 1959, box 32, Aubrey Williams Papers; West to Weissman, Dec. 29, 1958, box 1, George Weissman Papers.

28. West to Woodward, June 4, July 23, 1960, box 21, C. Vann Woodward Papers, Manuscripts and Archives, Yale University Library, New Haven; Williams to Mary Jane Keeney (telegram), ca. June 1960, and West to Williams, June 6, 1960, both in box 63, SCHW Papers, Tuskegee; West to Bert and Family, May 19,1960, box 7, Bert and Katya Gilden Papers.

29. West to Woodward, June 4, 1960, May 25, 1961, box 21, C. Vann Woodward Papers; West to Williams, June 6, 1960, box 63, SCHW Papers, Tuskegee; SAC, Atlanta to Director, April 14, 1961, file 100-559, FBI Report 100-20396-199; Sue Thrasher interview with Don West.

30. Sue Thrasher interview with Don West; Alex Baskin interview with Don West, Feb. 5, 1975, Stony Brook, N.Y.; *Talmudist* (Baltimore: Talmudical Academy, 1961–62). Baltimore was one of several urban destinations for Appalachian out-migration, starting in the late 1930s. Williams, *Appalachia: A History*, 320, 330.

31. West to Bert and Family, Feb. 18, 1961, box 7, Bert and Katya Gilden Papers; Jacqueline Hall and Ray Faherty interview with Don West, Jan. 22, 1975, interview E-16, Southern Oral History Collection, Southern Historical Collection, Wilson Library, University of North Carolina, Chapel Hill; Sue Thrasher interview with Don West; "For These Sad Ashes," manuscript (bound volume of poetry), in Don West Papers.

32. Sue Thrasher interview with Don West; Alex Baskin interview with Don West; SAC, Baltimore to Director, FBI, Aug. 14, 1961, FBI Report, Feb. 20, 1963, SAC, Baltimore, Report, "Donald Lee West," Feb. 28, 1964, and SAC, Baltimore to Director, FBI, April 30, 1964, all in FBI Reports 100-20396-203, 205, 206, 207; West to Editor, *Autoharp*, March 23, 1964, box 14, Archie Green Papers, Southern Historical Collection, Wilson Library, University of North Carolina, Chapel Hill; Jennie Levine to Rich Behles, June 30, 2004, att. Rich Behles to Author, June 30, 2004.

33. West to Anne Braden, Jan. 4, 1963, box 72, Carl and Anne Braden Papers, WHS; West, *No Lonesome Road*, xxxviii. For an informed account of the SNCC's policy shift sending whites to work in white communities, see Lewis, *Walking with the Wind*, 381–83. West does not appear to have been actively involved in party work during the Baltimore years. Although the FBI consistently monitored his activities, reports from this period conclude that there was "no information indicating [West was] currently a member of the Communist Party." FBI Report, SAC, Baltimore, "Donald Lee West," Feb. 28, 1964, file 100-22392, Report 100-20396-206; Baltimore, "RE: Donald Lee West," May 5, 1964, Bufile 100-20396.

34. George Brosi, Afterword, in West, *No Lonesome Road*, 195–97; author interview with George Brosi, Feb. 9, 2004, Berea, Ky.

35. West to Williams, June 18, Sept. 30, 1964, box 15, Claude C. Williams Collection; "Community Organization," in Michael Gallantz to Friend, May 12, 1964; "Convention Registrants," box 4, Students for a Democratic Society (SDS) Papers, Archives and Manuscripts Division, Wisconsin Historical Society, Madison; Byerly, "'What Shall a Poet Sing?'" 358.

36. West to Williams, Nov. 20, 1964, box 15, Claude C. Williams Papers; "Conference Agenda," Nov. 13, 1964, and Southern Student Organizing Committee, *Newsletter*, Dec. 1964, both in box 5, Carl and Anne Braden Papers, Special Collections, Hoskins Library (SC, HL), University of Tennessee, Knoxville; Memorandum, "Southern Student Organizing Committee (SSOC)," box 53, National Sharecroppers Fund Collection; "A Resolution Concerning SDS's Role in the South and the Relationship between SDS and the Southern Student's Organizing Committee," ca. April 1964, box 4, SDS Papers.

37. Hedy West to Author, Aug. 19, 2004; "Hedy West Gives Benefit Concerts for Appalachian Miners," April 1964; "Eastern Kentucky Background Sheet," n.d.; Don West to Arthur Gorson, July 1, 1964, and Gorson to West, July 24, 1964, both in boxes 1, 2, Committee for Miners Papers, Archives and Manuscripts Division, WHS. Further evidence of Don West's fund-raising activity on behalf of the Committee for Miners as well as his dissatisfaction with the committee may be found in Hamish Sinclair to West, Sept. 1, 10, 1964, West to Sinclair, Oct. 2, 1964, and Gorson to West, Oct. 16, 1964, Feb. 11, 1965, all in box 2, Committee for Miners Papers.

38. Hedy West to Loyal Jones, March 17, 1964, box 121, Council of the Southern Moun-

tains Papers, Special Collections, Hutchens Library, Berea College Library, Berea, Ky.; Don West to Presh, Sept. 7, 1967 and Hedy West Diary, ca. 1969, Hedy West Papers; West to Gilden, Jan. 11, 1964, "Join the Unemployed Kentucky Miners," ca. Jan. 1964, and "Eastern Kentucky Background Sheet," ca. Jan. 1964, all in Bert and Katya Gilden Papers, box 7.

39. West to Williams, Aug. 5 and 14, 1964, box 15, Claude C. Williams Papers.

40. West to Williams, Aug. 5, 14, Nov. 20, 1964, all in box 15, Claude C. Williams Papers.

41. West to Williams, Sept. 30, June 18, Aug. 3, 1964, all in box 15, Claude C. Williams Papers; see also West to Gilden, Jan. 11, 1964, box 7, Bert and Katya Gilden Papers, and West to Hedy West, Sept. 7, 1967, Hedy West Papers.

42. Sue Thrasher interview with Don West; Alex Baskin interview with Don West; Sullivan, "Don West, Poet and Preacher," 47; West to Williams, Oct. 2, 1964, box 15, Claude C. Williams Papers; Byerly, "'What Shall a Poet Sing?'" 358.

43. West to Gilden, Jan. 11, 1964, box 7, Bert and Katya Gilden Papers; West to Williams, Oct. 2, 1964, box 15, Claude C. Williams Papers.

44. Sue Thrasher interview with Don West; Alex Baskin interview with Don West. West's observations on New York folk artists are from Don West to Hedy West, Sept. 7, 1967, Don West Papers, and Sullivan, "Don West, Poet and Preacher," 47. For quotations on *Appalachian South* see West to Gilden, Jan. 11, 1964, box 7, Bert and Katya Gilden Papers; Duke, *Writers and Miners*, 53; Buckman, "Don West, Peripatetic Educator," 25; Byerly, "'What Shall a Poet Sing?'" 358; and West, *No Lonesome Road*, xxxviii.

Chapter 13: Pipestem: Old Left, New Left, and a New Educational Activism, 1966–82

1. "A Proposal for an Educational Service in the Appalachian South to Develop Potential within Young People Who Drop Out of High School," ca. April 1966, "Dear Friend," ca. April 1966, and "West Touches People, Problems Through Poems, Books, Songs," March 26, 1966, all in boxes 64, 72, Carl and Anne Braden Papers, Archives and Manuscripts, Wisconsin Historical Society (WHS), Madison; Duke, *Writers and Miners*, 54–55, 64.

2. "Dear Friend," ca. April 1966; "A Proposal"; Alex Baskin interview with Don West, Feb. 5, 1975, Stony Brook, N.Y.; Knapik and Woodruff, "Mountaineers Fighting for Freedom," 13; West, *No Lonesome Road*, xxxviii. Sharply different from the missionary imperialism of Hindman or elitist selectivity of Berea, the Folklife Center shared more objectives with Highlander than Don would have acknowledged. Despite irreconcilable differences, Horton and West agreed on the importance of cultural awareness and direct engagement with the poor. Duke, *Writers and Miners*, 53–54.

3. Dombrowski to Carl and Anne Braden, May 2, 1966, and Dombrowski to West, May 2, 1966, both in box 2, James A. Dombrowski Papers, Archives and Manuscripts Division, Wisconsin Historical Society, Madison; Anne Braden to West, April 26, 1966, West to Carl Braden, April 18, 1966, James L. Hupp to Carl Braden, and "Dear Friend," ca. April 1966, all in boxes 64 and 72, Carl and Anne Braden Papers, WHS. By the time of West's approach to the SCEF, the organization was in the midst of the transition from the New Orleans to Louisville locations, which meant not only a drain on financial resources but also a set of priorities that stressed interracial work more than the cultural and educational thrust of West's project. For full discussion of the SCEF's status in 1966, see Fosl, *Subversive Southerner*, 305–6.

4. For full treatment of the origins and early development of the Congress for Appalachian Development, see Whisnant, *Modernizing the Mountaineer*, 220–37; see also William

C. Blizzard, "Dawn over Appalachia," *Charleston Sunday Gazette State Magazine*, Sept. 6, 1966, and "Congress for Appalachian Development," *Appalachian South* (Spring and Summer 1967), both in box 71, Congress for Appalachian Development (CAD) Papers, Eastern Tennessee State University, Johnson City (Archives of Appalachia). For further discussion of grass-roots organizing in Appalachia, see Stephen L. Fisher, "Grass Roots Speak Back," in *Back Talk from Appalachia*, ed. Billings et al., 206; see also Williams, *Appalachia*, 350–52; and Drake, *A History of Appalachia*, 209–10.

5. West to Harry M .Caudill, Aug. 30, 1966, Caudill to West, Jan. 12, 1966, both in box 7, Harry M. Caudill Papers, Special Collections, University of Kentucky Library, Lexington. Although West and Caudill agreed on goals, they were very different activists, Caudill a liberal lawyer, and West a radical educator-organizer. There is some evidence that West had reservations about Caudill due to his profession as well as his tendency toward elitism, yet the two were close collaborators in promoting CAD. Author interview with Hedy West, Aug. 8, 2004, Narberth, Pa.; author interview with George Brosi, Feb.9, 2004, Berea, Ky.; Whisnant, "The Folk Hero in Appalachian Struggle History," 44–45.

6. West to Anne Braden, April 28, 1970, West to Carol Stevens, July 4, 1965, and West to Carl Braden, July 3, 1965 and June 15, 1966, boxes 72, 65, 60, Carl and Anne Braden Papers, WHS; West to Williams, ca. Oct. 1966, box 15, Claude C. Williams Collection, Walter P. Reuther Library, Archives of Labor and Urban Affairs, Wayne State University, Detroit; Fosl, *Subversive Southerner*, 305.

7. West to Williams, Nov. 4, ca. Oct. 1966, box 15, Claude C. Williams Collection.

8. Blizzard, "Dawn over Appalachia"; West to Horton, Oct. 5, 1966, box 99, Highlander Research and Education Center Papers (Highlander Papers), Archives and Manuscripts Division, Wisconsin Historical Society, Madison; Bruce Crawford to Ann Williams, Oct. 1, 1966, Don West Papers; Whisnant, *Modernizing the Mountaineer*, 228–29.

9. Fraley to Caudill, Sept. 18, 1966, box 71, CAD Papers.

10. Horton to West, Sept. 26, Oct. 10, 1966, Horton to Milton Ogle (Appalachian Volunteers), Dec. 2, 1966, and West to Horton, Oct. 5, 1966, boxes 99, 100, Highlander Papers.

11. West to Carl Braden, Oct. 11, 1966, box 72, Carl and Anne Braden Papers, WHS.

12. "C. A. D," ca. Oct. 15, 1966, Minutes, Steering Committee Meeting, Congress of Appalachian Development, Charleston, W.V., and Blizzard, "Dawn over Appalachia," all in boxes 1, 71, CAD Papers; Whisnant, *Modernizing the Mountaineer*, 229; "Certificate of Incorporation of Congress for Appalachian Development, Inc.," Nov. 25, 1966, folder 1, Paul Kaufman Papers, Archives of Appalachia.

13. West to Caudill, Feb. 10, 11, 1967; Caudill to West, Feb. 7, 1967, all in box 7, Harry M. Caudill Papers; West to Horton, Feb. 7, 1967, box 102, Highlander Papers.

14. *Appalachian South* 2 (Spring–Summer 1967); West to Anne Caudill, Feb. 13, 1967, and "Congress for Appalachian Development," ca. Feb. 1967, both in box 7, Harry M. Caudill Papers.

15. West to Caudill, Feb. 14, 1967, Horton to West, Feb. 1, 1967, and Joyce Dukes to Caudill, Feb. 1, 1967, all in box 7, Harry M. Caudill Papers; see also box 102, Highander Papers, and folder 33, series 3, record group 1, Highlander Research and Education Center Archives, New Market, Tenn. (Highlander Archives). For Caudill's acceptance of the Horton-West recommendation that CAD concentrate on organizing the poor, see Caudill to Horton, Feb. 8, 1967, box 102, Highlander Papers, and West, "'One Gallus' and 'No-Gallus' Folk," *Appalachian South* 2 (Spring–Summer 1967).

16. West to Carl and Anne Braden, ca. Feb. 1967, West to Dave and Pat, Feb. 13, 1967, and West to Carl Braden, Oct. 17, ca. Oct. 1966, all in box 72, Carl and Anne Braden Papers, WHS.

17. Anne Braden to West, March 8, 1967, West to Braden, ca. Feb. 15, Feb. 23, 1967, and West to Caudill, Feb. 14, 1967, all in box 72, Carl and Anne Braden Papers, WHS.

18. Braden to Caudill, March 19, 1967, box 8, Harry M. Caudill Papers; West to Anne and Carl Braden, March 26, 1967, box 72, Carl and Anne Braden Papers, WHS.

19. Minutes, CAD Board of Directors, March 25, 1967, box 8, Harry M. Caudill Papers; "Background Information on the Congress for Appalachian Development," n.d., box 71, CAD Papers; Whisnant, *Modernizing the Mountaineer*, 233. Horton again criticized CAD for the absence of poor people on the board and concluded that there were "two divergent points of view," the elitist vision of Ebersole and Austin's more democratic view of a grass-roots organization that would shape policy from the bottom up. "Report on Myles' Appalachian Trip," March 24–26, 1967, box 102, Highlander Papers.

20. "A Proposal for an Appalachian People's Congress," Oct. 14, 1967, box 8, Harry M. Caudill Papers; Ebersole to Parley Ayer (CSM), Aug. 1967, and "Proposal," boxes 135, 277, Council for the Southern Mountains Papers; Caudill to Ebersole, July 7, 1967, Appalachian Volunteers Papers, box 44, Special Collections, Berea College Library, Berea, Ky.; "Brief Report on Meeting to Consider an Appalachian People's Congress," ca. May 1967, box 3, Committee for Miners Papers, Archives and Manuscripts Division, WHS; see also (from box 8, Harry S. Caudill Papers) Austin to "Advisory Committee for the Appalachian People's Congress" and Austin to Caudill et al., both June 21, 1967, and Tom Rhodenbaugh to Advisory Committee, Appalachian People's Congress, July 7, 1967; Whisnant, *Modernizing the Mountaineer*, 233–34.

21. Minutes, CAD Board of Directors, Oct. 14, 1967, and West to Anne Caudill, July 14, 1967, both in box 8, Harry M. Caudill Papers.

22. Whisnant to Leigh, Nov. 22, 1972, box 72, CAD Papers; Whisnant, *Modernizing the Mountaineer*, 234–35. By 1969 Caudill and Austin had concluded that CAD was "finished" and the struggle had illustrated the "phoniness of the old liberals" in the labor unions and public power districts, none of whom gave the organization assistance. Caudill to Ebersole, March 24, 1969, box 9, Harry M. Caudill Papers.

23. "The Universal Christian Church," *Appalachian South* 2 (Spring–Summer 1967); see also "The Universal Christian," draft, 1970, Don West Papers.

24. Author interview with David Stanley, Aug. 7, 2004, Beckley, W.V.; author interview with Yvonne Farley, March 13, 2004, St. Albans, W.V.; author interview with Mildred Shackleford, June 22, 2004, New Market, Tenn.; "Report on Myles' Appalachian Trip"; *Charleston Gazette*, June 17, 1967.

25. Author interviews with David Stanley and Mildred Shackleford; author interview with P. J. Laska, March 12, 2004, Beckley, W.V.; author interview with Yvonne Farley; author interview with Warren Doyle, Sept. 25, 2003, Chapel Hill, N.C.; Margie Hutchens to author, Oct. 29, 2004; author interview with Frank T. Adams, Nov. 4, 2004, Asheville, N.C.; Author interview with Hedy West, March 10, 2004, Narberth, Pa.; Hedy West interview with Lillie Mulkey West, Feb. 1976, Blairsville, Ga., Hedy West Papers; see also Brosi, Afterword, in West, *No Lonesome Road*, 201–3; and West, *No Lonesome Road*, xxxix.

26. "Pipestem Log," July 30–Aug. 3, 1970, folder 2002, Archie Green Papers, Southern Historical Collection (SHC), Wilson Library, University of North Carolina, Chapel Hill; *Charleston Sunday Gazette*, Sept. 1, 1968; *West Virginia Hillbilly*, Oct. 26, 1968, Sept. 3, 1969;

"Pipestem Folk Festival Draws Fiddling, Singing Crowd," Charleston *Sunday Gazette-Mail*, Aug. 3, 1969; "The West Virginia Folk Festival," Aug. 1–3, 1969, box 1, series 3, record group 1, Highlander Archives; author interviews with David Stanley, Mildred Shackleford, Yvonne Farley, and Warren Doyle.

27. Sue Thrasher interview with Don West, July 10, 1974, Highlander Research and Education Center Archives, New Market, Tenn.; author interviews with David Stanley and Yvonne Farley; "Appalachian Cultural Heritage Summer Camp," 1970, box 8, James A. Dombrowski Papers; West, *No Lonesome Road*, xxxviii; Duke, *Writers and Miners*, 64; West to Doyle, ca. 1983, Don West correspondence file 1, Warren Doyle Papers, Hays, N.C. (private collection). The Heifer Project is described in *Heifer Project International* (Little Rock: Heifer Project International, n.d.) in Hedy West Papers. See also Byerly, "'What Shall a Poet Sing?'" 365–66.

28. Author interview with David Stanley and P. J. Laska; author interview with Donald Rasmussen, Oct. 15, 2004, Beckley, W.V. For evidence of the program's organizing component, see "Poor People's Workshop on Mountain Labor History and Poor People's Organizing," May 12–18, 1969, box 31, Mike Ross Papers, Southern Labor Archives, Special Collections, Georgia State University, Atlanta.

29. Sullivan, "Don West, Poet and Preacher," 51; Knapik and Woodruff, "Mountaineers Fighting for Freedom," 6; *Charleston Gazette*, Aug. 28, Oct. 2, 1968; *Princeton Times*, Aug. 8, Sept. 26, 1968; see also Constituents to Robert Byrd, Aug. 13, Oct. 4, Oct. 14, 1968, ca. Oct. 1968, Jan. 10, 11, 23, Aug. 13, 1969, all in FBI file 100-20396-(234–237); SISS files, record group 233, National Archives (NA).

30. Francis J. McNamara to Byrd, Oct. 11, 1968, SISS files, record group 233, NA; "Randolph Explains Purpose of Visit to Don West Farm," unidentified news clipping, ca. Oct. 1968, FBI file 100-20396-235. For Randolph's endorsement of West's programs, see Rasmussen, "Don West Does His Thing at Pipestem."

31. Dave Walls to Horton, Nov. 5, 1968, box 100, Highlander Papers; Charleston TACT Committee, "The Growing Communist Conspiracy," ca. Nov. 1968, and Jeanne Rasmussen to Horton, Nov. 5, 1968, box 1, series 3, record group 1, Highlander Archives; *West Virginia Hillbilly*, Nov. 16, 1968, and "Our Opinion," *Princeton Daily News* ca. summer 1968 (see also July 18, Aug. 1, 1968), all in Concord College Archives, Athens, W.V.; Byerly, "'What Shall a Poet Sing?'" 363–64.

32. Sullivan, "Don West: Poet and Preacher," 51; *Charleston Gazette*, Oct. 14, 1968, and Nov. 2, 1969; West to *Charleston Gazette*, Oct. 7, 1968, Don West Scrapbook, Ann West Williams Collection, Charleston, W.V.; West to Williams, Feb. 3, 1970, box 15, Claude C. Williams Collection; West to Laska, March 9, 1978, P. J. Laska Papers, Beckley, W.V.

33. Author interview with Billy Best, Feb. 8, 2004, Berea, Ky. (telephone); Sue Thrasher interview with Don West; and West to Williams, Feb. 3, 1970, Jan. 8, 1971, March 13, 1972, Feb. 9, 1974, all in box 15, Claude C. Williams Collection.

34. "The Free Forum," Nov. 4, 1968, Students for a Democratic Society (SDS) Papers, box 43, Archives and Manuscripts Division, Wisconsin Historical Society, Madison; draft memo, ca. Oct. 1968, box 64, Appalachian Volunteers Papers; West to Bob, Oct. 29, 1968, box 1, series 3, record group 1, Highlander Archives; Endorsement Letter and "'Fair Play for the Pipestem Center," ca. summer 1968, Concord College Archives; *Charleston Gazette*, April 19, Oct. 7, 13, 1968; *Princeton Times*, Oct. 3, 1968; Byerly, "'What Shall a Poet Sing?'" 364.

35. Duke, *Writers and Miners*, 56–57; Hodgson, "Mountain Voices, Mountain Days," 118–46; "Folk Center Teaches Cultural Pride"; Peeks, "Don West Seen in Different Light

These Days." For personal testimony to the powerful impact of Don West on students and co-workers, see author interviews with Mildred Shackleford, David Stanley, P. J. Laska, and Warren Doyle; see also Brosi, Afterword, in West, *No Lonesome Road*, 195–203; Margie Hutchens to Author, Oct. 29, 2004; Roger Hicks, "Why I Make French Toast," in Laska to Author, May 6, 2004; Laska, "Commemoration for Don West," P. J. Laska Papers; and Merry Tucker to Anne Braden, May 19, 1967, box 72, Carl and Anne Braden Papers, WHS. The board's character is described in John Crawford to Author, April 22, 2004.

36. Author interview with Donald Rasmussen; author interview with Michael Ross Jr. (telephone), Nov. 1, 2004; Alex Baskin interview with Don West. For West's interest in Miners for Democracy see *Miner's Voice*, Nov. 2, 1970 (excerpt), in box 2, Jean Rasmussen Papers, Archives of Appalachia. The development of Miners for Democracy and Arnold Miller's successful campaign to overthrow the Boyle machine are discussed in Green, *The World of the Worker*, 244–45; see also Drake, *A History of Appalachia*, 206. Don Rasmussen's pivotal role in the battle against black lung disease is discussed in Dotson-Lewis, "On the Wings of a Dove," in *Appalachia: Spirit Triumphant*, esp. 187–92.

37. Helen Lewis, comments, Appalachian Weekend, Craddock Center, Blue Ridge, Ga.; Hutchens to Author, Oct. 29, 2004; author interviews with Mildred Shackleford and Yvonne Farley.

38. Author interviews with P. J. Laska, Yvonne Farley, and Mildred Shackleford; Alex Baskin interview with Don West; Alice J. Gauldin, "Sixteen Year Old Is Finding Herself at Antioch," *Beckley Post-Herald*, ca. 1973, vertical files, Folk Schools file, Eury Appalachian Collection, Appalachian State University, Boone, N.C.; West to Laska, March 9, 1978, P. J. Laska Papers; West to Mike Ross, April 17, 1973, box 32, Mike Ross Papers; West to Williams, Dec. 4, 1971, box 15, Claude C. Williams Collection; "The Case for Antioch College/Appalachia," n.d., and "Southern Appalachian Circuit, Antioch College," 1975–76, both in Jeff Biggers Papers (Biggers Collection), Don West Collection; West, *No Lonesome Road*, xxxix.

39. Laska to Biggers, May 21, 2002, Biggers Collection; author interview with P. J. Laska; Laska to West, March 17, 1978, P. J. Laska Papers.

40. "Report to Our Friends," May 1972, box 31, Mike Ross Papers; West to Howard Klein, May 5, 1973, box 1399, ASFC folder, 1972–1975, series 200R, record group 1.3, Rockefeller Foundation Archives, Poncantico Hills, N.Y.; West quoted in West to Williams, Dec. 4, 1971, box 15, Claude C. Williams Collection.

41. West to Williams, Jan. 8, 1971, box 15, Claude C. Williams Collection; author interviews with P. J. Laska and Yvonne Farley; West, *No Lonesome Road*, xxxix, 66.

42. Author interviews with Warren Doyle and David Stanley; Sue Thrasher interview with Don West; Alex Baskin interview with Don West; John Crawford to Author, Oct. 23, 2004; Anne Braden to West, March 8, May 12, 1967, Anne Braden to Carl Braden, May 13, 1967, and Memo to New York Office, SCEF, Nov. 21, 1966, all in boxes 72 and 74, Carl and Anne Braden Papers, WHS; West to Howard Klein, Dec. 12, 1970, box R1399, ASFC folder, 1970–1971, series 200R, record group 1.3, Rockefeller Foundation Archives.

43. Knapik and Woodruff, "Mountaineers Fighting for Freedom," 13; Alex Baskin interview with Don West.

44. "Grant in Aid to Universal Christian Church," June 14, 1972, June 1, 1973, box R1399, ASFC folder, 1972–1975, series 200R, record group 1.3, Rockefeller Foundation Archives.

45. Author interview with Warren Doyle; Doyle to Author, Sept. 22, 2003; Doyle and

West, "Memorandum," Jan. 31, 1983, Don West Papers; Sullivan, "Don West: Poet and Preacher," 48, 51, 54; West to Klein, May 5, 1973, box R1399, ASFC folder, 1972–1975, series 200R, record group 1.3, Rockefeller Foundation Archives; Blais, "West Recites Tender, Compassionate, Moving Poetry"; Doyle to "Dear Friend," March 3, 1983, West to Doyle, ca. 1980, Sept. 29, 1980, and Carol Tuttle to Doyle, March 3, 1983, all in Don West lecture tour files 1 and 2, Warren Doyle Papers; see also Don West correspondence file 2, and American Friends Service Committee file, Warren Doyle Papers.

46. West to Leo Kirschner, March 20, 1975, and West to Klein, Nov. 27, 1974, both in box R1399, ASFC folder, 1972–1975, series 200R, record group 1.3, Rockefeller Foundation Archives; "Report to Our Friends," Feb. 1974, box 1, George Weissman Collection, Walter P. Reuther Library, Archives of Labor and Urban Affairs (ALUA), Wayne State University, Detroit; see also Appalachian Folklife Center Reports File, Warren Doyle Papers; *Bluefield Daily Telegraph*, Jan. 23, Feb. 28, 1974; and *Beckley Post-Herald*, Jan. 23, 1974.

47. West to Williams, Sept. 16, 1976, Claude C. Williams Collection; West to Weissman, Nov. 25, 1978, May 23, 1981, box 1, George Weissman Collection, ALUA; West to George Meyers, Jan. 7, 1977, box 1, folder 1, series 1, George Meyers Papers, Special Collections, Frostburg State University Library, Frostburg, Md.; Klein to West, Jan. 2, 1975, box R1399, ASFC folder, 1972–1975, series 200R, record group 1.3, Rockefeller Foundation Archives; "Dear Friend," ca. summer 1977, Don West Scrapbook.

48. West to Meyers, Jan. 7, 1977; West to Williams, Sept. 16, 1976, box 15, Claude C. Williams Papers; *Charleston Gazette*, July 14, 1978, Meyers Biography file, Reference Center for Marxist Studies, New York; author interview with Yvonne Farley; Crawford to Author, Oct. 23, 2004. For discussion of George Meyers's background as a Communist Party activist in Maryland see Pedersen, *The Communist Party in Maryland*, 94, 171–80.

49. West to Laska, Nov. 22, 1981, P. J. Laska Papers. Myers's perspective and Crawford's views are discussed in Crawford to Author, Oct. 23, 25, 2004; see also author interviews with Yvonne Farley and David Stanley.

50. Doyle to West, ca. Jan. 1983, Don West correspondence file 2, Warren Doyle Papers; see also Doyle to West, Feb. 2, 1983 and Don and Connie West to Friend, Feb. 1983, both in Appalachian South Folklife Center Annual Report, 1983–1984, vertical files, Folk Schools file, Eury Appalachian Collection; West to Ann West Williams, Feb. 1982, Don West Scrapbook; author interview with Warren Doyle.

51. Author interviews with Warren Doyle, David Stanley, Yvonne Farley, and Hedy West; author interview with Ann West Williams, Aug. 8, 2004, Charleston, W.V.; see also Mere to Don, Oct. 25, 1973, Don West Papers.

Chapter 14: Literary Maturity: An Artist in Full

1. West, "Some Final Reflections," unpublished comment, July 1965, "West's Unpublished Writings" file, Jeff Biggers Papers (Biggers Collection), Don West Collection.

2. Duke, *Writers and Miners*, 49.

3. Ross to Bro, March 20, 1966, box 31, Mike Ross Papers, Southern Labor Archives, Special Collections, Georgia State University, Atlanta.

4. Rubin, "Voice of the Cracker," 213–16; West quote from West, "Romantic Appalachia; or, Poverty Pays If You Ain't Poor"; see also *West Virginia Hillbilly*, March 29, 1969; West,

No Lonesome Road, xli; Whisnant, "The Folk Hero in Appalachian Struggle History," 45–46; and Duke, *Writers and Miners*, 54.

5. West, *People's Cultural Heritage in Appalachia*, in folder 20002, Archie Green Papers, Southern Historical Collection, Wilson Library, University of North Carolina, Chapel Hill; West, *Southern Mountain Folk Tradition and the Folksong "Stars" Syndrome*, in box 31, Mike Ross Papers; Don West, "Jesus, the Quiet Son of Man," reprint from *Orion Magazine*, 1967, spc. pam. 1688, George Meyers Papers, Special Collections, Frostburg State University Library, Frostburg, Md.

6. Whisnant, "The Folk Hero in Appalachian Struggle History," 46; "Appalachian Movement Press," n.d., folder 2002, Archie Green Papers, Southern Historical Collection, Wilson Library, University of North Carolina, Chapel Hill.

7. West, "Poverty War Pennies and Baby Sitters," ca. 1970, and West to Williams, ca. 1970, both in box 15, Claude C. Williams Collection, Walter P. Reuther Library, Archives of Labor and Urban Affairs, Wayne State University, Detroit; West, *Romantic Appalachia; or, Poverty Pays If You Ain't Poor;* Alex Baskin interview with Don West, Feb. 5, 1975, Stony Brook, N.Y.

8. Laska, "Don West: People's Poet"; Laska, "Don West, Revolutionary People's Poet"; see also Biggers, "The Fugitive of Southern Appalachian Literature."

9. Rubin, "Voice of the Cracker," 217; West, *No Lonesome Road*, xxxix; West, *O Mountaineers!* 272; Knapik and Woodruff, "Mountaineers Fighting for Freedom," 12–13.

10. Willard Uphaus, "*O Mountaineers*," *Come Unity* (March 1977), 17, in Don West miscellaneous writings file, Warren Doyle Papers, Hays, N.C. (private collection).

11. Bob Henry Baber interview with Bob Snyder, ca. early 1980s, courtesy of Peg Snyder, and Peg Snyder to Biggers, May 13, 2002, both in Bob Snyder file, Biggers Collection; Laska to Biggers, May 21, 2002, author's files; Snyder, "The Soupbean Poets," 6.

12. Sullivan, "Don West: Poet and Preacher," 56.

13. Author interview with Warren Doyle, Sept. 25, 2003, Chapel Hill, N.C.; Roy Smith, "Introduction," in West, *A Time for Anger.*

14. Henson, "'Naked Words That Have No Subtle Meaning,'" 57, 59.

15. Rubin, "Voice of the Cracker," 213–14; Wald, *Exiles from a Future Time*, 32.

16. West, "For These Sad Ashes" and "Automated Miner," *O Mountaineers!* (1974), both in *No Lonesome Road*, 159, 168.

17. West, "Obituary for Despair," "Appalachian Blues," and "There'll Be a Tomorrow," all in *No Lonesome Road*, 157, 175, 176; Rubin, "Voice of the Cracker," 213.

18. West, introduction to *O Mountaineers;* see also Aubrey Williams, introduction to 1964 edition (draft in box 64, Carl and Anne Braden Papers, Wisconsin Historical Society [WHS], Madison).

19. Sullivan, "Don West: Poet and Preacher," 56; West, "No Copyright" and "Introduction," *In a Land of Plenty*, frontispiece and 15; Wald, *Exiles from a Future Time*, 30–31; West, *No Lonesome Road*, xlii.

20. Order blank from *In a Land of Plenty; Worker Writer* 2 (Spring 1980): 3, John Crawford Papers, Albuquerque, N.M. (private collection); Crawford quoted in West, *No Lonesome Road*, xlii, and Crawford to Author, Oct. 23, 2004.

21. West, "I Cannot Sing," in *In a Land of Plenty*, 209; Wald, *Exiles from a Future Time*, 31; West, *No Lonesome Road*, xliii.

22. West, "I Dare Not Say I Love the Lord," "Free Enterprise Poverty," and "Question Mark," all in *In a Land of Plenty*, 210–13.

23. West, "Away Down South," *In a Land of Plenty*, 217.

24. West, "There'll Be a Tomorrow," *In a Land of Plenty*, 220.

25. Marius, "Don West's Sermon on the Mount"; *People's Daily World*, Oct. 28, 1982; Roediger, cover comment for West, *In a Land of Plenty*. For a discussion of the impact of West's didacticism and romanticism on the popular reception and critical reaction to his work see Wald, *Exiles from a Future Time*, 30–31, 33; and Duke, *Writers and Miners*, 66.

26. Laska, "Don West, Revolutionary People's Poet"; Laska, "Don West, People's Poet."

27. Mike Henson, "Prose and Poetry from an Appalachian Chronicler," *Guardian Book Review Supplement* (Summer 1983), in Don West correspondence file 2, Warren Doyle Papers.

28. *St. Petersburg Independent*, March 12, 1982; West to Meyers, March 10, 1986, box 1, folder 2, series 1, George Meyers Papers; West to Ann West Williams, Feb. 1982, Don West Scrapbook, Ann West Williams Collection, Charleston, W.V.; West to Laska, Nov. 22, 1981, P. J. Laska Papers, Beckley, W.V.; author interview with Ann West Williams, Aug. 8, 2004, Charleston, W.V.

Chapter 15: Letting Go: Journey's End, 1983–92

1. "Appalachian Writers Association Award," and Leon Ginsburg to West, Dec. 2, 1981, both in Don West Scrapbook, Ann West Williams Collection, Charleston, W.V.; Cleve Benedict, "Don West, Preserver of Appalachian Culture," *Congressional Record*, June 24, 1982, Benedict to Doyle, March 9 and 17, 1982, and Loyal Jones to West, all in Warren Doyle Papers, Don West file 2 and correspondence file 1, Hays, N.C. (private collection); *Charleston Gazette*, Aug. 6, 1977, May 25, 1978.

2. Author interview with David Stanley, Aug. 7, 2004, Beckley, W.V.; Brosi, "Afterword" in West, *No Lonesome Road*; author interview with Warren Doyle, Sept. 25, 2003, Chapel Hill, N.C.; Laska, "Commemoration for Don West," n.d., P. J. Laska Papers, Beckley, W.V.

3. Stuart to Still, Oct. 11, 1975 and Jan. 10, 1976, Don West file, box 15.4, James Still Papers, Special Collections, Morehead State University, Morehead, Ky.; West to Laska, May 3, 1978, P. J. Laska Papers; author interview with Frank T. Adams, Nov. 3, 2004, Asheville, N.C.; author interview with Warren Doyle; George Brosi Notes, Jeff Biggers Papers, Don West Collection; author interview with Hedy West, March 10, 2004, Narberth, Pa.; West to Byerly, May 28, 1990, Don West Papers.

4. The following are all in Mountain Freedom School file, correspondence file 1, and Don West lecture tour file, Warren Doyle Papers: Don and Connie West to Friend, Feb. 1983, Appalachian South Folklife Center Annual Report to Friends, 1983–84, West to Mike Shannon-Thornberry, CORA, Feb. 11, 1982, "The Mountain Freedom School," Mary to West, April 18, 1982, Phyllis M. White to Doyle, Jan. 28, Feb. 5, 1983, Doyle to White, March 24, 1983, and Doyle to Friend, March 3, 1983. See also Duke, *Writers and Miners*, 66.

5. West to Doyle, Jan. 1, May 2, 1983, correspondence files 1 and 2, Doyle Papers.

6. Author interview with Ann West Williams, Aug. 8, 2004, Charleston, W.V.; Mere to Ann, Nov. 7, 1983, West to Ballard, Jan. 1, 1982, and West to Meyers, Nov. 14, 1986, all in Don West Scrapbook, Ann West Williams Collection; West to David Stanley, Sept. 21, 1986, Don West Papers.

7. West, "Visit Shatters Myths about Soviet Union"; West to Doyle, Jan. 1, 1983, correspondence file 2, Doyle Papers; author interview with Yvonne Farley, March 13, 2004, St. Albans, W.V.; Byerly, "'What Shall a Poet Sing?'" 366; West, *No Lonesome Road*, xliv.

8. Author interview with anonymous source, March 13, 2004; West, "Visit Shatters Myths about Soviet Union."

9. West, "Visit Shatters Myths about Soviet Union"; Cratis Williams to West, March 9, 1984, box 12, Cratis Williams Papers, W. L. Eury Appalachian Collection, Carol Grotnes Belk Library, Boone, N.C.; author interview with Yvonne Farley; Byerly, "'What Shall a Poet Sing?'" 366.

10. West, "Visit Shatters Myths about Soviet Union."

11. Hedy West to Author, Aug. 19, 2004; *St. Petersburg Independent*, March 12, 1983; author interview with Ann West Williams; Byerly, "'What Shall a Poet Sing?'" 367.

12. Hedy West to Author, Aug. 19, Dec. 9, 2004; author interviews with Yvonne Farley, Hedy West, and Ann West Williams; West to Ann West Williams, May 17, 1986, Correspondence Book, Ann West Williams Collection. The artwork of Mabel Constance West is held in scattered locations, most of it in the possession of family members or the Appalachian South Folk Life Center. Some paintings and sketches are now in the hands of Hedy's daughter, Talitha West, in Spring Lake Heights, N.J., and Ann West Williams of Charleston, W.V. A few may be viewed at the Folklife Center in Pipestem, W.V. Unfortunately, a portion of her work was destroyed in the 1974 fire at Pipestem. In 2006 and 2007, a Connie West retrospective exhibit was held in Charleston, W.V.

13. Author interviews with Warren Doyle, Yvonne Farley, and Hedy West; author interview with Mildred Shackleford, June 22, 2004, New Market, Tenn.; Hedy West to Author, Dec. 9, 2004; Mere to Ann, Sept. 21, 1983, Correspondence Book, Ann West Williams Collection; Ann West Williams to Hedy West, Aug. 28, 1989, Hedy West Papers, Athens, Ga.

14. Carrie Nobel to Hudson, Oct. 28, 1984, Hudson to Hardy Scott, Oct. 15, Nov. 17, 1982, Jan. 2, 1986, all in box 1, Hosea Hudson Papers, Reference Center for Marxist Studies, New York; author interviews with Warren Doyle and David Stanley.

15. Author interviews with Warren Doyle, David Stanley, and Yvonne Farley; author interview with Donald Rasmussen, Oct. 15, 2004, Beckley, W.V.

16. West to Lowell Kirby, Feb. 7, 1985, and West to Stanley, Sept. 21, 1986, both in Don West Papers; Farley to Author, March 31, 2004; author interviews wth Warren Doyle, David Stanley, and Yvonne Farley; *Charleston Sunday Gazette*, March 24, 1985; Doyle to Author, Oct. 27, 2004; Nobel to Hudson, Oct. 28, 1984, box 1, Hosea Hudson Papers.

17. Author interviews with Donald Rasmussen, David Stanley, and Yvonne Farley.

18. Author interviews with David Stanley and Warren Doyle; Ann West Williams to West, May 15, 1987 and West to Stanley, Sept. 21, 1986, Don West Papers; West to Meyers, Feb. 27, 1987, box 1, folder 2, series 1, George Meyers Papers, Special Collections, Frostburg State University Library, Frostburg, Md.; see also author interview with P. J. Laska and Doyle to Author, Oct. 27, 2004, Jan. 20, 2005.

19. West to Doyle, ca. 1983, correspondence file 2, Warren Doyle Papers.

20. West to Meyers, Nov. 14, 1986, Correspondence Book Ann West Williams Collection; see also Don West Papers; author interview with Ann West Williams; Byerly, "'What Shall a Poet Sing?'" 368; Farley to Author, March 31, 2004; and Crawford to Author, Oct. 25, 2004.

21. West to Meyers, Nov. 14, 1986, Feb. 27, 1987, ca. 1989, Feb. 26, Dec. 26, 1991, all

in Correspondence Book, Ann West Williams Collection, and box 1, folders 2 and 3, series 1, George Meyers Papers; see also George Brosi Notes.

22. Author interview with Hedy West; West to Meyers, Jan. 1, 1992, n.d. 1991, series 1, box 1, folder 3, George Meyers Papers.

23. Quoted in Byerly, "'What Shall a Poet Sing?'" 370; West to Meyers, n.d. 1991, series 1, box 1, folder 3, George Meyers Papers.

24. Author interview with Hedy West. For comment on West's commitment to Marxism and obscure relationship to the Communist Party, see author interviews with Yvonne Farley and David Stanley. See also Crawford to Author, Oct. 23, 24, 2004.

25. West to Meyers, Jan. 1, 1992, series 1, box 1, folder 3, George Meyers Papers; Crawford to Author, Oct. 23, 2004. The indigenous roots of American communism in the 1930s and early 1940s are explored in Ottanelli, *The Communist Party of the United States*, 212–15. The Party's near collapse in the postwar era is discussed in Starobin, *American Communism in Crisis*, esp. 155–94.

26. Author interview with Ann West Williams; see also author interviews with P. J. Laska and Warren Doyle, and author interview with Billy Best, Feb. 8, 2004, Berea, Ky. (telephone); Brosi, "Afterword," in West, *No Lonesome Road*, 197. If, as Aileen Kraditor maintains, there were three varieties of American communists (those driven by hatred of the system, those motivated by love for the common people, and those who were blissfully naïve), Don West seems to have been an amalgam of the first two. Kraditor, "Jimmie Higgins," 41–43.

27. West to Meyers, Sept. 17, 1991, ca. Aug. 1991, and Dec. 9, 1989, box 2, folders 2, 3, 4, series 1, George Meyers Papers; D. T. to "Presh," April 28, 1990, Hedy West Papers.

28. Author interviews with Frank T. Adams and Ann West Williams; author interview with John David, Feb. 6. 2005, Kincaid, W.V. (telephone); Ann West Williams to Meyers, Oct. 1992, box 1, folder 3, series 1, George Meyers Papers.

29. *People's Daily World*, Oct. 17, 1992; *Atlanta Journal-Constitution*, Oct. 2, 1992; *Charleston Gazette*, Oct. 1, 1992; *The New York Times*, Oct. 2, 1992.

30. *Charleston Gazette*, April 29, 1993; author interview with John David.

31. Baber, "Remembering Don West"; *Charleston Gazette*, April 29, 1993.

32. Author interview with Mildred Shackleford.

33. Hutchens to Author, Oct. 29, 2004.

34. Author interview with Warren Doyle; Baber, "Remembering Don West"; Laska to Biggers, May 21, 2002, and Laska, "Commemoration for Don West," P. J. Laska Papers; author interview with P. J. Laska.

35. Author interviews with David Stanley and Warren Doyle; see also author interview with John David.

36. Author interview with Helen Lewis, Aug. 5, 2003, Morganton, Ga.; author interview with Yvonne Farley.

37. Merry Tucker to Anne Braden, May 19, 1967, box 72, Carl and Anne Braden Papers, Archives and Manuscripts, Wisconsin Historical Society, Madison.

38. Tucker to Hedy West, Nov. 20, 1967, Hedy West Papers; Author interview with Merry Tucker, Feb. 23, 2005, New York (telephone).

Bibliography

Manuscripts and Archives

Alabama
Alabama Archives: Clifford and Virginia F. Durr Papers
Tuskegee University: Southern Conference for Human Welfare Papers

California
Stanford: Hoover Institution on War, Revolution, and Peace Archives; Paul Crouch Papers

Connecticut
Yale University, Bienecke Rare Book and Manuscript Library, New Haven: Langston Hughes Papers
————, Sterling Memorial Library Department of Special Collections, New Haven: C. Vann Woodward Papers

District of Columbia
Library of Congress Manuscripts Division: Herbert Benjamin Papers; Civil Rights Congress Papers; W. E. B. Du Bois Papers (microfilm edition); National Association for the Advancement of Colored People Papers; Russian State Archive of Social and Political History, Communist Party of the USA Records (microfilm)

Florida
University of Florida Department of Special Collections, George A. Smathers Library: Lillian Smith Papers

Georgia
Atlanta History Center: Don West File
Atlanta University Center, Robert Woodruff Library Special Collections: Commission on Interracial Cooperation Papers; Southern Conference for Human Welfare Papers
Berry College: Berry College Archives

Emory University: Mary Barker Papers; James C. Davis Papers; Theodore Draper Papers; Harvey Klehr Papers; Ralph McGill Papers; Mary Raoul Millis Papers; Glenn Rainey Papers; Louise Patterson Papers; Celestine Sibley Papers; Josephine Wilkins Papers
Georgia State University, Southern Labor Archives, Pullen Library: AFL-CIO Region 8 Papers; Stetson Kennedy Papers; John Ramsey Papers; Mike Ross Papers; Southern Conference Educational Fund Papers; TWUA Northwest Georgia Joint Board Papers; United Textile Workers of America Papers
Oglethorpe University: Oglethorpe University Archives
University of Georgia Library, Hargrett Rare Books and Manuscripts Library: Byron Herbert Reece Papers; Lillian Smith Papers; Don West Papers; Hedy West Papers
University of Georgia Library, Richard B. Russell Memorial Library: Herman Talmadge Papers; Henderson Lanham Papers
Young Harris College Duckworth Library: Byron Herbert Reece Papers

Illinois
Southern Illinois University: John Howard Lawson Papers

Iowa
University of Iowa Library Special Collections: C. B. Baldwin Papers; Lement Harris Papers; Stetson Kennedy Papers; Hugh C. MacDougal Papers; Progressive Party Papers; Henry A. Wallace Papers

Kentucky
Berea College Library Special Collections: Appalachian Volunteers Papers; Council of the Southern Mountains Papers; Hindman Settlement School Papers (microfilm)
Morehead State University Library Special Collections: James Still Papers
Murray State University Pogue Library Special Collections: Jesse Stuart Papers
University of Kentucky Library Special Collections: Harry Caudill Papers; A. B. Chandler Papers; James Still Papers
University of Louisville Library Special Collections: Jesse Stuart Papers

Louisiana
Tulane University, Amisted Research Center: Race Relations Department Archive

Maryland
Frostburg State University: George Meyers Papers

Massachusetts
Smith College Sophia Smith Collection: Ann Burlak Timpson Papers

Michigan
Wayne State University, Walter P. Reuther Library, Archives of Labor and Urban Affairs: David Burgess Papers; Richard Jensen Papers (Miners for Democracy); Raymond and Charlotte Moscowitz-Lucien Koch (Commonwealth College) Papers; National Sharecroppers Fund Papers; George Lavan Weissman Papers; Claude C. Williams Papers
University of Michigan, Harlan Hatcher Research Library, Labadie Collection: Aaron Kramer Papers; Michael Gold Papers; Miners for Democracy File

New Jersey

Princeton University, Seeley Mudd Library: American Civil Liberties Union Papers (microfilm)

New York

Franklin D. Roosevelt Presidential Library: Lorena Hickok Papers; Harry Hopkins Papers; Franklin D. Roosevelt Papers; Aubrey Williams Papers; Henry A. Wallace Papers

George T. Arents Library, Syracuse University, Special Collections: James L. Adams Papers

New York Public Library, Schomburg Center for Research in Black Culture: Benjamin J. Davis Papers; Hosea Hudson Papers; International Labor Defense Papers (microfilm); Stetson Kennedy Papers

Reference Center for Marxist Studies, New York: Benjamin J. Davis Jr. Papers; Hosea Hudson Papers; George Meyers Biography File; Pamphlet File (all in Taimement Institute Library Collections)

Rockefeller Archive Center: Rockefeller Foundation Archives

Tamiment Institute Library, New York University Elmer Bobst Library: James Allen Papers; Cedric Belfrage Papers; Daniel Bell Papers; Arnold Johnson Papers; Clarina Michelson Papers; Oral History of the American Left Collection; Mark Solomon–Robert Kaufman Papers

North Carolina

Appalachian State University, Carol Grotnes Belk Library, W. L. Eury Appalachian Collection: Helen Lewis Papers; Cratis Williams Papers; Vertical Files

Duke University, Perkins Library Special Collections: Operation Dixie: The CIO Organizing Committee Papers, 1946–53 (microfilm); J. B. Matthews Papers; Socialist Party of America Papers (microfilm)

Private collections: Warren Doyle Papers, Hays, N.C.

University of North Carolina, Wilson Library, Southern Historical Collection: John L. Anderson Papers; Frank Porter Graham Papers; Archie Green Papers; Paul Green Papers; Hosea Hudson Draft Transcripts (Nell Painter); Clyde Johnson Papers; Howard Anderson Kester Papers; J. Spencer Love Papers; Myra Page Papers; Junius Irving Scales Papers; Southern Tenant Farmers Union Papers; Olive Stone Papers

Pennsylvania

Swarthmore College Peace Collection: Nevin Sayre Papers; Fellowship of Reconciliation Papers

University of Pennsylvania Annenberg Rare Books and Manuscripts Library: Theodore Dreiser Papers; Howard Fast Papers

Rhode Island

Brown University, John Hay Library Special Collections: Bert and Katya Gilden Papers

Tennessee

Disciples of Christ Historical Society: Alva Wilmot Taylor Papers

Eastern Tennessee State University, Archives of Appalachia: Congress for Appalachian Development/Gordon Ebersole Papers; Paul Kaufman Papers; Jean Rasmussen Papers

Fisk University, John Hope and Aurelia Elizabeth Franklin Library Special Collections: Julius Rosenwald Fund Papers
Highlander Research and Education Center, New Market: Highlander Research and Education Center Archives
Lincoln Memorial University: Lincoln Memorial University Archives
Tennessee State Library and Archives: Highlander Folk School Collection
University of Tennessee, Hoskins Library Special Collections: Carl and Anne Braden Papers; May Justus Papers
Vanderbilt University Heard Library Special Collections: Donald Davidson Papers; John Egerton Papers; Vanderbilt University Archives

West Virginia
Concord College Archives; P. J. Laska Papers, Beckley, W.V.; Don West Scrapbook (Ann West Williams Collection), Charleston, W.V.; Ann West Williams Papers, Charleston, W.V.

Wisconsin
Author's Possession: Jeff Biggers Papers (Don West Collection)
Wisconsin Historical Society: Frank T. Adams Papers; Anita McCormick Blaine Papers; Carl and Anne Braden Papers; Robb Burlage Papers; Paul Booth Papers; Committee for Miners Papers; James Dombrowski Papers; Highlander Research and Education Center Papers; Myles Horton Papers; Textile Workers Union of America Papers; Students for a Democratic Society Papers; George L. Weissman Papers

Interviews

Georgia
Author: Jane Ross Davis, Atlanta; Wynelle Dollar, Winder; Ruth Tribble Forestor, Pulaski; Philip and Mildred Greear, Helen; Helen Lewis, Morganton; Lula Students Group Interview (Guenivere Chapman, Genevieve Duncan, Bobbie Moore, Clyde Moore), Lula; Mark Pace, Dalton; Marcelle White, Dalton
Emory University Special Collections: Junius Scales; Glenn Rainey; Mike Ross
Georgia State University, Southern Labor Archives, Pullen Library: Joseph Jacobs; Mike Ross; Stetson Kennedy; Nannie Leah Washburne
University of Georgia Library, Hargrett Rare Books and Manuscripts Library: Don West (by Alex Baskin); Don West (by Hedy West)

Kentucky
Allen McElfresh (by Mildred Shackleford)
Author: George Brosi, Berea; Billy Best (telephone), Berea; David Palmore (telephone), Erlanger

New York
Author: Merry Tucker (telephone)
Tamiment Library, Elmer Bobst Library, New York University, Oral History of the American Left Collection: Clarina Michelson; Willard Uphaus

North Carolina
Author: Warren Doyle, Chapel Hill; Frank T. Adams, Asheville
University of North Carolina, Wilson Library Southern Oral History Collection: Ellis
    Arnall; William Terry Couch; Frank Porter Graham; Paul Green; Hosea Hudson; Clyde
    Johnson; James Spencer Love; Al Murphy; Olive Stone; Don West

Pennsylvania
Author: Hedy West, Narberth

Tennessee
Author: Mildred Shackleford, New Market
Eastern Tennessee State University: Don West, with Hedy West (taped)
Highlander Research and Education Center: Don West (by Sue Thrasher)
University of Tennessee Hoskins Library: May Justus

West Virginia
Author: Jon Karl Baldwin (telephone); John David (telephone); Yvonne Farley, St. Albans;
    P. J. Laska, Beckley; Donald Rasmussen, Beckley; Michael Ross Jr. (telephone); David
    Stanley, Beckley; Ann West Williams, Charleston

Wisconsin
Wisconsin Historical Society: Myles Horton; Dorothy Swisshelm

Unpublished Government Documents

Georgia Archives, Clayton: Governors' Correspondence; Ellis Arnall; Marvin Griffin;
    Eugene Talmadge; Herman Talmadge; Record Group 37, Records of the Georgia
    Education Commission
FBI Records Obtained through Freedom of Information Act Request: FBI File 100–20396,
    Donald Lee West; FBI File 61–7511, Highlander Folk School, Tennessee State Li-
    brary
Hall County, Ga.: Minutes, Hall County Board of Education, Gainesville
National Archives, Washington, D.C.: Record Group 9, Records of the NRA, entry 402,
    Records of the Textile Labor Relations Board, Records Relating to Labor Disturbances
    in the Textile Industry, 1933–37; Record Group 69, Records of the Work Projects Ad-
    ministration; Record Group 233, Records of the House Committee on Un-American
    Activities; Records of the Subcommittee to Investigate the Internal Security Act and
    Other Internal Security Laws

Published Government Documents

U.S. Congress, House. Committee on Un-American Activities. "Communism in the Mid-
    South: Hearings before the Subcommittee to Investigate the Administration of the
    Internal Security Act and Other Internal Security Laws." 85th Cong., 1st sess., 1958.
U.S. Department of the Army. *U.S. Military Intelligence Reports: Surveillance of Radicals in
    the United States, 1917–1941* (microfilm). Frederick, Md.: University Publications of
    America, 1984.

Published Primary Sources

Allen, James P. *Organizing in the Depression South: A Communist's Memoir.* Minneapolis: MEP Publications, 2001.

Baber, Bob Henry. "Remembering Don West (1906–1992)." *Appalachian Heritage* (Spring 1994): 27–30.

Basso, Hamilton. "About the Berry Schools: An Open Letter to Martha Berry." *The New Republic*, April 4, 1934.

Belfrage, Cedric. *A Faith to Free the People.* New York: Dryden Press, 1944.

Commencement Program. Fifty-seventh commencement, Vanderbilt University, June 8, 1932.

Harris, Lement. *My Tale of Two Worlds.* New York: International Publishers, 1986.

Herndon, Angelo. *Let Me Live.* New York: Random House, 1937.

Hicks, Granville et al. *Proletarian Literature in the United States: An Anthology.* New York: International Publishers, 1935.

Hodgson, Brian. "Mountain Voices, Mountain Days." *National Geographic Magazine* 176 (July 1972): 118–46.

Holman, Edwin. "Berry Schools Students Foil Attempts to Foment Strike." *Atlanta Constitution*, Oct. 8, 1933.

Horton, Myles. *The Long Haul: An Autobiography.* New York: Teachers College, Columbia University, 1998.

Hughes, Langston. *Arna Bontemps–Langston Hughes Letters, 1925–1957.* Edited by Charles H. Nicholas. New York: Dodd, Mead, 1980.

Kester, Howard. *Revolt Among the Sharecroppers.* New York: Covici-Friede, 1936.

Klehr, Harvey et al. *The Secret World of American Communism: Russian Documents Translated by Timothy D. Sergay.* New Haven: Yale University Press, 1995.

Lewis, John, with Michael D'Orso. *Walking with the Wind: A Memoir of the Movement.* San Diego: Harcourt Brace, 1998.

McGill, Ralph. "Add Don West's Subversive Associates." *Atlanta Constitution*, June 24, 1948.

———. "All Right, Here It Is!" *Atlanta Constitution*, Oct. 18, 1948.

———. "Don West Signs Himself a Communist." *Atlanta Constitution*, June 27, 1948.

———. "It Is Now Officially Communist." *Atlanta Constitution*, Sept. 28, 1948.

———. "The Unitarians Have Reason to Fret." *Atlanta Constitution*, Aug. 13, 1948.

Meyers, George. *Appalachia U.S.A.: A Study in Poverty.* New York: Publishers New Press, 1960.

Painter, Nell, ed. *The Narrative of Hosea Hudson: The Life and Times of a Black Radical.* New York: W. W. Norton, 1979.

Pickard, Walt. *Burlington Dynamite Plot.* New York: International Labor Defense, 1934.

Raymond, Harry. *The Ingrams Shall Not Die! A Story of Georgia's New Terror.* New York: Daily Worker, 1948.

Register of Vanderbilt University, 1931–1932. Nashville: Vanderbilt University, 1932.

Rosengarten, Theodore. *All God's Dangers: The Life of Nate Shaw.* New York: Alfred Knopf, 1974.

Scales, Junius Irving, and Richard Hudson. *Cause at Heart: A Former Communist Remembers.* Athens: University of Georgia Press, 1987.

Stuart, Jesse. *Beyond Dark Hills: A Personal Story by Jesse Stuart.* New York: E. P. Dutton, 1938.

———. *To Teach, to Love.* New York: World Publishing, 1970.

Sullivan, Ken. "Don West, Poet and Preacher." *Goldenseal* 5 (1979): 47–56.

Weissman, George L. "Pulpit for Unionism." *The Nation,* Feb. 25, 1956, 149.

West, Donald. *Between the Plow Handles: Poems.* Monteagle, Tenn.: Highlander Folk School, 1932.

———. "Build the New South." *Southern Worker,* Jan. 1937.

———. *Clods of Southern Earth.* New York: Boni and Gaer, 1946.

———. *Crab-Grass.* Nashville: The Art Print Shop, Treverra College, 1931.

———. *Deep, Deep Down in Living.* Privately published, ca 1932.

———. "Freedom in the Mountains." *Mountain Life and Work* 46 (Dec. 1970): 20–22.

———. "Georgia Wanted Me Dead or Alive." *The New Masses,* June 26, 1934, 15–16.

———. "I Am a Communist." *The Daily Worker,* March 13, 1934, 5.

———. "I Love the South." *The New Masses,* May 28, 1946, 3.

———. *In a Land of Plenty.* Minneapolis: West End Press, 1982. Reprint. Los Angeles: West End Press, 1985.

———. "Knott County, KY: A Thesis." Bachelor's thesis. Vanderbilt University School of Religion, 1932.

———. "'My Old Kentucky Home' of Miners and Unemployed in Harlan County." *Southern Worker,* Dec. 1936.

———. *No Lonesome Road: Selected Prose and Poems.* Edited by Jeff Biggers and George Brosi. Urbana: University of Illinois Press, 2004.

———. *O! Mountaineers.* Huntington, W.V.: Appalachian Press, 1974.

———. *People's Cultural Heritage in Appalachia.* Huntington, W.V.: Appalachian Movement Press, 1971.

———. *The Road Is Rocky.* Preface by Byron Herbert Reece; introduction by Roy Smith. New York: New Christian Books, 1951.

———. *Romantic Appalachia; or, Poverty Pays if You Ain't Poor.* Huntington, W.V.: Appalachian Movement Press, 1972.

———. *Songs for Southern Workers: 1937 Songbook of Kentucky Workers Alliance.* Huntington, W.V.: Appalachian Movement Press, 1973.

———. *Southern Mountain Folk Tradition and the Folksong "Stars" Syndrome.* Huntington, W.V.: Appalachian Movement Press, 1972.

———. "Sweatshops in the Schools." *The New Republic,* Oct. 4, 1933, 216.

———. "Taps for Private Tussie." *Mountain Life and Work* 20 (Spring 1944): 39.

———. *A Time for Anger: Poems Selected from* The Road Is Rocky *and* Clods of Southern Earth. Foreword by Tom Woodruff. Huntington, W.V.: Appalachian Movement Press, 1970.

———. *Toil and Hunger.* San Benito, Tex.: Hagglund, 1940.

———. "Visit Shatters Myths about Soviet Union." *Charleston Gazette,* Jan. 27, 1984.

West, Hedy. "No Fiddle in My Home: Lillie West Recalls." *Sing Out! The Folk Song Magazine* 26 (1978): 2–7.

Williams, Ann West. "My Father, Don West." *Traditions: A Journal of West Virginia Folk Culture and Awareness* 5 (1999), 40–42.

Wilson, Walter. "Atlanta's Communists." *The Nation,* June 25, 1930, 130–31.

Journals, Newspapers, and Magazines

Appalachian South, 1965– ; *Atlanta Daily World*, 1931–41; *Berry News*, 1923–26, 1932–33; *The Blue and the Gray*, 1928–30; *Charleston Gazette*, 1966– ; *The Daily Worker*, 1930–41, 1945–49; *Labor Defender*, 1930–38; *Mountain Herald*, 1928–30; *Mountain Life and Work*, 1963–74; *People's Press*, 1937–38; *Publisher's Weekly*, 1946; *Railsplitter*, 1927–30; *Southern Patriot*, 1942–48; *Southern Worker*, 1931–37; *Vanderbilt Alumnus*, 1932; *Washington Post*, 1954; *Work*, 1938–40; *The Workers Alliance*, 1935–36.

Author's Correspondence

Jeff Biggers, 2003–5; Klara Cook, 2004; John Crawford, 2004; Margie Hutchens, 2004; P. J. Laska, 2004–5; Harold Sowder, 2003; Hedy West, 2003–5; Ann West Williams, 2004.

Secondary Sources

Books

Adams, Frank T. *James A. Dombrowski: An American Heretic, 1897–1983*. Knoxville: University of Tennessee Press, 1992.

———, with Myles Horton. *Unearthing Seeds of Fire: The Idea of Highlander*. Winston-Salem: John F. Blair, 1975.

Anderson, William. *The Wild Man from Sugar Creek: The Political Career of Eugene Talmadge*. Baton Rouge: Louisiana State University Press, 1975.

Barrett, James R. *William Z. Foster and the Tragedy of American Radicalism*. Urbana: University of Illinois Press, 1999.

Bartley, Numan V. *The Creation of Modern Georgia*. Rev. ed. Athens: University of Georgia Press, 1990.

Bernstein, Irving. *The Lean Years: A History of the American Worker, 1920–1933*. Boston: Houghton Mifflin, 1960.

Biggers, Jeff. *The United States of Appalachia: How Southern Mountaineers Brought Independence, Culture, and Enlightenment to America*. Emeryville, Ca.: Shoemaker and Hoard, 2006.

Billings, Dwight B. et al., eds. *Back Talk from Appalachia: Confronting Stereotypes*. Lexington: University Press of Kentucky, 1999.

Blair, Everetta Love. *Jesse Stuart: His Life and Works*. Columbia: University of South Carolina Press, 1967.

Brattain, Michelle. *The Politics of Whiteness: Race, Workers, and Culture in the Modern South*. Princeton: Princeton University Press, 2001.

Buckmaster, Henrietta. *Deep River*. New York: Harcourt, Brace, 1944.

Carter, Dan T. *Scottsboro: A Tragedy of the South*. Baton Rouge: Louisiana State University Press, 1969.

Carter, Paul. *The Decline and Revival of the Social Gospel, 1920–1940*. Hamden, Conn.: Archon Books, 1971.

Chirhart, Ann Short. *Torches of Light: Georgia Teachers and the Coming of the Modern South*. Athens: University of Georgia Press, 2005.

Clowse, Barbara Barksdale. *Ralph McGill: A Biography*. Macon, Ga.: Mercer University Press, 1998.

Cobb, James C. *Away Down South: A History of Southern Identity*. New York: Oxford University Press, 2005.

Cobb, William H. *Radical Education in the Rural South: Commonwealth College, 1922–1940.* Detroit: Wayne State University Press, 2000.

Cohen, Ronald D. *Rainbow Quest: The Folk Music Revival and American Society.* Amherst: University of Massachusetts Press, 2002.

Conkin, Paul K. *Gone with the Ivy: A Biography of Vanderbilt University.* Knoxville: University of Tennessee Press, 1985.

Cook, Raymond A. *Mountain Singer: The Life and Legacy of Byron Herbert Reece.* Atlanta: Cherokee Publishing, 1980.

Craig, Robert H. *Religion and Radical Politics: An Alternative Christian Tradition in the United States.* Philadelphia: Temple University Press, 1992.

Crowell, Suzanne. *Appalachian People's History Book.* Louisville: Mountain Education Associates/SCEF, 1971.

Davidson, Donald et al. *I'll Take My Stand: The South and the Agrarian Tradition.* Reprint. New York: Peter Smith, 1951.

Davis, Benjamin J. *Communist Councilman from Harlem.* New York: International Publishers, 1969.

Denning, Michael. *The Cultural Front: The Laboring of American Culture in the Twentieth Century.* London: Verso Press, 1997.

Dennison, R. Serge. *Great Day Coming: Folk Music and the American Left.* Urbana: University of Illinois Press, 1971.

Dickey, Ouida, and Doyle Mathews. *Berry College: A History.* Athens: University of Georgia Press, 2005.

Dotson-Lewis, B. L. *Appalachia: Spirit Triumphant, a Cultural History of Appalachia.* West Conshohocken, Pa.: Infinity, 2004.

Drake, Richard B. *A History of Appalachia.* Lexington: University Press of Kentucky, 2001.

Draper, Theodore. *Roots of American Communism.* New York: Viking Press, 1957.

Duke, David C. *Writers and Miners: Activism and Imagery in America.* Lexington: University Press of Kentucky, 2002.

Dunaway, Wilma A. *Slavery in the Mountain South.* New York: Cambridge University Press, 2003.

Dunbar, Anthony. *Against the Grain: Southern Radicals and Prophets, 1929–1959.* Charlottesville: University Press of Virginia, 1981.

Durr, Virginia. *Outside the Magic Circle: The Autobiography of Virginia Durr.* New York: Simon and Schuster, 1985.

Dykeman, Wilma, and James Stokely. *Seeds of Southern Change: The Life of Will Alexander.* Chicago: University of Chicago Press, 1962.

Egerton, John. *Speak Now against the Day: The Generation before the Civil Rights Movement in the South.* Chapel Hill: University of North Carolina Press, 1995.

Engerman, David C. *"Modernization from the Other Shore": American Intellectuals and The Romance of Russian Development.* Cambridge: Harvard University Press, 2003.

Eskew, Glenn T., ed. *Labor in the Modern South.* Athens: University of Georgia Press, 2002.

Ferguson, Karen. *Black Politics in New Deal Atlanta.* Chapel Hill: University of North Carolina Press, 2002.

Flamming, Douglas. *Creating the Modern South: Millhands and Managers in Dalton, Georgia, 1884–1984.* Chapel Hill: University of North Carolina Press, 1992.

Folsom, Franklin. *Impatient Armies of the Poor.* Niwot: University of Colorado Press, 1996.

Fosl, Catherine. *Subversive Southerner: Anne Braden and the Cold War South*. New York: Palgrave Macmillan, 2002.

Gaer, Joseph. *The First Round: The Story of the CIO Political Action Committee*. New York: Duell, Sloan and Pearce, 1944.

Gilbert, James Burghardt. *Writers and Partisans: A History of Literary Radicalism in America*. New York: John Wiley and Sons, 1968.

Glen, John M. *Highlander: No Ordinary School, 1932–1962*. Lexington: University Press of Kentucky, 1988.

Grant, Donald L. *The Way It Was in the South: The Black Experience in Georgia*. Secaucus, N.J.: Carol Publishing, 1993.

Green, Archie. *Only a Miner: Studies in Recorded Coal Mining Songs*. Urbana: University of Illinois Press, 1972.

Green, Chris, Rachel Rubin, and James Smethurst, eds. *Radicalism in the South since Reconstruction*. New York: Palgrave-Macmillan, 2007.

Green, James R. *Taking History to Heart: The Power of the Past in Building Social Movements*. Amherst: University of Massachusetts Press, 2000.

———. *The World of the Worker: Labor in Twentieth Century America*. New York: Hill and Wang, 1980.

Griffith, Barbara. *The Crisis of American Labor: Operation Dixie and the Defeat of the CIO*. Philadelphia: Temple University Press, 1988.

Hall, Jacqueline Dowd et al. *Like a Family: The Making of a Southern Cotton Mill World*. Chapel Hill: University of North Carolina Press, 1987.

Harkins, Anthony. *Hillbilly: A Cultural History of an American Icon*. New York: Oxford University Press, 2004.

Heale, M. J. *McCarthy's Americans: Red Scare Politics in State and Nation, 1935–1965*. Athens: University of Georgia Press, 1998.

Henderson, Harold Paulk. *Heritage of Gilmer County, Georgia, 1832–1996*. Ellijay, Ga.: Gilmer County Heritage Book Committee, 1996.

———. *The Politics of Change: A Political Biography of Ellis Arnall*. Athens: University of Georgia Press, 1991.

Herndon, Jerry A., and George Brosi. *Jesse Stuart: The Man and His Books*. Ashland, Ky.: Jesse Stuart Foundation, 1988.

Hevener, John W. *Which Side Are You On? The Harlan County Coal Miners, 1931–1939*. Urbana: University of Illinois Press, 2002.

Hickey, Georgina. *Hope and Danger in a New South City: Working Class Women and Urban Development in Atlanta, 1890–1940*. Athens: University of Georgia Press, 2003.

Hodges, James A. *New Deal Labor Policy and the Southern Cotton Textile Industry*. Knoxville: University of Tennessee Press, 1986.

Holmes, Michael. *The New Deal in Georgia: An Administrative History*. Westport, Conn.: Greenwood Press, 1975.

Horne, Gerald. *Black Liberation, Red Scare: Ben Davis and the Communist Party*. Newark: University of Delaware Press, 1994.

Horton, Aimee Isgrig. *The Highlander Folk School: A History of Its Major Programs, 1932–1961*. Brooklyn: Carlson Publishing, 1989.

Hunt, Philip Mulkey. *The Mulkeys of America*. Portland, Ore.: Hunt, Marquis, Mulkey Family Association, 1982.

Inscoe, John C. *Mountain Masters, Slavery, and the Sectional Crisis in North Carolina.* Knoxville: University of Tennessee Press, 1989.

———, and Gordon B. McKinney. *The Heart of Confederate Appalachia: Western North Carolina in the Civil War.* Chapel Hill: University of North Carolina Press, 2000.

Irons, Janet. *Testing the New Deal: The General Textile Strike of 1934 in the American South.* Urbana: University of Illinois Press, 2000.

Jackson, Alan. *Byron Herbert Reece (1917–1958) and the Southern Poetry Tradition.* Lewiston, Me.: Edwin Mellen Press, 2001.

Kahn, Albert E. *The Matusow Affair: Memoir of a National Scandal.* Mt. Kisco, N.Y.: Mayer-Bell, 1987.

Kelley, Robin D. G. *Hammer and Hoe: Alabama Communists During the Great Depression.* Chapel Hill: University of North Carolina Press, 1990.

Kirby, Jack Temple. *Rural Worlds Lost: The American South, 1920–1960.* Baton Rouge: Louisiana State University Press, 1987.

Klehr, Harvey. *The Heyday of American Communism: The Depression Decade.* New York: Basic Books, 1984.

Kraditor, Aileen S. *"Jimmie Higgins": The Mental World of the American Rank-and-File Communist, 1930–1958.* New York: Greenwood Press, 1988.

Krueger, Thomas A. *And Promises to Keep: The Southern Conference for Human Welfare, 1938–1948.* Nashville: Vanderbilt University Press, 1967.

Kuhn, Clifford M., and Harlon E. Joye, eds. *Living Atlanta: An Oral History of the City, 1914–1948.* Athens: University of Georgia Press, 1990.

Lewis, George. *The White South and the Red Menace: Segregationists, Anticommunism, and Massive Resistance, 1945–1965.* Gainesville: University Press of Florida, 2004.

Lichtman, Robert M., and Ronald D. Cohen. *Deadly Farce: Harvey Matusow and the Informer System in the McCarthy Era.* Urbana: University of Illinois Press, 2004.

Lorence, James J. *Organizing the Unemployed: Community and Union Activists in the Industrial Heartland.* Albany: State University of New York Press, 1996.

Malone, Bill C. *Don't Get above Your Raisin': Country Music and the Southern Working Class.* Urbana: University of Illinois Press, 2001.

Martin, Charles H. *The Angelo Herndon Case and Southern Justice.* Baton Rouge: Louisiana State University Press, 1976.

Martin, Robert F. *Howard Kester and the Struggle for Social Justice in the South, 1904–1977.* Charlottesville: University Press of Virginia, 1991.

McCauley, Deborah Vansau. *Appalachian Mountain Religion: A History.* Urbana: University of Illinois Press, 1995.

Minchin, Timothy J. *What Do We Need a Union For? The TWUA in the South, 1945–1955.* Chapel Hill: University of North Carolina Press, 1997.

Mullen, Bill, and Sherry Lee Linkum. *Radical Revisions: Re-Reading 1930s Culture.* Urbana: University of Illinois Press, 1996.

———, and James Smethurst, eds. *Left of the Color Line: Race, Radicalism, and Twentieth Century Literature of the United States.* Chapel Hill: University of North Carolina Press, 2002.

Nelson, Cary. *Repression and Recovery: Modern American Poetry and the Politics of Cultural Memory, 1910–1945.* Madison: University of Wisconsin Press, 1989.

O'Brien, Michael. *The Idea of the Modern South, 1920–1941.* Baltimore: Johns Hopkins University Press, 1979.

Ottanelli, Fraser M. *The Communist Party of the United States: From the Depression to World War II.* New Brunswick: Rutgers University Press, 1991.

Parker, Ernest. *Days Gone By: Early Gilmer County, Georgia.* Ellijay, Ga.: Gilmer County Genealogical Society, 1999.

Patton, Randall L., with David B. Parker. *Carpet Capital: The Rise of a New South Industry.* Athens: University of Georgia Press, 1999.

Pedersen, Vernon L. *The Communist Party in Maryland, 1919–1957.* Urbana: University of Illinois Press, 2001.

Pells, Richard H. *Radical Visions and American Dreams: Culture and Social Thought in the Depression Years.* New York: Harper and Row, 1974.

Piven, Frances Fox, and Richard Cloward. *Poor Peoples Movements: Why They Succeed, How They Fail.* New York: Vintage, 1977.

Record, Wilson. *Race and Radicalism: The NAACP and the Communist Party in Conflict.* Ithaca: Cornell University Press, 1965.

Richardson, H. Edward. *Jesse: The Biography of an American Writer, Jesse Hilton Stuart.* New York: McGraw-Hill, 1984.

Romalis, Shelly. *Pistol Packin' Mama: Aunt Molly Jackson and the Politics of Folksong.* Urbana: University of Illinois Press, 1999.

Roper, John Herbert. *Paul Green: Playwright of the New South.* Athens: University of Georgia Press, 2003.

Salmond, John A. *The General Textile Strike of 1934: From Maine to Alabama.* Columbia: University of Missouri Press, 2002.

———. *Miss Lucy of the CIO: The Life and Times of Lucy Randolph Mason, 1882–1959.* Athens: University of Georgia Press, 1988.

———. *A Southern Rebel: The Life and Times of Aubrey Willis Williams, 1890–1965.* Chapel Hill: University of North Carolina Press, 1983.

Schrecker, Ellen. *Many Are the Crimes: McCarthyism in America.* Boston: Little, Brown, 1998.

Shapiro, Henry. *Appalachia on Our Minds: Mountains and Mountaineers in the American Consciousness, 1870–1920.* Chapel Hill: University of North Carolina Press, 1978.

Sharp, Jean Bell, comp. *The Georgia Mulkeys.* Talledega, Ala.: A. and T. Printing, 1996.

Singal, Joseph. *The War within from Victorian to Modernist Thought in the South, 1919–1945.* Chapel Hill: University of North Carolina Press, 1982.

Smethurst, James. *The New Red Negro: The Literary Left and African-American Poetry, 1930–1946.* New York: Oxford University Press, 1999.

Solomon, Mark. *The Cry Was Unity: Communists and African-Americans, 1917–1936.* Jackson: University Press of Mississippi, 1998.

———. *Red and Black: Communism and Afro-Americans, 1929–1935.* New York: Garland Publishing, 1988.

Starobin, Joseph R. *American Communism in Crisis.* Cambridge: Harvard University Press, 1972.

Sternsher, Bernard. *Hitting Home: The Great Depression in Town and Country.* Rev. ed. Chicago: Ivan Dee, 1989.

Teel, Leonard Ray. *Ralph Emerson McGill.* Knoxville: University of Tennessee Press, 2001.

Tindall, George B. *Emergence of the New South.* Baton Rouge: Louisiana State University Press, 1967.

Turk, Stephen G. N. *Beyond Atlanta: The Struggle for Racial Equality in Georgia, 1940–1980.* Athens: University of Georgia Press, 2001.

Wald, Alan M. *Exiles from a Future Time: The Forging of the Mid-Twentieth Century Literary Left.* Chapel Hill: University of North Carolina Press, 2002.

Ward, George Gordon. *The Annals of Upper Georgia Centered in Gilmer County.* Nashville: Parthenon Press, 1965.

Whisnant, David E. *All That Is Native and Fine: The Politics of Culture in an American Region.* Chapel Hill: University of North Carolina Press, 1983.

———. *Modernizing the Mountaineer: People, Power, and Planning in Appalachia.* Boone, N.C.: Appalachian Consortium Press, 1980.

Wiggenton, Eliot, ed. *Refuse to Stand By: An Oral History of Grass Roots Social Activism in America, 1921–1964.* New York: Doubleday, 1991.

Williams, John Alexander. *Appalachia: A History.* Chapel Hill: University of North Carolina Press, 2002.

Woods, Jeff. *Black Struggle, Red Scare: Segregation and Anti-Communism in the South, 1948–1968.* Baton Rouge: Louisiana State University Press, 2004.

Zieger, Robert H., ed. *Organized Labor in the Twentieth Century South.* Knoxville: University of Tennessee Press, 1991.

Articles

Baxandall, Roslyn. "The Question Seldom Asked: Women in the CPUSA." In *New Studies in the Politics and Culture of U.S. Communism,* 151–59. Edited by Michael E. Brown et al. New York: Monthly Review Press, 1993.

Biggers, Jeff. "The Fugitive of Southern Appalachian Literature: Reconsidering The Poetry of Don West." *Journal of Appalachian Studies* 5 (Fall 1999): 159–80.

Bernd, Joseph L. "White Supremacy and the Disenfranchisement of Blacks in Georgia, 1946." *Georgia Historical Quarterly* 66 (1982): 492–513.

Blais, Linda. "West Recites Tender, Compassionate, Moving Poetry." *Campus Lantern,* March 26, 1981.

Burger, Nash. "Homespun Poem of the South." *New York Times Review of Books,* July 18, 1946.

"Control of How Party Instructions Are Carried Out." *Party Organizer* 3, no. 1 (1930): 13.

Flynt, Wayne. "Religion for the Blues: Evangelicalism, Poor Whites, and the Great Depression." *Journal of Southern History* 71 (Feb. 2005): 3–38.

"Folk Center Teaches Cultural Pride." *Youth Magazine* (Sept. 1976): 19–23.

"Four Gifts for Man." *Stormy Petrel,* Nov. 6, 1946.

Gosse, Van. "They Organize in Every Neighborhood: The Gender Politics of American Communists between the Wars." *Radical History Review* (Spring 1991): 109–41.

Green, Christopher Allen. "Working Truth Inside Out: Don West, Muriel Rukeyser, Poetry, and the Popular Front in Appalachia, 1932–1948." *Journal of Appalachian Studies* 8 (Fall 2002): 382–406.

Haynes, John Earl, and Harvey Klehr, "The CPUSA Reports to the Comintern." *American Communist History* 4 (June 2005): 21–60.

Henson, Michael. "'Naked Words That Have No Subtle Meaning: Poetry and Teaching in the Writings of Don West." In *The Appalachian Experience: Proceedings of the Sixth Annual Appalachian Studies Conference,* 54–60. Boone, N.C.: Appalachian Consortium Press, 1983.

Hill, Rebecca. "Re-evaluating the CPUSA's Answer to the Woman Question." *American Communist History* 3 (June 2004): 145–51.

James, Sheryl. "A Radical of Long Standing." *St. Petersburg Times*, March 22, 1989.

Knapik, Michael, and Tom Woodruff. "Mountaineers Fighting for Freedom: An Interview with Don West." *Mountain Life and Work* 47 (Jan. 1971): 13.

Leab, Daniel J. "United We Eat: The Creation and Organization of the Unemployed Councils in 1930." *Labor History* 8 (Fall 1967): 300–315.

Lechlitner, Ruth. "Overalls Poet." *New York Herald Tribune Weekly Book Review*, Sept. 8, 1946.

Lorence, James J. "Mobilizing the Reserve Army: The Communist Party and the Unemployed in Atlanta, 1929–1934." In *Radicalism in the South since Reconstruction*. Edited by Chris Green, Rachel Rubin, and James Smethurst, 57–82. New York: Palgrave-Macmillan, 2007.

"Lula Author Sued on Libel Charge." *Atlanta Constitution*, Oct. 22, 1946.

Marius, Richard. "Don West's Sermon on the Mount." *Appalachian Journal* 10 (Summer 1983): 361–62.

Martin, Charles H. "White Supremacy and Black Workers: Georgia's 'Black Shirts' and the Great Depression." *Labor History* 18 (Summer 1977): 366–80.

Martin, Harold. "West's Poems Raise a Controversy." *Atlanta Constitution*, Oct. 14, 1946.

Moore, John Hammond. "Communists and Fascists in a Southern City: Atlanta, 1930." *South Atlantic Quarterly* 67 (Summer 1968): 437–54.

Naison, Mark. "Claude and Joyce Williams: Pilgrims of Justice." *Southern Exposure* 1 (1973): 38–50.

Patrick, Robert Pierce Jr. "A Nail in the Coffin of Racism: The Story of the Columbians." *Georgia Historical Quarterly* 85 (Summer 2001): 245–66.

Patton, Randall L. "The Governorship of Ellis Arnall." *Georgia Historical Quarterly* 74 (Winter 1990): 599–621.

Peeks, Edward. "Don West Seen in Different Light These Days." *Charleston Gazette*, May 25, 1978.

"Pipestem Folk Festival Draws Fiddling, Singing Crowd." *Charleston Sunday Gazette-Mail*, Aug. 3, 1969.

Rasmussen, Jeanne M. "Don West Does His Thing at Pipestem." *West Virginia Hillbilly*, Oct. 26, 1968.

Rayford, Julian Lee. "Jesse Stuart: Kentucky's Immortal Chronicler." *American Book Collector* 9 (Sept. 1958): 5–7.

"'Ridiculous,' West Says of Libel Suit." *Atlanta Constitution*, Oct. 22, 1946.

Rosenzweig, Roy. "Organizing the Unemployed: The Early Years of the Great Depression, 1929–1932." *Radical America* 10 (July–Aug. 1976): 37–61.

———. "Radicals and the Jobless: The Musteites and the Unemployed League, 1932–1935." *Labor History* 20 (Fall 1979): 52–77.

———. "Socialism in Our Time: The Socialist Party and the Unemployed, 1929–1936." *Labor History* 20 (Fall 1979): 485–509.

Rossinow, Doug. "The Radicalization of the Social Gospel: Harry F. Ward and the Search for a New Social Order." *Religion and American Culture* 15 (Winter 2005): 63–106.

Rubin, Rachel. "Voice of the Cracker: Don West Reinvents the Appalachian." In *Left of The Color Line: Race, Radicalism, and Literature of the United States*. Edited by Bill Mullen and James Smethurst, 205–21. Chapel Hill: University of North Carolina Press, 2003.

Salmond, John. "The Burlington Dynamite Plot: The 1934 Textile Strike and Its Aftermath in Burlington, North Carolina." *North Carolina History Review* 75 (Oct. 1998): 393–434.

Sibley, Celestine. "Neither Red nor Scout Organizer, Poet Don West Answers Questions." *Atlanta Journal*, Aug. 14, 1952.

Storch, Randi. "'The Realities of the Situation': Revolutionary Discipline and Everyday Political Life in Chicago's Communist Party, 1928–1935." *Labor: Studies in Working Class Histories of the Americas* 3 (Fall 2004): 19–44.

Snyder, Bob. "The Soupbean Poets." *The Sow's Ear: Poetry Review* 2 (Winter 1990): 6.

Troy, Bill, and Claude Williams. "People's Institute of Applied Religion." *Southern Exposure* 4 (1976): 46–53.

Torrey, Ben. "Tribute to Reuben Archer Torrey, III." http://www.jesusabbey.tv/Library/rat3_splash.jsp; jsessionid=OAOIGCGEDBCD (accessed on March 20, 2007).

"The Universal Christian Church." *Appalachian South* 2 (Spring–Summer 1967).

Uphaus, Willard. "O Mountaineers." *Come Unity* (March 1977): 17.

Weisenburger, Steven. "The Columbians, Inc.: A Chapter in Racial Hatred from the Post–World War II South." *Journal of Southern History* 69 (Nov. 2003): 821–60.

Whisnant, David E. "The Folk Hero in Appalachian Struggle History." *New South* 28 (Fall 1973): 30–47.

Wright, Ann C. "The Aftermath of the General Textile Strike: Managers and the Workplace at Burlington Mills." *Journal of Southern History* 60 (Feb. 1994): 81–112.

———. "Strategy and Structure in the Textile Industry: Spencer Love and the Burlington Mills, 1923–1962. *Business History Review* 69 (Spring 1995): 42–79.

Zehavi, Gerald. "Passionate Commitments: Race, Sex, and Communism at Schenectady General Electric, 1932–1954." *Journal of American History* 83 (Sept. 1996): 514–48.

Unpublished Material

Bell, Brenda, and Fran Ansley. "The Story of the Davidson and Wilder Coal Miners Strike of 1932–33." Highlander Research and Education Center Archives, 1973.

Buckman, Kathie. "Don West: Peripatetic Educator of the Appalachian South." Seminar paper in history. Henderson State University, 2004.

Byerly, Victoria Morris. "'What Shall a Poet Sing?': The Living Struggle of the Poet and Revolutionary Don West." Ph.D. diss., Boston College, 1994.

Dickey, Ovida, and Doyle Mathis. "History of Martha Berry College." Archives, Berry College.

Green, Chris. "The Social Life of Poetry: Pluralism and Appalachia, 1937–1948." Ph.D. diss., University of Kentucky, 2004.

Guthrie, Carol Anne. "Education and the Evolution of the South: A History of the Berry Schools, 1902–1970." Ph.D. diss., University of Tennessee, 1994.

Harbison, Stanley Lincoln. "Social Gospel Career of Alva W. Taylor." Ph.D. diss., Vanderbilt University, 1975.

Klibaner, Irwin. "The Southern Conference Educational Fund: A History." Ph.D. diss., University of Wisconsin, 1971.

Laska, P. J. "Don West—People's Poet." Paper presented at the West Virginia Festival of the Book, Charleston, March 16, 2004.

———. "Don West, Revolutionary People's Poet." Copy in author's files.

Leibman, Wilma B. "The Workers Alliance of America." Senior thesis, Barnard College, 1971.

Perry, Vernon S. "Labor Struggle at Wilder, Tennessee." Master's thesis, Vanderbilt University, 1934.

Shadron, Virginia A. "Popular Protest and Legal Authority in Post–World War II Georgia: Race, Class, and Gender Politics in the Rosa Lee Ingram Case." Ph.D. diss., Emory University, 1991.

Index

Grant, Edmonia, 133–34
Grattan, Steve, 93
Green, Archie, 192
Green, G. Leland, 9–10
Green, Leonard, 60, 62
Green, Paul: as ally in bomb plot defense, 57–58, West and, 58
"Greens," 200
Greensboro, N.C., 54, 60
Green, William, 69
Griffin, Gov. Marvin, 161, 171
Grundtvig, Bishop Nikolai, 23
Gurley, Rev. Melville, 9–10

Hagglund Press, 88
Hansel, Pauletta, 197
Harlan County, Ky., 49, 63–64, 72, 84, 87
Hathaway, Clarence, 39–40
Hazard, Ky., 178–79, 185
Hearst, William Randolph, 137
Heifer Project International, 192
Henderson, Donald, 41, 101, 103
Henson, Michael, 207–8, 212, 225
Herndon, Angelo, 242n34; as communist organizer, 37; Georgia Supreme Court action on, 48; and ILD, 39, 49; and unemployed movement, 37, 39–40; West and defense of, 37–38, 43, 47–50
Highlander Folk School, 171–72, 175, 183, 219, 268n15, 271n2; local attitudes toward, 30–31, 34; naming of, 28–29; origins of, 27–29, 237n24; program, 29–30, 32–33; West's departure from, 34–36, 40
"hillbilly" image: West's objection to, 6, 17, 77, 110, 122, 172, 180; West's use of, 78, 110–11, 123, 180, 226
Hille, Waldemar, 112
Hindman, Ky., 21–23, 233n13
Hindman Settlement School, 21–23, 233n13
"hippies," 193–94, 198
Hitler, Adolf, 49, 95, 101, 131
Hitler-Stalin Pact, 1939, 94, 99
Hod Carriers Union, 68, 70
Home Missions Council, 147–48, 150
Hoover, J. Edgar, 150, 162–63, 174
Hoover, Herbert C., 76
Horton, Gov. Henry H., 25
Horton, Myles, 27, 31–32, 36, 52, 120, 171, 194; attitude toward Congress for Appalachian Development, 187, 189–90, 272n15, 273n19; as co-founder of Highlander Folk

School, 27–29; relationship with West, 30, 34–35, 43, 95–96, 130–31, 183, 187, 271n2
House Committee on Un-American Activities (HUAC), 134–35, 151, 153, 159, 163, 172–73, 222, 269n6
Hudson, Hosea, 47, 196, 217–18
Hudson, John, 48
Hughes, Langston, 126, 147; and Arna Bontemps, 111; on poor white "crackers," 110; and Rosenwald Fund, 111, 113; as West's ally, 110–11
humanism, 5, 13, 146–47, 191, 206, 232n7
"hunger marches," 69–70
Hunter, Floyd, 139
Huntington, W.V., 197–98
Hupp, James L., 184
Hutchens, Rev. Margie, 196–97, 224

ILD. See International Labor Defense
I'll Take My Stand (Davidson et al.), 82
imperialism, 179, 216
In a Land of Plenty (1982, West), 209–12
Ingram, Rosa Lee: Communist Party and, 136–37; Connie West on, 136; Georgia Citizens Committee support for, 136; Henry A. Wallace support for, 137; prosecution, 136; trial and West's support, 136–37
insurrection law, in Georgia, 37, 48, 62
International Labor Defense (ILD), 47; and Burlington bomb plot defense, 57–60; and Herndon case, 38–39, 44; West's ties with, 39, 49, 62

Jackson, Cong. Donald L., 193–94
Jackson, Molly, 72, 86
Jacobs, Joseph, 129
Jesus, 24, 96, 100, 192, 205, 262n58; West's concept of as a revolutionary, 5, 52, 68, 95, 98–99, 101, 191, 201, 207, 228
Jim Crow, 47, 140–41; as bar to interracial organization, 138; union adaptation, 130
John C. Campbell Folk School, 21–22, 29
John D. Rockefeller Foundation, 199–200
Johns Hopkins University Medical Center, 179–80
Johnson, Arnold, 67, 71
Johnson, Clyde, 45; and Berry strike, 41–42; in unemployed movement, 47; as West ally, 41, 47
Johnson, Lillian, 28–29, 31, 34
Johnson, Lyndon B., 179, 184–85

JAMES J. LORENCE is professor of history, emeritus, at the University of Wisconsin–Marathon County, where he taught modern U.S. history. From 2001 to 2005 he served as Eminent Scholar of History at Gainesville State College in Georgia. Specializing in labor and radical history, he has published eight books. One of them, *Suppression of "Salt of the Earth": How Hollywood, Big Labor, and Politicians Blacklisted a Movie in Cold War Ameria* (1999), received the Western History Association's Robert G. Athearn Award for Best Book on the Twentieth Century West in addition to the Council of Wisconsin Writers' Kenneth Kingery Award. In 2001 he received the Wisconsin Humanities Council Governor's Award for Excellence in Public Humanities Scholarship. He is at work on a study of community organizing in Georgia during the Great Depression.

The University of Illinois Press
is a founding member of the
Association of American University Presses.

Composed in 10/13 Janson Text
with Helvetica Neue Condensed display
by Jim Proefrock
at the University of Illinois Press
Designed by Paula Newcomb
Manufactured by Thomson-Shore, Inc.

University of Illinois Press
1325 South Oak Street
Champaign, IL 61820-6903
www.press.uillinois.edu